PRIVATIZING WELFARE IN THE MIDDLE EAST

T0341972

Indiana Series in Middle East Studies
MARK TESSLER, GENERAL EDITOR

Privatizing Welfare in the Middle East

KIN MUTUAL AID ASSOCIATIONS
IN JORDAN AND LEBANON

Anne Marie Baylouny

INDIANA UNIVERSITY PRESS
Bloomington and Indianapolis

This book is a publication of

Indiana University Press
601 North Morton Street
Bloomington, Indiana 47404-3797 USA

www.iupress.indiana.edu

Telephone orders	800-842-6796
Fax orders	812-855-7931
Orders by e-mail	iuporder@indiana.edu

∞The paper used in this publication meets the minimum requirements of the American National Standard for Information Sciences—
Permanence of Paper for Printed Library Materials, ANSI Z39.48-1992.

Manufactured in the United States of America

LIBRARY OF CONGRESS CATALOGING-IN-PUBLICATION DATA

Baylouny, Anne Marie.
    Privatizing welfare in the Middle East : kin mutual aid associations
in Jordan and Lebanon / Anne Marie Baylouny.
        p.   cm. — (Indiana series in Middle East studies)
    Includes bibliographical references and index.
    ISBN 978-0-253-35472-3 (cloth : alk. paper) — ISBN 978-0-253-
22195-7 (pbk. : alk. paper) 1. Social institutions—Jordan. 2. Social
institutions—Lebanon. 3. Charities—Jordan. 4. Charities—Lebanon.
5. Middle class—Jordan. 6. Middle class—Lebanon. I. Title.
    HN661.A8B39 2010
    361.7'6095692—dc22   2009045228

1 2 3 4 5   15 14 13 12 11 10

To my husband, Amer,
and my father, Raymond,
for their unwavering support

CONTENTS

ACKNOWLEDGMENTS

My thanks in completing this book go first to Kiren Chaudhry, for her help and intellectual example throughout. I thank Beshara Doumani and David Collier for all their generous advice and help. I benefited from constructive discussions and manuscript advice from colleagues including Kent Eaton, Jeff Knopf, Mike Malley, Vali Nasr, Harold Trinkunas, and Rob Weiner. My department at the Naval Postgraduate School furnished valuable support. Thanks go to the interlibrary loan and research staff at Knox Library, Irma Fink, Zooey Lober, and Greta Marlatt. My numerous requests were always met graciously.

My gratitude also goes to the Abdelhaq family in Jordan for all their support and aid during my stay there; Rana Taha, for helping me to connect with important resources; the Center for Strategic Studies, Amman, for all the help and resources it provided; and Karam Karam in Lebanon and several research assistants there. I thank my brother, John Baylouny, for scanning the family trees, and Evan Jernagan and Dianna Beardslee for crucial help for the flow chart on the welfare opportunity structure.

Innumerable friends and family made me laugh and survive the process, particularly Anshu Chatterjee and Ellen Amster. My parents, Raymond and Kathryn Baylouny, continually supported me in my career goals; I owe them a debt of gratitude beyond words. My brother James and his family supported and encouraged me without fail. My husband, Amer, arrived in my life only in the last few years, but soon made me wonder how I had survived without him. His patience and support know no end.

Research for this book was completed with the aid of the Sultan Committee on Arab Studies dissertation writing grant, Center for Middle East Studies, Berkeley; Fulbright, Institute for International Education dissertation research fellowship; the Simpson Memorial Dissertation Research Fellowship, Institute for International Studies,

Berkeley; the Social Science Research Council, Near & Middle East Section pre-dissertation grant; Mellon Foundation Moral Economy of Islam travel grant, Institute for International Studies, Berkeley; the Center for Middle East Studies Mellon Foundation travel grant, Berkeley; and a Research Initiation Program grant at the Naval Postgraduate School, Monterey, California. All opinions and errors are mine alone.

PRIVATIZING WELFARE IN THE MIDDLE EAST

Introduction: Organizing for Security

Identity politics is one of the most salient issues of our time. The Arab world, a region often viewed as driven by enduring and sometimes violent identities, is witnessing the reorganization of identities as a result of practical economic concerns. The end of public social provisioning in Jordan and Lebanon caused people to construct their own solutions for social insurance in the absence of private market options for welfare: formal mutual aid associations organized around kinship.[1] A large portion—over one-third—of Jordan's and Lebanon's civil societies now consists of these recently constructed kin organizations based on re-created identities, registered as nongovernmental organizations (NGOs). Leaders research and alter definitions of kin, uniting thousands of individuals engaged in strikingly different occupations and classes. Genealogies have been rewritten, sometimes reaching back more than a thousand years, to redefine the present kin group. Lineages were split apart or pieced together without regard to prior legacy. Some individuals are startled to find themselves belonging to a family they viewed as completely separate from their own, and in some cases even hostile to it. These identity ties are proactive, intended for future economic security, not reflections of tradition or existing ties.

These mutual aid associations represent not a mere increase in the salience of kin-based identity in politics but the reorganization of identities, their institutionalization, and the takeover by kin organizations of duties previously performed by the state. Despite the superficial similarity to tribal institutions and the idiom of tradition, these are new organizations with services geared to contemporary market and labor needs. Their establishment corresponds closely to state welfare and urbanization; the organizations only formed after groups moved to the cities and in the absence of public welfare. They entail significant democratic control. Cultural repertoires were reworked to fundamentally change the power balance from the leadership to members. Existing or inherited kin leaders are supplanted by rising new elites subjected to member approval. The associations unite a diverse range of social classes and occupations; informal street vendors and government ministers are now fellows in the same association. They are listed in membership records, assessed annual dues, and together charged with electing a board of directors. The associations provide members with emergency aid, loans, health and accident aid, job networks, pensions, and marriage and funeral aid. Some furnish regular unemployment payments and monthly support for the poor and for widows.

Like cooperatives and rotating savings associations, these contribution-based organizations furnish participants with a right to financial aid. Unlike patron-client relations, the associations horizontally link members to one another more than they tie members to the association leader. Members not only redistribute but also connect one another to jobs in a volatile and insecure labor market. In these service economies jobs with general skill requirements can be obtained through connections far afield from one's own specialty. Broad networks make sense amid an environment of general skills work, as individuals can move into a wide range of jobs. The major actors behind this trend are the educated middle class, urbanites, and youth without alternative job or profession-based social insurance. These social-class and employment categories are economically vulnerable. Many of them previously eschewed kin-based associations; they now participate en masse.[2] Numerous participants disagree with organizations based on kinship, preferring alternatives. Interviews revealed that members were conscious of the costs and benefits to joining, and were willing to join a kin institution when the prospect of going it alone financially appeared worse than the added obligations to kin.

Changes in social provisioning, furnished at the state and militia level in Jordan and Lebanon, set in motion the search for new solidarities to institutionalize in mutual aid organizations. This removal of collective welfare signaled an increase in economic insecurity for households and a decrease in the aid to cope with such risk that would continue indefinitely. Economic reforms downsized precisely the policies that served as social insurance for much of the population just when the labor market was also contracting. Between the initial impetus and the kin solution lies the context of alternatives in which individuals choose. Job- or profession-based collective solutions were not available for most people owing to the characteristics and skill profile of the labor market. Given the lack of legal and contract enforceability for the average person, market alternatives were likewise not viable. Without job or market alternatives, individuals were willing to join collective institutions for economic security, but the absence of legal capacity meant that informal mechanisms would be necessary to ensure commitment among the group. Kinship is able to provide informal guarantees for duties that the legal system cannot. At the same time, kin provide one another employment connections, valuable in a generalized service-sector economy where individuals move across diverse jobs with ease. The shared identity in kin mutual aid associations creates networks of obligation based on expectations of future reciprocity.[3] The institutionalization of this relationship furnishes members with a somewhat enforceable claim to social aid through informal mechanisms. Abstract potential networks become physical reality and duties.[4]

Mutual aid through lineage or hometown village is an attempt to cope with national changes that affect individual prospects and future economic security. Yet the organizations do not address the national level directly, demanding changes in policy as occurred with welfare changes in industrialized states. Indeed, the new associations hardly address the state at all but instead withdraw into disconnected private spheres, approximating states within the state. They occupy an intermediate realm between conscious withdrawal from involvement with the state and full engagement.[5] Their goal is to secure individual livelihoods, and to do this they replicate many roles previously fulfilled by the state. The organizations aspire to monopolize members' needs and demands from aid to recreation. Kin mutual aid associations furnish a concrete institutional base for mutually exclusive subnational identities, turning individuals inward in their quest for services and potentially fragmenting the domestic realm. The presence of these institutions, claiming to provide aid for the populace, channels future demands into the same path, removing social insurance as a mobilizing issue from other types of private or public institutions. Since redistribution has been a central demand on the state historically, often linked to appeals for representation, this could further complicate the Middle East's already troubled path toward representative political institutions. Violence and stability may be affected as well, since these identity associations can aid in subnational conflict. As militia mobilization in the Lebanese civil war and Gaza's clans currently show, kin associations can enter violent politics wholesale, furnishing thousands of foot soldiers as they take a side in subnational divisions.[6] The organizations fundamentally affect and change the composition of society that forms the basis for mobilization as well as engagement in, or removal from, national politics.

The large-scale trend of kin mutual aid associations was not antici-pated in economic liberalization, and these organizations diverge sharp-ly from the ideal depicted in the NGO and civil society literature. In economic reform, international development organizations advocate removing the state from welfare and instead promote decentralization through local organizations taking up the slack. The growth of NGOs would strengthen civil society, which in turn was believed to be linked to popular representation and democracy. The belief that civil society will emerge as a bulwark against authoritarianism pervades the literature on liberalization.[7] Funding for NGOs thus exploded to billions of dollars in the 1990s.[8] Mutual aid associations have a long history in democratic countries, but as exclusive membership organizations, limited by lineage criteria, kin associations depart from the idea of voluntary and charitable NGOs aiding civil society. Indeed, their classification as civil society is questionable. Because they are redistributive organizations based on membership dues, they do not aid the public at large. Their purpose is not charity to the less fortunate, unless those needy persons happen to be members of the association. Kin associations are self-help, coopera-tive institutions, straddling the NGO–business divide. They are marked off from most local development associations in that their membership criterion is based on kinship through genealogy or place of birth.

Social safety nets, instituted to accommodate the negative impact of economic reforms, have focused on poverty alleviation, not social insur-ance, which leaves the middle classes unaided. Private charity, promoted by states and the international community in economic liberalization, cannot guard against a decline in status for the middle class; it can only be accessed once the family has dropped into poverty. Charity in these regions is focused on social services for the poor, and few NGOs are ac-cessible to the middle class.[9] Charity also is not insurance or an entitle-ment. In fact, the middle stratum more often participates as a provider of voluntary aid, whether in secular or Islamist charities.[10] Nor would the middle class want to accept charity for fear of loss of status and reputa-tion, upon which much livelihood depends.[11] Requesting aid stigmatizes the household as a business and credit risk that is unable to fulfill its obligations. This jeopardizes the central resources of the self-reliant mid-dle class: friends, family, neighbors, and credit from the local merchant. Even for middle strata in the developing world, cash-flow shortages and periodic inability to pay bills are normal.

The motivations and conditions facilitating kin mutual aid organiz-ing in these cases are increasingly common, especially in developing countries, as new economic needs arise in liberalizing economies with limited state reach.[12] Despite the advocacy of market and civil society to fill in for declining state social provisioning, private-sector alternatives are not always available. Further, legal contract enforcement is ineffective in many regions and arguably unsuited for certain collective goods. Virtual and geographic areas are escaping state provisioning, and many are outside state monitoring. The result is often not anarchy but instead the rise of new institutions to address popular needs. Left to their own governance, new neighbors can develop solutions to collective problems.[13] The specific institutional form of the solution varies with incentives in the labor market, available resources, and repertoires of collective organizing. The particular institutional form of kin groups, witnessed here, may differ in regions where repertoires of kin are absent or kinship is a non-starter for organizing, but the incentives and mechanisms can push toward alternative solidarities. The implications of the institutions for state, civil society, and the individual are yet to be explored.

This book examines the rise and fall, motivation, and design of new identity institutions in Jordan and Lebanon since independence, drawing primarily on the political economy of labor and skills, economic institutionalism, and welfare regime literatures. I concentrate on the period of economic liberalization since the end of the 1980s, as it presents a stark example of the withdrawal of social provisioning in contrast to the previous period, along with abundant ethnographic data on kin organizing. Jordan and Lebanon offer a wealth of comparative outcomes among social groups within the national sphere. Earlier periods demonstrate crucial variation among social groups in the presence of social insurance. In this introductory chapter, I more fully describe the kin association outcome and the associations themselves. I then examine explanations for new identity institutions, reviewing cultural, state, elite, and societal variables in light of these cases. Though the usual explanations do not fit the path of kin identity associations, identity politics conclusions indicate that political representation, material goods, and labor networks can cause identity organizing and changes. Lastly, I discuss the data, research methodology, and justification for case selection, and sketch the outline of the remaining chapters.

THE VARYING FATE OF KIN ORGANIZING

Jordan and Lebanon present a puzzle of altering lineages and changing kin groups whose analysis generates insights into the relative causal importance of culture, economics, and political agency in the creation of identities and institutions.[14] The formation and predominance of kin associations followed social welfare and urbanization. As social groups urbanized, their preference for establishing kin mutual aid associations depended on the presence of alternative social insurance. Without viable alternatives, individuals responded to economic hard times and no social insurance by expanding or creating familial networks and formalizing reciprocal obligations for aid and job connections. For those who had social insurance from the state until economic reforms, the establishment of kin associations soared long after urbanization had destroyed many kinship ties. Kin identity had to be re-created among many of these families, whereas others changed their operative kin identities out of a need for resources and informal monitoring. Large kin groups split apart to form more viable enforcement networks, and small families searched for allies and enlarged their definition of kinship to obtain more resources. Some associations advertised publicly for members to acquire the requisite numbers.

Kin associations in Jordan and Lebanon went from a small presence to striking proportions beginning at the end of the 1980s, encompassing around 40 percent of these populations.[15] They outpace all other organizational types. In Jordan, in 2003, out of a population of 5.5 million, there were almost eight hundred kin associations, of which 60 percent were established in less than a decade and half since economic reforms began in 1989. In 1996 only 10 percent of the population belonged to any type of civil society organization such as professional associations, voluntary organizations, sports, youth, and cultural clubs, unions, or religious associations.[16] Professional associations, often cited as a powerful force in the country, involved just over 1 percent of the population in 1995.[17]

Lebanon has more than 1,500 kin associations, 70 percent of which were formed after the war ended in 1990, among a current population of 4.5 million. Although at the start of the war there were approximately 477 kin mutual aid associations, 500 additional associations formed in the first five years after the war alone.[18] This number is all the more striking given the relatively constant population size of 3 million in Lebanon before and after the war. According to some analysts, the kin association phenomenon has altered the face of Beirut.[19] These associations, moreover, are concentrated among 60 percent of the population, those without alternative means of social insurance. The Shi'a, Lebanon's largest community, forms few kin associations, and currently receives social insurance and services from the Islamist group Hizbullah.[20] This pattern contrasts sharply to this social group's organizing in the 1950s, when, as they urbanized with no source of social services, they avidly formed associations.[21] With far more professional and worker associations than Jordan, Lebanon demonstrates the trade-off between mutual aid associations and alternative sources of social welfare. The well-developed charitable sector shows that mutual aid associations do not result from a vacuum of alternative organizing forms. Further, the tight economic circumstances during the Lebanese civil war demonstrate that not austerity but the lack of social provisioning is responsible for the creation of alternative private institutions. Just as the economy was at its worst, for the populations under the purview of the major militias, alternative welfare institutions declined dramatically as militias took over social provisioning. The Christian Lebanese Forces, the Palestine Liberation Organization, the Progressive Socialist Party, and the Shi'a Hizbullah provided crucial welfare services to the populations under their control.[22] After the war, as the militias and their social programs were dismantled save one, the formation of mutual aid associations skyrocketed.

Unlike tribal institutions, kin associations are collectively owned membership organizations, registered as NGOs and built on exclusive identity criteria for membership. They have elected boards of directors, computerized membership records, published treasury reports, and regular dues. Funding comes from members. Members and beneficiaries are one and the same. Group ownership and financing of the association empower members in a way that previous institutions did not. Thus the organizations are horizontal networks, not charity or favors done by patrons. Because of member control, members view kin associations as more accountable, democratic, and transparent than charities.[23] Organization members recounted that the idea of a charity found no takers, whereas a mutual aid association was readily embraced.

Since identity idioms cross class and job and can entail normative duties, they permit individuals to cast a wider net for employment and business contacts and informally guarantee that people repay their obligations. Through shared identity, potential informal networks become formalized institutions with enforced reciprocity for locating jobs and securing emergency aid. Scarce and valuable, these goods necessitate strong ties that combine monitoring and enforcement mechanisms. Trust revolves around reputation and is secured through membership. In order to effectively monitor commitments the organizations remain small, including around one thousand to two thousand members. Though the organizational form and purpose is singular, the particular form of identity varies. Village of origin, present village, and lineage are all spun as aspects of enduring primary relationships. The form of kinship varies with the possibilities for creating a substantially large group.

These mutual aid associations furnish numerous services for their members. Their activities begin with the establishment of a central location or hall for the family to meet regularly and as venues for pivotal events in the life-cycle such as weddings and funerals. The associations provide various types of financial aid, for example, emergency money and loans; regular monthly support for the poor, unemployed, and widows; and seasonal help during holidays, the beginning of the school year, and the onset of winter. Emergency assistance is given for accidents or illness, regular or monthly support for widows or those unable to work, and yearly gifts to needy families during religious occasions. The associations give a small amount of aid to poor families at other times and loans to meet household expenses or for business purposes. Increasingly kin associations take over responsibility for services previously provided by the state.

The specific configuration of services for each association differs according to the membership and its needs, and reflects the contracted labor market and austerity. Some associations paid its members' medical bills. In the event of a funeral, the associations prepare food for those paying their respects, which otherwise is a large financial burden on the family. The associations fund weddings, at least for the poor, and all members usually use the hall free or for a nominal fee for their weddings and funerals. Meetings to discuss political matters, raise emergency funds, or elect a new leadership are held in the center. Other formal services include educational loans, schools, child care, medical and dental clinics, ambulances, hearses, savings funds, computer and other training programs, sports activities, and even summer camp. Informally the associations create job and business networks. In urban areas they offer single, middle-class women employment training programs. In the rural regions poor married women put their toddlers in the association's day care while they manufacture goods for low wages.

To arrive at this form of redistributive association, Jordanians and Lebanese combined diverse modes of organizing, altered them, and added new forms of organizing, all the while turning the previous power structure on its head. Structure, power, purpose, and frequently identities differ from prior institutional models. The dominant functions are now mostly economic. Ceremonial and negotiation roles attached to older kin institutions have been downgraded; economic need is now the stated priority for establishing the organization. The name has changed also. Instead of the former terms *rabita* or *diwan*, "association" (*jama'iyya*) is now used, and some older, established associations are officially changing to the new term. Elite leaders have been displaced. Structural power has altered to provide members leverage over leaders and one another. Historically kin organizations were funded through the benevolence of the tribal leader.[24] Leaders are not inherited, nor do they ply their authority unhindered. The elites setting up mutual aid associations are new, not from the traditionally powerful elite families. Nor are these associations family firms, extended families, or elite families. Thus, although these institutions absorb varying trappings of older institutions, well analyzed by the concept of institutional conversion,[25] they are substantively innovative, are led by new socioeconomic groups, and serve new purposes.

CAUSES OF IDENTITY CHANGE:
THE STATE, ELITES, AND SOCIETY

At first blush the dominance of kinship groups in the Arab world would appear expected. Family and tribal ties seem perennial, and much Middle East literature is based upon the importance of family, tribes, and personal connections in politics. Using the language of tradition and culture, the new arrangements appear old, a "return" to the past. However, cultural continuity would predict differing lines of aggregation than the small kinship groups resulting in Jordan and Lebanon. Some of the new groups unite previously unrelated or unfriendly groups and others break them up to the detriment of the group's electoral chances. Although cultural perspectives would suggest a solidification of identity along lines drawn in war,[26] Lebanon demonstrates otherwise. After a civil war dividing the population by religion, Lebanese organized within religious sects and across them in small kinship organizations despite the apparent increase in political confessionalism.[27] Societal organizing during the civil war itself also confounds cultural concepts of allegiance. War in a kinship-oriented culture could be expected to increase family feeling, but, in fact, kin feelings and kin organizing declined during the Lebanese civil war, 1975–90.[28] Further, most organizing here is in the Lebanese Christian community, whereas observers have noted that culturally, Muslims were more prone to ally along family lines.[29] In Jordan, national origin or tribe would be anticipated historically.[30] Kin organizing contradicts that prediction, splitting tribes and joining national origin groups. Indeed, if Arab cultural stereotypes were in force, then these kin organizations would be unnecessary: informal coercion would not be required for kin to live up to cultural obligations to provide aid to one another. Nor is individual ideological stance regarding the organizations a significant determinant of kin organizing. A large number of the participants in kin organizing disagree with the framework but participated nonetheless. In Jordan a number of leftists have begun to use this form of organizing, as do the most politically active and those formerly opposed on principle to kin-based organizing.[31] Many mentioned the disadvantageous side effects of membership in a kin association, including being drawn into fights with other families, the traditional nature of the institution, and its imposition of political and social rules on members.

A diverse set of situations has been linked to the rise of identity politics. Explanations for identity change and organizing locate causes in the state, elites, or society. Individuals can espouse identities in order to benefit materially or succeed politically. Societal-level explanations contribute most to explaining the Jordan and Lebanon cases. Focused on the grassroots and daily life, societal perspectives identify economic factors responsible for altering identification or creating new lines of cleavage separate from politics and state institutions. Labor networks are particularly important. Whereas state-level incentives, both material and political, are minimal and constant across the fluctuating kin association trend, labor networks and economic need align with interviews, reasons for founding the associations, and the time line of the trend. Kin associations have multiple uses and benefit members and leaders differentially; elite incentives are a part of the story, but they have remained fairly constant. Cultural frameworks are integral to collective action, providing various repertoires or models of action, but how they are used and changed varies.[32] Why different identities are activated or why organizing based on identity is marginalized at different periods remains to be explained.[33] What has changed in these cases is the incentive for members to join or push for kin mutual aid.

The state is the focus of many identity explanations. Political or electoral goals can cause identity organizing for patronage networks and electoral support. Electoral institutions, resources and goods from the state, and direct state promotion can determine whether groups mobilize and the makeup of the groups themselves. For Posner, incentives of political institutions interact with individual expectations of identity salience for individuals to then choose one dimension of their identity as more likely to secure election to political office.[34] This choice is determined by the size of the identity group and probability of success, a calculus affected by the character of the party system as singular or multiple. Local, tribal, or district-level identities triumph in single-party systems. In India, Chandra finds that numbers and the mobilization for votes are important factors in determining if an ethnic party can succeed. She incorporates the observation that ethnicity itself is not fixed since numbers of votes are primary, so identities can be chosen.[35] Political incentives are responsible for ethnic rioting, which is planned for electoral purposes in Wilkinson's account.[36] Elections are also causal in the transition to democracy, as aspiring elites utilize nationalistic appeals to sell an agenda for their own political prominence when media institutions are an unconstraining variable.[37] Similarly, Northern Italian territorial alliances were not preordained but were directed by political mobilization.[38]

Material goods from the state are also important. Patronage is a long-standing explanation for the constitution of groups.[39] In the Middle East the availability of rents has been a powerful explanation for changing identities and renewed tribalism.[40] Groups organized to receive economic resources and jobs in Kazakhstan. Economic problems and shortages, caused by neoliberalism, spurred regular meetings on holidays or generated rotating credit associations in the late 1980s.[41] Rearranged clans developed as networks for goods from the state administration in Tajikistan.[42] In Latin America previously nonpoliticized groups mobilized when their situation vis-à-vis the state diminished in new citizenship regimes.[43] In Africa competition for resources encouraged new ethnic mobilization among groups.[44] Internally, descent groups also altered, accepting new members, as they became state lobbying groups for goods attached to agricultural production and also determined access to land.[45] The Soviet state recomposed communities and identities along territorial and administrative lines in Tajikistan.[46] The equation can work in reverse, from the state to a subnational region as the provision of goods is transferred there. In the European Union the role of subnational regions increased when tasked with social services.[47]

States can channel activism in preferred ways, toward or away from particular identities and forms of mobilization, explaining persistent cross-national differences.[48] In a now famous study, Laitin found that colonial authorities could politicize different forms of identity.[49] Elite battles to retain control amid interactions with ruling and colonial powers can change a society's main identity cleavage, yielding a sectarian system in Lebanon.[50] States promoted and channeled benefits to their own subnational or ethnic group as in Saudi Arabia.[51] In Egypt and much of the Arab world, Islamist organizing was promoted to counter the leftists.[52] Regime type can influence organizing as well, either overtly or through example, as societies mimic state organization through isomorphism.[53] Small-scale kin organizing would be expected in authoritarian regimes, as it could escape political strictures by organizing in *diwaniyya* in Kuwait.[54] However, while the state may have an interest in promoting societal divisions to control social actors, it cannot be presumed to unilaterally impose its will upon society. The state does not always get its wish; outcomes are often adverse to state intentions, as historical institutionalists well know. A relevant example is the persistence of clans despite Soviet attempts to eliminate them.[55]

How do these state-level explanations fare in accounting for the outcomes in Jordan and Lebanon? The role of the state in these cases differs from that posited in other works on ethnicity and the politicization of identity. The state is not absent, and continually asserts itself in the monitoring, approval, and registration of members, however the organizations focus inward, channeling redistributive demands away onto themselves instead of the state, and very few rely on the state for funds. Financial benefits from the state are minimal, and state identity promotion, institutional legacy, and elections would predict different identities than kin groups. While economic rents have provoked the reorganization of lineages to tap the state's coffers, in Jordan and Lebanon economic liberalization and privatization were depleting this revenue source when kin organizing was rising. Neither do the associations mobilize to monopolize a diminishing pie; instead, they largely withdraw from interaction with the state and focus on internal financing and private-sector jobs. Little funding is available in Lebanon, and more in Jordan. Whereas state-building in some Arab countries has relied upon tribes and thus activated them, here kin groups are organizing amid the withdrawal of key state public goods.[56] Many kin associations arose outside and even in opposition to the state.

Regime encouragement of kin organizing and tribalism does not explain the trajectory of the phenomenon. Kin associations remained a marginal organizing form during the martial law period in Jordan, when they were one of the only types of organizations permitted. A constricted organizing field does not explain kin organizing, as the bulk of organizing in Jordan and Lebanon occurred precisely during periods when organizing strictures were loosened: in Jordan, during liberalization post-1989; and in Lebanon, before and after the civil war. A pattern of state formation in Jordan and Lebanon that did not combat the use of kinship or tribes, as did other countries in the region, may have indirectly aided the kin association trend; patronage politics may have kept the repertoire alive. In Lebanon government promotion of kin associations occurred after the war toward the Sunni community, and does not explain the massive kin organizing among the Christian population. Further, these states encouraged sectarian or national origin divisions, not the organizing occurring currently, and this promotion did not substantially waver through time. In Lebanon religious allegiances were institutionalized in the political system. Jordan promoted national origin distinctions and religious organizing, solidifying the former in preferences regarding public-sector employment and allowing the latter to organize throughout the martial law period, most of the state's history.[57] Indeed, some maintain that the state created Jordanian national identity.[58] Yet this does not account for why organizing along kinship lines remained marginal and confined to the minority groups until economic liberalization, or why kinship identities changed as people formed kin mutual aid associations. Jordanian Muslims, deemed by scholars to be the most tribal of Jordan's social groups and encouraged in this by the state, only formed kin associations in the 1990s with economic reforms.[59] Identity promotion and the formation of organizations using identity solidarities are distinct processes and do not necessarily coincide.

The influence of electoral politics is more complicated. Although leaders of kin associations do occasionally stand for national and local elections, their success is limited unless they utilize a broader base than these small-scale organizations. This result comes as no surprise to those familiar with the identity politics literature: elites have incentives to increase their group. Large-scale votes and national-level allegiances are the determining factors for the use of ethnicity. Neither Lebanon's multiparty politics nor Jordan's unified opposition are situations shown to encourage local over national issues and mobilization. The alliances expected from electoral insights counter those identified in the Jordan and Lebanon cases. Instead, from the identity politics literature, large tribes or regional groups would be expected to organize in Jordan, and religious groups or regions would be expected to do so in Lebanon. Religions had been mobilized during the Lebanese civil war, the period prior to a sharp rise in kin organizing. Breaking large religious groups into small kin associations would not be anticipated. Overall, the vast majority of kin associations do not attempt electoral involvement, and, in fact, politics is a divisive internal issue for kin associations.

Many state-level political incentives turn on the decisions of elites. Elite choices have been important variables in changing identity. Elites obtain prestige through the provision of collective goods,[60] but what form of organization or to whom they provide the goods is left unspecified, since this social group has choices for its venue of social promotion. Social status can often be more easily achieved among small groups than in national competition. Decentralized government affords opportunities to ethnic and small-scale entrepreneurs.[61]

The decision to espouse one identity over another, to assimilate or assert a particular identity, can depend on public reputation and vary along with a necessary portion of the populace.[62] Cultural entrepreneurs selling various identity wares often exist, but they are drawn upon when the circumstances alter to give pride of place to that version of identity.[63] Cascades of individuals choosing minority identification or assimilation occur when a critical mass has been reached.[64] What causes the original decisions, before the tipping point is reached, remains a question. Why is a particular identity or language embraced as the new vogue for social advancement?[65]

Elite-based explanations are also inadequate for these cases. The incentives of potential leaders were relatively constant while members' interests in joining changed through time. Elites could benefit from kin organizing by creating symbolic capital and reputation easier than through national or party organizing, a situation that continued through both states' histories. Kin associations represent a shortcut to entrance in the accepted elite, and many leaders had been pushing for the associations for years. Leaders stated that they could not get relatives to agree for decades to form an organization. Then, in hard times, potential members suddenly changed their minds. While in previous decades Jordanian and Lebanese elites attempted to build prestige and networks through sporting, cultural, and professional clubs, in the 1990s idioms of family began to seem a reasonable basis for organizing even for those ideologically opposed to kin organizing. Former leftists, one imprisoned for years for his beliefs, initiated these associations despite considering them "traditional" and "backward." Politically, professional associations and political parties have been more effective as springboards to elected office. In some cases, elites were literally pushed by their relatives to assume the role of leader and organizer of mutual aid organizations.

The analytic focus on the state as the object of societal demands and the agent that structures society often overlooks both the subnational and the individual levels, and cannot explain organizations that ignore or bypass the state. Some states have little to offer, or societal groups are unable to gain access to state goods. The cases analyzed in this book confirm the centrality of material goods and aid identified in the rent-seeking literature on state-level incentives for identity changes, but here the locus of material goods is transposed to society, not the state. Horizontal, member-to-member networks furnish goods. Thus these institutions cannot be classified strictly as patron-client. Although they may contain elites and benefit those leaders, the primary sources of goods are members aiding one another.

Numerous circumstances in society have been shown to cause a shift in identity salience. Chief among these situations are jobs and economic welfare. In these cases, creative mixes of economic interests and identity have been used to generate exchange networks. Migration is a prime motivator of changing and activated identity.[66] Migrants utilize expanded versions of identity to network in the new environment and stay connected with home, obtaining aid in the host country and maintaining links with home. Mexican and Haitian immigrants formed hometown associations in the United States,[67] and Chinese used family associations in San Francisco.[68] Through these associations, Latin Americans and Haitians invested in their home villages.[69] Urban migrants similarly utilized new identities in the city. Migrants in Turkey and Sudan in need of services joined together in new solidarities borne of urbanization.[70] Ancestral native place has been used to tie rotating savings associations, or ROSCAs, in Korea and Taiwan.[71] The substance of these institutions varied with the services provided by the country and the migrants' condition, and were born of urbanization, not carried over from the past.[72] Some began with employment contacts, translation, and mediation, and then moved into the educational and social fields. Many provided aid and loans, or helped members in negotiating aid from banks.[73] Even mutual aid associations in the United States became identities. According to some analyses, the new solidarities were more important than extended family.[74]

Forms of work and economic ties have altered senses of identity. Long-distance trade motivated conversion to Islam in parts of Africa.[75] Differing types of agricultural production altered the bounds of the family in West Africa.[76] In Turkey family and neighborhood networks became interpreted as kin, to be used as safeguards against the precarious labor market.[77] Similarly, flexible and unstable work has led to the use of idioms of kinship and family to secure ties for work in northern-central Italy.[78] Work in southern Italy was conditioned on entering identity and familialistic networks.[79] Nonmigrant but urbanized groups created new tribal identities to furnish social welfare in Iraq during the sanctions period and the removal of state aid. So newly generated were they that the new leaders were dubbed sheikhs made in Taiwan.[80]

The trajectory of kin organizing does not correspond to migration waves, agricultural labor, or productive manufacturing networks. The bulk of the associations formed long after the period of migration, among the socially well integrated, and the trend includes rural, nonmigratory areas.[81] It is not urbanization itself but the lack of social insurance in the new urban environment that generates organizing. More important, the societal examples leave the cause and dynamics of the new affiliations unaddressed. Why do migrants organize among themselves and what determines the specific identity used, whether it is village, region, religion, ethnicity, or nationality? The lack of opportunities explains the pull of organizations that assist migrants, but how do they manage to collectively pool their resources without the problem of free riders? Kinship and ethnicity have been taken for granted as providing easy collective action, a black box of assumed cooperation. If identity can change or multiple bases for identity organizing exist, we can no longer posit that individuals act together out of a long-standing cultural or normative duty to help others from the same identity group. Indeed, on the ground much effort goes into securing obligations and creating solidarity among members.

SOCIAL INSURANCE ORGANIZING AND IMPLICATIONS

Social insurance, or buffers against economic upsets and risk, is a popular priority demonstrated in the identity and welfare literatures.[82] Not only does poverty spur the search for social insurance and welfare, but economic vulnerability and the threat to current economic status also inspire organizing or demands for protection.[83] Economic liberalization reforms in the 1980s and 1990s signaled the progressive end of state social policies for Middle Eastern non-oil countries. These economic reforms dismantled generous public employment, consumer price supports, and subsidies, all of which had served as buffers against economic downturns. The end of the Lebanese civil war translated into the same result, as militia services for the bulk of the population ended. The reforms occurred just as regional labor markets contracted, markets that had served as an outlet for unemployment and provided income from labor remittances. The result was increasing vulnerability for a significant portion of the population, middle class and poor alike, who lack alternative sources of social insurance.[84]

Because public welfare was provided through different mechanisms than the specialized social insurance of industrialized states, its role in supporting these countries' middling strata has been overlooked. State provisioning helped the entire populace, not merely the poor, and thus was economically inefficient for the purposes of targeted support. It had provided a market buffer to the middle classes, however. Poverty grew.[85] Still, national economic growth and poverty statistics do not tell the full story. The percentage of the population that is vulnerable even to minor fluctuations in expenses and the job market has increased dramatically. Not only was the removal of welfare more drastic in the developing world than in the industrialized countries, but also fewer resources exist to cope with emergencies.[86] As in other developing contexts, more economic risk and variability in employment and income exist in these economies, even when individuals are employed regularly; households "move in and out of poverty."[87] Not being paid for months, despite continued work, is normal, in addition to job instability. Labor market insecurity increased and pension coverage declined. The mythical traditional family has been unable to prevent the rise of poverty and the decreasing middle class.

Varying in importance by economic conditions and resources, obtaining social insurance can motivate the formation of new institutions and networks, and alter existing identity legacies. Kin institutions were abandoned, embraced, or created along with the presence or absence of social insurance. The chain of institutional creation is set off by changes in the level of economic risk. For collective institutions to be established, there must be a commonly felt risk. The withdrawal of state social policies altered the economic calculus of individuals, introducing popular economic vulnerability as in other cases of welfare removal.[88] New needs and a loss of prior buffers, entailed in state and militia welfare services, provided an opportunity and demand for institutions to respond, or claim to respond, to unmet requests. As in other cases, the quality of new services may not be good or even adequate, but it is better than nothing.[89]

The kin institutions arise amid the dearth of private market and labor-based alternatives for social insurance, within the context of ineffective judicial institutions to enforce contracts. The characteristics of nonprofessional service work dominating these economies complicate the search for social insurance and pensions through guilds or associations based on human capital assets. Work is not steady or necessarily formal, precluding employer-based social insurance. Job changes are recurrent. Neither can these employees organize around common skills as professionals do; service jobs are not tied to a particular knowledge base. With generalized skills, they move among jobs in the service sector with ease. Today's waiter is tomorrow's taxicab driver. A hospital administrator can become a tour guide or a retail employee. Typical is the situation of one Lebanese interviewee who is both a professor and a green grocer. This skill structure also means that cross-class, cross-sector organizing makes economic sense, bringing the possibility of wide-ranging networks, unlimited by skill or know-how, furnishing employment. Thus the relevant category of labor is not class but risk categories within classes. Those at higher economic risk because of vulnerable employment and lack of social insurance are the ones interested in kin associations. Skilled labor can utilize professional associations and unions for insurance and aid.

New kin identities yield face-to-face credible expectations for reciprocal aid. Institution members provide help because they trust that others will also. Personal relationships and reputation have been instrumental in securing work amid insecure, precarious labor markets. Networks of commitment and duty to find employment for others have taken the form of fictive kinship and friendship. These informal webs of reciprocity were institutionalized, and that institution's shape conforms to the size, communication, and identity variables delineated by economic and rational institutional analyses. This design creates enforcement mechanisms holding individuals to their promises, which in turn generates outcomes superior to those individuals could achieve alone. What differentiates the networks in this case from manufacturing networks is their time line of creation and professional makeup. Networks to obtain these goods, jobs, and loans are not necessarily preexisting but can be created for that purpose. The kin idiom generates reputational effects or cascades, allowing initial trust and faith that others will abide by their commitments, since the institution also entails monitoring and communication—in other words, gossip that a person is shirking her commitments.[90]

The effects of these organizations are far-reaching, including a rise in the use and salience of subnational identity economically, socially, and politically, and deepening obstacles to good governance and state transparency. Politically the organizations can marginalize participation in political parties and demand allegiance internally at this subnational level. At the same time the organizations reinforce corruption and nepotism, chief rallying cries of the Islamists. In a shrinking labor market, subnational groups can attempt to segment the market and decrease its competitive character to the profit of the smaller group. Benefits and jobs can remain within that identity group.

The changing circumstances that generate new accommodations and institutions in Jordan and Lebanon provide an opportunity to view institutional creation and the dynamics of societal change in action. These cases identify powerful incentives linking micro-level pressures and collective action, revealing popular preferences regarding economic risk and vulnerability, and making clear when those risks outweigh costs of contributing to the welfare of a collective. As such, they highlight practical incentives for organizing that are often overlooked in economic planning. Though specific outcomes and institutional forms differ across regions, classes with resources are strongly motivated to avoid economic vulnerability, and the context generating these incentives is increasingly important for internationally connected economies. This mechanism of searching for social insurance is globally relevant to policy makers and social scientists as states withdraw their social provisioning.[91] The type of work prevalent in developing societies—irregular, informal, and general skills service work—must be overtly brought into theorizing the institutions that arise to govern the economy. In many areas, market sources of social insurance cannot be presumed to exist, and state economic safety nets omit the middle class, a main actor in welfare demands. Discovering that economic factors underlie some motivations for identity organizing engages the relationship between subnational organizing and state-building, economic growth, and democratic aspirations.

RESEARCH DESIGN

Jordan and Lebanon were chosen for practical and theoretical reasons. Both countries have histories of economic liberalism, and their market institutions are more prominent than in similarly placed Arab states. They also have relatively large public spheres, histories of secular organizing,[92] and are implementing economic liberalization reforms combined with targeted antipoverty safety nets.[93] Jordan and Lebanon are often praised as approximations of democracy, and their legacies of minimal economic interventions are viewed as boding well for long-term market success, in contrast to neighboring socialist states. Moreover, they are not hampered by single-party regimes.[94] The two small countries share similar economic circumstances that could plausibly lead to association formation. Both are labor-rich, capital-poor, and internationally oriented, dependent on international services and remittances. Both are resource-poor, with urban, educated labor forces and a substantial middle class. The bulk of income comes from the service sector, with a large percentage of self-employment, informal labor, small-scale industries, and multiple jobs per worker.[95] Neither country effectively encouraged manufacturing and both have a small rural population, the lowest in the Middle East and

North Africa region.[96] Jordan and Lebanon are also (relative) regional leaders in the provision of market loans, pensions, and insurance.

The countries share common cultural models of collective action, and are rich in social groups with divergent positions to state welfare and the labor market. These religious and ethnic subnational divisions provide significant variation through time. Jordan and Lebanon experienced various periods of state or state-like social insurance across time that allows a more thorough treatment of alternative arguments for formal identity groups. Chief among these is the Lebanese civil war, which is presumed to increase feelings of identity, but kin organizing declined during this period. On the macro domestic level, Lebanon witnessed two changes in social provisioning, the first when welfare began for much of the population during the war and the second when it was removed. Jordan experienced one major change at this level, the end of state social provisioning. Thus, in the current period, the two states' outcomes correspond, both demonstrating a rise in kin mutual aid associations. However, this is not only a case of similar outcomes but of numerous cases within those countries compared across time. Subnational comparisons of social groups and their corresponding relation to state welfare reveal variance and furnish evidence that supplements the macro change in national social welfare. This within-country variation minimizes the influence of regime type, history, and culture in the determination of those varying social outcomes.

Differences between the countries help eliminate country-specific explanations. While both countries are family-oriented, they became so from divergent histories. In Lebanon, family prominence is associated with confessionalism and the role of religion in daily life. In Jordan, it has been attributed to tribal legacies. Cosmopolitan Lebanon has a longer history of interaction with the West, economic development, and a vibrant civil society. Its economic sector is further developed and it hosts a larger working class than Jordan. Lebanon also has a higher per capita income. Jordan is a newer, and some would say more invented, state.[97] Its trade and political links look eastward. Jordan has a larger family size and birth rate, factors that could conceivably contribute to mutual aid through identity. Lebanon's average household is small (approximately 4.5 members).[98]

This book is based on more than two and a half years of fieldwork, including close to four hundred formal interviews and questionnaires (see Appendix I for details).[99] The data include dozens of formal interviews with individuals who are not members of a kin association, and surveys and profiles of cultural and charitable organizations. To avoid deriving conclusions solely based on functions or explanations driven by current conceptions, I examined decision-making processes, member opinions and reasons for the institution at the time of establishment, and the benefits received or expected. I analyzed the work, income, and educational background of members and leaders, and of a sampling of nonmembers. I reviewed association records and family histories, including financial data, membership lists, promotional publications, annual reports, original registration data, and internal administrative reports detailing activities and funding. In order to assess alternative explanations, I used nonmember interviews and compared the timing of these institutions with other posited motivations. I employed a targeted questionnaire, written in Arabic and reviewed by several Jordanian and Lebanese social scientists (see Appendix II). The questions were open-ended and codified subsequently, after all were completed, to allow for maximum flexibility in responses. The questions overlapped, approaching the same subjects from different angles and wording. Through this method I was able to combine ethnographic data with a systematic analysis of the sample associations, yielding a more representative and complex picture of kin associations, their causes, and their role in daily life.

The changing factors driving this identity trend are made all the more clear by cases where identities themselves are reorganized to yield a mutual aid association. My hypothesis, that the welfare opportunity structure determines individual choices in the presence of economic risk, is testable. Maintaining the economic sector as a constant, kin mutual aid associations should vary with major changes in state welfare, credit, and the demand for labor. The massive influx of U.S. aid to Jordan after 2003 demonstrates this variability. The use of mutual aid associations temporarily declined as jobs, credit, and money became more available. If kin associations became a dominant trend while either state welfare was being provided or among economic sectors with alternative economic organizations, my claim would be falsified. Supporting my hypothesis, middle- and lower-income groups engaged in a skill-specific business were uninterested in these associations, expressly stating their preference for overtly economic affiliations. Further, individuals opted out of these kin associations when they were financially able to plan their middle-class future without the social insurance provided by formal kin groups.

OUTLINE OF THE BOOK

The theoretical background for my explanation of kin associations is delineated in chapter 1, where I review the welfare regime literature and economic institutionalism. I describe a welfare opportunity structure of individual preferences that prioritizes available private-sector alternatives, skill analysis, and the character of the labor market. Many options for welfare are tied to the type of labor and job stability. Given existing possibilities in this context, economic institutionalism explains the specific design of the new kin associations, a design that attempts to generate commitments among members backed up by the monitoring power of the association. Identity provides the solidarity that allows members to be obligated, and hold one another to account, for providing aid to the collective.

Chapter 2 focuses on the public provision of welfare, the first of the welfare opportunity structure variables. Using the welfare regime literature, I examine state and militia social policies beginning from independence. Jordan's welfare system differed significantly from that of developed economies but resembled social policies in Latin America, Southern Europe, and other Middle Eastern states. Lebanon's experience of welfare for the middle classes came mainly through the militias during the civil war, as the major militias initiated complex social policies comparable to those in the advanced democratic states. In 1989 Jordan's welfare policies began to be dismantled with the beginning of economic liberalization. Lebanon's welfare policies ended in 1990 with the dismantling of all but one militia (Hizbullah) and the accompanying social services. In economic liberalization, state social provisioning has been limited to targeting antipoverty measures, encouraging private charities, and increasing benefits to military employees. Chapter 3 examines the private sector's potential to fill in for state welfare. Here I analyze the potential of labor-based alternatives and market possibilities. Employment-based options for insurance are not viable for much of the population because of the character of labor. Outside the professions, the bulk of labor is intermittent, seasonal, and irregular, and local markets for credit and private insurance are lacking.

Chapter 4 traces the trajectory of mutual aid organizing, its rise and fall. This time line corresponds to the presence or absence of collective social provisioning laid out in chapters 2 and 3. I compare kin association services and numbers with nongovernmental charities, demonstrating that mutual aid associations exceed charities in popular participation and that the two types of organizations cater to different social groups and services. Chapter 5 delves within the associations, presenting ethnographies of associations. Examined here are the dynamics of institutional creation and the social strata responsible for the establishment of the associations. I analyze how the organization incorporates and departs from prior collective organizing models, and also explain the income-pooling or insurance functions of kin associations and the motivations of members. The services of mutual aid organizations demonstrate their link to gaps in the labor and credit markets, including pensions, periodic aid, and loans. Job provision holds pride of place in the organizations, and leaders must be able to furnish employment contacts.

Chapter six explores the associations' potential political motivations and social implications. New elites consciously aid in the reorganization of identity and the establishment of the associations, and benefit primarily by establishing social prestige for themselves. Social implications stem from the priority of demonstrating commitment to the kin association. The informal monitoring of members translates into a privileging of kin identity solidarity, even if newly created, that can reduce involvement in politics outside the group's solidarity. Because political allegiances differ among the membership, political involvement and ideologies are marginalized to preserve group unity. They sometimes can, and do, join in temporary blocs of independents allied for a common, short-term cause. State institutions also weigh in on the kin association trend, biasing funds in that direction. The effect of kin associations is broader than formal politics, as social senses of identity and individual behavior can be affected. Indeed, the associations turn demands for welfare goods inward and away from the state.

The book concludes with a review of the findings, and the theoretical and policy implications they imply. I examine the theoretical lessons regarding the ability to establish diverse organizations, the boundaries of created identities, the role of culture, and the responsibility of elites. Also discussed is the scope of the independent variable of social welfare, the core of economic risk, and the applicability of social welfare to other regions. I analyze the general civil society implications of kin mutual aid, examining the counterintuitive conclusion that internally democratic organizations may themselves be incapable of effective demands on the state, and instead facilitate the maintenance of authoritarian regimes. Yet these outcomes are not inevitable. Policy makers have options to discourage kin association formation without sacrificing comprehensive economic reform.

1

Welfare, Work, and Collective Action

The rise and fall of kin mutual aid organizing within a country and within the same social group across time is a powerful indicator of an association's variability in terms of purpose, viability, or attractiveness. That the institution is created actively by altering and combining existing templates is another sign of changing incentives. How can we explain new organizing variously at odds with political incentives, institutional legacy, and cultural heritage? The review of identity politics literature in the introduction shows that identity changes and new organizing on the basis of identity can occur for political representation, material goods, and labor networks. Emotional and cultural attachments to identity do not preclude strategic action or the rational calculus of benefits: identity and interests are not mutually exclusive. Individuals hold a wide range of identities simultaneously. Though somewhat elastic, these identity possibilities are not infinite but are confined within parameters marked by the historical context.

Three theoretical literatures together explain the re-creation and mobilization of kin solidarities in Jordan and Lebanon—the welfare regime literature, economic institutionalism, and labor asset analysis, combining historical and economic approaches at different levels.[1] This book concludes that individuals seek protection from economic risk and vulnerability, created and signaled with the end of collective social protection, by forming new mutual aid institutions. The shape of these institutions is explained by economic institutionalism, whereas the choice of identity rather than job or profession as the means of solidarity is explained by the employment profile and collective organizing repertoires. Historical patterns of organizing alone cannot explain the choice of kinship for social insurance. Economic institutionalism's analysis of institutional design accounts for the shape of kin identity and the changed institutional form, and historical analyses provides the emphasis on the middle, institutional, or state-level policies, analysis of the context of cultural repertoires, and delineation of the national implications for the new institutional trend.

Historical approaches argue that culture and institutional legacy prefigure the available options known or considered possible or appropriate, their repertoires.[2] Yet culture permits a wide range of potential choices. Further, culture, legacy, and group solidarity cannot negate problems highlighted by micro-level analyses such as the moral hazard problem, free riders, or overuse of commonly pooled resources. The institutional power structure may be set in advance of choices, but this constricted universe of options does not mean that collective action need not be explained or that the selection of one institutional form over another is predetermined. Individuals can choose instrumentally from their existing repertoires. Recent work on identity problematizes both the institutional and individual levels, attempting to account for systemwide incentives and personal choices. This new trend of joining the middle or state level, analyzed by historical institutionalists, and the individual level, often considered the preserve of rational choice theorists, holds the promise of enduring and portable explanations.[3] As Geddes states, work such as David Laitin's on Russia "uses some of the tools provided by economic models to help understand otherwise puzzling or seemingly irrational actions and . . . it also explores in depth and detail how people perceive their situations."[4] Rational choices can coexist with intense feelings of identity and institutional trajectories.

I first examine the welfare regime literature and economic institutionalism, which explain the initial cause for identity organizing and changes in identity solidarities themselves. The welfare regime literature demonstrates that formal state provisioning comes through different policies. In many areas, continuing welfare through interest-group pressure on states is not viable. Instead, individual and collective nonstate options serve as welfare for much of the globe. Analyzing collective welfare organizing in the private sector necessitates understanding what keeps individuals to their commitments, since legal guarantees backing informal contracts are not present. The economic institutional literature explains what is needed for effective informal monitoring of commitments. Trusting that others will be held accountable, individuals join and volunteer to help, allowing for the long-term success of the institutions. Using insights from these bodies of literature together with political economic skill analysis, I then formally fashion the argument. I delineate a theoretically informed hierarchy of choices facing individuals to secure their future, mapping a welfare opportunity structure (WOS).[5] This matrix of alternatives consists of state social policies, markets for credit and insurance, and the potential for professional or job-based insurance. The turn to kin and not profession is explained by the skill profile of the labor market, making identity a rational allegiance for employment seekers. I focus on the variable of collective social protection in Jordan and Lebanon, with particular emphasis on the recent period of economic liberalization and after the civil war beginning in 1989 and 1990, respectively. This recent period provides ethnographic data on individual preferences, and the outcome is stark. Both countries ended social provisioning for the general populace, gradually or all at once. Although that social insurance was furnished through different sources, the state or militias, the altered economic incentive for kin associations was clear in interviews. This end of public social provisioning generated and signaled a rise in vulnerability and financial risk, creating an interest in social protection among large segments of society.

WELFARE REGIMES AND SOCIAL INSURANCE

The identity politics literature and welfare regime analysis both emphasize the causal importance of social insurance and material security. The key variable in welfare demands is the sense of vulnerability or exposure to risk and the resulting willingness to contribute to collective institutions.[6] The deprivation of basic foodstuffs continually causes uprisings and food riots, and goods-based patronage has been a staple of political analysis. Social protection mitigates and buffers individuals against life-cycle and abnormal economic risks, that is, periods when existing household funds cannot cover expenses because of downturns or extraordinary expenditures. Typical recurring risks for the poor include unemployment, death, divorce, old age, and illness. Imperiling the middle class are education costs, expenses for funerals and weddings, accidents, and un- or underemployment. Industrialization and urbanization gave way to large-scale collective risks, which voided village-level mechanisms while creating the need for new types of risk-protection. Focused at the state level, the welfare regime literature tells us that financial security for individuals and households is often a priority, that the middle class is a major constituency for welfare, and that social provisioning can be furnished through different policies, all buffering the individual experience of relative prices and hard times. Changes in economic vulnerability or insecurity, as those following the end of public social provisioning in Jordan and Lebanon, can generate demands for collective protection and the turn to individual social insurance options.

More broadly, scholars of the welfare state in advanced economies have noted the analytical insight of this lens into the distributive, power, and class battles that make the country's politics. Lines of conflict are established and politicized. In- and out-groups are set, the substance of citizenship and rights determined, community integration or autonomy solidified.[7] Distinguishing categories of welfare policies has provided insights into the trajectory of production regimes as well as their economic prospects.[8] Different welfare regimes have varying, long-term consequences on the development of skills, labor capacities, and political and social organizing.[9] The welfare regime literature can tell us about the national-level implications of changes in state provisioning for the economy and potential societal unity.

Welfare studies highlight three key factors in the configuration of state social provisioning: economic interests and organizing, the economy itself and the type of capitalism, and regime type or the array of political institutions. Haggard and Kaufman highlight the role of the first variable, the power resources theory, privileging distributive coalitions and the relative strength of classes as determinants of welfare policy.[10] Thus they assert the important role of groups such as labor, and the lasting legacy of stakeholders entailed in particular benefits and the resulting partisan politics.[11] Additional factors are the economy, strong or weak, and the particular form of capitalism, the country's production profile, its place in the international system, and employer preferences regarding skilled labor. Political voice is important in creating and maintaining welfare. Organizing on the basis of economic demands was a key factor in the form of social protection from the state. Democracies appear to be more responsive to social groups than non-democracies, but autocracies are not immune to the pressures of politically important groups, whether organized or not. In fact, state-building, or the search for a coalition to support the state, has been an important consideration in providing welfare in developing countries. In Latin America the forces responsible for state-building were reflected in the pattern of social insurance.[12] In the Middle East the political creation of a national identity in the process of state-building was a goal of social policies in many states.[13]

Middle classes are often at the center of social provisioning, despite common conceptions that social insurance policies serve as protection for the poor. Notwithstanding their interest in social insurance, the ability of the poor to mobilize for it and their weight in policy making has lagged. The politically noisy middle class, often presumed to be averse to taxation and state spending, was a prime actor behind state welfare policies in the West. When economic uncertainty became intolerable, this stratum threw its lot in with the lower classes, demanding state welfare. Industrialization and its displacements spurred initial social insurance laws across the globe.[14] Welfare acts as insurance, a spreading of financial and labor market risk. Foregoing a portion of present income for future insurance collected by the state, for these classes welfare is insurance, not redistribution.[15] Future orientations are particularly important for the middle classes, since they lack independent security through ownership of fixed assets or wealth. Unlike the poor, they have resources to invest for tomorrow, but they lack the hereditary privileges of the upper class. Together, the "shaky independence" of the middle classes vis-à-vis the market, the fear of losing status and descending into poverty,[16] and having resources to invest in the future give this class both incentive and ability to press for social security. As Baldwin demonstrates, preventing the middle class from falling into poverty is the motivating force behind the welfare regimes in industrialized democratic states. Welfare secures aid as entitlement, not charity, at vulnerable times in the life-cycle.[17]

In the developing world the methods of providing social welfare differ sharply from those of the industrialized countries, with the result that they have only recently been identified as forms of welfare.[18] Various policies not specifically termed "welfare" provide social insurance. Many countries furnish social goods and assure a minimal living through guaranteed low prices and employment. Rodrik finds that the secure jobs entailed in public employment are the most common means of social insurance in developing countries.[19] These jobs also provide pensions, in contrast to informal and unstable employment in the developing world. Likewise Huber finds that pensions, health care, and price supports and controls were central to social provisioning in Latin America.[20] Haggard and Kaufman also conclude that pensions and health insurance constituted the main social policies for welfare, in addition to the state's provision of social services such as education.[21] Rudra similarly highlights the effect of pensions in stabilizing income through market changes, along with various other policies such as housing subsidies and education.[22] Redistribution and insurance are related and can serve the same purposes.[23]

Middle Eastern social provisioning has been called a social contract, trading political rights for economic goods, and shares many commonalities through the region.[24] The central characteristics of Middle Eastern welfare have been the setting of prices and protection of consumers, and, second, the provision of employment in privileged public-sector institutions—the bureaucracy, the army, and often a small elite of industrial workers in top industries. Public employment, though poorly paid, carried additional coveted benefits generally unavailable in the private sector, including job security, pensions, health coverage, access to inexpensive consumer goods, and the ability to get advances on pay. Some jobs offered subsidized education and housing as well. This created a dual system, wherein a minority of workers were well furnished with social welfare, whereas the majority had minimal or no coverage. Outside of public employment, pensions and health insurance are rare. Thus the states with the highest public employment are also those with the most social insurance coverage, as public employment is the main and virtually only way of providing pensions.[25] The average coverage of pension systems in the Middle East and North Africa is around one-third of the labor force, with high levels of coverage where public employment is also elevated.[26] Public employment was privileged in rich oil rentier and poorer states alike, although the former furnished a more extensive array of services. In the Middle East public nonmilitary employment exceeds the global average.[27] Pension systems there suffer from design flaws and numerous plans; they are also costly and incur debts to the government. Pension coverage is low, social insurance overlooks the informal and agricultural sectors, and the benefit amount is decreasing as a result of inflation. The high is 50 percent among the active labor force in Egypt. Increasing demographic pressures because of high birth rates will further strain available resources.[28]

Demands on the state for social policies differ from the model of industrialized countries, which helps explain the ineffectiveness of protests calling for continued social aid during economic reforms. The political voice variable is affected not only by the overwhelmingly authoritarian character of states in the Arab world but also because of the differences in organizing based on economic interests. Economic organizing is weak. Smaller percentages of society are mobilized in unions or professional organizations, and many Arab states have little manufacturing. Service-sector employment, containing the bulk of labor, presents distinct difficulties for organizing workers, not least because of the lack of specialized skills and the dearth of job stability.

Social insurance can be provided not only by the state but also by nonstate actors, a dynamic increasingly relevant to the Middle East and to the developing world in general.[29] Collapsed, failed and weak states, and civil wars give rise to states within states which often provide state-like services.[30] Many territories have witnessed the establishment of new institutions of law and order along with social provisioning, including

Somaliland, Eritrea, Savimbiland, and FARClandia.[31] Militias substituted for the state in Lebanon, providing a wealth of social services and welfare that path dependence and isomorphism cannot explain: militia services bore no resemblance to the state's previous lack of social policies.[32]

Market and nongovernmental social insurance exists for households and groups as well. Private-sector formal options for self-provisioning increased in the last half-century in industrialized countries, as the markets for insurance, pensions, and loans have become available to the middle to lower classes, including the use of credit for emergencies. Life insurance became available in the eighteenth century in the United States, and, in the nineteenth century, mutual insurance societies aided the working class with resources to spare.[33] Some were religious, combining prayer societies with insurance and health aid.[34] The large number of African American fraternal associations provided mutual insurance.[35] Individual families can undertake certain social protection solutions such as migration, marriage into different labor markets to balance out risk, and loans to smooth income and accommodate periodic financial needs.[36] Credit substitutes for insurance, providing needed cash in downturns.[37] In some cases this can be reciprocal, and can smooth the variability in income and consumption that is inevitable for much of the world.[38] Indeed, one reason that charity is not an option for middle-class households, in addition to their not qualifying, is their fear of losing access to credit. Livelihood, overall, depends on status and the reputation of being able to pay debts.[39]

Because individual and market solutions are often absent or insufficient, nonstate collective accommodations for insurance have proliferated, joining subgroups of the national populace. Among them are professional associations, guilds, unions, mutual aid associations, and village and migrant organizations. People organized along agricultural village or employment lines pooled resources to purchase pension programs and insurance, and furnish mutual loans. Such associations include village cooperatives for agriculture, mutual aid and unions for workers, guilds for artisans, fraternal societies for the upper-middle classes, and professional associations for the highly skilled. Village associations shared risk, albeit incompletely, but did provide some aid.[40] Historically professional associations, unions, and guilds lobbied on behalf of members and attempted to provide for their future. In fact, guilds and professional associations were precursors of state welfare in the West, and many industrialized countries based their welfare systems upon pensions and insurance provided by employers.[41] Even in the informal sector, with enough collective worker power, employers can be pushed to provide credit, sick leave, and bonuses.[42] Rotating savings and credit associations (ROSCAs) are one form of nonmarket, relationship-based economic organizing that exist in many countries around the globe: in numerous African countries and throughout the Middle East, Latin America, and South and East Asia. In Yemen local villages pooled their finances in the absence of state services to provide public goods.[43] The definition of solidarity varied, but all shared an interest in insuring against common risks.

BUILDING INSTITUTIONS WITH CREDIBLE COMMITMENTS

Private-sector collective social welfare arrangements such as rotating savings associations, mutual credit, village mutual aid, and migrant association depend upon individuals keeping their word and contributing to the collective. Individuals must repay loans without legal contracts, help others against their own short-term self-interest, or contribute labor to common projects. In the real world, no matter how tight the solidarity, institutions that last have ways of insuring that individuals abide by their commitments. Where formal legal protection is available, contracts can guarantee loan repayment. But when courts and police do not function for the average person without powerful connections, other means of securing repayment must be found. In short, positing an identity solidarity or culture does not erase the prospect of moral hazards and free riders. Collective action analyses, rational choice, and game theory have problematized the black box of group cooperation.[44] Assuming automatic cooperation is particularly problematic when the group is not preexisting but contains newly generated solidarities.

Informal reciprocity helps villagers, kin, and friends through hard times, but it is often mythologized.[45] Community and family are frequently assumed to be automatic sources of aid. What motivates people to help and when they do so are not questioned. In reality, village reciprocal aid is incomplete and often breaks down; network members attempt to hide assets or misinform on their ability to help.[46] Individuals do not give more than they must to stay on good terms and be able to count on aid from the network for themselves. Internal conflict occurs; differences in power and gender are variables that complicate the peaceful community image. Indeed, even relations within the household are contentious, as members differ over expenditure priorities and the allocation of responsibilities.[47]

Rational approaches can help explain cooperation but need to be combined with network and institutional perspectives. Micro-level decisions are not based on the individual alone but on networks, future concerns, and benefits derived from these institutions. Micro-level theories have contributed much to understanding new collective institutions across the globe precisely because they take changing individual interests into account. While the assumption of rationality gives agency to individuals, individual rationality in isolation cannot accommodate the networks and interpersonal exchanges that pervade daily life. Preferences do not aggregate neatly and arithmetically. Economic institutionalism advanced economics' rational, self-serving, and calculating concept of the individual beyond the individual herself to include networks and institutions.[48] Markets are not seamless, information is costly and asymmetrical, and contracts are sometimes unenforceable or inappropriate for particular types of relationships and goods. The insight that formal contracts and property rights may not be enforceable through legal institutions opens a wide field of research for the developing world. The state and market institutions taken for granted in other areas are not present or are inadequate here, creating the potential for alternative institutions to act as substitutes. Without such acknowledgment of differing market and contract conditions, many outcomes in the developing world would be unintelligible. The lack of regulatory and legal institutions, often assumed to exist in micro-level analyses, could be behind many institutions that appear cultural.[49] These nonmarket solutions to the principal-agent problem can be more efficient than market contracts in situations of incomplete and private information.[50]

Institutions that limit individual behavior while providing benefits to members can generate cooperation. Institutions enable collective action, facilitating greater benefits through a collective coordinating body than an individual could achieve alone.[51] They do so by imposing rules on members, backed by informal methods of enforcement. Often these institutions are informal, such as the relationship between neighbors. Mutual help and reciprocity is characteristic of such relationships, which can be modeled as ongoing, iterative games. Informal mechanisms monitor, enforce, and punish in the event of nonparticipation or moral hazards.[52] In a closed, linked network, word of mouth transmits information on the individual's business worthiness and her ability to work within the informal understandings of the group.[53] Essentially this is done through the threat of exclusion from the network, that is, a denial of access to network business opportunities or services. Because neighbors see one another repeatedly, they trust that they will not cheat or hurt one another, since the relationship provides long-term benefits superior to short-term advantages or selfish behavior.[54] In these relationships people will make every effort to demonstrate their trustworthiness, with the understanding that fellow neighbors will reciprocate.[55] Loaning money, conducting long-distance trade, or merely aiding a coworker all entail trust in reciprocity. Exchanges are not immediate and involve faith that the other party will fulfill her obligations at a later date. Giving goods or services without immediately receiving something in return stems from expectations of future aid, based on institutional understandings of the relationship and its obligations. Unlike market transactions, reciprocity has a longtime horizon and the exchange is not terminated in one encounter. They are not equal transactions in the short term but tend to even out in the longer term. These are not altruistic favors but are part of an implied, informal contract. Exchanges are carefully remembered and counted.[56] Though tallies are usually not formally kept, the individuals involved and the community have a value measure for favors done and remember what favors are owed.[57]

Clearly not just any relationship can become committed reciprocity. The potential to institute such enforcement mechanisms is an important consideration for the choice of solidarity in organizing. Long-term, continuous relationships are qualitatively different from fly-by-night ones.[58] The ties must be strong, with the potential for in-group policing; that is, network members must be capable of monitoring one another's behavior. To establish this group of people, bound by informal obligations with ongoing peer monitoring, individuals must be unable to escape the group. Otherwise, members can "take the money and run," skipping out on their obligations. Sanctions and relations that are unavoidable make shirking more difficult.[59] Maintaining the boundary of insiders and outsiders is crucial in such trust networks. If not, monitoring and enforcing cannot be sustained and the group will not last.[60] These mechanisms are person-specific—there is some way that the individual cannot avoid being in the group in the near term. These relationships can be modeled formally. Akin to repeated iterations of a game, superior results are achieved through cooperation in ongoing relations. As Weingast summarizes, "By tying behavior today with (negative) consequences tomorrow, trigger strategies alter the trade-off between defection and cooperation."[61]

Geographic proximity satisfies these requirements, if neighborhood residents are not fly-by-night. Family, often presumed as obliged to provide aid, actually constitutes a minority of informal networks in many areas.[62] Home and job can trump close kin who live a distance away, since kin can disappear and neighbors and coworkers must be seen daily.[63] More complete information can be obtained by sharing work or residence. Social networks of the poor in Chile and women's pooling networks in Egypt consisted not of extended family but of common neighborhood.[64] Strong ties can be based on home neighborhood, occupation, friendship, a small religious group, or close kin.

Yet, to function as trustworthy members, the groups need not already exist or be based on current close ties. Institutions, through reputational effects, allow people to interact as if they were engaged in trusted, long-term relationships.[65] Reciprocal trust is normally built over time through repeated personal interactions where good faith and reliability are demonstrated. But idioms of identity can serve as shortcuts to reciprocal trust if they entail monitoring to convince members of one another's commitment. Identity can serve as a marker or sign of future behavior. As Landa states, "Under conditions of contract uncertainty, where the legal framework for enforcement of contracts is not well developed, the identity of potential trading partners matters."[66] Boundaries marking groups are important. People in the group are at pains to demonstrate their group identity, that they really belong and are playing the same game, with the same expectations of action and reciprocity.[67] For Kuran, identity groups can create reputational cascades pushing individuals in the group to demonstrate that they belong to that group by manifesting group behavior and dress. Members privilege relations with their own group over outsiders.[68] These expectations of the fellow ethnic's behavior are accompanied also by the expectation that sanctions will be imposed for not behaving according to norms. Thus, even if the individuals are not related, the use of kin idioms strengthens the relationship by enshrining it in noninstrumental terms. Using the language of family highlights the special and close relationship between the parties, drawing the new relatives into a web of commitment that decreases their ability to resist claims on their time or money.[69] To solidify the obligations, rituals and gift-giving are often used to avoid movement in and out of the group, and to reinforce obligations for future reciprocity.[70]

A rich literature attests to the role of monitoring and informal enforcement in grass-roots, private-sector accommodations for social welfare and mutual aid that commonly operate outside enforceable contracts and legal regulation. Migrant associations in Sudan contain checks and balances, furnishing accountability to the membership of hometown associations through widespread participation.[71] Immigrant communities in the West, through associations built on village or ethnicity, provide credit on the basis of character references. If it is not repaid, the member is cut off from the community networks and the association's aid.[72] Clans in Central Asia provide access to goods in shortages, and sanction, monitor, and informally coerce members.[73] Long-distance trade and labor market recruitment for migration enforce and monitor by utilizing the overlapping categories of friends and kin in the same ethnic group.[74] Personal relationships and reputation are used to guarantee credit and loans.[75] Such character loans carried the threat of exclusion from the group should the member not repay.[76] Reputation figured prominently in evaluations of credit worthiness in early capitalism. Credit was provided to those of good reputation, not those with collateral, in early capitalism.[77] Reputation indicated that the individual could be relied on to repay her debts. Who the individuals are and information on them are crucial: their family, reputation, consumption practices, social behavior, and income level.

Analyses of institutions that solve collective-action problems show that size, communication, relationships, reputation, and idioms of solidarity distinguishing the group from outsiders are all important factors in successful informally enforced institutions.[78] Several design variables are involved. First, a method of monitoring individual behavior and knowledge of financial status must be in place. This necessitates communication to the group, gossip even, on the reputation of the participants and their track record in living up to their commitments. For communication to be manageable in an informal institution, the size of the group must be limited, otherwise both communicative and enforcement mechanisms may not function. Size matters for collective action; large groups have more difficulty acting collectively than smaller ones.[79] Information on reputation must easily and quickly pass through the network to keep track of violations. This communicative mechanism functions best when enforcement power and information are equally distributed throughout the group, as in a network of peers.[80] Reputation mechanisms function best in situations of inside information among those of like status. This provides informal power throughout the group, facilitating both information and sanctions. Thus the more individuals overlap in identity and role categories, the better.[81] Even close neighbors may not satisfy the requirements of having sufficient information on one another, and proximity may be inferior to employment in the same field for information purposes.[82]

Second, the institution must have repercussions for individuals reneging on obligations and benefits for fulfilling them. The group needs to provide goods that the member prizes, improving member circumstances through aid, favors, job or business opportunities, rights to land, or inclusion in the community, benefits the individual cannot achieve alone. Exclusion from the group is the threat that keeps members in line. For this to be a negative incentive, the ongoing benefits to inclusion must outweigh the short-term temptation to refuse participation, free ride, lie, or cheat. In other words, the group must have something the individual wants in the long run.

Third, the group must share common desires or risks binding them to similar desires. The needs of the group must also be parallel, with members sharing the same interests so that they can to come together and act collectively. Often this means that they are also subject to similar vulnerabilities or economic risks. If the risks or benefits differ throughout the group, calculations of the relative cost of cooperation or reneging will differ, preventing uniform compliance and destroying trust. For example, if the economic situation of some members alters, such that they no longer need the benefits of the group, they can operate on short-term calculations, cheat on the group, and destroy the other members' faith that they will cooperate.

Fourth, to function optimally, group unity and solidarity should be reinforced and elevated above allegiances to outsiders in order to reinforce commitments and group norms. This entails creating and expressing idioms of the group, including the use of rituals and celebrations. Translating or coding sanctions and economic benefits into emotional and identity idioms elevates them beyond mere economic calculations, making it more likely that individuals will cooperate when tempted to cheat. This is demonstrated in the numerous rituals involved in fraternal organizations and the reinforcement of solidarity in mutual aid organizations based on identity.

THE WELFARE OPPORTUNITY STRUCTURE

The desire for social insurance explains the impetus for the organization, and economic institutional analyses account for the design of the organizations and changes in kin identity, but a central question remains: Why is kinship the basis for collective welfare institutions? We can answer this question in the context of state and market alternatives, and the character of the labor market. The skill profile of the labor market is central to the opportunity structure for social insurance. This eliminates many collective options for the majority of the population while also

TABLE I.I. WELFARE OPPORTUNITY STRUCTURE AND OUTCOMES

Welfare Opportunity Structure Variables			Outcomes (provided resources exist)
Universal Social Insurance	Employment or Job-based Insurance	Credit and Loans	Mutual Aid Identity Associations
Yes	No	No	No
No	No	No	Yes
No	Yes	No	No

providing benefits to nonoccupational forms of mutual aid, like identity, that cross economic sectors and classes. Without the levers professional associations are able to wield, identity associations must guard against cheating and noncompliance in other ways. The need to informally hold members accountable pushes the design of the kin institutions toward a version of kin identity that often differs from established ideas. The resulting kin identity and organizational form provide for ongoing communication of reputation, sanctions for noncompliance, prioritization of group solidarity, and a group size both manageable for communication and with resources to aid members. These alternatives for securing social insurance are modeled as a welfare opportunity structure (WOS), depicted in Table 1.1 and Figure 1.1.[83] These variables were derived from the literature on welfare and social protection at the grassroots, including economic studies of village mechanisms reviewed above.

The WOS includes state welfare, the relative stability of employment, the skill profile of the labor market, the domestic credit market, and the legal or regulatory structure of the judicial system. Private-sector collective accommodations are of three types: individual market and legal institutions with open memberships, available for all; employment-based, dependent on membership in the profession or job; and personal or relationship-based through trust institutions. The particular configuration of these social insurance options forms the background for individual choices to secure a financial future. Except for state welfare, these choices depend upon the presence of resources that individuals can devote to new arrangements or for pooling finances. The WOS models the decision-making path, beginning with the initial change at the national level that caused a widespread alteration in the calculus of collective welfare solutions. Alternative means of securing social protection and aid were known and preferred by many; kin was not the only example available

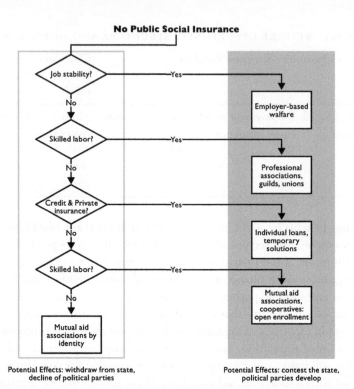

No Public Social Insurance

Job stability? —Yes→ Employer-based walfare

No ↓

Skilled labor? —Yes→ Professional associations, guilds, unions

No ↓

Credit & Private insurance? —Yes→ Individual loans, temporary solutions

No ↓

Skilled labor? —Yes→ Mutual aid associations, cooperatives: open enrollment

No ↓

Mutual aid associations by identity

Potential Effects: withdraw from state, decline of political parties

Potential Effects: contest the state, political parties develop

FIGURE I.I. Welfare Opportunity Structure and Outcomes. This dynamic presumes the populace concerned has resources to organize, and the imperative of organizing is exacerbated during bad economic times and extreme job flexibility.

for mutual aid. Yet the vast majority of the population was unable to utilize these other forms of social aid. I first investigate individual possibilities for securing aid, positing that this will be preferred given the costs of collective organizing and the infrequency of collective kin organizing historically, particularly its demise in good times. The welfare literature shows that credit can be used as a substitute for social insurance and periodic hard times.[84] Nonkin options for social insurance do not end there, but extend to occupational collective organizing such as professional associations, unions, or employment-based insurance. Likewise, pensions through job, the state, or market insurance are overt possibilities for social insurance.

Consumer credit, private pensions, and market insurance for health and life, to name a few, can take the place of state social welfare. Individual options for aid and insurance cover little of the population in Jordan and Lebanon. Loans and retail credit are important in these circumstances, helping to meet intermittent life-cycle needs owing to the variability of income over time. Off-seasons are commonplace. Even when the work is steady, the flow of income is usually not. Financial reputation matters here, as many households are in mutual debt relationships to local stores, family, and neighbors. However, the lack of regulatory structure prevents the development, to date, of credit markets for the general public. Only a few have the collateral for loans, most hospitals do not take insurance, and fraud is a problem. Borrowing another's health card or faking one's own death to collect on insurance is relatively easy. The credit and insurance markets here are extremely weak, despite being regional leaders in these industries. Interest rates average 20–40 percent for the few individuals able to provide collateral, and the states' lack of regulatory capacity prevents private insurance as moral hazards could proliferate.[85] The middle class cannot afford housing loans in Lebanon.[86] The development of private life and health insurance similarly suffers from market credibility problems, and are utilized by a very small proportion of Jordan's and Lebanon's populations. One-tenth of Lebanese have private health insurance, and up to 60 percent have no insurance at all.[87] Only 4 percent of Jordan's health expenditures come through private insurance.[88]

The lack of regulatory capacity that hinders market sources of aid also mitigates against collective mutual aid organizations that rely upon legal institutions for members to repay loans or pay dues regularly. Whereas in the United States and Europe open mutual aid societies developed in the nineteenth century supported by a developed judicial infrastructure, here individuals cannot be prosecuted or even located in order to be held to their commitments. Indeed, for private-sector insurance to function, information must be perfect or nearly so.[89] Asymmetrical information facilitates the moral hazards that prevent market insurance from functioning and being profitable. Instead, in Jordan and Lebanon contract enforcement is still largely informal and dependent upon powerful connections (*wasta*). For business accountability, the World Bank ranks Jordan and Lebanon in the fifty-ninth and fortieth percentiles, respectively.[90] It takes an average of 689 days in Jordan and 721 days in Lebanon to enforce a business contract, dealing with 39 and 37 procedures, respectively.[91] These figures are for business contracts; civil or consumer suits are in even worse conditions, and are novelties, not the norm for the average individual to use.

Collective social insurance can also be obtained through employer or skill group, but this covers only a minority of these populations.

Common labor relations often lead to mutual aid organizations, as these relationships entail shared interests in mitigating the same risk. Job-specific social insurance, professional associations, guilds, and unions all organize on the basis of employment and skills. Occupational organizing provides superior information on others in the same sector, helping to lessen information asymmetry problems, and furnishing guarantees or internal regulation. People who shirk their repayments can be barred from future participation or even work. Common employment generates information on the activities of members surpassing even that of the extended family, making loans and aid more viable.[92] Because they require significant investment, specialized skills often lead to mobilization to protect those valued assets.[93] Professional associations and unions can provide insurance for those with specific skills, playing the role of insurer even absent formal employ or job stability. Similarly, long employment tenure could motivate company employees to unite. Long-term firm employment facilitated organizing with like-situated workers; moving firms but working the same job allowed workers to recognize their interests as alike.

Most people in Jordan and Lebanon are unable to utilize these methods. Lack of job stability and worker bargaining power in Jordan and Lebanon, as with much of the rest of the region, do not facilitate insurance through employers. Skill groups have joined in professional associations and furnished insurance through these organizations. Indeed, since economic reforms, skill-based associations have expanded beyond their base among engineers, doctors, lawyers, and manufacturing workers to even smaller professions such as newspaper writers and Internet providers. Existing and new associations organize to provide social security, pensions, and credit for members. Yet few are covered in these specialized associations. At most 13 percent of Jordanian labor is included under such associations and far less in Lebanon.[94] Manufacturing employs a minimal portion of the working population, and it is unable to serve either as a constituency for pressuring elites for welfare or, through unions, as a source of welfare itself. Only a small percentage of the population is unionized, 10 percent in Morocco and Tunisia and an exceptional one-quarter in Egypt.[95] Jordanian unions encompass no more than 4 percent of workers in any one sector, with one exception, where workers are concentrated in a single southern town.[96] Manufacturing plays a slightly larger role in Lebanon than in Jordan, but almost all industries are micro- or medium-sized. Agricultural work is similarly nonunionized and employs a small number of workers, 6–7 percent in Jordan and Lebanon.[97]

SKILLS, OCCUPATIONAL ORGANIZING, AND IDENTITY NETWORKS

The skill structure of an economy is an important consideration for social insurance options. Occupation-based organizing is problematic in many developing countries, particularly the Middle East. The economic impetus for professional associations, unions, and even regional production networks is clear. Shared economic interest has often been a prime source of collective solidarities and, in particular, common exposure to similar income risks. They organize around economic interests derived from career, profession, or work in the same field or job. Labor unions, business associations, professional associations, and agricultural village cooperatives bind members to share economic risk. Specialized skills promote investment in those skills and association with others of like interests.[98] Yet nonprofessional service workers, who dominate the labor market in the Middle East, have no economic motivation and can see no benefit in joining together by profession, in contrast to those invested in particular skills.[99] Lacking specialized skills and partaking in multiple labor markets, it would not pay to join a binding association on the basis of any one of them.

The majority of jobs in the Middle East are in the nonprofessional service sector, requiring generalized and minimal skills. Work in various forms of non-traded services prevails—tourism, retail, administration, recreational sectors, construction, and contracting. Services constitute two-thirds or more of employment in Lebanon and Jordan, and the vast majority is non-professional.[100] Jobs are intermittent, irregular, often informal and almost all in micro-enterprises. Informal work in the Middle East as a portion of labor had increased by one measure from one-third in the 1970s to three-quarters in the 1990s, and the Gulf countries demonstrated the opposite trend. Self-employment is between 30 and 40 percent.[101] In Egypt about half the workers have no contracts.[102] This work profile demonstrates that employment-based insurance is not viable for a large portion of the populace. The tightness of the labor market was exacerbated during economic liberalization, as it coincided with the constriction of the regional labor market and the decline in international aid. Jordan's and Lebanon's economies made them vulnerable to regional and international changes, since they remain closely tied to markets outside the domestic arena. Still, labor remittances sustain much of the region, topping $160 billion in 2004.[103]

Job or career security is absent. Since work is often of indeterminate length, seasonal or part-time, workers keep one foot in another occupation. Multiple sources of income are the norm in these insecure service economies. Almost 80 percent of the Lebanese I surveyed cited a second source of income, usually in unrelated occupations. Other sources put supplementary, nonwage sources at over 40 percent of income in Lebanon.[104] Less than half the households in a Jordanian rural town depended on a single income source.[105] Only half the Lebanese labor force had permanent employment and a further 10 percent were on fixed-length contracts. Thirty percent were self-employed or contractors.[106] The mix of occupations can be striking, as noted earlier: professors are also green grocers or farmers; landowners are tailors; and journalists, drivers, and butchers sideline as merchants. In Jordan a budget controller is also a freelance merchant, real estate brokers were previously car salesmen, an accountant used to be a traveling salesman, merchants were mechanics or accountants, and a salesman was a radio and TV technician.[107] Such irregular jobs or nonstandard employment do not provide enough for a family but form only one of many sources of income. Economic sectors are not thriving to the extent that workers switch from one job to another in the same field. Downturns are experienced by the sector as a whole. Taxi drivers do not moonlight as drivers for another company; their second job is completely different from their main one.

The required skills for these various service-sector jobs are portable and can be carried over into other firms and work.[108] Generalized capabilities such as literacy, basic arithmetic, organization, administration, presentation, and interpersonal skills move an individual successfully from receptionist to taxi driver to waiter, and even into higher administrative positions. There is no economic incentive to unite in an association on generalized skills, and what the common denominator for such an association would be is unclear. Class standing and the location of those with similar economic interests are hazy. Generalized service workers are left without options to organize along work lines.

Economic organizations are not viable for most of the population, and identity organizing further provides benefits of cross-class and cross-sector networks that aid in job seeking. Indeed, the generation of work networks in informal and flexible labor markets has often seen the use of kin and identity idioms. In these service economies, jobs with general skill requirements can be obtained through broad connections. The competitive and insecure nature of the labor market pushes individuals to broaden their own personal connections to insure a livelihood, and one's profession or class need not limit the resulting networks.[109] Broad networks make more sense amid an environment of general skills work, as individuals can move into a wide range of jobs. Work here is flexible or insecure, informal, and seasonal—what could be called nonstandard work, although it dominates many developing countries.[110] This service sector is similar to informal, competitive, and open labor markets in that numerous contacts and community relationships are needed to obtain employment.[111] The literature on flexible specialization affirms the need for wide-ranging personal networks to locate opportunities in these labor market conditions. Intense competition for jobs and goods creates clientelism.[112] The more irregular the labor market, the more important identity and reciprocity networks and contacts become. Contacts serve as the main source of capital.[113] From Silicon Valley to the Third Italy, personal relations are collateralized, turning trust into financial opportunities and contacts. In Chile fully one-third of all network ties were used for locating employment.[114] New networks form specifically for the purpose of locating work in scarce labor markets; however, casual contacts will not suffice.[115] Unlike Granovetter's weak ties, which pass information about jobs over loose networks or between friends of friends, for example, here the ties must be strong.[116] Only close relationships will insure that a job goes to a particular individual in a competitive job market.[117]

Yet the literature on economic organizing suggests that kin ties are a second-best option, a ranking substantiated by interviews in Jordan and Lebanon. In the presence of stronger long-term potential for self-reliance, from state provisioning and market loans, individuals often eagerly forego indebtedness to family and identity solidarities. In the United States private-sector organizing through fraternal and mutual aid associations in the late nineteenth and early twentieth centuries all but disappeared when the risk calculus changed with the new national Social Security Act.[118] As Beito states, "By assuming fraternal welfare burdens, governments had undermined much of the reason for the existence of societies and thus for people to join."[119] Other studies have demonstrated that borrowing from kin relatives is avoided if other options are available so as not to incur debts to relatives.[120] Even in presumably traditional societies such as Yemen, the poor most often turn to loans and mutual debt from neighbors and retailers.[121] Similarly local nonkin sources, as opposed to extended families, are the basis of most aid in the Palestinian territories.[122] In some regions, fishing community households withdrew from reciprocal networks of aid and loans when one member obtained a stable, nonfishing job.[123] In others, as credit markets along with steady jobs become available, informal risk-sharing institutions became defunct.[124] With stable jobs, migrants opted out of these organizations and ceased remitting to their home villages.[125] Interviews in Jordan and Lebanon revealed that kin associations were a last resort for many of the members, and that, during good economic times, elites had problems finding takers for the kin association idea.

CONCLUSION: INSTITUTIONAL DESIGN AND KIN IDENTITY

The motivations and economic interests inherent in nonprofessional services profoundly affected the type of network that formed for mutual aid in these cases. Instead of organizing sectorally to pursue economic interests, service-sector workers here united in groups that cross various economic industries, using idioms of identity as their organizing instrument. How they organized and what repertoire or model of organizing they used demonstrate the requirements for successful institutions and the malleability of cultural models and inherited identity. These institutions could not rely upon third-party or external regulation; legal institutions and the state could not force informal promises to be met. Institutional design explains the size of identity and changes in legacy in the Jordan and Lebanon cases, altering existing identities and institutional legacies to yield a group of horizontal membership power, ongoing communication and monitoring, and sufficient resources for mutual aid. As the theory discussion showed, the key to informal enforcement lies in internal monitoring of members and levers of benefits and punishments. Such monitoring entails good communication among members. This is often achieved through horizontal relationships diffusing the power of monitoring and thus sanctioning throughout the group. Networks are primarily horizontal, not vertical or patron-client. Thus the operative elements of the institution are solidarity, communication among members, horizontal networks of member power, and limited group size.

Kin is clearly present as an organizing idiom in the Arab world, available for use more so here than in most industrialized countries. In those other areas, kin ties have been cut or loosened through movement for work over several generations. The mere presence of kinship as a model or repertoire of organizing is only part of the answer to why kinship was used, often in altered form, in mutual aid associations. Kin idioms allow the creation of an information network that includes monitoring and enforcement mechanisms. Faith in peer sanctioning and communication allows members to trust one another as if they had repeated, ongoing relationships, even when they are strangers without an existing identity tie. Exclusive identity is promoted within the organization to generate binding commitments and minimize shirking. The group's size and the identity definition are integral to maintaining communication networks. The group cannot expand too much or else monitoring the numerous members becomes effectively impossible. The importance of interpersonal trust and extra-legal policing comes in the size of the group and the ability to hold people accountable to one another through face-to-face communication.

Kin identity changes, and is often re-created to accommodate the needs of size, but it is not created from scratch. It changes at the margins. A new identity can be defined as all those whose grandfather was so-and-so or everyone from a certain village. Families can join together that historically have had close ties and often are of the same religion.[126] In that case the association can carry the names of all the families. The number of members included in a particular identity definition can shrink, when families split off from a larger clan, or it can increase, when families band together or kin definitions become broader. Potential members are alerted and invited to join a kin association. Some associations advertise publicly in newspapers, starkly demonstrating the newness of the allegiance. Once formed and while the association is active, the kin identity is taken seriously and members act as long-established kin, despite not previously having met or considered the other a relative.

The identity must be large enough to provide for members but small enough to guarantee that others maintain the bargain. Possible identity bases include village of origin, neighborhood or village of residence, religion, region, national origin, and numerous levels of kinship from extended family to large-scale tribe. Cultural legacies included all these potential solidarities in Jordan and Lebanon. Religion, national origin, region, and levels of kin genealogy such as tribe unite large groups in these countries, making internal accountability for mutual aid problematic. These solidarities do serve as bases for organizing, but those organizations are characterized either by horizontal participation networks of charity, aiding others as in Islamist social services, or vertical patronage without member control. The others, village of origin, current residence, and smaller levels of lineage, are all used in mutual aid associations and spun as kinship. In other words, village of origin and even neighborhood are reinforced as family units, related individuals genealogically. The idiom of kinship provides a right to monitor relatives' behavior and share the information, or gossip, with other kin, in the Arab world.

The associations use an idiom of group solidarity to reinforce the duties of members to one another and prioritize commitments to the institution.[127] A marker, such as ethnicity or religion, is needed to elaborate the difference of the group and its separate need to compete in the political system.[128] This helps to insure that the membership is internalized apart from overt monitoring, making compliance and internal solidarity more likely. A collective identity,[129] separate and distinct from the rest of society, is used to enforce norms of mutual aid among the group. Utilizing this terminology reinforces and reminds members of their commitment to contribute to the group. The creation of obligations under the idiom of family abounds even in developed economies with little direct experience of kin economies. Networks using idioms of kinship and family have been useful in flexible specialization, solidifying trust and establishing stable, cooperative relations among producers and subcontractors.[130] Encoding relationships in the language of kinship and family solidifies obligations for aid within the network.[131]

Cultural repertoires were selectively molded and reworked to furnish an institution with enforcement, altered to yield a horizontally linked group instead of a top-down organization (see chapter 5). In the new organization, members have power over one another instead of a leader holding the power position over members. Optimally this organization is relatively democratic, giving members the ability to vote leaders in and out of office regularly. Internal elections are vibrant, more so than the national electoral arena. Regular meetings allow a constant flow of communication, and cultural events offering rituals of identity reiterate the group's unity. Plays, cultural lectures, holiday festivals, wedding celebrations, and funerals all further develop the identity. Less-established organizations are only approximations of this model and lean more heavily toward the leader.

2

State and Militia Welfare and Their Demise

Social insurance is a prime concern of the Jordanian and Lebanese populations. After the end of the Lebanese civil war, a remark heard often among Lebanese in East Beirut was that they missed the war, that life had been better economically during the war years.[1] It was not war and destruction that they missed, of course, but the welfare services that militias[2] had provided during the war. For many Lebanese the war was the one time public goods were provided by a state-like administration, despite the militias' brutality.[3] Jordanians likewise decried their loss of welfare with economic liberalization. Contrary to analysts' expectations, the constituencies in Jordan who historically had supported the regime and served as its military were the very same ones that rioted against the lifting of price subsidies on basic goods.[4] The Palestinians, whose loyalty the state and observers presumed to be questionable, were noticeably quiet in the consumer price riots of 1989 and 1996.

The analytical lens of social insurance makes these outcomes intelligible. Social policies in Jordan and militia welfare in Lebanon provided buffers for segments of the middle class. Both furnished significant aid to the middle classes, not just the poor, and this assistance was valued in these volatile and insecure economies. Clearly social services provided by militias in Lebanon were not state welfare but they were state-like: for the populations under militia purview, welfare was based on inclusion in the political collectivity. Social services were furnished to the middle class, a crucial actor in establishing social welfare institutions. This chapter concentrates on the time line and social groups benefiting from state social welfare, delineating the policies through which welfare was provided and their withdrawal during economic liberalization. State welfare is the first of the welfare opportunity structure variables, and the periods of state and militia welfare demonstrate variability in the provision of collective social welfare.

In this chapter I show how and when Jordanians and Lebanese benefited from public social aid. These experiences of social welfare were never complete. Social policies did not encompass the entire populations, but, rather, the beneficiaries were stratified by social group. The differential positions of these social groups to state provisioning were determined by the requisites of state-building, or the need to build support for the state among influential sectors. This picture of the social groups included and excluded by collective social aid yields a time line that corresponds to the rise and fall of kin mutual aid associations outlined in chapter 4. The lack of social insurance paved the way for new institutions to dominate civil society.

I first discuss the welfare regime insights and state-building in Jordan and Lebanon, and then take the countries in turn, elaborating social policies and their beneficiaries. Jordan's path is typical of developing countries and the wider Middle East. Social policies were geared to demographic groups important to state-building, particularly the military and the Jordanian populace, also called "East Bankers" or "Transjordanians," who were privileged in public employment. The state also protected consumers through price subsidies. Lebanon's initial state-building was geared to the Christians and urban Sunnis, but little aid was provided by the state. Lebanon's social welfare differs from general Middle Eastern and developing country welfare, as only minimal social provisioning existed. Large-scale public welfare was only secured during the Lebanese civil war through the militias, to the constituencies within their mini-states. Social policies in these cantons exceeded the Lebanese state's own welfare. In both countries the welfare that peaked during the 1970s and early 1980s was dismantled in the 1990s. In 1989 Jordan initiated structural adjustment policies removing price supports and cutting public employment. As occurred in economic liberalization elsewhere, Lebanon's postwar reconstruction policies concentrated on removing the state from the economy, since the war had involved the state deeper in the economy than before. The new social policies in liberalization consisted of the countries channeling funds to nongovernmental organizations (NGOs) and targeting aid to the poor. These policies, inadequate even for the limited antipoverty goals, exclude the middle class. As the state-sponsored realm of inclusion narrowed, the states increasingly emphasized their militaries, whose privileges and social welfare have expanded in economic reform. For Jordan, this is a reversion to the state's initial welfare, whereas in Lebanon the heightened profile of the military can serve as a new mechanism of social provisioning and support for the state.

Social policies are linked to state-building for much of the developing world. Welfare regimes differ in their component policies, mechanisms, and targeted social groups.[5] The specific mix of social provisioning is shaped by historical patterns of state-building, economic trajectory, political representation, and administrative capacity.[6] Welfare can be composed of varying combinations of credit or emergency financing, health care, educational aid, employment security, pensions, and future professional viability. All welfare regimes provide some form of risk-mitigation and long-term security for organized segments of society, from the state or in combination with private-sector business arrangements. Central to welfare is the minimization of risk owing to market downturns or inevitable life-cycle events. The expenses of weddings, births, old age, and funerals affect the populace universally.[7] Accidents, illness, and unemployment affect some more than others. Social policies are closely linked to political divisions. The main beneficiaries of welfare are those groups central to state-building, often distinct in national origin or religion from the remaining society in the Middle East. Vocal and important groups for the new state receive welfare first, with the military often the earliest covered.[8] In Latin America the squeaky wheel was the one that got oiled; as fears of labor disruption grew, the most organized electoral constituencies were the first to receive benefits.[9]

State social policies have been well acknowledged in the Middle East literature, termed a social contract providing economic goods in return for the sacrifice of political voice.[10] Colonialism left the Middle East and North Africa with welfare states, further inspired variously by the Soviet model or Western Keynesianism.[11] Middle East states furnished welfare along differing lines than the industrialized states do currently. The lack of effective regulation and prevalence of informal work prohibited many forms of welfare, such as social security withdrawn from paychecks. Social provisioning was made up of an aggregate of policies, which together mediated market volatility. Middle Eastern social provisioning has mainly taken place through employment and consumer protection—price supports and subsidies. As in other developing countries, public employment is the main source of welfare, providing credit, health insurance, pensions, and low-cost goods. Even when it is poorly reimbursed, such employment is coveted because of these accompanying welfare goods.[12] Remaining household members are then free to supplement this secure and steady income with irregular and seasonal jobs. These benefits are attached only to those in public employ; those in the private sector are not covered. This leaves at least half the population without formal social insurance or pensions. On average, only one-third of the labor force is covered under pension systems.[13] As in Latin America, social policies first targeted government employees and urbanites. In most of the Middle East, self-employed and agricultural workers are not covered. The general population was aided by consumer subsidies, artificially keeping prices on key goods low. Oil rentier states developed more generous systems than their non-oil counterparts in the Middle East. These measures, though expensive and benefiting the non-needy as well as those in need of welfare, did raise the standard of living for the populace, increasing education and life expectancy.

Scholarship on the southern European variant of social provisioning provides a fitting comparison to begin analyzing Middle Eastern welfare.[14] Like Jordan, the welfare regime in southern Europe is only weakly developed, and it is focused mainly on residual protection. State welfare comes through the formal employment of a male breadwinner; women's social rights are "derived" rights from a male relative.[15] Often clientelism is the method of accessing state insurance, including the exchange of votes for welfare services and the prevalence of personal connections to negotiate the bureaucracy.[16] Social security and pensions form the bulk of welfare expenditures, on top of salaries to state employees. Within the national system, large territorial differences exist side by side with a dual system of welfare provision: a minority of workers is well furnished with social welfare, and the majority has minimal or no coverage.[17] Such "peaks of generosity" are apparent for segments of the public sector in the Middle East.[18]

Compared to other countries in the region, the public social insurance systems in Jordan and Lebanon are long-standing. Lebanon's began in the 1960s, Jordan's in the late 1970s.[19] Yet these are unable to capture much of the population. In the Middle East the welfare regimes operated along social group lines, allocating benefits by group and identity.[20] State welfare was indirect and segmented, circumscribed to one social group considered full citizens. Crucial to the state were East Bankers in Jordan, and Christians and Sunnis in Lebanon. In both countries access to state services and bureaucracy has depended heavily upon personal connections and patron-client relations. Welfare was obtained through employment, not citizenship, making the connection to the labor market crucial. Outside of employment for the privileged, all society benefited from the subsidies on consumer goods in Jordan, and some minorities had limited access in obtaining government jobs, such as Christian Jordanians. In

TABLE 2.1. GROUP WELFARE STATUS IN JORDAN

Social Group	State Welfare Status Pre-1989
Palestinians	Limited (subsidies only)
Jordanian Christians	Medium (subsidies, some employment)
Jordanian Muslims	Complete (subsidies, employment)
Rural communities	Complete (subsidies, employment)

Lebanon during the civil war [1975–90] military welfare provided social services to many along with expanded government spending for the general populace. The experience of welfare here depended largely on the ruling militia. Christians, Druze, Palestinians, and the Shi'a in the southern suburbs of Beirut all benefited from militia welfare.

STATE WELFARE IN JORDAN

In Jordan state social provisioning was split along the groups deemed important to the state. It was furnished completely for Jordanians of East Bank origin, partially for Christian Jordanians and other small minorities considered regime supporters, and only through general subsidies for Jordanian Palestinians (Table 2.1).[21] Dominating the rural areas of the country, East Bankers received privileged state civil and military employment, reaching 90 percent of all employed in some areas, in addition to consumer price subsidies. The only qualification for employment was their status as "sons of the country."[22] Small minorities such as the mostly urban Christians had limited access to state employment, and inhabited both private- and public-sector labor markets.[23] The urban Palestinians, after 1970, were excluded from state employment and worked in the private sector, sending a significant number of laborers to the Gulf states. Subsidies began in the 1970s and benefited the entire population. Thus the welfare regime and labor market were effectively split by national origin.

Jordan's initial welfare regime, set during British indirect rule and the immediate post-independence period, centered on the Jordanian population. These so-called East Bankers or Transjordanians formed the state's main support, in contrast to the population of Palestinian origin. "Jordanian," "East Banker," and "Transjordanian" are all terms for those tracing their origin to the area now known as Jordan. Palestinians trace their ancestry to the West Bank, the Gaza Strip, or within the boundaries of Israel, arriving in Jordan beginning in 1948. Until political liberalization in 1989, welfare was simultaneously the basis for the social contract supporting the regime—trading political rights for economic considerations—and the foundation for labor market choices for these groups. For the East Bank population, welfare meant public-sector employment.

Despite the East Bankers being reputedly more tribal in organization, tending to mobilize through kin, they did not set up formal, exclusive kin associations until economic liberalization withdrew their privileged welfare. The Palestinians, largely relegated to the private sector and employed in the Gulf states, set up such organizations, increasing in number as the hard times of the 1980s affected their main employment in the Gulf. Minorities—the Jordanian Christians, for example—were the forerunners of this mutual aid pattern. Dependent on the private sector, they organized early to provide for kin. During the 1970s welfare extended to subsidies on basic goods benefiting the entire population.

Public employment was furnished in the state administration and the army. Along with a steady income, these jobs provided access to health care and inexpensive consumer goods. In the 1970s, with increasing inflation and rising incomes among Palestinians working in the Gulf, the state took several additional measures to aid the poor and the state-employed Jordanian population. Blanket subsidies on basic goods were implemented, and specialized institutions were created to filter low-cost goods to employees of the state and the military. Together, foreign aid propping up the state sector and remittances to the private sector ended the contest over who would control the state after previous military battles had failed to do so. "Political rent" flowed in to support these social welfare policies; that is, the Gulf provided foreign aid to the state in return for Jordan's hosting the Palestinian refugees and for its border conflict with Israel.

Jordanians had long received welfare through state employment, dating from the mandate era and initial state formation, when the state purchased loyalty through carrot-and-stick policies. Antigovernment tribes were settled and made economically dependent upon the new government. John Bagot Glubb, the British officer charged with subduing the Bedouin, recruited those desert tribes into the Arab Legion, offering benefits unavailable elsewhere, particularly when the British created famines.[24] The state not only provided employment and food for the general population, but special benefits were also granted to tribal leaders. Continuing the British colonial-era strategy of incorporation,[25] heads of tribes or sheikhs received cash allowances, along with subsidies and agricultural resources to farm their new land, in exchange for their allegiance to the new regime. Large landowners received support, loans, and aid from the government, particularly via irrigation projects in the Jordan Valley (the East Ghor).[26] Favorable mortgages were also granted to West Bank landowners supporting the new Hashemite state.[27] Owner-operator farms, which comprised the vast majority of farms, did not receive such support.[28]

The army, the institution that integrated and employed the local population, forcibly put down tax revolts. Military personnel, some of whom had been mercenary in origin, often hailing from outside Jordan, became regime supporters. So integral was the army to state-building that some contend it effectively created the Jordanian state.[29] Already in the 1950s the military was the largest employer, after agriculture, of village workers. Indeed, by 1960 almost 30 percent of men in one sample village worked for the military.[30] Employment in public works projects was another means to incorporate the tribes. Government investment and planning was predominantly directed at the East Bank, neglecting the Palestinian West Bank during Jordan's period of administrative rule there.[31]

After the 1970–71 clashes between the PLO and the Jordanian Army, the Jordanian state began a "Jordanization" project, prioritizing East Bankers in government positions and minimizing the Palestinian presence in public administration and the military.[32] Jobs were won based on connections, or *wasta*, not qualifications, operating through tribal leaders or compatriots in the state administration.[33] In fact, some assessed state employment to be the defining characteristic of East Banker identity.[34] This process was given free rein as Palestinians left the country for work abroad. By 1985 the number of employees in the civil service had tripled since 1970, not even counting the expansion of the military, which had increased threefold between 1961 and 1975.[35] In 1975 one-fourth of the domestic labor force was in the security services.[36] The importance of East Bankers to the government is apparent in the state budgets of this time, one-third of which was directed to a mere 10 percent of the population in the southern regions, an area dominated by East Bankers and among the least populated in the country.[37] In addition to having high levels of direct employment in state institutions, these regions also benefited from military construction and works projects that filtered government funding to them. The rural, Jordanian areas thus enjoyed a guaranteed, steady income, integral to the household's ability to cope.[38]

Employment with the state provided access to a range of welfare goods including social security, health care, and access to emergency loans. State employees could also take advances on earnings, which constituted the main form of loans. These funds were used to meet extraordinary expenses such as weddings and funerals. The average family could not undertake these expenses on its own, and most lacked the collateral needed to borrow from banks. Military service, in particular, provided extra social benefits. In addition to health care, employees of the military and their families were eligible for state-subsidized (essentially free) higher education, with seats reserved for them through quotas.[39] Government-subsidized housing also accompanied military employ. The military itself was seldom a lifelong career. At retirement, around the age of thirty, former army personnel were free to seek other employment while continuing to receive a pension. Health and social security benefits covered the entire family of a male employee.[40] The state's health and education spending amounted to $163 per person in 1983, significantly higher than in other developing countries.[41] Social security, established by law in 1978 to begin functioning in 1980, covered much of the domestically employed population not otherwise provided for through government institutions.[42]

The oil boom spurred another of the state's welfare mechanisms, subsidizing and regulating consumer prices. The flood of currency from abroad, through remittances sent home to relatives and foreign aid to the state, had increased domestic inflation. State salaries could not keep pace.[43] In the decade following 1972, the cost of living increased by 300 percent.[44] After troubles in the army arose over this, the state established the Ministry of Supply in 1974 to administer subsidies on goods considered basic or politically "sensitive."[45] The Ministry set maximum retail prices and imported goods that it then provided below cost through civil and military cooperatives to which public-sector employees had access.[46] This had the additional effect of depressing market prices.[47] Prices were first fixed for wheat, sugar, and petroleum and subsequently for a host of items, including powdered milk, bread, poultry, meat, cheeses, soda, rice, pasta, coffee and tea, soap, cigarettes, car parts, and school notebooks.[48] Progressive rates were set for electricity and water services, and high customs duties were imposed for luxury goods.[49] The population as a whole benefited from these subsidies, although only state employees could purchase from the cooperatives.

The End of State Welfare in Economic Liberalization

The regional oil bust of the 1980s altered Jordan's welfare expenditures. In line with the fate of its neighbors, after the prosperous, state-led period of the 1970s Jordan succumbed to the regional recession of the mid-1980s.

In Jordan the regional oil price decline translated into a drop in foreign aid and labor remittances. Jordan's administrative detachment from the West Bank in July 1988 further contributed to the currency's devaluation.[50] The dinar decreased in value by over a third by 1989, subsequently declining further. The country went into debt, as the state borrowed to avoid decreasing its social services to regime-supporting groups. When unable to borrow further, Jordan turned to the International Monetary Fund (IMF) and began structural adjustment policies. Negotiations yielded a structural adjustment plan that included the removal of subsidies, privatization of public-sector investments, cuts in state employment, and the gradual elimination of customs duties. Jordan began to implement these piecemeal, increasing at the end of the 1990s. Hiring in the public employment sector declined and shifted toward the military, and civil service pay did not increase in line with the rising price of living caused by initial economic reforms. Combined with the regional recession, the effect of partial reforms in state provisioning was exacerbated.

Welfare withdrawal came first through ending certain subsidies and increasing taxes on cigarettes, alcohol, and soft drinks, among other goods. These policies met with resistance from regime supporters, those benefiting from state welfare. Increases in fuel prices, a main ingredient of the package, sparked immediate riots in the regime-supporting southern town of Ma'an in 1989.[51] The economy of Ma'an, a transportation center, was built on trucking goods between Iraq and the port of Aqaba. Residents not working in transport were employed either by the state, the army, or in agriculture. Government jobs provided small, borderline-poverty incomes, which did not keep pace with inflation that was rising at rates of 30 and 50 percent. Price increases reached 50 percent on fuel, cigarettes, phone bills, and residential water, compounding the effect of the dinar's depreciation.[52] Farmers were hit hard by increased prices for irrigated water and fertilizer,[53] and plans called for the removal of subsidies on meat the following year.[54]

In 1996 the decline in welfare expanded with the removal of additional subsidies. This again led to riots in the Jordanian areas.[55] Three days after the removal of wheat subsidies, which effectively tripled the price of bread, riots began in the key regime-supporting area of Karak, whose labor force depended almost entirely on state and military employment.[56] Rioters selectively targeted symbols of luxury and the government, such as banks and the Ministry of Education, which had just raised school fees. Police in riot gear suppressed the mainly peaceful crowds.[57] While King Hussein blamed foreigners and the Ba'th political party, others suggested that the populace was rioting out of fear of hunger.[58] Bread is the staple of the lower classes, and the price increase occurred on top of declining opportunities for state jobs, alongside the whittling away of other subsidies. Price increases affected all food items using wheat as an input such as dairy, poultry, and meat.[59] By this point poverty had reached around 30 percent.[60] In 1997 educational fees again rose, as did prices on health care products and services.[61] By 2000 the food subsidy was eliminated and the agency responsible for it was dismantled.[62] Overall the food subsidy declined from 3.4 percent of the GDP in 1990 to 0 percent at the end of the 1990s.[63]

For economic growth and the generation of employment, the government pinned its economic hopes on foreign investment. Economic laws were quickly rewritten in time for accession to the World Trade Organization (WTO) in the winter of 1999–2000. Customs duties were scheduled to slowly decline to 30 percent by 2010 to meet European Union (EU) and WTO requirements.[64] Duties on cars were scheduled to sink to 20 percent by 2010.[65] The industrial sector complained that customs remained on many intermediate goods used in manufacturing.[66] Lost duties were partially recovered through the imposition of a sales tax and increased fees for government services.[67] The sales tax, which won popular approval over the alternative proposed income tax, was believed by much of the populace to be less regressive than the latter, as shown in media debates, but in fact it was not. However, an income tax would have affected public-sector and formal employees more than informal and private workers, who would be able to avoid such taxes as their wages are not registered. Thus a sales tax was preferable for the regime's support base, public employees. In 1994 the consumer tax, which had begun in 1989, turned into a sales tax of 10 percent. It subsequently increased to 13 percent, became a value-added tax,[68] and later rose to 16 percent. Bread and food was now taxed.[69] Fees also increased. An annual tax was placed on public transportation vehicles, heavily affecting taxi drivers.[70]

Overall Jordan reduced its public employment while continuing to privilege some policies geared to regime supporters during the initial years of liberalization. Employment in the public sector decreased from about half to 35 percent of all jobs between 1987 and 1996, and Jordan's reforms along with Morocco's were classified by the World Bank as the most far-reaching reform of public employment in the Middle East region.[71] Still the salary and current expenditures portion of the budget, which comprised 60 percent of the total, was not touched in early reforms,[72] whereas investment and capital expenditures were cut.

Privileged employees who remained were better compensated. Plans to build low-cost housing for public-sector employees proceeded.[73] Civil and military cooperatives still provided low-cost goods for those employed in state institutions,[74] selling goods on installment to the detriment of local business.[75] In response to civil servants' demands, their salaries increased slightly at the beginning of 1996,[76] but employees of certain public-sector companies received salaries significantly higher than those of civil servants. The Phosphate Mines Company, for example, were paid wages ten times those of the average civil administration employee.[77] Privatization of state enterprises did proceed, however, late in the 1990s, in telecommunications, water, electricity, and the national airline Royal Jordanian.

Welfare after Liberalization: The Military and the Poor

Structural adjustment policies attempted to rationalize Jordan's state expenditures, aligning its policies with neoliberal ones. In this process the specific conditions of a developing country based on service employment were not recognized. Formal pensions continued for those in state employment, since their employment is regulated and on the books. For those outside state employment, however, coverage is nonexistent. Economic reforms for the poor established targeted antipoverty schemes and vouchers. These omitted the middle classes entirely, however, and in fact provided inadequate and only sporadic coverage for the poor. The main group that continues to benefit from the state is the military.[78]

Instead of subsidizing Jordanians or East Bankers in general, the state began to target its social largesse to a subgroup of East Bankers—the military. The military and security services are the only sector growing in structural adjustment. Subsidies, pensions, and employment in the military increased, and these benefits were targeted to East Bankers. Military conscription was eliminated in 1992, allowing for Jordanian domination of the army once again.[79] Alongside shrinking social service allocations, the military's budget increased. The military's reported budget for 1998, almost $700 million, equaled one-quarter of the total government budget.[80] That year the government gave an additional month's salary to all employees in the defense and security fields. Pension expenditures also increased that year, on top of previous large increases.[81] Benefits for retiring soldiers increased, with up to ten times more officers receiving a one-time payment of $28,000 in housing aid. The Jordanian military also diversified into subcontracting, training Palestinian Authority police and participating in UN peacekeeping forces throughout the world, highly paid positions. Later, after the Iraq War, Jordan instituted a peacekeeping training institute to teach cultural awareness for coalition forces in Iraq.[82] In 1997 military employment reached 10 percent of the labor force.[83] In rural areas 20 percent of the labor force work in the army.[84] About 9 percent of the GDP was devoted to defense expenditures.[85]

Social welfare for military personnel and their families has been maintained and enhanced. Scholarships are reserved for the military and their dependents, along with free medical care and military cooperative stores selling goods at preferential prices.[86] All military employees have pension coverage, whereas only around 40 percent of Jordanians have pensions. The Social Security Corporation (SCC) for the private sector and civil servants covered almost 24 percent of the labor force in 2000. Added to this is the military, which covers 6.4 percent, and the civil system, which covers 8 percent.[87] Since 2002 the military pension system was closed to new entrants, who were directed to the SSC. The same applied to the civil service scheme since 1995.[88] Pension spending amounted to 1.3 percent of the GDP in 2001 for the SSC, and the combined military and civil service spending came to 3.5 percent of GDP.[89] The public pension system is not directly connected to contributions but is subsidized by the government. In recent years Jordan announced its intention to reform this system.[90] Severance is one month for every year of service, or a month and a half after ten years of service.[91]

Further, Jordan initiated its own defense industry in 1999, whose main purpose is not to aid the country's military capacity but to increase its economic capability.[92] The King Abdullah II Design and Development Bureau (KADDB) would be called on to produce equipment, services, training, and research for the military in Jordan and ultimately regionally for the Middle East and North Africa. Whereas the qualified industrial zones cater mainly to foreign, unskilled workers, this industry would be staffed by a smaller number of Jordanians with some skills and educational background.[93]

The provision of health care mirrors the focus on the military and the poor in other social services. These segments, accounting for less than half the population, have public health insurance.[94] The distribution of coverage is skewed by social group, leaving most of the population in the poor Palestinian areas excluded from the formal health care system.[95] Pension and social security receipts continue to be highest in East Bank areas and lowest in the areas of Palestinian concentration.[96] The covered poor receive health care at low, or occasionally no, cost by applying to the

Ministry of Health. Almost 333,000 people had cards from the Ministry of Health in 1992.[97] However, public hospitals are last resorts and health services have eroded in liberalization. The wait is typically five hours long, months if the need is not urgent, and managing the bureaucracy is burdensome. Much of the population avoids going to the hospital unless it is imperative, resorts to home-based remedies, or finds a way to purchase services through the private system.[98] During the Ma'an riots in 1989, public health centers were targeted.[99] Efforts to upgrade the facility have been under way since the late 1990s, but this still leaves health care for the middle class unaddressed.

Specialized welfare programs target the unemployed poor but rely on the initiative of the poor themselves to come forward, and the programs are inadequately funded. Less than 20 percent of the needy are aided through social assistance.[100] To benefit, they must provide numerous documents verifying their income status. The program covers forty-five thousand households, providing cash aid that totaled 0.2 percent of the GDP in 2000.[101] For other qualified families, the Family Income Supplement program provides cash supplements, replacing the former system of food coupons that started in 1990.[102] Around $130 annually is allocated to the head of the household in families of 6 earning less than $700 per month. The money is automatically added to state employees' paychecks; others pick it up at banks.[103] The National Aid Fund provides monthly cash payments to qualified families, generally the unemployable poor. In 1998, for example, fifty thousand families benefited. Families receive between $35 and $70 per month.[104] The Zakat Fund, which is run by the government but financed privately, provides regular, small amounts of aid to three thousand households, an average of $11 each.[105] Around three hundred people received help from one of these government programs or from private, NGO charities at the end of the 1990s.[106] Observers have criticized these programs as ineffective and unable either to reach all the poor, particularly those in rural areas, or to provide adequate assistance to those they do reach.[107] Because social assistance is limited to families without a male who could be employed, many poor families are not able to utilize this source of aid in the event of unemployment.[108]

Other aid measures are indirect. Microfinancing of private initiatives is a popular trend, promoted by international institutions as one way to alleviate poverty. Several programs attempt to provide developmental aid, especially for women's enterprises,[109] including the National Aid Fund, the Small and Micro Enterprises Development Program, the Training and Employment Support Program, the Community Infrastructure

Development Program, and the Social Productivity Program; the latter is the main one.[110] The Development and Employment Fund lent money for five hundred projects in 1993, the bulk of which were in Amman and the service sector.[111]

SOCIAL POLICY IN LEBANON

Lebanon, for most of its history, purposely did not provide state welfare; rather, state aid came through small measures before the civil war and through government spending during the war to mitigate the war's economic effects on the population. Some important measures were initiated in the reform era of the 1960s. Chiefly collective provisioning came during the civil war from the major militias. During the civil war only populations under a territorially consolidated militia benefited from their social policies. Those differing from the militia's social group, Christians in a Druze-controlled area, were usually excluded.[112] State employment benefited some, but social policies were mainly accessed indirectly by a host of agencies and subagencies in state ministries. Patronage, as in Jordan, was rife, but this did not equal social insurance as it lacked continuity and breadth of coverage. The key attribute of long-term security is missing in patronage, as it cannot be assured from year to year. The population was generally left to communal aid as social groups urbanized, both before and after the war. This self-reliance is reflected in both time periods spurring the formation of alternative collective assistance, particularly community charities, political parties affiliated to aid associations, and kin mutual aid associations.

Lebanon was created through a compromise that entailed a minimal, noninterventionist state leaving social aid to charity and privileging the Christians and upper-class Sunnis in political power and access to aid. Lebanon's heterogeneous population failed to agree on a definition of the nation, neither pro-Arab nor pro-West.[113] Contrary views of the state's proper role in the economy accompanied these divisions. Financial and service-sector elites, mainly Christians with some Sunni Muslims, were unconcerned with rural development and preferred a minimalist state with low taxes and services. Their deal entailed a "bargain" regarding the country's identity, necessitating that its foreign policy was neither pro-Arab nor pro-Western in return for a minimalist state favoring the growth of the financial and service sector.

The government began providing support to stem increasing poverty and income polarization just prior to the beginning of the civil war in

1975 and continued during the civil war. The mechanism of welfare took the form of the developing country model, similar to Jordan's. In other words, the Lebanese state provided some subsidies, price supports, and benefits to employees. The main development of social policy occurred during the tenure of the reformist president Shehab in the 1960s. Most subsidies were administered through the Ministry of Education and the Ministry of Health. These subsidies absorbed almost the entire budget of the former and 60 percent of the latter's.[114] Shehab's reformism included a national social security treasury in 1963, for state employees. This was expanded in subsequent years prior to the war to include family allocations and illness and maternity provisions.[115]

At the end of the 1960s the state started purchasing primary goods at low prices, and began stabilizing sugar and fuel oil prices. Government salaries were increased in response to protests and inflation, as was the minimum wage.[116] Tobacco remains subsidized. Other programs included the Green Plan to promote agriculture, hydroelectric projects for the Litani River, irrigation, and increased social welfare aid in the rural areas.[117] The Social Development Office was also established during this period of the 1960s. Social security programs also began just prior to the civil war. The system included the National Social Security Fund (NSSF) for private-sector employees; the Cooperative of Public-Sector Employees; the Social Services System of the Army and Internal Security Forces; and special services offered by the Ministries of Health, Social Affairs, and the Displaced by the High Relief Committee and the Council of the South. The first two mainly provided hospitalization and health care, which represented about half the aid they offered.[118] The government also provided interest-free loans for lower-income groups to establish cooperatives, and then started rent control in the 1970s. Since the mid-1970s one-third of the working population has had pension coverage.[119]

The main episode of state largesse occurred during the war, in an effort to offset the negative impact of the civil war. The government stepped up its aid during the civil war in an attempt to steady the economy and prevent wholesale disaster. The civil war began in April 1975; it officially ended with the signing of the Ta'if agreement in October 1989, but battles continued for another year. During this time the government continued to pay salaries amid the general absence of employees from work, and broadened consumer subsidies on basic goods. The government further established price controls on oil, flour, beets, and other essentials in the late 1970s.[120] Other funds were pumped into the economy through the Council of the South to compensate for damage from Israeli attacks, rent controls, housing subsidies, easy credit, and tax breaks. Army employment itself aided 250,000 people, including families, even though many military personnel did not serve during the war.[121] Transfers and the fuel subsidy made up 38 percent of the government's expenditures in 1990, which was itself seven times its revenue. Wages made up over one-quarter of expenditures.[122] Subsidies were maintained on wheat, energy, and fuel, costing the government even while it saved by not collecting fees for electricity.[123] Sugar was also subsidized. In 1985 gas subsidies were removed, increasing prices by three-quarters within two years amid an inflation rate of 600 percent in 1987.[124] Fuel subsidies increased from under one billion LL (Lebanese Lira) in 1982 to 99 billion LL in 1989.[125]

The government maintained some investment in minor areas, with loans, subsidies, and tax deferrals for tourism, and some for manufacturing. The public sector increased from 15 percent of GDP in 1974 to 50 percent in 1989.[126] Wages even increased from time to time for state employees but not enough to compensate for inflation. The pension system ran a deficit, as people did not contribute but filed for compensation. Militias even collected contributions. Housing credit was extended for purchase or home repair, at rates better than inflation. Many borrowers defaulted.[127] Income from customs was removed from the state as militias took over the ports.

Militia Welfare in the Civil War

It was the militias who were the main provider of social welfare for many Lebanese during the civil war. In their attempt to establish ministates, create legitimacy, and forestall popular protest against their rule, militias furnished varying degrees of social services. Populations living in militia territory received different amounts of welfare, social insurance, health care and education, law and order, clean streets, public beaches, and even consumer protection. The militias efficiently provided a wider range of public goods, effectively discrediting the Lebanese state (Table 2.2).[128] Militias in the civil war spent much time and effort after obtaining territory to develop complex revenue-generation and social policies, far more detailed and thorough than the state's measures had been. The original impetus for the new policies was to secure the health of militia soldiers and take care of their families. The extension of this welfare to the broader population under militia control was to create public acquiescence to militia rule. This dynamic is demonstrated by one of the only public surveys done at the time. Public approval of the Lebanese

TABLE 2.2. GROUPS AND MILITIA WELFARE IN LEBANON

Militia and Social Group	Time Line of Militia Welfare
Christians (LF, East Beirut)	1976–1989
Palestinians (PLO in the camps, southern Lebanon)	1969–1982
Druze (PSP, Lebanese Mountain)	1983–1989
Shiʻa (Hizbullah, southern suburbs of Beirut; Bekaa valley)	1983? (est.) to present
Sunni	No militia welfare

Forces dropped significantly when militia services were unable to keep pace with inflation in 1988. This militia lost half its prior support, and its response, tailored to increase militia support, was to plan even more elaborate social service programs.[129]

The four territorial militias established complex political and economic institutions and administrative structures, de facto mini-states within the Lebanese state. The ideologically center-right Christian Lebanese Forces engaged in the same blanket services as the others, the Druze socialist organization and the Palestinian developmentalist one. Under the banner of Islam, Hizbullah now furnishes a similar set of services, albeit more thoroughly and efficiently. Even the small militias tried to establish some form of social assistance such as aid to soldiers' families. The parameters of the militia territorial system were laid in the first two years after the war began in 1975. More than one hundred militias were active at some point during the war, but only a few consolidated territories or cantons and established an infrastructure of service provision. These were the Lebanese Forces (LF) in Christian East Beirut from 1976 to 1989; the Palestine Liberation Organization (PLO) in the refugee camps from 1969 to 1982; the predominantly Druze Progressive Socialist Party (PSP) in southern Mount Lebanon, particularly from 1983 to the end of the war (1989); and Hizbullah in the southern suburbs of Beirut, termed the Dahiyya from about 1983 to the present.

Between one-fourth and one-third of the population was directly supported by the militias through either their military or civilian administration. Militiamen numbered thirty thousand, receiving benefits economically, socially, and in health care. In addition, there were fifteen thousand to twenty thousand Palestinian forces. Sunnis were mostly dependent on other militias, apart from their own small militias. An estimated three-fifths of expenditures were on military needs, including food and health care for the fighters and their families, and the remainder was divided equally between social services and public relations.[130] The militias controlled an estimated one-third of the Lebanese GDP. Total revenues were estimated at $40 billion for the fifteen-year period.[131]

The PLO was the first to develop a mini-state and prolific services. PLO institutions developed in the Lebanese refugee camps mainly after the 1969 Cairo accord in which the government conceded operational autonomy within the camps to the PLO. The areas were now outside the jurisdiction of the Lebanese Army. This situation lasted until the Israeli invasion of 1982, when PLO forces were expelled from Lebanon. From its start in the mid-1960s, the PLO was charged with caring for refugees and their families, serving a population of more than three hundred thousand. Without a vote and prohibited from working in more than seventy job categories, the Palestinians were shut out of the Lebanese workforce. Responsibility for infrastructure—water, electricity, garbage, bomb shelters, and road services—also fell to the PLO.[132] At its height the PLO's annual budget was estimated as larger than that of the Lebanese state itself. Around $300 million was spent on PLO and allied Palestinian militias.[133]

PLO social institutions concentrated on education and child care, including extensive prenatal and postnatal care, kindergartens, and orphanages. Its educational programs included vocational and technical education, training for women, as well as summer camps, sports, and literacy drives.[134] Ninety women's centers offered literacy classes, job training, and other instruction specifically for women. For health care, the Palestine Red Crescent Society provided free medical care or charged only nominal fees, care that included sophisticated surgeries. In the early 1980s sixty thousand to eighty thousand individuals received treatment each month.[135] Dental care was provided, and prosthetics for the injured were so advanced that they were manufactured in the camps.

About two-thirds of the Palestinian labor force was employed in PLO and movement institutions.[136] The Palestine Martyrs Works Society (SAMED) ran industrial and agricultural enterprises, producing items ranging from military uniforms to toys, blankets, and handbags. Five thousand workers were employed in SAMED factories, and six times that number received training there. Additional workers labored in experimental farms. More than three thousand employees worked in social services, and a few thousand more in the institutional administration of the PLO itself. Other divisions supplied some ten thousand jobs.[137] The military contained around three thousand paid regular militia forces, in addition to fifteen thousand regular Fatah soldiers. They received monthly salaries along with a number of benefits such as medical treatment, salary advances, housing, and school and university scholarships. Seven consumer cooperatives had a combined membership of twenty-five thousand. The Social Affairs Institution, which before 1979 had been named the Society for the Care of the Families of Martyrs and Prisoners, assisted twenty thousand families with payments and regular stipends, ran three orphanages housing some 850 children, eleven daycare centers, and organizations for the blind.[138]

The next militia group, the Lebanese Forces, was a coalition of Christian militias supporting the Lebanese state and the status quo. Shortly after the civil war began, the Christian militias began developing social policies to ameliorate community conditions. By 1978 there were 142 Popular Committees, providing security, health care, repairs, street cleaning, and garbage collection. In 1977 the Popular Committees opened a Department of Consumer Protection, checking meat, drugs, and foodstuffs. In 1987 the Social Welfare Agency was established to target the needy. With thirty-five branch offices, the agency aided twenty-five thousand families regularly.[139] Toward the end of the war, massive inflation resulted in displeasure with LF rule, and the militia attempted to improve its public image through enhanced social services.[140] Other LF institutions focused on media, transportation, a refugees' bureau, and economic development think tanks. To deal with the effects of the war, the LF established summer camps for children to escape the war, programs to combat drug use, emergency phone centers, and centers to provide emotional support, in addition to career guidance for youth, public beaches, and consumer protection agencies. Prices on goods were monitored to prevent overpricing, and fuel stations were monitored to ensure that the fuel delivered was of the quality promised.[141]

By the end of the war the Lebanese Forces equaled the state's military, the Lebanese Armed Forces, in size and surpassed it in weapons, equipment and parts, and tax resources.[142] Salaries for the militias ranged from $60 for part-timers to $350 at the higher-ranking levels of the LF.[143] Toward the end of the war the civil administration of the LF employed about four thousand. The LF spent 200 million LL a month on its militiamen, 50 million LL per month went for social welfare, and a like amount was spent on the LF-created public transport system.[144] As of 1982 LF revenues exceeded $100 million.[145]

The third major militia to establish social services was the Progressive Socialist Party, based heavily in the Druze community and founded in 1949. Ideologically socialist and nonsectarian in origin, the PSP had been the main coalition member of the Lebanese National Movement, the forces opposing the Lebanese Forces at the start of the war. Always heavily Druze, the sectarian nature of the party became more dominant as the National Movement was eclipsed by opposing forces in the war; the coalition then split into its constituent sects. In 1976 the PSP briefly set up the Popular Administration to provide social welfare. This short experiment was followed in 1983 by the extensive services of the Civil Administration of the Mountain (CAOM). Half the CAOM's budget went to social services.[146] In the mid-1980s the PSP had five thousand armed forces. The CAOM employed three thousand and had a civil budget of $200 million.[147] Health care institutions in the PSP began with living room dispensaries and communal cooking for fighters.[148] Care for the dependents of the militia fighters followed. Basic services and education expenditures represented 40–45 percent of the PSP's budget, and included Public Inspection and consumer protection. Services provided included loans, monthly family support, grants, scholarships, and payments to the families of three thousand soldiers. Though at the start of the war production was not central to the Druze areas, the PSP began building industries that gave rise to a new industrial sector. More than a hundred industrial firms were established, twenty-nine of them sizable, employing more than twenty-five workers. All told, the PSP employed fifteen thousand to sixteen thousand workers in its various companies and the administration. In addition to industry, the PSP invested in agriculture, real estate, and a retail and household goods chain store of the CAOM.[149] The party also built new schools and repaired homes.

The last and only militia that currently continues to function is Hizbullah. Hizbullah is an umbrella group of various Shi'a religious groups founded between 1982 and 1985, whose union was spurred by the Israeli invasion of 1982.[150] The organization turned into a political party for the postwar elections, but without sacrificing its social welfare and military components. Indeed, Hizbullah is well known for its extensive social provisioning. In 1987 Hizbullah provided eight thousand student grants, provided assistance to martyrs' families, and furnished health and other aid worth $12 million per month.[151] The main institutions furnishing the aid were the Social Services Unit, the Reconstruction Campaign, and the Islamic Health Organization. The Reconstruction Campaign rebuilt almost eleven thousand institutions including homes, schools, and hospitals, and constructed seventy additional new ones. The Health Units of the Islamic Health Organization have benefited an average of 400,000 people yearly. Medical visits and tests are discounted, and patient bills are subsidized. An Educational Unit provides financial aid, furnishing an average of 5 billion LL a year.[152] The party provided basic services, including sewage, water, and electricity. Agricultural centers have provided aid to farmers and veterinary services in the underserved rural areas. In 1992 Hizbullah established a free transport system, restaurants with free meals for the poor, low-price supermarkets, pharmacies, and clinics.[153] The party further has supplied about seventy-five hundred small loans a year, more than any other NGO in Lebanon.[154]

The End of Militia Welfare and Economic Reform

Economic reforms began after the end of fighting in 1990. Militia civil institutions and social services ceased, for all save Hizbullah. The Lebanese state itself exited the war in debt, a new situation for the country. The state borrowed to fund reconstruction programs, privatized the industries acquired through the war, cut subsidies, customs duties, and public employment, and increased indirect taxes such as fees and sales taxes. Economic liberalization accompanied unprecedented increases in national debt, as Lebanon took international loans to rebuild the country. Privatization and increased fees did not cover the rising government expenditures. National debt increased to encompass most of the budget, totaling 185 percent of the GDP in 2004.[155]

Lebanon came out of the war in debt, a new situation for the country. The state's role in ownership of enterprises and employment had increased during the previous fifteen years of civil war, and this increase was the target of economic reforms. Transfers and the fuel subsidy made up 38 percent of government expenditures in 1990 or seven times the government's revenue. Wages made up more than one-quarter of expenditures.[156] One-third of the state's budget went to paying employees, and over half the rest went to financing the debt.[157] The state now owned various businesses that, because of legal proceedings or bankruptcy, had come under its control during and after the war.[158] The government also owned Middle East Airlines and operated several cell phone companies. Government loans extended to Middle East Airlines by the Banque du Liban made the bank its effective owner, along with owning other failed banks.[159]

However, government expenditures were slated to increase further in order to reconstruct the country's infrastructure and rebuild damaged sectors. The cost of the war was estimated at $25 billion.[160] Postwar reconstruction focused on rebuilding infrastructure and promoting commerce, primarily in the capital region, and accomplishing economic reform through fiscal tightness. Horizon 2000 ($60 billion in public and private funds) was initiated in 1993 to rebuild the country, under the Saudi-made business tycoon Prime Minister Rafiq Hariri. Connections and corruption were the code words, cronies and clients of the prime minister benefited, and the private company seemed unaccountable.[161]

To raise money and encourage business, the government increased taxes on a number of goods while lowering income taxes and corporate taxes. In light of Lebanon's extreme dependence on imported goods, decreasing customs duties entailed in economic liberalization removed a major revenue source for the government. Corporate taxes were reduced to less than 7–8 percent in the late 1990s and early 2000s. The government reduced social security contributions by employers from 38.5 percent of salary to 23.5 percent.[162] The tax structure, previously regressive, became more so. Social spending decreased to 5.7 percent of the GDP over the 1990s. Indirect taxes and fees increased, including taxes on gasoline, car registration and inspections, mobile phone minutes, and imported cigarettes. The yearly car tax was increased by four times.[163] A 5 percent interest tax on all deposits was introduced in 2003. A 6 percent real estate registration tax was instituted at the end of the war, and excise taxes increased from 5 to 30 percent between 1993 and 1995.[164] In February 2002 a value-added tax of 10 percent was introduced, along with multiple fees on work permits, driving licenses, passports, and a road tax.[165]

At the same time the state's role in the economy declined in employment, social services, and subsidies. Thirteen percent of government expenditures went for social policies in the mid-1990s. Expenditure on sickness and maternity is half the amount it was in 1974, and even then it was only 2 percent of the GDP.[166] Funding for public enterprises was cut by 11 percent, and there were additional reductions in the slim agricultural funds. Public-sector wages were frozen, civil employment decreased, and the sixty-four state-run enterprises laid off employees or were being privatized. These include Lebanon's national Middle East Airlines (MEA), the Intra Investment Bank, the state television channel Tele-Liban, electricity and water utilities, and cell phone companies.[167] The state withdrew almost all subsidies in 1995, on flour and other goods, and gave up its monopoly over communications and gas importation. The long-lasting sugar subsidy, dating from the 1950s, ceased in 2001 but was reinstated temporarily in 2004 as a result of pressure from the farmers.[168] The allowance for Members of Parliament (MPs) ended, which had been used for patronage public works programs.[169] Together cash and in-kind aid totaled just 1 percent of the GDP.[170]

A partial aim of economic liberalization was to make the country friendly to business, aligning its policies to the requirements of international trade organizations and joining international economic agreements. Lebanon plans to join the future Arab Free Trade Area and the WTO, and has signed a partnership agreement with the Euro-Mediterranean Partnership (Euro-Med). In 2002 it signed an association agreement with the EU. The role of the IMF was only partly official because of the difficulty in reaching political agreements on the subject. Foreign aid propped up the government's efforts. Donors agreed to lend $4.3 billion, most going toward debt restructuring. Lebanon received slightly more than half that amount, and has used it to pay off and maintain its debt.[171] Substantial aid has been received from the Paris II group, which agreed to $4.4 billion in loans and debt restructuring.[172] The United States has donated around $35 million annually between 2001 and 2005, increasing the donations dramatically after the 2006 war with Israel.[173]

Welfare after the War: Military and Community Aid

Welfare in economic reforms in Lebanon consists of subcontracting aid to communities for health and social services and support for the military. Indeed, the military is the one area where the state's role has increased. Ironically Lebanon in economic liberalization and reconstruction has converged to become increasingly similar to neighboring Arab states in its emphasis on military employment. The military's role has heightened since the war, for the first time in the country's history. Historically the laissez-faire and merchant orientation of the economy granted little state money for the unproductive military sector, and the compromise sustaining the state allowed no use of the half-Christian, half-Muslim army. This changed with the Taif Agreement that ended the civil war. The armed forces increased in size from twenty thousand at the start of the war in 1975 to forty-five thousand in 1995. By 2003 the ranks of the military had reached seventy-two thousand.[174] New military clubs were established, one in the high-priced real estate section of Beirut's Corniche in 1998, and another was expanded significantly in Byblos. Though a draft was instituted in 1993, it was shortened in duration from eighteen to six months in 2004 and allowed significant exemptions for those in universities or overseas. Thus, as in the Jordan case, only those desiring to serve and those in the poorer segments form the ranks of the military. Social insurance, military hospitals, and cooperatives funnel privileges to this sector, benefiting the military families. There is a military hospital for soldiers and a cooperative, which serves 150,000.[175] Security and military personnel totaled about 66,000 in 1994, and, with their families, represented about 370,000 Lebanese.[176] A large and increasing portion of the state budget goes to the military. When internal security spending is included, defense spending reaches 40 percent of the budget.[177]

Outside government employees, few have state-organized pensions. Lebanon's pension system covers 20 percent of workers, below the regional average of 34 percent, exclusive of security and military workers. Coverage by the National Social Security Fund (NSSF) dropped from 38 percent of the labor force before the war to 28 percent in 1996. Most of those covered are in the greater Beirut area. Severance also declined by two-thirds.[178] Lebanon provides a maximum of ten months severance salary, one month per year of work. Overall about 30 percent of income is secure in retirement pensions. The income of the remaining majority is uncertain upon retirement.[179]

For community health care, government ministries subcontract through NGOs to provide clinics and health care. These NGOs, formally categorized as community social welfare organizations, are mainly kin and village mutual aid associations. Few government hospitals exist, and there is no public emergency ambulance service. Most primary care is handled by NGOs and more than seven hundred local clinics. The public sector and the NSSF both cover 15 percent, and private insurance accounts for about 9 percent.[180] The ministry spends most of its budget for expensive treatments in private hospitals. To receive services one must obtain written proof of one's poverty from a community official. About seven hundred thousand benefited from the NSSF, which covered 20 percent of outpatient care and 40 percent of in-hospital care. The share of health funding grew from a manageable amount even during the war (7% in 1987) to half the expenditures in 1994 for the state insurance plans.[181]

Lebanon also provides aid through the Council for the South, most of whose expenditures are for electricity, the Ministry of the Displaced, and the High Relief Committee, which coordinates NGOs and public agencies. The Social Development Ministry and the Ministry for Public Health mainly operate through subcontracts with NGOs and its own Development Services Centers (between 65 and 85 of them). About 60 percent of its annual budget of $60 million went to contracts. Almost 150 community social welfare institutions had contracts with the Ministry in 1994, benefiting an estimated thirty-five thousand persons.[182]

CONCLUSION

The time line of social groups provided with public welfare indicates those who were included and those who were left to their own resources. The beneficiaries of state welfare did not form kin mutual aid associations while they received welfare. Only when welfare was withdrawn did they initiate private-sector organizations to solve their welfare problems. In liberalization, both states began promoting and funneling support to their militaries. Lebanon now cultivates the military as a new base of support, as Jordan had early in its history, and Jordan is currently narrowing its regime base to this one, historically central, social group.

The literature on the social pact in the Middle East asserts that state services aided the populace in accepting the regime as legitimate. Yet social policies accomplished far more. They served as social insurance for a crucial segment of the population, buffering the costs of life-cycle and market risks. The Jordanian version of welfare is typical of that of the broader Middle East, and holds many elements in common with welfare regimes in Latin America, southern Europe, and developing countries, whereas Lebanon's experience of militia welfare is comparable to other regions with civil wars and regional autonomy. Welfare through employment and consumer subsidies was economically inefficient. Unrecognized as welfare, state policies benefiting the middle classes were cut by economic neoliberal reforms. Lower classes are partially—but inadequately—aided through a targeted social safety net implemented along with economic reforms. The lower classes are often presumed to be the group mostly affected when state services end, but this perspective neglects the middle classes, which can be prime actors in civil society and in establishing new institutions. They have resources and motivation to insure themselves against shocks from the market and life-cycle events that threaten to plunge them into inescapable debt and poverty.

In Lebanon both before and after the war, state provisioning was minimal for the entire population. As groups urbanized, they began to form alternative aid organizations. The civil war in 1975 spurred several state attempts to pump money into the population in order to offset the decline in popular standards of living, such as continuing to pay salaries even though no one showed up for work. Though these measures helped to a degree, they were insufficient in the climate of rampant inflation. The significant factor aiding many during the war was the provision of social services by the militias. This covered only those living in territory consolidated by a major militia, and only aided co-nationals or co-religionists. Those not living in a militia territory or excluded because of a different religion or national origin formed alternative social aid organizations. After the war, as three of the major militias disbanded their arms and social welfare, such mutual aid organizing soared. Thus the periods before and after the war demonstrate the consequences of lack of public welfare on social organizing, as does the experience of those excluded from militia welfare during the war. However, the current period of economic liberalization demonstrates the additional impetus for alternative organizing owing to regional and domestic hard times, as jobs became scarcer.

In Jordan the time line of welfare is simpler: a period when state welfare was provided and then gradually withdrawn. Jordanian Muslims were provided full welfare, minority regime supporters such as the Christians were partially included, and the Palestinians were left out of all but general consumer subsidies. This welfare regime lasted until the 1989 economic reform, when IMF structural adjustment policies began to align state spending to neoliberal guidelines. Generous employment and subsidies began to be dismantled, with subsidies ending first and employment adjustments trailing slowly. The main change in employment occurred in the replacement of the East Bank, Jordanian population as a whole by the privileging of one segment of East Bankers, those in military employment. While civil employment halted and began to decrease, military employment and its benefits, staffed by East Bankers, increased.

The legacy of Jordan's welfare regime is the solidification of one segment of the population's dependence on the state, and hence its vulnerability. The state, able to easily establish a support base through employment, did so, particularly since this form of social provision did not contradict a prima facie free market orientation. While supporting the regime's allies, the welfare system contributed to labor market configurations that in economic liberalization bode poorly for this very constituency. In economic liberalization the fate of the formerly privileged East Bank Jordanians, the base of the regime, became tenuous as the public sector declined. The labor market onto which they were thrown had been altered in the intervening decades, and the regional economy left underdeveloped. With the impending end of generous public employment, these workers face scarce employment opportunities. What was initially a reward is fast becoming a curse under the new economic arrangements. Palestinians, left out of state welfare, had a jump on private-sector employment.

3

Hard Times and Private-Sector Welfare Options

Economic liberalization in Jordan and the end of the civil war in Lebanon signaled the end of public social provisioning. State welfare policies conflicted with neoliberal economic reforms. Consumer subsidies and the bloated bureaucracy had to be abandoned. Such a reduction in state social welfare is based on the premise that the private sector, together with government antipoverty safety nets, can take the place of welfare. Welfare is often equated with aid to the poor, who are assumed to be the group primarily affected by economic liberalization. But economic reforms also leave the middle class to fend for itself. In the industrialized world the middle class can rely on consumer credit, insurance companies, and job-based benefits in hard times. What private-sector options were available to secure social insurance in these economies?

This chapter investigates the private-sector avenues of welfare and intermittent aid that could be used to survive difficult economic circumstances, temporary or long-term. Many of the private-sector possibilities are tied to the character of employment, such as job-based insurance and pensions, or profession-based options joining those in a single field. As demonstrated in chapter 2, social welfare addresses market risks such as unemployment and life-cycle expenses. General life-cycle expenses begin with paying for marriage, children, and possibly education. Unexpected and periodic expenses relate to illness, health care, and the death of a breadwinner, to name a few. Inflation and an increasing cost of living make all these expenses harder to bear. Jordan and Lebanon's removal of welfare in economic reforms coincided with and exacerbated hard economic times. Expenses grew because of new and higher government fees, the removal of subsidies, and the termination of state welfare policies, while at the same time the cost of living increased. Similarly employment vulnerability grew. Regional economic downturns and the search for non-Arab guest workers decreased job availability in other Arab countries, while the state shrunk its own share of jobs as a result of economic reform. Cutting employment with the state was problematic because of the absence of alternatives jobs. Just as economic reforms began, regional and domestic labor markets were contracting. Gulf countries, formerly the providers of employment for Jordanians and Lebanese, are attempting to nationalize their labor forces, decreasing their use of non-national Arab laborers and using more Asian labor. Meanwhile, high birth rates indicate that the Arab labor force is growing, causing severe population pressures that distinguish this region from other labor markets.[1] Vulnerability and the cost of living rose while the ability to cope with these economic burdens declined.

Opportunities for social insurance through the market or job are scarce in Jordan and Lebanon because of the character of the economies. The contributor-based social insurance typical of the industrialized states is not feasible in these countries, as in much of the developing world, as a result of absent administrative and regulatory institutions. The state is unable to enforce private business contributions to payroll taxes or, in fact, to tax at all. Social security deductions are only feasible for public-sector work, where the state pays and withdraws in one stroke. In Jordan and Lebanon those jobs that are available are informal, precarious, and in the service sector, and this sector is growing.[2] Agriculture declined and manufacturing stabilized at low levels.[3] The predominance of services, common to the developing world, is exceptional in its domination of labor in the Middle East, owing to historical development patterns and resource endowments. Evading legal monitoring by its nature, informal workers do not have recourse to occupational welfare.

Those with specialized skills invest in professional associations to preserve their investment.[4] These associations can be used to furnish health insurance, pensions, and other benefits, as they often do in the Middle East. Skilled professionals are motivated to organize in order to guard their investment. They make demands on the state concerning their profession and secure its continued importance in their lifetimes.[5] Likewise, unions provide for manufacturing workers, but the potential reach of these institutions is limited in Jordan and Lebanon. Unlike in Latin America, where organized labor played a key political role, little manufacturing exists in the Middle East.

Nor are market provisions of credit, home loans, and pensions forthcoming. Loans can substitute for insurance,[6] providing needed cash in downturns. Much of the industrialized world relies on credit to fund temporary or investment expenses such as sudden health crises or education. However, no cash-advance and quick-loan stores litter the developing world as they do industrialized countries. In the developing world, the lack of regulatory structure makes these market services unprofitable. The only similar institution is microfinancing, which has been promoted in the development literature. Contrary to its intent, these small, one-time loans are generally utilized not as business capital but to meet periodic emergencies in the life-cycle.[7] They are not widely available to serve this purpose. After more than two decades of economic reforms, market mechanisms for welfare have still not emerged.

Below I examine the private-sector welfare opportunity structure variables, showing that occupational and market social insurance were not viable in Jordan and Lebanon. First, I demonstrate the existence of economic hard times, an increasing cost of living and decreasing income, just as the state began to withdraw from social provisioning, clearly signaling an end to state popular aid. The populace in general, and not merely a few individuals, experienced this economic vulnerability. I then examine the potential for occupational welfare, collective organizing through common skill, or company of employment to furnish health care, pensions, and other social welfare goods. I analyze job stability and the profile of skills required for these economies. Insecure and changing jobs require multiple contacts to obtain work, and expanding personal contacts and obligations to provide jobs is a key feature of the kin mutual aid associations that are formed to provide welfare. Skilled labor does make use of professional associations for occupational welfare. Uniting on the basis of common profession, they do not need to utilize kin networks for welfare. Many of these individuals are active in national politics, as the professional data on Islamists demonstrate.[8] Lastly, I examine individual attempts to cope, through loans and private insurance, neither of which is readily available or widespread.

RISING COST OF LIVING AND INCOME SQUEEZE

The termination of state welfare in Jordan and the end of the war and militia economy in Lebanon removed a main source of market security for much of the two countries' populations. Also motivating the search for new social welfare institutions was the decreasing ability of households to make ends meet because of economic reforms as well as regionwide economic trends. Since 1990 poverty has increased in both countries, particularly in the rural areas. The income distribution has worsened, leaving a smaller middle class and a larger lower class. Few are able to cover their basic expenses.[9] Those in the middle class who remained moved to preserve their status.

Poverty, which the World Bank declared had effectively been eliminated in Jordan in the mid-1980s, reached 20 percent in 1991 and is currently 30 percent.[10] The working poor, about half of them in state employment, comprise a significant portion of those living in poverty. The largest number of poor families resides in the capital region, not surprisingly, since most of the populace lives there.[11] Proportionally, however, the capital has the lowest incidence of poverty; the highest rates are in Mafraq in the north, then in Karak in the south, followed by Balqa, Irbid, Tafileh, and Ma'an. The same general distribution holds for families in absolute or abject poverty. The line between the poor and the non-poor is extremely thin. An added expense of $20 per month would send thirty-two thousand families below the poverty line, increasing the poverty rate by 4.2 percent. The wealth gap is wide: the top 10 percent of the population spends the equivalent of the poorest 54 percent.[12] Official per capita income went from more than $1,500 in the mid-1980s to less than $1,000 in 1990, and further decreased over the 1990s to $850 in 1998. The average income in the rural areas was less than three-fourths of that in urban areas.[13] Not only did the lower classes stop eating red meat, but they ate chicken only rarely.[14]

Jordanians consider their worst problem to be the increasing difficulty for even middle classes to cover expenses.[15] Household debt to friends, family, and the local grocer has increased in structural adjustment. Poorer households delayed paying water and electricity bills, and moved out of titled property into squatter settlements to save on expenses.[16] Expenditures on essential goods absorbed a larger portion of the family budget. Food prices increased almost 80 percent from the economic reform in 1989 to 1992.[17] From 1992 to 1997 prices doubled for food, education, rent, and health care, and heat and electricity increased by 150 percent. The consumer cost of living index went up by 73 percent overall between 1987 and 1993. Clothing costs were three times as high as in 1986. Prices of cereal products doubled between 1994 and 1998, which had an inflationary effect on most other food items as well.[18] Even these numbers underestimate the actual impact, since the index excludes imports. Jordan depends heavily on foreign goods, importing 60 percent of its needs. Already in the early 1990s consumption was cut by around one-quarter.[19] Spending on food, drink, fuel, and rent increased, whereas spending on clothes, furniture, and personal care declined. Most individuals have only $1.40 in discretionary income, a sum insufficient even to purchase a book or see a movie.[20] In line with the distribution of poverty in the kingdom, those in Maʿan and Karak in the south spend the highest proportion of their income, over 55 percent, on groceries.[21] In Amman, families of all income groups spend the least on these items. By the late 1990s newspapers were commenting on the absence of demand in the marketplace, the sudden appearance and flourishing of stores selling "everything for a dinar," and the newly common sight of beggars on the streets of the capital.[22]

In Lebanon the war drove prices up. Rampant inflation increased the cost of consumer goods 150 times from 1974 to 1989; from a baseline of 100 in 1974, the consumer price index grew to more than 73,000 in 1990.[23] The economy had also become completely dollarized. After the war ended, inflation worsened to 120 percent annually. The currency further depreciated, stabilizing later in the 1990s at LL (Lebanese lira) 1500 to U.S.$1. Prior to the war the lira's value had been higher than the dollar.[24] Inflation had reached triple digits in the late 1980s and early 1990s. The cost of a standard bundle of goods, used to measure inflation, went from LL 10 in 1974 to LL 1500 in 1989. The consumer price index reached over 73,000 in 1990 from a baseline of 100 in 1974. Creeping up during the beginning of the war, annual inflation reached 100 percent in 1986 and jumped to 500 percent in 1987.[25] Spending on food grew as a percentage of the family budget from 27 percent to 34 percent between 1966 and 1997, and enrollment in substandard public schools increased as private schools became unaffordable.[26] Health care costs doubled in Lebanon in the first few years after the war. Indeed, out-of-pocket expenses for health care amounted to over 80 percent in 2001. Land prices increased with the demand for real estate; one estimate found real estate price increases in the Bekaa of up to 1400 percent in the first half of the 1980s, or close to 400 percent when the general inflation rate is taken into account.[27]

The income structure in Lebanon has been reversed and is now more polarized than before the war. The lower class has increased and the middle class has decreased, albeit still constituting a significant portion of the population. The lower-income category increased from 22 percent of the population before the war to 62 percent in 1999. The middle-income category declined during the same period, from a high of 68 percent in 1973 to less than 30 percent in 1999. The upper-income group stayed basically the same during the period.[28] Poverty was about 42 percent in 2000.[29] Thirty percent of the population is in debt in order to meet their basic needs.[30] The northern and rural regions are particularly poor, and poverty rates reach 60 percent in some areas.[31] Poverty rates for Palestinians in Lebanon are high. The Palestinian population is poorer than the Lebanese population and has little access to employment. Poverty among Palestinians was estimated in the early 1990s at 60 percent, and data from later in the decade indicate that the rate reached as high as 80 percent.[32] Most Palestinians are in mutual debt and buy their basic goods on credit.[33]

LABOR SKILLS AND JOB STABILITY: SERVICE-SECTOR WORK AND REGIONAL EMPLOYMENT

The bulk of labor in the Middle East is intermittent, seasonal, and irregular, characteristics that bode ill for long-term security and private-sector social insurance. The largest and most dynamic sector is services, much of which is informal. Service-sector workers lack the employment longevity or occupational skills to organize either by employer or occupation. No specific skills unite service workers, thwarting attempts to establish guilds or associations based on human capital assets. Required skills are portable, and can be carried over into other firms and work.[34] Service jobs include office workers, repair personnel, retail shop workers, and vendors.[35] Further, service and informal employment is notorious for its seasonality and instability. Continuity of employment for firm-level insurance is absent, as job changes are recurrent.[36] Unemployment and disguised unemployment is pervasive, and employment elasticity is high.[37] Generalized service workers are left with no clear option for economic organizing.

The labor market in Jordan and Lebanon is broadly similar. The labor markets are service sector,[38] with a large percentage of self-employment, informal labor, small-scale industries, and multiple jobs per worker. Both countries are labor-rich, capital-poor, and internationally oriented, dependent on international services and remittances. This international connection centers not on the production of goods but on the migration of labor and the importation of goods. Neither country effectively encouraged manufacturing, and both have a small rural population—the smallest in the Middle East and North Africa region. The overwhelming majority of the labor force is urban. Scant labor is in manufacturing, and a large portion of educated labor is geared toward work in the region and internationally. The retail sector is particularly fragmented and prominent, employing only a few workers per establishment. Over 60 percent of business owners invest in the service sector in, for example, tourism, commerce, bank notes, and real estate.[39]

Unlike in other countries, service employment in Jordan and Lebanon is entirely unconnected to manufacturing. The sector is not expansive, and it generates low wages and unstable work.[40] The services include tourism, the airline industry, hotels, restaurants, hospitals, travel agencies, and public relations representatives of foreign concerns; professions such as doctors, lawyers, administrative officials; and retail businesses and merchants including Internet cafes and computer programming. Informal labor represents between one-third and one-half of all work in Jordan, and a few percentage points less in Lebanon.[41] The economies are heavily linked to the regional and international economies for imports and remittances. Worker remittances are 20 percent of the GDP in both countries.[42] Both have an excess of qualified skilled labor, much of it geared to emigrate overseas. The two countries import goods: in Lebanon imports constitute about 40 percent of the GDP and exports comprise only 12 percent, and Jordan imports almost 70 percent of its GDP and exports 40 percent.

Multiple sources of income are the norm in these insecure service economies. Almost 80 percent of the Lebanese I surveyed cited a second source of income, usually in unrelated occupations.[43] Lawyers in Lebanon benefit from agricultural income; an office owner paints off-hours; a factory owner, who used to be a journalist, sells handicrafts; and journalists, drivers, and butchers sideline as merchants. Company employees also work as real estate brokers; lawyers run retail stores; a pharmacist operates an international trading company; an information engineer sells produce; and a barber is a car salesman. Almost 60 percent of surveyed members in Jordan relied upon an irregular source of work income. In one rural Jordanian town, less than half the households depended on a single-income source.[44] Supplementary sources, not wages, account for more than 40 percent of income in Lebanon.[45] As one interviewee put it, everyone is always semi-employed and on call for work, which is a boon to the thriving cell phone business. Often individuals occupy diverse employment fields simultaneously. Taxi driving is a particularly widespread second or third job. Further, credit is highly important in these circumstances, as the flow of income is not steady, even if the work is. Yet off-seasons are commonplace. Many households are in mutual debt relationships to local stores, family, and neighbors.

Jordan's welfare regime centers on the population of Jordanian origin, the "East Bankers" or "Transjordanians," who provide the state's main economic support, in contrast to those of Palestinian origin.[46] Palestinians and Jordanians occupy different labor markets, the private sector and the public sector, respectively, owing to historical processes of national inclusion and employment.[47] In fact, a near dichotomy of employment opportunities characterizes the country's rural and urban regions. Jordanians inhabit the rural northern and southern regions, working primarily in the army and in state employment; Palestinians live in the central, urbanized area of the country, where the bulk of private employment and industry is concentrated. This central region contains the majority of the population, a mix of Palestinians and Jordanians, and is home to the capital, Amman. It is by far the most densely populated area in the country.[48] The southern and northern regions, rural and Jordanian, are home to a small proportion of the population. The southern region contains 10 percent of the total, and the north around 27 percent.[49] The south is also sparsely populated, compared to the central region and parts of the northern regions. Population density varies between three and fifty-nine people per square kilometer there.[50]

As refugees, the Palestinians settled in the urban areas of Jordan, where most refugee camps came to be located; the camps are administered by the United Nation Relief and Works Agency (UNRWA), whose expenditures are mainly directed toward education but some toward health care. These camp settlements would often re-create prior village and neighborhood residences that had existed in Palestine.[51] Later waves of refugees, in addition to living in the camps themselves, settled nearby to receive services provided by the UN organization.

The UNRWA recognizes ten official and three unofficial Palestinian refugee camps. The main camps are in East Amman, Balqa, and areas nearby Amman, in Madaba and Zarqa.[52] Around 72,000 registered refugees live in the most prominent camp, Wihdat, located in the eastern part of the capital. Balqa, a rural area, houses the largest camp, containing 79,000 registered displaced people.[53] Although the housing facilities in the camps were intended to be temporary, they have become permanent. The camps and surrounding low-income areas, all overwhelmingly Palestinian, are overcrowded and underserved regarding electricity and running water.[54] An estimated 13 percent of all refugees, around 275,000 persons, live in the camps.[55] About 10 percent of the Jordanian population lives in one of the low-income areas, which include the thirteen refugee camps and fourteen squatter settlements.[56]

As shown in chapter 2, most domestic employment in Jordan prior to economic reforms was with the state, accounting for around half of all employment.[57] Eleven percent of jobs were in industry in the mid-1980s, mainly in phosphate and other raw material extraction.[58] Some three-fourths of East Bankers nationwide worked for the government in some capacity, and outside Amman this proportion reached staggering heights. The public sector was virtually the only source of employment in these regions. At the advent of structural adjustment, 92 percent of the domestic labor force in Karak worked in the public sector; 99.5 percent in Tafileh; 90 percent in Ma'an—all in the southern region.[59] By contrast, the central areas of Palestinian concentration—Amman, Zarqa, and Balqa—had a much lower percentage of public employment, 56–58 percent. In 1985 only one-quarter of workers in refugee areas were in any salaried employment. Most of the remainder were casual wage laborers and petty traders.[60]

The main private employment within the country was agriculture, which declined in the 1970s oil boom. Higher salaries were available with the government during the oil boom, pushing farming out of the realm of viable employment. From one-third of all employment in the 1960s,[61] agriculture sunk to less than 10 percent of domestic labor in the 1980s[62] and represented only 6 percent of employment in 1993.[63] The field was surrendered to foreign workers or became part-time, seasonal work for Jordanian women, children, and the elderly. The agricultural products from these farms were primarily used in home consumption, supplementing the main income from government jobs.[64] Domestic unemployment dropped to almost nil during the boom, and Jordan began importing workers. Not strictly replacement labor, these migrants filled positions that paid poverty wages, which the domestic population rejected.[65]

Many worked abroad, and Jordan was highly reliant upon regional employment. In the early 1980s, 40 percent of the Jordanian labor force worked outside the country. In the late 1970s Jordan's labor remittances were $0.50 billion, and in 1980 they were $0.75 billion. Reported remittances averaged a yearly $220 per resident in the 1970s.[66] At their highest, reported remittances during this period equaled 124 percent of Jordan's trade exports. This foreign-earned pay provided around one-third of the GNP, at times outpacing foreign aid and funding a negative balance of trade.[67] Foreign earnings from those in the Gulf dropped at the end of the 1980s, bottoming out in 1991.[68] Still, such labor receipts formed the largest component of national income at liberalization. Foreign-earned paychecks sent back to the country constituted 20 percent of the GDP in the 2000s, amounting to $2.5 billion in 2005.[69] In Palestinian refugee settlements, the majority of families had at least one member employed in the Gulf. Displaced Palestinian farmers, now in the city, found informal, irregular, service-sector work, particularly in construction, health care, and retail.[70] Their income was supplemented by relatives working abroad, who sent money through kin networks. Fifty-two percent of expatriate workers in Kuwait, for example, aided four or more family members.[71] The investment profile of the migrant leans heavily toward consumption, not investment, spent on land and housing construction, for example. Family members used these funds to purchase household necessities and consumer goods, and to fund higher education.[72]

In economic reforms, unemployment went from almost zero in the 1980s to 28 percent in the late 1990s. Rural areas dependent upon state employment are particularly vulnerable as structural adjustment proceeds.[73] For rural Jordanians, agriculture had served as the main alternative to state employment prior to the oil boom. However, low-paid agricultural work is no longer an option as a main source of income.[74] Urban Jordanians, living in the central region, enjoyed the widest employment potential. Not only did they receive preference in public employment, but the bulk of private business and industry is located in the center. Suffering from reduced state employment and declining possibilities abroad, much of the professional class is now unemployed. Forty percent of agricultural engineers are unemployed, and the rest have an average monthly salary of less than $170, which border the poverty level. Thirteen percent of dentists are unemployed.[75]

Services continued to dominate the economy. In the 1990s, 70 percent of employment and value-added was in services. Manufacturing was 12 percent of employment, and its contribution to national income was 13 percent.[76] The scarce manufacturing that existed prior to economic reforms—pharmaceuticals, for instance—has been hurt by recent policies.[77] Much of Jordan's labor force is highly educated, geared toward regional and expatriate professional service work. At any one time, 28 percent of eighteen- to twenty-three-year-olds are enrolled in higher education.[78] Engineers represent a large portion of qualified labor. Out of a labor force of less than one million, forty thousand are engineers. Jordan has five times the international average of dentists per population.[79]

The Iraq–U.S. Gulf War and subsequent sanctions on Iraq affected Jordan economically. The 1991 war increased the domestic labor force, as expatriate workers were expelled from Kuwait upon its recapture from the Iraqis. Overnight three hundred thousand workers carrying Jordanian passports, mostly Palestinians, "returned" to a country many had never inhabited but only visited on holidays. The former Gulf workers brought large amounts of capital, worth about $1 billion, much of which was used to establish small-scale and retail businesses.[80] During the 1990s the transport industry, in particular, suffered from the Iraqi sanctions.[81] Work opportunities in the Gulf decreased as nationals replaced expatriate workers.[82] Aggregate numbers of Jordanian expatriates, after declining sharply, rebounded to the 1989 level, but the percentage of the Jordanian labor force employed abroad has dropped, and the value of remittance receipts has eroded.[83] The amount of camp residents receiving remittances from abroad decreased from a majority of families to one-third in the 1990s. Currently, about 30 percent of Jordanian qualified labor work outside the country. Unemployment is high for them, as is underemployment and working in jobs outside their field.[84]

To make up for declining public employment, the government has promoted its cheap labor to attract business. Qualified trade zones were set up to encourage foreign investment, with duty-free entrance into the U.S. market as an enticement. The goal was political, namely, to encourage joint ventures with Israel; investment from both Israel and Jordan was needed to qualify for duty-free export status.[85] These industrial zones are disconnected from the main economy, effectively exempt from labor laws and social insurance payments, and female and child labor is common. In addition to poor working conditions and no job security, the women are paid below the minimum wage, only $70–$84 per month. Although Jordan technically has a minimum wage of $112 per month, or about 70 percent of the poverty level, it is not enforced. In one documented case, workers received wages of less than $24 per month for years.[86] Indeed, that children have begun working in these zones is an indication of family poverty levels and the pressing need to sacrifice children's education in order to survive.[87] In the end, despite the extent to which the zones add to stability and growth, their success may well be temporary. Though firms located in Jordan to gain access to the U.S. market, that advantage ended with the termination of the Multi-Fiber Agreement in 2005.[88]

These industrial zones mainly employ woman, as the dominant industry there is textiles.[89] The companies in Jordan's roughly twelve industrial zones are mostly East Asian. Of sixteen thousand workers in the highest-producing zone, six thousand are Chinese, Filipina, or

Bangladeshi women. Despite managers' complaints that Jordanian labor is inferior, Jordanian labor has now taken up half or more of the work in the zones.[90] Child care remains a problem, however. In order to work in these zones, the women rely on inexpensive child care services. In one factory, twenty-five women utilize the industrial zone's own nursery for their children, and many others put their children in nurseries in their home villages. Many of these nurseries, including the one in this industrial zone, are unregistered and unregulated. Further, even if women are employed, men, particularly in the rural areas, are still without jobs.

Salaried public-sector work, and indeed all formal employment, has declined in the Palestinian camp areas, leaving only unemployment and irregular income. Much of the informal sector, particularly for the lower-income Palestinian areas, is in construction work, which moves in tandem with regional trends. Other employment in the central region—trade and hotels—is seasonal and precarious. Taxi driving is a coveted irregular activity. Women work in sewing, knitting, and cooking enterprises, for which the market is saturated. Further, even when the work is steady, the pay is irregular; months often pass without a paycheck, and so this work cannot substitute for other sources of income.[91]

POPULATION AND EMPLOYMENT IN LEBANON

Lebanon's population has been estimated at 4.4 million nationals, with another 200,000 to 300,000 noncitizen Palestinians, half of whom live in twelve camps.[92] Lebanon's population growth has remained level because of the large out-migration, war deaths, and lower birth rates relative to neighboring countries. Lebanon's population is composed of nineteen recognized sectarian groups, generally broken down into four main sects—Christians, Sunni Muslim, Shi'a Muslim, and Druze—in addition to the Palestinians who do not have citizenship. The outdated census on which the country's political institutions are based was conducted in 1932, and showed a slight majority of Christians. No official population counts have succeeded that census, but most estimates including those of the U.S. government maintain that Shi'a Muslims are now the largest sect. The trend of growing Shi'a numbers, currently an estimated 38 percent of the population, and the decreasing number of Christians will likely continue, given the former's slightly higher birth rate and the latter's continued emigration.[93] Christians were estimated at 32 percent of the population in 1992; Sunnis, at 23 percent; and Druze, at 7 percent.[94] The population is overwhelmingly urban (84–90 percent) and is heavily concentrated in the greater Beirut region (40–50 percent). One-fifth of the population is in the north, the most poverty-stricken area of the country.[95]

Income was skewed by sect at independence, with Shi'a the poorest group by more than one-third and comprising more of the poor than all the other groups. But the gaps between the groups have diminished since independence. At that time Christians comprised three-quarters of the upper class but had decreased to only 60 percent at the start of the war.[96] Currently a new class of rich is rising because of money made through emigration and the financial effects of the civil war. Shi'a have become wealthier through increased education, urbanization, and work abroad, and are now moving into state civil-service jobs in large numbers.[97]

Service jobs made up between two-thirds and three-quarters of the national income, and accounted for at least two-thirds of employment in Lebanon.[98] Employment in industry and agriculture were both around one-fifth of the labor force. One-quarter of workers were independently employed in 1970.[99] Lebanon's working class was larger than Jordan's in 1975, as a percent of population; in Lebanon it was 5 percent and in Jordan 1 percent. In Lebanon, however, the "working class" was defined to include small business owners, the self-employed, and family workers.[100] Until then manufacturing had not been dynamic, creating only 23,000 jobs out of 120,000 new workers in the labor force during the 1960s. At the same time agriculture was declining as workers left the rural areas for the cities.[101] Companies remained small, averaging five employees. Medium- and micro-sized industries represented 99 percent of all industries.[102] Eighty percent of retail stores in greater Beirut in 1968 were small-scale, employing an average of 1.5 persons. The employment structure was largely based on self-employed taxi drivers, peddlers, and shop owners, and remained so during and after the war.[103]

Migration was the country's solution to unemployment. Large numbers of Lebanese left the country for work in the West, Africa, and the Gulf, and households depended on remittance income from family members.[104] Emigration averaged ten thousand individuals a year in the early 1970s, forty thousand a year during the war, and decreased again to ten thousand a year in the 1990s.[105] Income remitted from abroad constituted a significant portion of the country's national earnings. In 1950 worker remittances constituted more than one-fifth of the GNP, and by 1975, one-third of the GNP.[106] Before the start of the civil war, remittances totaled $150 million, soaring to over $2 billion in 1980.[107] In 2004 remittances totaled $5.6 billion, or 20 percent of the GDP.[108]

During the civil war the demographic landscape changed significant-ly, but the fundamental economic emphasis on services did not. Instead of the previous centralization and urbanization, the war spurred the de-centralization of people with businesses fleeing the cities to suburbs and villages.[109] Up to one-quarter of the population was displaced during the civil war,[110] which strengthened religious segregation. Large popula-tion movements occurred up to and during the war; indeed, between 33 and 45 percent of the population moved.[111] Despite official encour-agement and funding, most were hesitant to return and remained in their new homes.[112] The predominantly Shi'a southern population fled north before and during the war as a result of Israeli bombings and the poor economic conditions of agriculture in the south. They settled in the southern suburbs of Beirut, now simply called "the suburbs," or *al-Dahiyeh*. The area, long devoid of any state services or official infrastruc-ture, is Hizbullah's stronghold. Christians left West Beirut and southern parts of Mount Lebanon for East Beirut, and Muslims left the East, the southern area occupied by Israel, and other Christian-controlled areas. Percentages of Christians decreased from 55 percent to 5 percent in some areas, and Muslims in the East declined to 1 percent of the population there.[113]

The economy became extremely decentralized and tied to the mili-tias during the civil war. Duplicate institutions and branches were estab-lished in the hinterlands, creating new enclave economies. Universities established multiple campuses throughout the country, accommodating a populace no longer free to travel. Seventy percent of a Lebanese's regu-lar activities were restricted to his or her immediate neighborhood.[114] Economically militia rule diminished but did not destroy the country's GDP, which dropped to less than LL 3 billion in 1990 from LL 8 billion before the war. Services, including the drug trade, remained the main-stay of the economy.[115] The average monthly wage dropped from $200 in 1980 to $30 in 1987.[116] Work in the militias or the newly self-sufficient small local economies absorbed many of the unemployed.

Postwar reconstruction has neither altered Lebanon's labor market nor changed its dependence upon emigration. Unemployment is esti-mated at 20 percent, although some put the figure at 30 percent.[117] Wag-es have declined compared to their prewar level. In 2003 the minimum wage—$81 at the end of the war—was raised to $200 per month; the average monthly salary for a Lebanese national is $400.[118] Agricultural employment accounts for around 7 percent of employment.[119] Those working exclusively in agriculture, without a job in another sector, are most vulnerable, yet little employment exists outside agriculture in the rural areas to stem the tide of urbanization.[120] Three-quarters of agricultural workers without secondary employment are poor.[121] In the south, tobacco is the crop on almost all the land. Sixty percent of the workforce there is in agriculture, the majority of which are peasants working on small plots.[122] Rural populations often depend upon remittances for survival. In one village in southern Lebanon, half of all household income comes from foreign remittances, and 60 percent of households had two or more workers abroad.[123] Emigration continues to run at over one hundred thousand annually since the war.[124] Public administration comprised 11 percent of employment in 1997, and industry and construction employ 22 percent.[125]

Only half the workers were permanently employed in 2003. About 10 percent have a fixed length for their job. Almost 30 percent are in liberal professions, which, in Arabic, means self-employed contractors. Independent workers continue to constitute one-fourth of labor, as they did before the war.[126] The most sought-after occupations are in the service sector, where many jobs are seasonal or dependent upon networks. Hotel management, information, accounting, nursing, electricians, and electronics are the most popular.[127] Thirty percent of the unemployed are from the commerce sector. Like Jordan, Lebanon has a disproportionate number of skilled professionals—doctors and engineers—and few technicians and vocational workers. Between fifty thousand and sixty-three thousand individuals are professionals.[128] At any time, over one-third of the population is enrolled in school, one-quarter of them in higher education, and the country has some ten thousand professors.[129] A large percentage of graduates emigrate for work abroad, since less than half the twenty-five thousand graduates each year find employment in the local market.[130] Thirty percent of information technology graduates leave immediately upon obtaining their degrees, and an additional 30 percent follow a while later. The information technology field in Lebanon employs fewer than three thousand persons.[131]

Palestinians are particularly vulnerable. Around 5 percent of Palestinians in Lebanon are regularly employed.[132] Earnings are meager, according to one estimate averaging an inadequate $54 per month.[133] Unemployment for Palestinians is estimated to be between 50 and 65 percent.[134] Restricted from employment in seventy-two occupations, Palestinians have worked in construction and agriculture as day laborers, in addition to being self-employed and engaging in informal work.[135] In the summer of 2005, after the departure of Syrian migrant workers whose situation had become insecure with the end of the Syrian occupation, Palestinian employment was opened to the working-class jobs previously performed by the Syrian migrant workers.

WELFARE THROUGH PROFESSIONAL ASSOCIATIONS

Professional associations are another means of social welfare in the private sector. The number of skilled professionals and manufacturing workers is small in Jordan and Lebanon, limiting the potential for collective solutions based on work. At most 13 percent of Jordanian labor is covered under such associations, and the percentage is far less in Lebanon.[136] In Jordan membership in the associations is mandatory for those employed domestically. Externally oriented labor, working abroad, is less concerned with unions or social security.[137] Lawyers were the first to form a professional union, in 1950; physicians unionized shortly thereafter. The social activities of the unions began in the 1970s, starting with housing. Engineers began the first housing cooperative for engineers who had left the West Bank in the 1967 War. The next priorities were pensions and health insurance. In 1965 the physicians rejected this proposal based on the rationale that all doctors are prosperous, but it was instituted just a few years later in 1971. The physicians association now provides pensions, insurance, and loans to member physicians and their families. In the 1990s the associations began providing credit for consumer goods and increased their range of social welfare services.[138]

Since economic reforms, skill-based associations have expanded beyond their base among engineers, doctors, lawyers, and manufacturing workers to even smaller professions such as newspaper writers and Internet providers. Existing and new associations organize to provide social security, pensions, and credit for members. Associations have been formed for newspaper writers, pharmacists, and Internet providers. The Pharmacists Association recently voted to cover the costs of funeral services and to provide an investment fund. There is a demand for small loans from the association.[139] Though many associations are small, they nonetheless try to establish social security, pension, and credit provision. The Agricultural Engineers Association is now establishing a Social Interdependence Fund, as is the Association of Certified Public Accountants; the Nurses and Midwives Council recently began pension and social security programs. Most associations have only a few hundred members. The total membership of professional associations in Jordan is 80,000, but fewer are full, dues-paying members.[140] Workers' unions, for which only private-sector workers are eligible, have voluntary membership with the exception of the Land Transport and Mechanics union, the largest of them all. Anyone who holds a public transport license must be a member of this union, which has 175,000 members throughout Jordan. In all, the seventeen unions have a membership of 200,000.[141]

Lebanon has some five hundred professional organizations, of which about half are workers unions.[142] Some professional associations have mandatory membership if one wants to work in that particular field; in workers unions, membership is optional, as are membership dues. In the mid-1990s the Association of Engineers had twelve thousand members, only half of them current dues-paying members, and the Beirut Bar Association had six thousand members.[143] Labor unions have a low membership, only about 7 percent of workers. Trade unions capture less than 40 percent of their target group, and the mandatory professional associations of lawyers, doctors, and engineers obtain almost 90 percent.[144] The largest professional associations—engineering, legal, dentist, doctor, pharmacist, and nursing associations—have a combined membership of thirty-eight thousand.[145] Specialized labor requiring less education, such as fishermen, organize among themselves.

INDIVIDUAL SOLUTIONS: CREDIT AND PRIVATE INSURANCE

Even though Jordan and Lebanon were regional leaders in private insurance and banking, individual options for intermittent borrowing and long-term insurance are not available.[146] Both loans and private insurance are hindered by the lack of legal coverage to insure business practices. In order for private-sector insurance to function, information must not be asymmetrical, providing the potential for fraud.[147] Few individuals in either country have the necessary collateral for loans, which would require permanent employment or title ownership of fixed assets. Interest rates in Lebanon have been high, around 40 percent in the early 1990s and decreasing to 20 percent by the end of the decade.[148] The middle class cannot afford housing loans, for example.[149] Large businesses monopolize loans in Lebanon.[150] Less than 2.5 percent of bank depositors accounted for 40 percent of all deposits at the end of the war, and 60 percent by 2002.[151] Credit and loans are predominantly (about three-quarters) extended to large service-sector companies overwhelmingly in the Beirut area.[152] Micro-enterprises find loans difficult to obtain.[153] Micro-loans in Jordan are geared toward established businesses, not small or new companies.[154]

Life insurance and private health insurance is similarly lacking. Lebanon's insurance market is highly fragmented, with high premiums and laws that are difficult to enforce.[155] Jordan's insurance market is not well developed, although the sector is crowded.[156] Claims outpace premiums, and fraud is difficult to prove.[157] A mere 1.7 percent of Jordanians had life insurance in 2000.[158] The Jordanian state provides health insurance to more of its population than does Lebanon for its citizens, mainly because of Jordan's greater number of civil and military employees. Only about 14 percent of Lebanese had adequate private insurance coverage in 1997.[159] The numerous private insurance companies in Lebanon covered around 7–8 percent of the population in 1995 and operated entirely in the Beirut region.[160] An estimated 44–60 percent of Lebanese are not covered by a health system according to the Ministry of Health. Ninety insurance companies furnish insurance to 450,000 Lebanese, or one-tenth of the population.[161] The excluded population relies on the private pay-as-you-go system, which is where the bulk of money on health care is spent despite representing a much smaller percentage of population served.[162] Private insurance as a percent of health expenditures is 12 percent in Lebanon and only 4 percent in Jordan. The vast majority of hospital care is in the private sector. Ten percent of Jordan's GDP is spent on health care, and 12 percent is spent in Lebanon. Of total health expenditures, private sources account for just over half in Jordan and three-quarters or more in Lebanon.[163]

CONCLUSION

As the Jordanian state and Lebanese militias withdrew their welfare services, the lack of private options for social security became apparent. What recourse do individuals have in these countries for a secure economic future? Middle classes in these economies are often in precarious positions, living a decent lifestyle but unable to save and barely meeting expenditures. State social policies effectively serve as a form of social welfare and insurance against hard times, providing a range of goods furnished under other social welfare systems. When protests for the return of social provisioning achieved nothing, people turned to the private sector to organize. Those with money purchased club memberships. Gated communities furnished upper-class Lebanese with parks, sports facilities, law and order, and water and electricity.[164] The poor have few options, borrowing from friends and working more.[165] Those in professions or with specialized skills unite for pensions and loans. Previously unorganized occupations are mobilizing in economic liberalization for this purpose, and established professional associations are expanding their social services. Left uninsured are nonprofessional service workers. Their options for private insurance, consumer credit, and job-based pensions are meager. Organizing on the basis of work is problematic, as work is unsteady and the skill base is minimal.

Private-sector credit and insurance are not options for most of the population in Jordan and Lebanon. Market institutions are incapable of providing aid for the middle class, particularly in these fluctuating service economies. The character of the labor market heavily influences private-sector options for social welfare. Collective solutions along occupational lines are also not viable because of the lack of longevity in companies and occupations. With long-term employment scarce, most households must rely upon numerous sources of irregular income. To date, the economies have proven little able to absorb growing numbers of entrants to the labor markets.

As a result of the labor and market structures, the bulk of the middle and lower classes are without work or market-based possibilities for social insurance. One civil-society type of association that has provided social aid in other countries when markets did not fill in the gaps is mutual aid associations. In the United States and Europe, mutual aid associations and fraternal organizations were rife in the late nineteenth and early twentieth centuries. These types of organization depended on members paying their dues and repaying loans. The judicial system functioned better in those countries at that time than legal institutions function currently in Jordan and Lebanon. Legal recourse was backed up by the additional techniques of rituals reinforcing solidarity and loyalty to the organization, most of which were local.[166] These methods of joining individuals in mutual aid provided support and social insurance for those with extra resources to invest in a collective endeavor.

In Jordan and Lebanon local, small-scale methods of social aid were altered to accommodate larger groups of people furnishing aid and employment contacts. Identity idioms served both as a substitute for legal enforcement and fit with the prevailing character of employment. In contrast to specialized jobs or professions, which necessitate networks among the specialty only, work in the various facets of the service industry could be obtained through contacts in employment far afield from one's present job. Identity idioms, linking individuals across the economy, could profitably lead to jobs in these economies.

4

Kin Mutual Aid

Changes in social insurance caused much of the population in Jordan and Lebanon to orient their demands onto reconstituted identity organizations. The time line of kin association formation and decline corresponds to the existence of collective social provisioning furnished either by the state or militias and the urbanization of the social group. Village mechanisms, well documented elsewhere,[1] aided village residents prior to urbanization, albeit incompletely and selectively. Arriving in the city, people organized anew. Instead of joining up with others according to economic interests, service-sector workers in Jordan and Lebanon united on the basis of their identity and so united in groups that crossed various economic industries.

Although identity and kinship often take priority over economic concerns when individuals organize collectively, they will often forsake kinship when alternative, long-term solutions for their social insurance needs are available. When welfare and market buffers exist, the populace eschews formal kin organizing, and when state social insurance policies are withdrawn and times are hard, the populace will invent these institutions where they did not exist. Alternative institutional designs are well known. Guilds, professional associations, business groups, and religious and family trusts all provided welfare. In the minority communities, communal organizations assisted members. Though many preferred private market options, they were not available. Charity, called upon in economic liberalization to combat poverty, misses the mark: welfare's main function is as redistributive insurance, not charitable handouts.

I being this chapter by tracing the time line of the groups forming kin associations in Jordan and Lebanon, their labor market position, and the type of kinship used.[2] The operative kinship or family consists of relatives relevant to daily life, those one can turn to in times of need. Other relatives may still be acknowledged as kin, but they are not included in the kin association. Thus "family" incorporates and excludes relatives.

The group's relation to state welfare determines when kin associations are formed; the precise version of kinship embodied in the association is a consequence of the members' labor market position. After breaking down the trend by social group and time period, I compare the presence of mutual aid associations and participation in them to the countries' use of charities and other organizations. Mutual aid associations, it turns out, encompass far more of society than do traditional NGOs or civil society associations. I then delineate the typical services of kin mutual aid associations, which have become one-stop institutions for an array of social services, newly generated in economic liberalization and austerity. The associations substitute for other single-issue charities, state services, and class organizations. The relation to labor market needs is clear in their training programs and child care services, which were established to aid women newly employed in the qualified industrial zones. All these services are ideals; the existence of an organization and its provision of a service should not be taken as proof that the needs are covered. The associations are often ill-equipped to assess labor market needs, as demonstrated in the training programs and the lack of adequate funds to devote to services. The primary purpose of these associations remains insurance and job connections for the middle classes, discussed in chapter 5.

JORDAN'S MUTUAL AID ASSOCIATIONS

The formation of mutual aid associations, as noted, corresponds to the labor market position and welfare needs of the social group in question. Jordanians received state welfare until at least 1989, and so, until that time, kin associations were rare among this population. From the 1970s to 1989 Jordan's residents all benefited from consumer subsidies, which buffered their experience of market prices and insured a modicum of financial stability. The state's main support base, Jordanian Muslims, did not form mutual aid associations for most of Jordan's history. For them, kin organizing prior to 1989 took place in large-scale organizations similar to tribes organizing informally. These were vertical organizations, dominated by a leader. After 1989 the pattern changed. This same group created smaller organizations based on horizontal networks, excluding many who had previously been considered kin. The organization style of other groups differed. Jordanian minorities—Christians, for example—received limited state employment. Mainly based in the private sector, they put together social insurance organizations shortly after the state of Jordan was formed. With somewhat privileged access to the state, these groups used narrow, genealogical definitions of kinship. Palestinians organized primarily after 1967, using broad definitions of kin to maximize resources and contacts. Palestinians were largely denied state employment from the 1970s on, and they worked in the private sector. They formed large networks in their kin associations, organizing on the basis of village of origin.

The current form of mutual aid association first appeared in Jordan in the early twentieth century.[3] By the 1950s it was formally organized. Minorities, including Jordanian Christians and Druze, were behind the initial movement.[4] Though they supported the regime, these groups were not the primary social base of the Hashemites. Their ability to tap state welfare was circumscribed. Few were employed in the public sector, but those who were held mid-level management positions with significant influence. By and large, these minorities attained work in the service sector as employers, owners, and professionals, and are not heavily involved in regional migration. To provide welfare for their families, they formed associations using a restricted version of kinship, and turned welfare and access to the state bureaucracy into a club good.

The Jordanian Christian cooperative Aal al-Naber Association exemplifies this group.[5] Despite having migrated twice, first from Yemen to Karak in 1710 and then to Amman in the twentieth century, the family is defined by strict patrilineal descent starting from the generation that arrived in Amman. Their family tree (Figure 4.1) lists the first names of all members on the branches; the trunk is reserved for those who originally migrated to the capital. There are currently 580 members. Some family members live in the West Bank, but no attempt has been made to incorporate these relatives.[6] Another Christian family came to Jordan from Syria in 1605. They identify themselves as Jordanians and staunch supporters of the Hashemites. After praising the family lineage and history, they state that current residence, not the family's original location, defines their identity.[7] In this way they effectively narrow the realm of kinship.

The Palestinians, left out of state-provided social welfare, drew on broad kin networks to obtain social insurance in their precarious economic condition. Arriving mainly in 1948 and 1967, Palestinians found domestic, international, and regional employment primarily in services such as construction, administration, and professions. In the 1960s, and especially the 1970s, some Palestinian family associations were established that had no significant ties to the state. Separated from the land that had formed the basis of their livelihood (most had been farmers), the migrants pursued a professional education that would allow

FIGURE 4.1. al-Naber Family Tree. "Compiled by Father Elyas al-Naber in 1950; completed by the steering committee of the Aal al-Naber Cooperative Association in 1971; finalized in 1988." *Courtesy of the al-Naber Family Cooperative, Amman, Jordan, n.d.*

them mobility so that they could practice anywhere. Unable to count on state largesse for jobs, Palestinians sought work in the private sector. Wide-ranging employment contacts were necessary for these positions, not only domestically but also within the region and internationally as Palestinians searched for work outside their new residence. Inclusive kinship aided their life chances in statelessness. Coping techniques included the wife's kin, an innovation in family practices, along with additional selected kin. As Ghabra states, "family became the means by which the Palestinians were able to respond to the conditions of the diaspora."[8]

Almost always the family that was used to cope with diaspora living was based on village of origin, casting a wide net and drawing in thousands of members. In the refugee camps, Palestinians settled among former neighbors and villagers. Jordanian state practices furthered this grouping based on home village, since the government used the village leader, or *mukhtar*, as an administrative intermediary.[9] Family associations in Jordan served as transit and networking centers for kin to or from the West Bank, and some associations came to have branches in Kuwait and even the United States.[10] Lifta, a village outside Jerusalem, formed a charitable society in 1969. The family tree (Figure 4.2) lists the names of the major families in the village, broken down by tribe

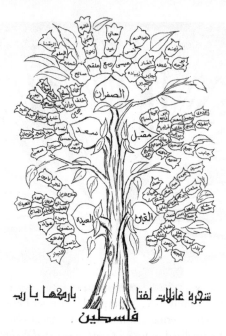

FIGURE 4.2. Lifta Family Tree. *Courtesy of the Lifta Charitable Association, Amman and Zarqa, Jordan, n.d.*

(the large leaves on the tree) and then family name (the smaller leaves). An estimated 15,000 of the village's descendants live in Jordan. The association has branches in Amman, Zarqa, and the West Bank, and two in the United States.[11] Silwan village, named after the original village in the West Bank, formed an association in 1975 and has continually added families to its family tree (Figures 4.3 and 4.4) as more are included in the association.[12] The names on the trunk are tribes, and the leaves on the branches are family names. Al-Ramla, a village from inside the pre-1948 borders of Palestine, formed its association in 1971. Originally containing merely 37 members, the association increased incrementally to 212 in 1981. In the following decade the membership doubled, and then more than doubled again in the 1990s to its present membership of 1,100. A branch opened in Zarqa in the north in 1987, and one in Balqa camp in 1997 (both areas of high Palestinian concentration). The association puts the descendants of al-Ramla village at 150,000, spread out among 500 families.[13] The association contains only those from al-Ramla who are interested in collective organizing and pay dues. In general, only the head of the nuclear family in this association pays membership fees, as is the practice with many other associations.

شجرة عائلات باركها يا رب

FIGURE 4.3. Silwan Family Tree (version 1). By 'Ali 'Ayyash. Silwan Social Development Association. "22nd Annual Report for the Fiscal Year 1998." Amman: al-Dustoor, 1998. *Courtesy of the Silwan Charitable Association.*

FIGURE 4.4. Silwan Family Tree (version 2). "Family tree designed and executed by Engineer 'Ali 'Ayyash." "Gift of Engineer 'Ali 'Ayyash." *Courtesy of the Silwan Charitable Association.*

Mutual aid associations remained a marginal phenomenon in the 1970s and throughout most of the 1980s, even though they were the only organizing form permitted by the state (for the growth of kin associations, see Figure 4.5). The core regime base and those with state welfare, the Jordanian Muslims, did not embrace the trend despite often being identified as more kin-oriented and tribal. Indeed, observers noted a decline in tribal and kin allegiances prior to economic reform in 1989.[14] The impetus for kin mutual aid was slight, since the state provided the general population with urban consumer subsidies and some employment and health care. The Palestinians had access to plentiful work opportunities in the Gulf. Economic liberalization introduced the main stimulus for kin organizing. Then previously unorganized Palestinians established family associations, and those that had an organization for the individual family (*rabita* or *diwan*) joined with others to form a larger association based on a broader kinship. The return of expatriate workers as a result of the 1991 Gulf War and political liberalization indirectly contributed to the rise of kin associations.[15] Individuals returning to Jordan, from the West or the Gulf, having migrated for political or economic reasons, represented an expanded pool of potential kin.[16]

In the period of liberalization, Jordanian Muslims, the regime's main allies, have narrowed kinship to smaller identity groups. Until liberalization ended the unrestricted welfare Jordanian Muslims enjoyed through public-sector jobs, they remained unorganized. Before liberalization, they sometimes organized informally in extremely inclusive associations. Now, in urban and suburban areas, tribes began dividing into smaller units, often the *hamula* or seven-generation family,[17] and registering this as the kin association. One tribe traces its descent back to 1717 in Palestine. Acknowledging the various potential bases for defining his family, which could include inhabitants of the West Bank, the author of the tribe's history instead delineates the family exclusively, eliminating many potential kin.[18]

Last to organize were the rural communities. Until economic liberalization these areas were employed steadily in the civil service, public companies, and the military. For the rural population, the configuration of classes and services differs. Because of their earlier production profile, the rural areas are largely devoid of a middle class and lack the participatory character of urban associations. Association membership is smaller, often only a few dozen, and leaders are generally retired army officers or local government officials. Members' dues and participation are largely absent, and association attendance was low in the late 1990s.[19] The use of kinship as the idiom of solidarity is the same, and, in fact, many are composed of one or two families.[20] One association of this type is Um Batma, founded in 1990 by local government officials. An East Bank association based on community residence overlapping with kinship, it has a current membership of three dozen and its elections are uncontested.

Demonstrating the economic role of kin organizations, some associations temporarily fell into disuse as large amounts of aid flowed into the country from the United States in 2004. Approximately $1 billion came into Jordan that year. In line with the hypothesis that kin associations are social insurance mechanisms for hard times, many individuals pursued their own separate interests and abandoned their kin associations. One association in my core 2004 survey had not had meetings for a year.[21]

Governorate	1960s		1970s		1980s		1989		1990s	
	coop	char	coop	char	coop	char	coop	char	coop	char
Mafraq	1	-	-	2	-	9	-	1	9	26
Irbid	2	17	9	29	6	19	-	1	31	37
Jerash	1	-	-	6	3	5	-	-	27	6
Ajloun	2	-	-	3	2	4	-	1	4	13
Total Northern	6	17	9	40	11	37	-	3	71	82
Amman	12	9	21	14	5	23	2	1	55	55
Balqa	-	-	2	3	2	10	1	1	12	14
Zarqa	2	2	5	2	3	11	-	1	6	11
Madaba	-	-	6	2	3	2	-	-	18	10
Total Middle	14	11	34	21	13	46	3	3	91	90
Karak	-	6	2	5	2	6	-	1	13	23
Tafileh	-	-	-	1	3	6	-	1	4	5
Ma'an	-	5	2	2	2	15	-	-	12	7
Aqaba	-	-	-	1	-	-	-	-	2	6
Total Southern	-	11	4	9	7	27	-	2	31	41
Total	20	39	47	70	31	110	3	8	193	213

FIGURE 4.5. Number of Jordanian Kin Associations by Region, cooperatives and charities. Data calculated from interviews with officials, various dates in 1999–2000; General Union of Voluntary Societies, Directorate of Research and Social Studies. "Directory of voluntary societies and social development in the Hashemite Kingdom of Jordan (updated)." Amman: Ittihad al-'am lil-jama'iyyat al-khayriyya, 1999; Jordan Cooperative Corporation. "List of cooperatives by type and governorate (internal documents)." Amman: al-Mu'assasa al-t'awuniyya al-Urduniyya, al-Ma'had al-t'awuni, 2000; updated computer-generated list from General Union of Voluntary Societies, mimeo, 2003. Numbers err on the conservative side and most probably underestimate the phenomenon. Cooperatives from 2000–2003 are not included because of the inability to obtain data from the Cooperative Corporation.

Numbers of Associations and Participation

Numbers and participation in kin mutual aid associations outpace all other types of organizing in Jordan. In 2003 there were 789 kin mutual aid associations in Jordan, 472 (60%) of which formed since liberalization in 1989 (see Figure 4.5). The vast majority of charities established since economic liberalization has been based on kinship. In fact, charities not based on kinship are almost completely limited to the most urbanized areas, the capital Amman and nearby Zarqa to the north. NGOs in other regions of the country overwhelmingly consist of kin associations. Some areas are without more than one non-kin charity. Comparing these numbers to other types of organizations demonstrates the relatively large breadth of the phenomenon. The related organization and precursor to the current kin association, the guesthouse, *madafa* or *diwan*, numbers at most 293 in the country. Kin associations outnumber both cooperatives and charities. The total number of cooperatives increased to 1,000 by the year 2000[22] and charities numbered around 800,[23] and these figures include kin-organized charities and cooperatives.

A significant portion of Jordan's population, about 40 percent, participates in kin associations.[24] This figure correlates with the findings of the Fafo Institute for Applied Social Science that 34 percent of the population has a kin association. According to the Fafo report, between 19 percent and 45 percent of men attend their kin association. Similarly the surveys of the Center for Strategic Studies found higher numbers: 40 percent of Jordan's population had a kin association in 1997 and 50 percent in subsequent years. Over 60 percent of Jordanian members attend monthly, and more than one-fourth attend every three months. Of these, two-thirds gathered regularly at the association, and three-fourths or more attended for a funeral. Thirty percent took part in internal disputes or discussions.[25] Moreover, membership has increased. Whereas previously only a handful attended yearly meetings, a much larger portion of the membership is now active. According to one association leader, attendance at meetings went from fifteen to hundreds of attendees by 2000.[26]

LEBANON'S MUTUAL AID ASSOCIATIONS

As in Jordan, the trajectory of kin mutual aid associations in Lebanon follows urbanization and a lack of social welfare. In Lebanon's case the state did not provide welfare, and for some groups social aid came mainly during and just prior to the war. The labor market is almost completely private sector; state employment is not the fiefdom for state supporters that it is in Jordan. Here, too, poorer groups utilized expansive definitions of kinship. This usually took the form of village of origin, used by both the Palestinians and Shi'a migrating from the south. Richer groups closed the circle tighter. The first groups to urbanize even before the founding of the state were the Christians. The Sunnis then organized, followed by the Shi'a. Palestinians arrived in 1948 and 1967 but received welfare from the Palestine Liberation Organization until 1970 to 1982. This source of social welfare ended in the middle of the civil war. The UN, through UNRWA, continued to provide some aid, particularly for the most vulnerable. Hometown or village organizations were established soon after the Palestinians' arrival in 1948, but the importance of these organizations diminished sharply as the PLO took over welfare, only to rise once more again when the PLO again left in 1982.

Lebanon's kin associations date from the mid-nineteenth century with the initial wave of urbanization in the contemporary era. Richer groups, with some ability to secure political connections and state employment (Christians), formed more exclusive, genealogical family associations, akin to the Jordanian Muslims at liberalization and Jordanian minorities in the 1950s. Others, with no access to state employment, organized inclusively. The Lebanese Shi'a, coming from the south, used village of origin as the basis of kinship, or even included several villages in close geographical proximity, to form a large group suited to securing private-sector connections.

The majority of the first wave of associations (71%) that formed before the 1940s were Christian, such as the Majdalani family (1939, Beirut).[27] Some Sunni families also organized. The Tabbara (1907) and Sinou (1920) families in Beirut established associations for social aid and health care. The 1940s and 1950s were the peak of Sunni Beiruti associations. The Kabbara Family Charitable Association is an example, formed in 1948 in Tripoli to care for the family's needy. Shi'a associations increased in the 1960s, the main period of migration for this group. Southern Shi'a organized by village of origin, much as the Palestinians traditionally had. Both the Shi'a and Palestinians experienced harassment and difficulties in locating employment. Shi'a in the Beka'a and the north, such as the Hamadeh (1960), organized by tribe, similarly yielding a large membership. The run-up to the war saw an increase in ideological associations in the late 1960s and early 1970s among the Shi'a and a decline in village associations. Instead, professional organizations, unions, political organizations and parties, and sectarian associations increased. This has been called the "golden age" of civil society organizations in Lebanon, particularly because of the increase in cross-confessional associations and employment-based unions.[28]

During the war, from 1975 to 1990, kin associations increased dramatically in the areas left unserved by militia welfare (see Table 2.2). Where no militia was able to consolidate a hold, numerous militias fought for hegemony, or if the population was denied access to the militia's social services, people organized to provide their own social security. For example, Christians living in the Druze-ruled areas of Aley and the Shouf did not receive equal access to employment or services, and so kin associations increased substantially among these excluded Lebanese.[29] Indeed, 40 percent of all organizations in the Shouf were Christian kin associations.[30] In the former Druze-controlled area of Aley, 31 percent of associations were family-based.[31] Over 60 percent of these were formed during and after the war, predominantly among Druze or mixed Druze-Christian families. Christian families formed associations in Baalbek (Syrian-controlled, with no service-providing militia) and Lebanese Muslims in Sayda (controlled by Palestinians). The Sunnis were mostly dependent on other militias, forming alternative associations based on kinship and neighborhood to provide for themselves.[32] In Beirut no militia secured dominance with the geographic reach or long-term tenancy to branch out into social provisioning. The result was an increase in kin and neighborhood associations among the Sunnis and the Christian orthodox (dominated by a group of well-defined families), providing services that were lacking.[33] Tripoli, with no dominant militia, had only seven kin associations prior to 1980. Subsequently at least sixty kin and village associations were established.[34]

By contrast, where militia institutions furnished social services for the middle class, the populations did not form kin associations and existing associations fell into disuse. This was the case for Palestinians in the camps during the PLO's tenure until 1982, for Christians in their militia canton during the war, for Druze after the establishment of a social administration in 1983 until the end of the war, and for Shi'a living under Hizbullah's jurisdiction since about 1984. For example, in Kisrawan, a Christian area with a consolidated service-providing militia, kin associations declined during the war.[35] Although a few Christian associations remained active in the Christian-controlled canton, most ceased their activities and new ones did not arise. One Christian association interviewee stated that although his family is large and strong, the association fell into disuse during the war.

Instead of enhanced familial and kin identity, which can provide protection and security during times of war and unstable economies, these ascriptive subnational identities decreased in areas under consolidated militia control. This led to complaints from familial and religious leaders, who, although they supported the militias themselves, saw militia institutions as challenges to the existing system. Individuals became less dependent upon traditional leaders' authority.[36] Kin relations strengthened only for the immediate family and among friends, not relatives, during the war.[37] Religiosity declined, even as the strength of confessional identity increased.[38] In some cases militias simply took over kin associations; in others they worked together, and the kin associations grew to become a regional association.[39] The militias surpassed both family and the state in service provision. None of the militias was democratic, and all quelled internal dissent. Yet some associations did form, in areas controlled by opposing militias and presumably suffering heightened repression compared to sects living among friendly militias. Kin associations also began forming in the last few years of the war, when the militias were unable to meet people's needs as standards of living plummeted and inflation spiraled.

When the war ended and the militia institutions disbanded, the formation of kin associations soared among all sectors of the population with resources, except for the Shi'a among whom the formation of kin associations lagged. For them, the militia continued to provide general public social welfare. Not all in need are able to form kin associations, of course. Palestinians turned to hometown mutual aid organizations after the PLO departed in 1982, and their establishment sped up after the Oslo Accords in 1993. But the associations have not been able to function well.[40] Because of irregular jobs, lack of employment, and a dearth of resources, redistribution and aid among Palestinian members is difficult, and most village associations do not succeed. Despite widespread poverty, the decline of UNRWA's services, and the end of PLO funding and institutions after the Oslo Accords, Palestinians have been unsuccessful in establishing alternative effective institutions such as village associations.

Number of Associations and Participation

With the end of the war came a sharp rise in the number of kin and village associations (see Figure 4.6).[41] Although Lebanon has far more associations of all types than Jordan does, kin associations are prevalent among a large portion of Jordan's population (almost 40%). More than 1,500 kin and village (hometown) associations[42] exist in Lebanon out of an estimated 4,000 associations.[43] Whereas at the start of the war there were approximately 477 kin mutual aid associations,[44] 500 additional associations were said to have formed in the first five years after the war alone.[45] According to some analysts, the kin association phenomenon has altered the face of Beirut.[46] Using the Social Development Ministry's (conservative) count, there are 570 kin associations. My tally from the official gazette concludes that 397 of these, or 70 percent, were formed during or after the war. There are an additional 962 local associations, either village- or neighborhood-based,[47] half of them established after the war. These neighborhood associations are effectively kin-based; they are not the community development associations of other regions in the world. Beirut alone currently has 300 registered kin associations and 60 neighborhood associations. In the 1950s there were only 3 neighborhood associations and 11 family associations.[48] Some analysts posit, moreover, that between 20 and 40 percent of Lebanese mutual aid associations operate without registering.[49] The majority of associations remain uncategorized

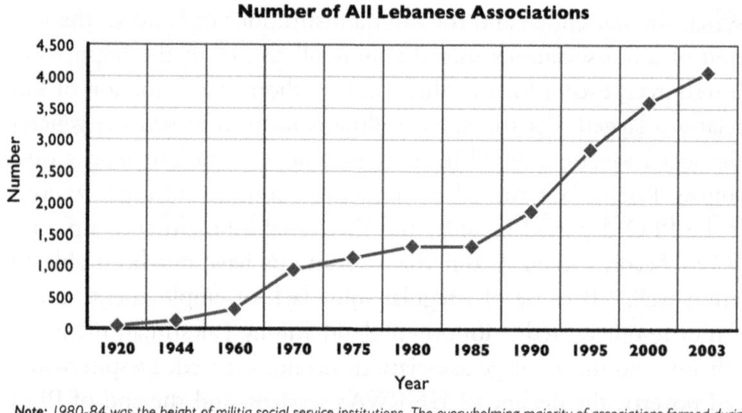

Number of All Lebanese Associations

Note: 1980-84 was the height of militia social service institutions. The overwhelming majority of associations formed during the 1960s and early 1970s, called the "golden age" of associations, was secular and non-kin. The opposite is true of the late war and post-war period.

FIGURE 4.6. Number of Lebanese Associations. The period from 1980 to 1984 was the height of militia social service institutions. The overwhelming majority of associations formed during the 1960s and early 1970s, called the "golden age" of associations, was secular and non-kin. The opposite is true of the late war and postwar period. *From Hashem al-Husseini, Abdullah Muhi al-Deen, and Munthir al-Haraka, "Dirasat mash minathamat al-qita' al-ahli fi Lubnan [Study of civil society organizations in Lebanon] (unpublished manuscript)." Beirut: Ministry of Social Affairs, 2002.*

by the Interior Ministry, and many have a general, nondescript name which makes identification difficult. Further, these numbers necessarily omit Palestinian associations since they are un-registered.

The increase in kin associations is particularly dramatic given the relatively constant population numbers, before and after the war, owing to emigration and war casualties. The single largest sectarian community in Lebanon, the Shi'a, who represent an estimated 40 percent of the population, now form significantly fewer associations than the other communities. In fact, among Shi'a, kin associations have all but disappeared.[50] Some attribute this to the role of militias, as opposed to family, in providing social mobility for middle class and new entrants to the elite.[51] This is in direct contrast to the prewar era (1950–1960s), when Shi'a kin and village associations were on the rise. It is among the Christian community where most local, identity organizations exist. Forty percent of all kin associations are in Mount Lebanon. Together with Beirut itself, the capital area surpasses all other regions in the number of associations (two-thirds of all types).[52]

Participation in kin mutual aid associations is high. More than half the Lebanese members interviewed attended their association within the past month, with only 8 percent not attending in the previous six months. Officials of the United States Agency for International Development (USAID) estimate that around two-thirds of the population belong to a kin mutual aid association;[53] a more conservative estimate puts the figure at one-quarter to one-third of the population. Mutual aid associations have higher average memberships than other NGOs. For example, one kin association, revived after the wartime lapse, had sixty voting members when it started in the mid-1990s. By 1998 meetings were attended by more than one thousand members.[54] In stark contrast, many NGOs are limited to a few dozen members.

SERVICES OF KIN MUTUAL AID ASSOCIATIONS

Kin associations are multipurpose furnishing numerous services. The activity of mutual aid associations begins with the establishment of a central location, a *maqar* or hall for the family to meet for funerals, weddings, and religious holidays, pivotal events in the life-cycle. These activities resemble burial societies worldwide. Newer associations lack a location entirely; others rent one. Well-established associations own a building for this purpose. Formal meetings of the general assembly are usually once or twice yearly, and as needed for emergencies. They serve to elect a board of directors, president, and subcommittees. Informally the association is used as a weekly meeting place or club for the men of the family. On religious holidays the family hall allows kin to meet in one place, saving the time-consuming necessity of visiting numerous houses to wish relatives well. Given the lack of public space, establishing a family meeting hall was viewed as a practical measure.

The associations provide various types of financial aid, including emergency money and loans; regular monthly support for the poor, unemployed, and widows; and seasonal help during holidays, the beginning of the school year, and the onset of winter. Emergency assistance is provided for accidents or illness, regular or monthly support for widows or those unable to work, and yearly gifts to needy families during religious occasions. The associations give a small amount of aid to poor families at other times and loans to meet household expenses or for business purposes. Members repay loans at face value or with minimal interest. Some associations paid members' medical bills for those unable to do so. In the event of a funeral, the association prepares food for those paying their respects, which otherwise is a large financial burden on the family. The associations fund weddings at least for the poor, and all members usually use the hall either free or for a nominal fee. Meetings to discuss political matters, raise emergency funds, or elect new leadership are held in the center. The same distribution of services holds for associations based on village of origin and for neighborhood associations in Lebanon.[55] Only a few of the very large and successful associations provide aid to non-kin. The Lifta Charitable Association (Palestinian) in Jordan supports orphans once kin obligations have been met.[56]

The specific configuration of services for each association differs according to the membership and its needs. All the associations in my surveys provided financial aid (see Figure 4.7). The first act of one Jordanian association president was to distribute a questionnaire inquiring about members' needs for services.[57] Popular services in Lebanese associations are providing small loans, emergency medical aid, educational funding, and jobs through owners of companies, traders, and retail store owners among the family. A number mentioned social security, insurance, or a treasury as key services. One Palestinian association in Lebanon runs a nursery, library, and ambulance. One Jordanian association runs a savings fund, yielding higher interest than the going rate, and offers personal loans up to $3,500.[58] In a Palestinian Jordanian association, children's clothes and books are provided seasonally, at the beginning of the school year, at the start of winter, and on religious holidays.[59] "Social

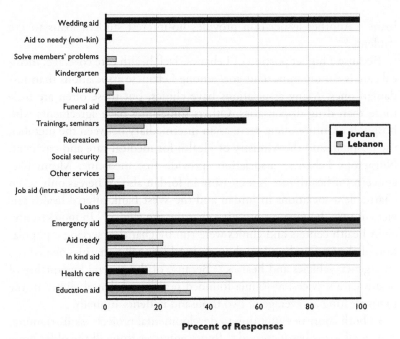

FIGURE 4.7. Formal Services of Associations. Compiled from my questionnaires.

meaning" and cultural lectures are occasionally mentioned among the associations' services, demonstrating the multiple natures of these associations, spanning economic and identity fields. More successful associations provide sports and recreational activities for youth. One provides a summer camp. Some associations offer computer training classes and Internet services

Educational loans are another priority. Future educated members will be indebted to the association and in positions of influence to help fellow members. One-third of Lebanese associations in my survey provide this help. One Christian association funds the total cost of education for males and half the cost for females.[60] A prosperous Sunni association helps members pursue higher education abroad. Most often aid is provided through loans or grants for some portion of the tuition. Other associations focus on younger children, purchasing schoolbooks and paying school fees. In Jordan, one-quarter of the surveyed associations provide educational aid. The Silwan Association provides yearly student loans or support for twelve university students, five at vocational schools, and thirty-three high schoolers, in addition to regular financial aid and loans.[61] Another association provides no-interest student loans to 170 students.[62]

Because a higher portion of Lebanese lack health care coverage, medical care is a more important goal among Lebanese associations than Jordanian ones. Many associations have clinics, but these often are little more than drug dispensaries. Others sometimes have agreements with hospitals or, more often, serve as an intermediary between the member, the hospital, and the Ministry of Health for medical care and payment. Numerous Lebanese associations provide free medicine. Meanwhile, concern for health care is increasing in Jordan also. Whereas only seven charitable associations in Jordan and the West Bank offered health services in 1987, by 1994 twenty-nine charities ran clinics.[63] In 1999 seventy-eight health centers and clinics were run by charities, serving a population of almost four hundred thousand. Additionally, charities owned 140 emergency vehicles and hearses.[64] Because of the general low quality of health care services, al-Ramla founded health and dental clinics in the 1970s treating an average of two thousand patients annually.

In both countries attention to developmental projects, skills-training, and small loans has increased.[65] Representatives from all the older organizations in Lebanon stated that services increased after the war. Some now regularly provide a fixed amount for needy kin. In Jordan associations have stepped up their activities, running training programs for girls and opening new branches, and some are building housing for students. The presence of more needy families was often cited as the reason for establishing an association or increasing services, along with a change in the types of people in need. In the past ten years the category of "needy" has grown and the forms of aid expanded.[66] One Jordanian kin association, established in 1989, was created specifically for the purpose of loaning money based merely on confidence rather than collateral.[67]

Investments, Training, and Production Programs

The associations invest to raise resources beyond the members' own potential. These investments are generally in the service sector, mainly in real estate and, in Jordan, reception halls, and stem from the basic need of kin associations to establish a central location for family gatherings. State funding supports this pursuit, furnishing aid for the maintenance or development of a building for the kin association. When associations rent out property in Jordan, the state is often the main renter. Other donations to the association commonly take the form of building or construction aid; donors subsequently receive much prestige for their philanthropic acts. In my survey, over 70 percent of Jordanian family associations had real estate holdings separate from the meeting hall, some quite extensive.

Some associations (15% in Jordan) turned their reception hall into a major commercial enterprise, renting it out to the general public. Family members usually are given access to the hall for a reduced rate. For many this is only a side activity, whereas others profit greatly. The Hebron charity Khalil al-Rahman charges $1,700 for one evening's use of its hall, exclusive of services and catering.[68] The Lifta Charitable Association runs a successful reception hall on its premises, which helps fund its other programs. The establishment of social reception halls for weddings and funerals reflects the changed situation of the middle class and the importance of symbolic capital and networks in a service economy. The rates for these halls have increased dramatically through the 1990s. In neighboring Syria this need, or preference, for a family hall is not felt, although reception hall rents are comparable. There, finances are pooled to rent a location, or the event is held in the home, however small.[69]

Training and productive programs are promoted as associations are called upon to alleviate the country's high unemployment. Funding women's programs is a high priority for international aid organizations, and the state has followed suit in promoting these projects. Royal NGOs in Jordan are heavily involved in producing goods for the tourism industry, mainly handicrafts. Training programs are mostly offered in sewing, beautician skills, secretarial work, and office management.[70] In a study of Irbid in northern Jordan, two-thirds of charitable associations offered training in sewing and knitting.[71] The associations provide access to sewing machines, a service increasingly necessary in light of high-priced consumer goods. Ten percent of the associations in my survey added productive projects or training programs between 1998 and 1999. A Jordanian Christian association brought tricot machines and made them available to all members in order to generate jobs, but finding people interested in this type of manual work was difficult. Another kin association in Jordan played the role of middleman in obtaining low-cost consumer products. The association purchased products wholesale and sold them to members, providing terms and credit otherwise unavailable to individuals.[72] Another ran stores to provide reasonably priced goods, employing association members in the stores.[73] A Lebanese association has projects for industrial production and Internet access.[74] Computer and sewing classes were also common in Lebanon.

The richer associations own land, especially for cemeteries but for other purposes as well such as real estate, schools, and nurseries. Of sixty-one associations in Lebanon responding to a survey, twenty-three owned their associations' center or hall; some as well owned land, a library, a clinic, a nursery, a garage, and a school. The remaining ones declared no possessions in the name of the associations, some renting and others attempting to purchase a hall. Kin mutual aid associations also run primary and secondary schools. In Jordan, the Khalil al-Rahman association (Palestinian) has three schools with a total of 1,280 students. Other schools are run by al-Quds, 'Ayn Karam (400 students), and al-Ramla, all Palestinian. These schools give priority to members of their own community, as teachers, staff, and students, and can undercut other schools in costs.[75]

Child care services are a high priority for the recently established rural associations in Jordan, and state funding is allocated for these programs. Kin mutual aid associations manage almost all of the sixty-seven existing nurseries, serving more than thirteen hundred children. These services have skyrocketed in the less-populated Jordanian and rural areas.[76] Nurseries in the northern regions, with 28 percent of the national population, increased from eighteen to thirty-four in the six years after 1993, and, in the south, with 10 percent of the population, the number increased from ten to sixteen.[77] Rural associations primarily provide child care to facilitate women's employment in the adjacent, newly established export-processing zones and in low-cost primary schools for older children. Nurseries, or *hadana*, are for very young children—under the age of four—and are primarily used as day care for poor working mothers. In the rural south, women have more young children and larger families than the national average, and their divorce rate (50%) is similarly higher than the rate for the nation as a whole.[78] Although women do not represent a large percentage of the Jordanian workforce, rural women work more than urban women (by 18%). Their jobs are also longer term, as rural women are less likely to quit after marriage than are their urban, white-collar counterparts. Married women work more than single women.[79] Officials in qualified industrial zones verified the need for working women to have a nursery. Associations are also taking over kindergartens, whose cost has risen with economic reform.

Problems in Providing Social Services

Kin associations and their activities increased as needs rose and state services declined, but the ability of kin associations to take on the requested social services varies greatly.[80] Funding can be scarce, and the organizations are increasingly overstretched. Associations' budgets are usually meager, limited by members' resources and the small size of the organizations. Smaller associations are necessary, however, to enable personal enforcement of obligations (see chapter 5). Apart from the few rich, high-profile associations, with budgets of $100,000 or more, the average association operates on only a few thousand dollars a year. Almost 40 percent of the Lebanese associations surveyed had budgets of less than $3,000 annually. A few receive funding from outside organizations. In Jordan the state provides some funding for specific services, but usually less than $1,000 annually.

Thus, because of their lack of resources and problems in obtaining full compliance among members, most associations are unable to compensate for the services that are lacking. Nor does the mere presence of a service mean that the population is adequately served in that realm. Kin associations, in effect, "check the box": they appear to be catering to the needs of some of the population and members continue to turn to them with demands. They fill a vacuum left by the lack of general, public social insurance, but they may be incapable of effectively furnishing social welfare. Even the richest associations complained of rising costs and the difficulty of providing quality services at low prices as requests increased. Associations complained that their limited economic capacity prevented them from meeting the needs of financially strapped members. In Lebanon, Palestinian associations noted that members' demands have increased dramatically at the same time that the associations' capacities to help have decreased, forcing them to cut services. Loans are particularly problematic. Many associations stated that members fought over who would receive the educational loans, and the recipients did not always repay. Some associations no longer provide this service. Medical clinics suffered chronic difficulties owing to high costs and competition, causing temporary closures and the resignation of doctors. Procuring medical supplies was another ongoing problem.

THE ROLE OF CHARITIES

How do these numbers and services compare to charities not limited to kin? The number of kin associations tower over that of other NGOs in Jordan and constitute 40 percent of all NGOs in Lebanon. Religious charities dominate the non-kin NGOs in these countries. Religious charities have typically relied upon the urban, professional middle class for voluntarism and donations.[81] The particular niche of kin associations, membership organizations providing social insurance, has little parallel among NGOs in Jordan and Lebanon.[82] Charities and mutual aid associations serve distinct purposes, provide different services, and are utilized by different populations. Charities are for aiding others; mutual aid is insurance. In kin associations, services are for members, not outsiders, similar to a cooperative. Charities both secular and religious focus on aiding the poor or concentrate on one specific issue of general concern. In Lebanon and Jordan most charities do not serve the middle classes. Kin associations provide a variety of services for specific individuals. Small loans, a service of kin associations, have been taken up by some NGOs, but apart from the religious charities, particularly Hizbullah in Lebanon, such loans are few and costly for the borrower. Outside of this, microfinance NGOs are available for business purposes.

Jordanian Charities

Apart from kin associations, charities and developmental NGOs are scarce in Jordan and dominated by religious organizations. Almost all the single-issue or specialized charities in the kingdom are located in the capital of Amman. Specialized charities include the Green Crescent (Red Cross), organizations for the disabled, those with developmental disabilities and illnesses, blood banks, cancer hospitals, foreign medical charities, and aid for university students. This contrasts with kin associations, which have numerous goals on a smaller scale and for a targeted population, taking the place of multiple specialized charitable institutions. Many of these single-purpose charities, such as women's organizations, are driven by foreign considerations.[83] Eighty-seven single-purpose charities exist in Amman; the remaining 176 associations in the capital are multipurpose, and, among these, mutual aid associations form the clear majority. An additional forty-one specialized charities exist in the kingdom as a whole.

Islamist charities stand out. They are well funded, with budgets unrivaled by other social organizations.[84] Three branches of the charitable wing of the Muslim Brotherhood, the Islamic Center Charity Society, had several million dollars in capital, surpassing all other charities except perhaps the royal NGOs, whose accounts are not publicly available.[85] On the eve of structural adjustment, Islamist organizations were concentrated in the central urban region, with scant institutions in the rural areas.[86] All but one of the Islamic Center Society's health services was located in Amman, Zarqa, or Balqa.[87] Educational institutions run by the Society have a similar geographic focus, with a slightly larger presence in the southern regions. Forty percent of these were established after 1989.[88] Following liberalization, however, Islamic NGOs spread into new geographic areas and began to bridge the urban-rural divide, employing urban funds and mobilizing bases to do so. During this period Islamist charities increased their presence in social services, providing higher-quality and less-expensive services than the private sector or other philanthropic charities. This heyday of Islamic charity lasted from 1989 to about 1993, and saw the establishment of Islamic Center Society branches and other Islamic charities in Zarqa, Amman, and Tafileh (in the south).[89] The Society for the Preservation of the Quran opened approximately one hundred centers.[90] Since 1993 only a few Islamic charities have been established.[91]

Other religious charities exist. Between 1982 and 1995 more than thirty thousand people received aid from the Fund for the Sick and the Poor, amounting to around $4 million.[92] Aid is parceled out to families in small amounts. The state-affiliated Zakat committees, furnishing aid from religious contributions similar to tithes, helped six thousand families in 1992 with between $14 and $42 a month. Altogether that year they spent about $900,000 in this endeavor. In Amman, over one-quarter of all Islamic charitable organizations were devoted to health care.[93] Some national nonreligious philanthropies also exist, most prominently the royal charities and the 'Abd al-Hameed Shooman Foundation.

Microfinancing has become a popular trend, particularly in funding women's projects.[94] Women are funded by international organizations to establish, for example, a new business of embroidery or spices.[95] USAID funded a position at the Ministry of Social Development for women, but after a brief time the money was absorbed into the general fund. Projects are funded for women to raise small animals, but the recipients often have difficulties keeping the money away from male family members.[96]

Lebanese Charities

Lebanon has numerous charities and NGOs in comparison with neighboring Arab states. Most are local social welfare NGOs; mutual aid associations represent the second largest category of organizing.[97] In the 1990s more than two thousand NGOs were established. Only a small percentage was cultural (10%), political (5%), or academic (2%).[98] The cooperative movement amounted to fewer than eight hundred organizations. Almost one-quarter of the associations were established for aid, and the primary goals of nearly another quarter were to set up schools, hospitals, and clinics, to provide funeral aid and training, and to assist orphans.[99] Half of all the NGOs provide health care and literacy aid, 15 percent offer job training, and no more than 10 percent are dedicated to social welfare, rural development, and aid to displaced persons.[100] Job and vocational training consists mainly of women attendees, who comprise three-fourths of the members and are enrolled in courses such as sewing, flower arranging, and beautician skills.[101]

Beneficiaries of these NGOs are almost exclusively the poor, and benefits are means-tested through spot checks and home visits. NGOs also confer with one another to verify that no one is "double dipping."[102] Funding for non-kin, secular NGOs is predominantly foreign, as secular organizations lack popular support and trust partly because of their lack of transparency.[103] Of the few prominent NGOs, most are specific to a community or religion. The Maqassed Society, founded in 1879, is a Sunni organization that provides education, general loans, health care, start-up loans, and investments. The Hariri Foundation, which is technically secular, subsidizes pilgrimage trips.[104] The Druze rely on the Druze Foundation for Social Welfare, and the many Christian denominations look to humanitarian associations.

NGOs and UNRWA serve the Palestinian community. UNRWA has long been the largest employer of Palestinians,[105] providing primary education and basic health care. UNRWA also provides aid for particularly poor refugee families, amounting to $40 annually and four rations of basic goods.[106] The arrival of NGOs is relatively new. The PLO provided aid and services that UNRWA did not, such as pre- and post-elementary education.[107] Prior to 1982, the end of the PLO's reign in Lebanon, only three NGOs served this community. With the exit of the PLO and its infrastructure, poverty increased and NGOs, both foreign and domestic, began forming. Even more were established after the Oslo Agreement in 1993, which signaled the end of PLO funding.[108] Hizbullah, the Sufi Ahbash, and a branch of Hamas also provide services in the camps. The Palestinian Red Crescent Society and twenty-nine NGOs run kindergartens, nurseries, health care centers, cultural and recreational centers, and vocational training centers.[109] The kindergartens cover about half the eligible children. The Coordination Forum of NGOs Working in the Palestinian Community, founded in 1994, also established the Health Care Society to provide medical services to this population.[110] Some Islamic NGOs operating with the Palestinians are reportedly increasing their provision of social assistance and pensions, in addition to medical facilities. NGOs are generally expanding to training and vocational programs (such as sewing, typing, hairdressing, vocational training in carpentry, radio and TV repair, computers, and office management).[111]

In line with much of the developing world, Lebanon's NGOs have begun offering micro-loans, with interest rates averaging at 20 percent. These usually amount only to a few hundred dollars each, and many merely pay for needed household expenditures. Others are geared toward women's productive projects, in agriculture or the service sector (e.g., hair salons). A small number of NGOs offer small loans for business purposes. One organization, al-Majmoua, provides short-term loans particularly to women farmers. Another, Ameen, loans to any type of business, but their fourteen hundred clients must have collateral. Many small-business borrowers are repeat customers.[112] The Catholic organization Caritas, one of the largest NGOs in Lebanon, provides about fifteen hundred loans. However, Hizbollah outstrips them all, providing about nine thousand small loans yearly for small projects.[113]

CONCLUSION

The fate of kin associations lies with the economic fortunes and alternative welfare possibilities of the society at large. The time line of kin associations demonstrates a strong correlation to state welfare and labor-market variables. Participation numbers also testify to greater attendance during economic difficulties. The associations strive to provide educational loans, business loans, and general aid for periodic life-cycle needs. Most of these services are geared toward those with spare resources and some ability to invest for the future, that is, the middle class. Indeed, though some services span middle and lower classes, medical and financial aid to the needy, for example, kin associations differentiate themselves from charities specifically in their provision of social insurance and services requested by those of the middle class. Large elaborate weddings and respectable funerals mark the organization as middle class or above, as the poor are less concerned with the prominent display of good economic fortune. For the middle class, such social demonstrations of financial ability aid in networking, business and social status.

This chapter provided data against the two main alternative explanations for kin associations, namely, cultural continuity and the psychologically jarring experience of urban life and modernity. The first is falsified by the record demonstrated in this chapter, the rise and fall of mutual aid associations based on kin. The changing content of who is considered family, which I analyze in chapter 5, reiterates this point. The second thesis, family as psychological support, fails the test of when such associations are established. Arguably city life is experienced as most shocking and severe when groups first urbanize, and yet in Jordan, for those with social welfare, the trend did not kick off until 1989. War is certainly traumatic, and if anomie was the driving factor behind kin associations, surely it would operate in times of war. Instead, where militias provided social welfare during the Lebanese civil war, mutual aid associations declined to the degree that church and family leaders complained about their absence. Claims that the Lebanese are culturally oriented to family and the Jordanians perennially tribal must be qualified by time period and social group. The next chapter reinforces these conclusions using data on changing kinship forms, and members' perceptions and purposes in joining and establishing kin associations.

5

Creating Kin and New Institutions

J ust as kin mutual aid associations rise and fall with the availability of social welfare and economic need, the internal structure of the association and the motivations of members also revolve around social insurance. The very form of the association was generated for social insurance purposes.[1] The kin mutual aid association is new, adapted from cultural models of organizing. Superficially similar to tribal guesthouses, the kin association transformed that organization, changing its power relations and ownership into a network of redistribution controlled by members. In many cases kinship itself is altered to maximize the social insurance potential of the organization, innovated by the individuals setting up the organization. Different forms of kinship can be used, limiting kin to those descended from a particular grandfather or removing qualifications on kinship and expanding members beyond those previously considered relatives. Kin associations can be established periodically upon need and later lapse, to be revived with another episode of need. The kin definition need not remain constant through all these periods, and can change in line with new needs and potential.

Kinship is a solidarity that communicates a duty to help fellow kin, and employment is high on the list of requests. Indeed, after social insurance through pooling dues and the distribution of aid during hard times, the next key role of kin associations is as an employment network. Member motivations demonstrate the desire to obtain jobs and business contacts through the association. As relatives, members privilege one another in employment and business deals. The kin association makes such preferential treatment central to membership while expanding the pool of relatives obligated to reciprocate aid. It creates a method and location for sharing information on potential employment and business. The employment-generating role of kin associations is clear in the qualifications necessary for an individual to be voted leader of the association. All are able to either provide jobs or job contacts for members.

In this chapter I first delineate the kin association as a new institution, describing how it draws upon existing models but transforms them to accommodate new actors and purposes. The shape of kinship itself is often a new creation, joining previously disconnected families or paring down tribes. Kinship in some associations is more apparently contrived than in others. In all, the goal is clear: establish a group large enough to redistribute but small enough for personal and informal monitoring of obligations. As with any collective endeavor, creating a kin association necessitates a combination of resources and historical luck. Many are unable to meet the requirements. I describe the associations' purpose and the reason they were founded, and show how their structure provides accountability through internal elections and elected boards of governors to implement objectives and oversee finances. The associations are attended and utilized heavily by the middle classes. Aside from helping those who are economically vulnerable and insuring against hard times, the members' secondary focus is work. I show the pivotal role of employment networks in drawing members into kin associations. I then profile the occupations of association leaders, further affirming the importance of jobs. Leaders and founders of the associations are those able to provide employment contacts, hailing predominantly from the private sector. More often than not, the new associations displaced individuals who were considered leaders of the kin group, replacing them with those holding market and professional assets benefiting the membership.

CREATIVE KINSHIP AND INSTITUTIONS

Social insurance is a strong incentive for organizing, and for generating change in institutions and existing identity legacies. The kin mutual aid organization is a new structure, encoding new power and responsibilities for members. This structure demonstrates the uses of the organization amid little effective legal regulation and a flexible labor market. Kinship definitions, who is considered a relative and who is not, have often changed to accommodate the new institutional form. Member power and horizontal networks translate into a size that is pushed to expand by the desire for resources but also limited in that expansion by the need to guarantee and monitor member obligations. The benefits of an economy of scale are limited by moral hazard problems. Although kinship changed to generate this medium size, it is not created ex nihilo. All the versions of kinship in these cases stretched existing definitions, limited them, or expanded to include others who were close geographically or by religion. In other words, a plausible story linked these members in a new solidarity viewed as primary. Not all could form associations, and usually the neediest were unable to do so. Resources, a potential kin group of sufficient size, and the absence of strong political affiliations or divisions among the group are necessary to establish and maintain a kin mutual aid association.

The new kin association first appeared in Lebanon in the late nineteenth century and in Jordan in the first half of the twentieth century. The association draws upon older repertoires of the tribal guesthouse or *madafa* and the family fund or treasury, or *sunduq al-'a'ili,* combined with the new model of the charity or cooperative.[2] Historically tribal organizations were funded through the benevolence of the tribal leader, who in turn relied upon the same income base as his tribe and depended on their support.[3] The tribal guesthouse, also known by various names including *rabita* and *diwan,*[4] was a place for receiving guests in the sheikh's home, funded by him.[5] The guesthouse was a location to socialize and visit during holy days. Wedding celebrations, engagement parties, funeral gatherings, political meetings, and negotiations were also held there.[6] Very large mutual aid associations that unite multiple clans or span geographical regions approximate this older association type.[7] The family treasury was a pooling of resources and a form of insurance for those able to set resources aside. Kin contributed yearly to a fund used for any family member in need. The fund could be used to finance extraordinary expenses, help less-fortunate members, and pay medical expenses or educational costs.[8] Through these institutions, distant relatives became active participants in the daily lives of other family members.[9] The similar institution of revolving funds or rotating credit and saving associations, often female-run, pooled assets among close friends, neighbors, and coworkers.[10]

Today's kin-based mutual aid association is a collectively owned membership organization using the idiom of charity. The kin institution no longer demonstrates the relative position of kin to the institution's leader, as did the prior *diwan,* but instead pits entire kin groups against one other. In doing so, it reinforces their differing corporate identities within society. Group ownership and financing of the association, formalized in elections, give members control in a way that previous institutions did not. Funding comes from members, and though dues can be symbolic, payment indicates approval of the association.[11] Members and beneficiaries are one and the same. Membership is exclusive, limited to kin by unstated qualifications. In the charter, the steering committee and often the original membership have the right to reject applications at will. The dominant functions have changed and are now mainly economic, in contrast to the previous ceremonial and negotiation roles of the *rabita* or *diwan*. Indeed, even the term is currently changing to the more common word "association" (*jama'iyya*).[12] The high level of institutionalization and formalization has made nonparticipation or free riders more difficult.[13]

All mutual aid associations organize along kinship lines, or attachments stemming from a belief in a common lineage, to cement the informal regulation of group members. However, kinship is neither straightforward nor constant. Not only do several bases exist for establishing kinship, but alterations that depart from past legacies now generate new lineages. Kinship in the Arab world, as in many other parts of the world, incorporates numerous levels of familial relations, all of them potential organizing bases. Kinship is situational, determined by practical social networks.[14] Matrilineal relatives can be included, as in many Palestinian families. Family can be defined through genealogy, tribe, village of origin, or, most recently, present village of residence. The number of generations included varies. Tribes, as multigenerational descent groups, include numerous organizing possibilities.[15] Clans, extended families, and *hamula*, the seven-generation level of lineage, are potential definitions of the relevant family. The ancestral village is another basis for kinship and can encompass several families, tribes, and unrelated individuals.[16] Immigration and urban migration have often produced organizing based on hometown or regional origin. Indeed, returning migrants in parts of Africa and the Sudan organized on the basis of home village. In the United States, Haitians and Latin Americans established hometown associations. The ancestral native place has been used to bind members in Korean and Taiwanese rotating savings associations.[17]

The size of the association, large enough to redistribute but small enough to maintain personal relations, is important for accountability and membership power, as discussed in chapter 1. Only a few of the associations in my Jordan survey exceeded the thousand-member mark. Almost three-fourths had 300 members or fewer; 61 percent had fewer than 150 members. However, a member often represents an entire household, and therefore the actual number of individuals involved is five or six times that number. Three-fourths of the Lebanese associations had a membership of 500 or less. Associations registered in the 1990s can be even smaller, with only a handful of members. Their newness partly explains their small size, as the older established associations also began with small numbers, or reflects their inability to redefine kinship in an inclusive way in order to generate more resources. Most organizations have a few hundred to a thousand members.

To arrive at this average number of members, kin associations simultaneously draw upon and alter existing ideas of the family. Most of these concepts differ only somewhat from previous ones but not enough to be seen as generating an identity from scratch. The associations combine families with a sense of historical closeness and intermarriage or geographical proximity, such as residence in the same village. Alternatively new kinship definitions split the previous group into smaller units as employment possibilities narrow. Even within seemingly stable kinship groups, a large degree of mobility is occurring below the surface. Marginalized branches rise to prominence as external success and ideology allow some to displace the nominal leader to become the de facto head of the tribe. Non-relatives have also been incorporated. These can be tied to the leader through networks or by membership in families historically close to the kin group.[18] Political differences or battles over leadership cause elites to choose differing bases for membership.[19] When numerous clans or families join in an association, seats on the executive board are apportioned by the relative weight of the subgroups.

The individuals starting or leading the associations were the ones to innovate the definition of kinship. Those who began the association, or the "idea people," *sahib al-fikra,* the ones pushing the kin association concept, were also often the association's future leaders. In some cases this occurred through clear attempts to create a new version of the family, as when leaders extensively researched the history of the family going back a thousand years. In other cases the simple need for a pool of resources to redistribute pushed leaders to search for more people to include. The group definition depends partly on the restrictions of compliance and internal cohesion, but it is often expanded in order to increase resource and labor market connections. Larger and more inclusive organizations are formed among less-privileged kin groups that wish to extend the pool as much as possible, again to increase contacts and resources. The broader the definition, according to association leaders, the greater the shirking and free riding. Kinship was often defined more narrowly when this expansion to generate resources was unnecessary, as in richer associations, or when a would-be leader wanted to break off from the established kin leader. A desire to maintain resources, whether money or jobs, generated a more exclusive organization that narrowly defined membership. Thus, those with privileged connections to a segment of the labor market, particularly public-sector work as its employment potential declined, formed smaller, more exclusive organizations. The political interests of kin elites can also enter the equation, generating a particular version of kinship. This is especially true when members are poorer and the leader shoulders a large portion of the association's resources or when the leader seeks to remove himself from the shadow of an existing kin leader.

The result usually does not fit the image of continuity given by traditional perspectives. Many kinship associations combine religious or national groups previously hostile to each other. In Jordan, Palestinians and East Bank Jordanians have joined together. One mutual aid association in Jordan actively recruited members to its family, reportedly requesting that individuals change their last names to that of the leader, according to one official. Families related by marriage, location, or common religion can form an association. In Jordan a Christian association, originally from Karak but currently residing in Amman, absorbed a smaller family that had long been associated with it through marriage. These and other families united on the basis of shared religion and origin.[20] Adding locations of family members is another method of increasing the size of the association. Some join family in "all of Lebanon" or "Amman and Zarqa." Others unite the domestic association with family or branches of the association abroad. One Jordanian Christian association, carrying a name unrelated to any one family, al-Azhar, is made up of fourteen families. Many associations revive a concept of kin membership that had long been forgotten, surprising members who are invited to join the association.

In Lebanon a sizable minority of associations contain members of other religious communities. Multireligious associations constituted 4 percent of my Lebanese survey. Using the same tactics as families in Jordan, 20 percent of the associations established between 1984 and 2005 in Lebanon expressly increased their family, using the name of a broader tribal level, specifying that they were including diverse branches of the family, joining multiple families in the name of the new organization, delineating multiple towns where the family or families resided, using a distant relative and calling to all descendants, or simply gathering all family members from all parts or regions of the country and overseas.[21] The Suwayd and Faris families in Aley (Muslims) joined an association in 1995, carrying both their last names. Similarly a Christian association that formed in Eastern Beirut in 1994 listed the names of five families. An association limited to a single family, established in the late 1960s, changed to the village name in 1993 to incorporate more members (in Byblos).[22] The League of United

Families joined together six families.[23] During the mandate period, one leader attempted to make his association as large as possible, utilizing the ancestry of Abraham, thereby enabling all with the common last name of Khalil to join.[24] In both Lebanon and Jordan, Palestinians generally use the broad category of village of origin to define kinship. Likewise, Lebanese Shi'a coming from southern Lebanon organized by village and expanded their contacts in the urban areas.

Other families attempt to limit or decrease the kin eligible for membership. In Lebanon 17 percent of associations registered between 1984 and 2005 specified precise limits on their kin group, excluding many potential members. To do so, they delineated the precise ancestor whose descendants were considered kin, using the first and last name, restricting membership to a town or geographic territory, or delineating a subgroup of those with the same lineage, for example, only those of a particular religion. A Christian organization (Lama'iyyah) formed before independence reworked its membership in 1982, only including those descended from a particular grandfather. Several associations for the same last name were registered, one specifying only the Orthodox (Christians) of that name. In one long-standing Shi'a family whose genealogy dates to the 1700s, a branch separated off and organized by itself in 1999 in northern Lebanon (outside Hizbullah's base). Branches of a family can pool their resources in separate associations. The Dakkash family name (Christian) is the basis for distinct associations in Lebanon: Byblos (1948) and Kisrawan (1964). Some neighborhood associations in Lebanon also organize along kinship lines. These are not place-based civil society organizations, but associations founded on exclusive membership criteria. They consist of families tracing descent to the original Beiruti inhabitants.[25] Their structure, solidarity, services, and purpose are the same as other kin associations, with the occasional addition of local policing functions. In Jordan rural associations take the village name but are controlled by a few prominent families in that village, or tribes limit heritage to a less-inclusive level of ancestry, splitting into clans and subgroups. They unite only part of the tribe or village.

Collective organizing requires resources, time, ability to negotiate the system, and someone willing to do the paperwork, often the organization's leader. Not only must people be aware of a potential solution to their economic predicament, but there must be sufficient interest in combining resources collectively. This only occurs during economic hard times; only then are enough people willing to forego individual options and incur collective obligations. Still, even when people desire a collective solution, they may be unable to achieve it. History, resources, and politics can prevent an association from forming. The accident of one's birth can determine the range of possibilities, as it may not be possible to unite a sufficient number of kin. Those from smaller villages or families, unable to unite with larger ones, are left out of this organizing form. One member complained that his association did not accomplish much because the family is spread out as a result of migration and the war in Lebanon. Some richer elites researched their history to rewrite kin lineages, but this cannot always be done. Resources limit the ability to undertake such research. Lacking that, it can be difficult to join several families into a group that can plausibly be considered a new kin identity. Disagreements over power and leadership in the association are common when combining families, and boards of directors are often split proportionally by the size of the member families. Despite these difficulties, many attempt and succeed at such alliances, demonstrating the strong incentive of mutual aid.

The necessity of resources limits the associations to the middle and higher classes. One-fifth of surveyed nonmembers were unable to form an association owing to lack of resources. Some stated that there was no time for it. One individual with a modest income reported that pursuing a living and the number of hours devoted to work drove people to focus on their individual affairs to the detriment of kin associations. Others said that they could not consider such an association, because they lacked money and thus would be unable to provide insurance or services to members. Gathering all our poor family relatives will not help to better our situation, another claimed. We are a small family and lack resources, reported another. One individual said that kin associations are a remote thought for the humble, that we poor rely on God and leave kin associations to the well-off. Rich families work to raise the standard of living of their own family members, another interviewee said. A sentiment often repeated was that rich families take care of their own. About 10 percent of surveyed nonmembers received charity or aid from the government, NGOs, or religious organizations. Most interviewees in the Lebanese Shi'a community also felt that they could turn to Hizbullah or Amal for help. The political party is a big family, providing security in hard times, another stated. According to another interviewee, the family gathers through Amal.

Politics can also prevent a kin association from forming or break an association apart. This is due either to political divisions among elites in the association or to concerns not to offend the reigning political parties.

Interviewees highlighted how politics can divide the group. "[When members are involved in national politics] politics inevitably enters the association and ruins it," stated one interviewee. In one example, a kin group had been working to start a family association prior to the 1996 elections in Lebanon. However, a prominent family member stood for parliament in those elections without asking the opinions of his kin, and this episode caused divisions and put an end to the kin association idea. In Lebanon an association split because of political divisions in 1958 caused by varying stances on the Baghdad Pact.[26] A Jordanian kin group was unable to form an association until two politicians in their midst both lost parliamentary elections. The family was divided in loyalties and unable to form until these candidates retired.

A KIN ASSOCIATION STORY

The strong role of the labor market in determining membership is apparent in one inclusive organization, Abna' al-Harith. In 1995 a Jordanian family joined with a Palestinian village to create a new association in Amman. The leader, Dr. 'Ali al-Hawamdeh, was born in Karak, Jordan. After hiring researchers to discover the family's history, they learned that their genealogical ancestry traced back to the Hijaz, in Saudi Arabia, in the seventh century CE. Part of this tribe had settled in Karak, Jordan, and others went on to the village of Yazour in Palestine, near present-day Jaffa. The descendants of this village who live in Jordan are considered kin. Thus the association includes individuals who consider themselves Jordanian as well as those who self-identify as Palestinian, all now identifying as relatives. Separate *diwan* had existed for the village kin from Yazour and those from Karak, and news of the establishment of kinship between the two came as a surprise to many future members. Although the identity affiliation of the Palestinians in this association was clearly new, emerging by surprise in 1995, in interviews a few years later, in 1999, young, male Palestinian members had internalized the identity and felt it was "real."

The Palestinians invited to join this association saw it as a chance to get connections, jobs, and aid. "Everyone else is helping each other, why shouldn't we?" one member stated. "We don't know each other, we don't have connections, we don't know where our relatives work," he added. The family members did not need convincing, as they already felt weak and wanted networks, another member stated. The female relatives, according to one woman, were uninterested in the new association.

Though they were generally well educated, they were not concerned with meetings and felt it was an activity for the men. The association contains both prosperous members and those who qualify for state aid to the poor. Most are middle class in income, and the youth are college-educated. At the monthly meetings for men, the association takes *talabat,* or requests, and members determine if anyone can help with services, connections, or jobs. Businessmen advertise in the association, and family members receive discounts for frequenting those businesses or referring customers. Most of these businessmen depend on contacts for business, such as retail owners or contractors. Participation in the association is expected, particularly at holiday times. The association also organizes cultural programs, explaining family history or stressing the importance of family unity. Women make handcrafted heritage items and participate in craft sales run by the association. The women keep their profits from these events. Further, upon the death of a member, the association provides aid for the funeral and for the preparation of food for mourners, an expensive undertaking. If members are poor, the association pays for their wedding.

The following example demonstrates how the Abna' al-Harith association is important for job connections. A Palestinian member went to see the president of the association, a hospital director, soon after the association's formation, requesting employment for his daughter. Although they had never met, the member used all the tropes of close kin, visiting without an appointment and telling his daughter that the association president was her uncle. The president found a position the same day for the newly graduated daughter by offering to fire the occupant of that position; when the father refused this course of action, the leader found another position with his son, also a hospital director.

The association's relationship with the state is mixed. Though it supports the opposition and Islamists, the association's prestige has won respect from the government. Dr. 'Ali al-Hawamdeh, the association's leader, was elected to parliament in 1989 from Amman (second district), and was affiliated with the Muslim Brotherhood. He formed the kin association after ending his stint in parliament. Though, as noted, he was born in Karak, Jordan, from a Transjordanian background, he was listed in 1989 parliamentary data as a Palestinian.[27] This may have been a mistake, but, even so, it was most telling. The family is mainly engaged in the private sector, and the leader directs two private hospitals. The leader is also allied with the Palestinians by extension of the leader's membership in the Muslim Brotherhood (which supports Palestinian causes).

He alternates in identifying as Jordanian or Palestinian. In the 1997 elections the association supported an opposition candidate, Toujan Feisal, a secular liberal woman, the only woman to be elected to parliament prior to the quota for women. They were united in opposition only. The association provided her space to campaign, but the Ministry of the Interior threatened to pull the association's license if it continued or if it allowed her sister, who was also running for office, to use the association. However, the new family pedigree gave it a small degree of prominence. In researching the family's genealogy, the leader discovered that the family was related to the Prophet Muhammad. After authenticating this claim, the Abna' al-Harith association received a letter acknowledging the family's lineage from the then Crown Prince Hassan, who suggested a meeting with the family's leader. Though the meeting never occurred owing to other circumstances, association members valued the perceived social prestige.[28]

WHY ASSOCIATIONS ARE FOUNDED AND THEIR ORGANIZATIONAL STRUCTURE

As noted, crisis and need are the motivating factors behind the establishment of kin mutual aid associations. Such need can be situational, arising only during hard economic times. One association (Lebanese Christian, in Zahleh) acknowledged the need for an association at various points in history and actually founded one at least five times, the earliest in 1886. The common goal of associations is to unify family members and provide assistance to one another.[29] Khuri notes that uniting family members by offering membership to the kin association is viewed as a major political event, altering the structure of responsibility, political allegiance, and the definition of those entitled to free services from kin.[30] Those wishing to unify the family state that they wish to do so in the spirit of cooperation or to create cooperation between the various branches of the family. Some state that they desire to build cooperation and duties with family members abroad.[31] Only 10 percent of surveyed members in one Jordanian kin association had pensions. For surveyed members and nonmembers alike, the decision to establish an association and the ability to sell the idea depended on whether they would receive services.

In Lebanon the oldest organizations formed in order to provide medical, educational, and other aid to the family. The main purpose of some was to provide members with social insurance in hard times. "Cooperation," "unity," and "mutual aid" were buzzwords for describing the purpose of an association. Only 20 percent of the associations established prior to the war cited unifying the family as a reason for forming; the rest cited various kinds of aid to the family, educational, medical, or insurance. Material reasons for founding were also clear after the war. The main reasons given for pooling resources were mutual aid, cooperation to provide aid, the deteriorated social situation, and need. Others stated that their chief purpose was to provide services, especially a medical fund for health care expenditures. Only one association mentioned an increased role in politics as the reason for forming. The rest cited need, the dire economic situation, and a desire to raise the status of family members in terms of their lifestyle and education. Almost all agreed that people's needs had increased after the war. One association changed its purpose in 2005, declaring that its new goal was to take care of the modern issues of the family and education.

Of the 112 kin associations listed in the Lebanese official gazette between 1980 and 2005 that provided a rationale for establishing their kin association, the vast majority—75 percent—stated material concerns as the sole reason for founding the association. Including those organizations that listed both material concerns and social cooperation as goals, the figure jumps to over 90 percent. Less than 10 percent declared unity or cooperation to be their goal for the organization. Further, existing associations changed their purpose from social to economic welfare. All six existing associations that altered their official goals during the same period declared material goals as their primary concern, such as raising the family's material level; aiding the family's needy; establishing a private school, hospital, or clinic; setting up a treasury; and providing loans, insurance, and educational aid. One association changed its goal in 1992 from raising the cultural level of the family to helping meet family needs. Only ten of sixty-nine associations in my questionnaire survey stated that they formed to unify the family. Economic services were the stated purpose for the rest.

In Jordan, prior to structural adjustment, the main goal of kin associations was to gather family members together in a central location and only secondarily to provide financial aid. This order has now reversed. Almost half the associations established since liberalization declared that their primary purpose was to help the family's poor. The primary goal of most of the others was a mix of gathering the family and helping poor kin. One association wanted to combine the financial abilities of kin, provide health services, encourage savings, run stores to provide consumer goods at affordable prices, produce and sell consumer goods, establish an emergency financial fund, and provide aid and loans. The goals of the Silwan Social Development Association (Palestinian) were to establish an occupational training center to train girls in sewing, secretarial work, typing, textile work, flower arranging, ceramics, and beauty techniques; provide student loans; encourage sports activities; help needy families; and establish a kindergarten. Another association listed as their aims the provision of social and financial services to the family's needy; employment training or rehabilitation for the head of the family; a sewing school for girls; a private hearse and aid for funerals; a health clinic, nursery, and kindergarten; aid to university students; and the encouragement of athletic activity. The Jordanian organizational files in the supervisory organization confirm the priority of financial aid. Social and cultural purposes were rarely cited except in rural governorates, where women's health education was the aim. Other studies verify this. Al-Faʿori's survey in Irbid, a northern, mostly Jordanian area, found that 17 percent of associations provided health services, and one-fifth provided financial help to the poor and unemployment services. Very few had programs such as aiding the physically disabled. Hamarneh reached the same conclusion in a study of all the charities in the kingdom. Without question the most common goal of charities was financial and in-kind aid. The next most common aims in order of frequency, almost half the previous number, were social and cultural goals and health education. Only 10 percent mentioned religious education, and this figure included all local associations in the kingdom and was consistent across governorates with only minor exceptions.[32]

The structure, size, and funding of the organization gives control to the members. Association elections for president and board of directors, along with the small size of the organizations, make association decisions relatively accountable and transparent. The creation of accountable obligations is what sets the mutual aid association apart from religious, charitable, or other nongovernmental organizations. In Jordan several richer associations stated that they could not raise interest for a charity but only for a cooperative since in that organizational form members retain title to association property upon dissolution. Members see kin associations as more accountable, democratic, and transparent than charities because of the differences in control.[33] Like mutual aid societies in the West, members eschew the stigma of charity in favor of fraternal reciprocity. All are in the same economic boat; members giving aid may later be receiving.[34]

The organizations generally charge a few dollars in dues per month, paid by either the head of the family or adult members.[35] Most charge between seven and twenty dollars a year. A few are wholly supported by donations and fund-raising events, and others require the purchase of large shares. Even for existing associations, sufficient income is necessary for the association to function. The negative economic situation caused individuals in one poorer kin group to look after themselves and withdraw from participation in the association, one member stated. Organizations unable to charge dues because of members' poor economic status are unable to provide services. Interviewees complained that no dues meant no budget and no ability to plan or enact programs beyond immediate aid. Funds raised by members are used exclusively for members. When a government ministry or the poor approached successful associations requesting aid, it was provided from a separate account of donations, not association dues; the two accounts are kept strictly separate.[36]

Internal association elections reflect member control. Elections are generally held annually for president and board of directors. When multiple families or kin groups make up an association, as is the case for villages or tribes with clan groups, positions on the executive board of directors are allocated on the basis of constituent kin groups and according to their membership numbers. (See Figures 4.2, 4.3, and 4.4; each large leaf or branch on the tree indicates a subgroup of kin.) Such accountability and member power is the ideal, approximated to varying degrees. Where no dues are charged, no elections for leadership positions are held. The balance of power shifts to the leader of the organization. This was the case in several new organizations, including some Shiʻa and Palestinian organizations in Lebanon. Similarly rural and large tribal associations have less accountability and power for the membership. They more closely resemble the tribal guesthouse of old, rural associations because of the lack of middle-class and dues-paying members. Too large an association pushes control away from the general membership, as the monitoring of members and leaders becomes more difficult. To remain accountable and enforce mutual obligations, organizations must be able to monitor through informal mechanisms. On the other hand, too small an organization limits networking capability and the generation of resources.

MEMBERS, ECONOMIC ROLES, AND JOBS CONTACTS

Kin associations create a method and location for the exchange of information, money, contacts, and jobs. Establishing a new network of obligation, members pool a portion of their funds and redistribute money to those in need while obtaining business and employment contacts.

Though leaders help with jobs, most members now rely more on one another than on the kin leader to obtain services or jobs.[37] These horizontal obligations marry informal dynamics to formalized institutions. Much of what they provide—information—is informal. Professionals are members, although a portion of them has access to a professional association for insurance and aid. As members of the identity group, they are partly drawn in through informal pressure once a majority of the group is interested. The sizable number of self-employed professionals benefit from networks and business promotion within the group. Interviewees pointed to nonprofessionals or those not in a professional association as pushing hardest for the establishment of a kin association.

Educated, urban, middle-class employees in the nonprofessional services dominate the membership. Members are not the old retired men people often associate with a kin association, but rather are middle-class and youth most concerned with future employment and financial security. Almost 60 percent of the Lebanese sample membership has a bachelor's degree or higher; 14 percent have postgraduate degrees; and 60 percent make lower-middle- to middle-class wages, as is common for young professionals. In Jordan more than half the active members from one association hold a bachelor's degree or higher. Similarly they earn lower-middle- to middle-class wages; only 10 percent, however, had a pension. Another Jordanian association reported that 90 percent of its members work for themselves or own their own businesses; in other words, only a few are employees. A survey in a northern Jordanian suburb found that young adults aged twenty-six to thirty-five frequent the kin association most.[38] Another study found that 82 percent of the educated youth surveyed, also in northern Jordan, attended their association regularly.[39]

Member opinions and benefits demonstrate the economic roles of the kin association and its material benefits (see Figure 5.1). The kin association allows individuals to exit from their tight circumstances, a Lebanese member stated. The association benefits those in need and the sick, another said. One interviewee stated that his kin association has raised members' standard of living. Another praised the association for aiding in members' education. Currently young people's situation has worsened, a leader stated. In kin associations, the members take care of one another. Individuals look there for help, and search no further.[40] Several leaders declared the dire economic circumstances of the 1990s to be the driving force behind kin associations.[41] Poverty has increased, one Lebanese interviewee stated, which drove the formation of associations and networks to aid the family. A member of a Maronite (Christian) kin

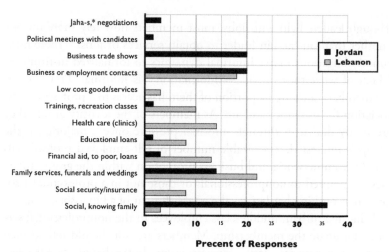

*A *jaha* is a negotiating delegation from one tribe that tries to reach a compromise deal with another tribe or family. It is used, for example, when a member of one family is injured by one from another family, or (sometimes) when proposing marriage.

FIGURE 5.1. Benefits Received by Members. Members cited more than one benefit. Leaders were not included. Appendix 2a. Questionnaire for Organizations, Jordan.

association reported that family members are newly interest in reviving their association, which had ceased to operate during the war.

Aid offered by associations includes employment and business contacts. In tight labor markets, individuals would be expected to eagerly broaden their networks to job-connected members and elites. Discovering unknown family members is intended to serve various economic purposes. Contacts and social ties translate into information about jobs, the attraction of start-up capital, customers, and higher incomes. In general, more links translate into higher individual income through greater job prospects.[42] Although in Jordan job networks are not officially advertised as playing a central role for the organizations, employment contacts are fundamental to kin associations in the urban areas.[43] Positions are advertised through the association.[44] Widening one's available circle of connections is very important, one Jordanian interviewee said.[45] These connections are used to obtain jobs, discounted services and goods, and potential customers; to cut through bureaucracy; and to wield political influence. These uses of family networks were implied by the expressed desire to know more family members, explicitly stated in long interviews. Further, government employees, with secure pensions and stable jobs, are underrepresented in the associations.[46] Young adults join as soon as they learn the benefits of knowing kin.[47] In several associations parties are held once or twice yearly to facilitate connections, or *tawaasul.* One member declared: "The family has expanded, and if we don't know each other, anything can happen to the *miskeen* [unfortunate] among us. There is no other source of social security."[48] The nature of Jordan's seesaw economy made organizing through family seem the only way to provide social welfare, stated one association leader. One member hailed his association for its large network of contacts; another stated that his association was good at activities and finding jobs for people. Priority is given to kin for jobs within the association itself or among its programs such as schools. Kin take precedence for student slots and teaching jobs.

Job seekers and employers who have positions to fill call upon kin leaders, and kin turn to one another at association meetings to find jobs. At meetings, requests are taken to see who is able to help and what services and connections people have to offer. Professionals and small retail and service businesses benefit greatly from the kin network. Forty-four percent from one urban association declared that increased business or employment was the primary benefit of belonging to the kin association. Reflecting this fit between particular labor markets and kin networks, a large portion of kin association attendees, 40 percent from a single association, were merchants or small business owners, including the owners of a supermarket, a pharmacy, and a money-changing establishment, along with a carpenter and computer software salesman. An additional 50 percent of attendees work in the professions or the services, jobs dependent on contacts for either continued business or employment.[49] For example, the kin association promoted a pharmacy owner's business, and he subsequently received business from kin. Kin consumers frequenting other family members' businesses receive a discount. In turn, they introduce friends to that business, advertising it and increasing the consumer base.[50] One member, recently returned from exile for (leftist) political activity, stated that he does not know who his kin are, and he could be purchasing from someone's store without realizing that it belongs to kin. Knowing who among the family owns stores would lead him to patronize those instead of other businesses.[51] Other members reiterated the desire to know which businesses their returned kin are in and the services they can offer. The more successful associations directly employ a number of people, sometimes dozens, in these endeavors, as teachers for example.[52] A Lebanese Sunni association finds jobs for members among family businesses and retail stores.

Lebanese associations were blatant about the role of kin associations in obtaining employment. Some associations publish lists of connections. Numerous associations stated that the association furnishes employment opportunities through members who own their own businesses and hire kin. One Lebanese association holds parties for young family members to get to know one another and utilize the network for contacts.[53] Youth are a particular priority, one interviewee in Lebanon stated. Employment aid was cited as a primary reason for many Lebanese associations formed in the post-civil-war era. A prominent member of a mutual aid association stated that he has received hundreds of requests for help in locating a job.[54] Professionals such as doctors, lawyers, and professors are newly active in the associations for the express purpose of increasing their business contacts and clients.[55] One Lebanese interviewee, a doctor, attributed his success to the kin association's networks. Lebanese Shi'a mutual aid associations based on village of origin assist newcomers to the city in finding jobs.[56]

LEADERS AND EMPLOYMENT

In a service-sector economy, power, privilege, and access depend on the capacity to provide jobs. Leaders are those with employment resources or connections to offer.[57] The ability to network is a key attribute of an association president. Money alone will generally not suffice. The leader should be socially known and well connected. By providing socially worthwhile goods, welfare, and employment aid, the elite create a general reputation for being socially responsible, helpful, and charitable (see chapter 6). Kin association leaders are generally young men,[58] averaging between their mid-thirties and late forties.[59] They come from a range of occupations reflecting both the local employment structure and the family's particular position in the labor market. All have obtained financial success or professional connections. They are socially active and often belonged to unions and other civil society organizations prior to their involvement in mutual aid associations. The financially successful generally hail from the private sector, occasionally accumulating resources through stints of migration to the Gulf or West Africa.[60] Those able to provide connections only are linked to state employment, particularly in the rural areas. This mainly applies to Jordan, with its larger public sector. Elites lacking services of employment, credit, or mediation do not succeed in their quest to form a kin association.[61]

Merchants and business owners, self-employed professionals who depend on contacts for business, and service-sector employees dominate the leadership of Lebanese kin associations, each category constituting almost one-quarter of the leadership. Notables and elite landowners comprise only 3 percent, and workers are almost completely absent. This distribution is the same among religious sects with only slight variations. The prominence of professions entailing contacts for success remains constant. The key founders of the organizations are concentrated among merchants and business owners (22%) and professionals dependent on contacts (21%). Politicians and government officials make up 11 percent of the leadership. Only in a few of the associations are notables the leaders.[62] Government employees make up a smaller percentage of leaders and key founders than in Jordan, as the state sector is smaller there. Women show up in the leadership of Lebanese associations more than in Jordanian associations. Among the Palestinian associations in my survey, professors appear more often, along with military (PLO) officers.

For example, a doctor, lawyer, contractor, and insurance company employee lead a Sunni association in Tripoli in the north. The owners of a factory, a garage, and a business association joined with merchants to lead a new Shi'a association. Teachers, housewives, and a moneychanger lead a Druze association. A Maronite association, originally founded by beer factory employees, a lawyer, and a landowner (who doubles as a tailor), is now led by a real estate broker, an insurance company employee, a contractor, mechanic, store owner, and driver. Another Maronite association was formed and is currently led by a furniture salesman, two business owners, and a contractor. Three merchants, the director of a bank, a banker, a doctor, an employee, and a retired military officer lead a long-established Sunni association in Beirut (Aal Tabbara).

The private sector dominates, even in Jordan where 50 percent of workers are employed by the government. The primary founder (*sahib al-fikra*, or "idea person"), the one who originally proposed establishing a kin association, is most often a businessman (merchant or business owner) or government official. Among Jordanians, retired army officers and farmers play a small role. Farmers show up only in organizations established after 1989. Studies of rural associations demonstrate the same trend. Though the presence of rural government officials is conspicuous, this social group is nonetheless smaller than its proportion of the labor market would imply. Given the stark characterizations of the labor market as divided—public sector for Jordanians and private for Palestinians—higher numbers of Palestinian government employees are among the founders than would be expected. However, most of these are older associations; Palestinian elites now establishing kin associations are almost all from the private sector. Similarly more Jordanian founders hail from the private sector than their occupational distribution would suggest.

The most frequent combination of professions among Jordanians establishing kin associations is government officials and retired army officers. In Palestinian-Jordanian organizations, merchants are paired with professionals, some government officials or high-level employees, and even retired army officers. Of thirty-two associations, Palestinian founders are divided mainly between government officials and business-men. Jordanian leaders come not only from business and government, but some are from the army and agriculture. Almost 30 percent of all founders are businessmen, just over one-fifth are professionals, and 13 percent are government officials. Primary founders are largely govern-ment officials (39%) and business owners (33%), along with some pro-fessionals (17%). One Palestinian association was started by a group of entrepreneurs and contractors, along with some professionals, retired government employees, and one official at the governmental newspaper. In another, a retired school director, a teacher who was a member of the writers' union, a private-sector doctor, and the treasurer of the driv-ers' union took the lead. A government official, a real estate owner, a lawyer, and three merchants founded Khalil al-Rahman. The Shuwayka Social Development Association was founded by a number of business-men and engineers—some from the electric company and one from the phone company—and a university president. An economics professor, a doctor, a bank director, and two retirees started the Silwan Charitable Association. The current president is retired from the army. Members of the Lifta Association's current board include five engineers, a doctor, a retired army officer, and two auditors. Four merchants and a doctor founded al-Ramla.

Palestinian associations in Jordan that formed in the 1990s reveal a more private-sector base. The owner of a restaurant, four merchants, and three employees started a Palestinian association registered in 1998. A salesman, a contractor, two merchants, a bank employee, and an accoun-tant led the formation of another the same year. The Na'leen Charity, from the Ramallah area of the West Bank, was established in 1991 by a group of doctors, engineers, store owners, merchants, and employees. Deir Yassin, a village from within present-day Israel, formed an asso-ciation in 1994, initiated by a retired employee, a merchant, a (retired) school director, and a UN employee.

The executive committee of al-Naber, an urban Jordanian association, is composed of professionals, a car dealership owner, merchants, small retail business owners, and the female owner of a reception hall. In another Jordanian association, the leaders (and authors of a book on their tribe) were professionals, one in the state administration and the other a psychiatrist.[63] By contrast, local government officials, retired or current, dominate Jordanian rural associations, including the mayor, president of the municipality, and former military officers.[64] One Jordanian community association was formed by numerous retired army personnel, an agricultural engineer, a pharmacist, and an electricity company (public) employee. The Tabarbour Charity, a Jordanian community association, was founded in 1992 by the president of the municipality, a real estate owner, a retired army officer, a bank director, and a lawyer. The mayor, a public-sector employee, and the president of the municipality founded Um Batma in 1990. In 1994 merchants, farmers, and a few employees (mostly with the government) formed a Jordanian kin association. This same distribution is seen in another association that was formed on the eve of economic liberalization in 1988. Traders, employees, and two individuals retired from the military founded a Jordanian Bedouin association in 1994. In 1993 a former mayor, a retired army officer, the president of the local sports club, and a retired engineer established another Jordanian rural association. A teacher, a grocery store owner, and a mechanic formed another in 1998.

CONCLUSION

The new kin association demonstrates the dynamics of institutional genesis and change. Resources, a favorable family history, and a lack of strong political allegiances are needed for individuals to form a kin association. Many who want to form an association are unable to do so, either because they lack resources or, through historical accident or political divisions in the family, they cannot unify a sufficient number of potential kin as members. As self-help organizations, they depend on members' ability to financially support the organization. Though the associations contain multiple classes, the driving force behind them are individuals from the middle class, as they are able to contribute money and provide contacts to the association's network and those in financial need. Members are also owners who pay dues and thus control the workings of the association. The middle class has enough resources to be future-oriented but is not sufficiently independent to secure itself on its own, as the upper class is. Having achieved a degree of status, the middle strata desire redistribution and entitlement insurance, not charity.

However, social class is just one way to pinpoint members. In line with observations in the welfare and collective action literatures, common risk and vulnerability can bind people. In the cases discussed here, this vulnerability is concentrated among the largest segment of the labor force, those in nonprofessional service work. Once nonprofessional workers constitute a large number of kin, peer dynamics carry the rest of the family along. Professionals benefit from the enlarged pool of contacts, but most are able to access insurance through their professional association.

Kinship itself can change in a number of ways, and the social groups forming kin associations do not define kinship in the same way. Kin definitions expanded or contracted in line with the desire for more resources and the need to keep track of members' contributions to the organization. Richer groups generally formed more exclusive organizations to avoid dissipating their wealth among less-privileged kin. Poorer groups and those with fewer employment connections broadened their definition of kin as much as possible to increase their networks and resources while still differentiating themselves from the general society. Larger associations report high rates of members not repaying loans or free riding by not contributing. Small associations lack resources to provide services and connections for members. The new, re-created family acts like old, well-established families, even though the new kin had never previously met or known of one another. New relatives can provide *wasta,* or influential connections, after a simple declaration of kinship based on the kin association, no matter how recently it was established.

6

Elites, Elections, and Civil Society

Although the primary reason for organizing in formal kin associations may be economic, these associations have far-reaching social and political effects. Kin associations are commonly attributed to the political designs of elites and their desire for patronage organizations to generate electoral support. But the interaction between kin associations and the political realm is not straightforward. For most associations, the connection to electoral politics is tenuous or even nonexistent; the associations were established prior to and separate from electoral motivations and thus are generally not successful as national political voting blocs. Elites do benefit, however, and they participate by providing significant resources, setting up the organization, researching lineages, and contacting potential members. These elites are newly established members of the upper class seeking social prestige and influence. Unlike patron-client organizations, most kin associations rely upon horizontal networks among members, not charity or favors done by leaders. The leaders can be held to account through informal techniques together with yearly elections. The role of leaders varies by the size and resources of the organization's membership. In large and very small associations, charity and potential patronage plays a larger role. Large organizations demonstrate more shirking and less obligation on the part of the membership to repay aid.

The political and ideological interests and positions of associations are wide-ranging. Tradition, religion, and subnational identity are all reaffirmed in the associations. The separate identity entailed in kin associations is utilized to promote mutual aid, convincing members to view group unity as vital enough to sacrifice short-term gains and alternative allegiances without legal enforcement. Many of the political and social effects of kin associations stem from this factor. Not only do they advocate separate subnational identities, but in order to function effectively kin associations must regulate members to assure that their behavior does not compromise the primary goal of mutual aid achieved through identity solidarity. Kinship provides the right to monitor and gossip on the behavior of other kin—in other words, to disseminate information through the group on members' activities. The organizations attempt to do this through frequent meetings and uniting members under the umbrella of kin solidarity.

This chapter assesses the role of elites in kin associations, the associations' effect on the formal political realm, and their potential implications for social identity. I begin by delineating leaders' motivations, the desire of new elites for symbolic capital. I then examine the record of kin associations in elections, a common explanation for the rise of kin associations. I place the effect of kin associations on electoral politics in context by discussing the background of political parties in Jordan and Lebanon. I then present data supporting the thesis that kin associations can act as rivals to political party activism. This is a popular belief socially in these countries, repeated by interviewees and the media. State bureaucratic institutions are not neutral in the kin sphere. Jordan for decades and Lebanon selectively have demonstrated a preference for organizing through kin. Kin associations can obtain a minor amount of funding from the bureaucracy and have sought it. Such funding can be important to the sustenance of small organizations. The effects of the increase in kin associations range from individual regulations on member behavior to the generation of new subnational identities that separate kin from others in the domestic sphere.

ELITE PRESTIGE AND IDENTITY ORGANIZING

Institutions do not arise effortlessly. Individuals set them up, complete the bureaucratic paperwork to register them, and sell the idea to potential members. Often concepts of identity are innovated, entailing costs as individuals research and alter lineages. It is new elites—not the traditionally dominant families—who undertake the establishment of kin associations in order to achieve social notoriety and break into the accepted upper-class clique. Through identity divisions, delineating insiders and outsiders, elites outside the traditionally powerful families capitalize on kin identity and build upon their service provision to amass a clientele. Indeed, those with established prestige, the some two hundred families consistently elected to Lebanon's parliament, for example,[1] are not the ones founding kin associations. Kin leaders are generally unconnected to past powerful families. This circulation of elites reveals changes in mobilization, incentives, and frames of organizing. A class of individuals has achieved success through new, fluid processes of market or state-created opportunities. Achieving social status, breaking into the structure of socially prominent families, is more difficult. By providing socially worthwhile goods, welfare, and employment aid, the elite create a reputation for being socially responsible, helpful, and charitable.[2] Some associations publish lists of the donors and their contributions. Their resulting influence makes them players to be reckoned with, whose interests should be taken into consideration, backed by the numbers of their kin group.

Individuals who have achieved success through market or state-created opportunities lead mutual aid associations. Since social status and the structure of socially prominent families are relatively rigid, leaders use these associations to demonstrate their good works and thus gain a place among the accepted upper class.[3] In contrast to the literature's dominant focus on notables or traditional ruling families with regard to kin organizing,[4] it is second-tier elites, social climbers, middle-status families, and the nouveau riche who establish the associations.[5] These new members of the upper class use the associations as springboards to social power, with or without electoral ambitions. Relative newcomers have usurped the position of the tribal leader or advanced their tribe against a previously dominant one. Traditional sheikhs, their descendants, powerful families, and family branches are challenged and marginalized in many cases. The professions of association leaders generally mirror those in society or the social group as a whole, with business professions overly represented. In earlier eras, the notables with financial resources but without job networks led mutual aid associations. They were displaced, however, as the organizations changed to their current emphasis on middle-class cooperative ownership and social insurance. Notables and landowners are now almost completely absent from leadership roles in the associations. This distribution of professional backgrounds is distinct from those of most Islamists. Islamist activists also hail from the new upper middle class, but most are professionals—doctors, professors, engineers, and lawyers. In Jordan, Islamist leaders hailed predominantly from the capital and urban areas. Unlike mutual aid association leaders, who furnish job connections, most Islamist leaders in Jordan are employed in education where jobs are limited.[6]

Bourdieu's concept of symbolic capital adequately captures this dynamic.[7] As opposed to "social capital," a term much used but little defined,[8] "symbolic capital" can be defined as societal "credit" or reputation that can be used for future economic benefit. One of the main methods of creating symbolic capital in both industrialized and less-developed countries is through public charitable works.[9] The political and reputation-building aspects of philanthropy have been well documented. Elite charity is not a reflection of abstract altruism but the desire to create or expand social prestige. Charitable giving represents a preoccupation with status and elite competition, forming an arena for cultural battles.[10] Philanthropy is a method for marking class and intraclass distinctions in status. Supporting an institution that is socially recognized as valuable and central to the society's self-definition is a way to bolster social status. Giving is tied to the desire for social prestige, mapping one's own cultural values onto society, including religious ones, and the attempt to attract a membership for political parties. Charity is not value-neutral but is often linked to religious or political aims in the domestic or foreign arena.[11] Political leaders emerge from charitable organizations, having acquired public exposure there.[12]

It is important that activities which increase symbolic capital are not recognized for what they truly are, namely, economic strategies. Exchanges, reciprocity, or gifts can all be interpreted as fiscal transactions or investments, but this monetary aspect of the deals must be obscured in order to function according to plan and increase the individual's stock of capital. Major events such as marriages are stages for the production of symbolic capital, a means to impress others and cement obligations of future reciprocity. This dynamic operates particularly in economies that are insecure and those in which reputation serves as the main economic guarantor.[13] A good reputation and influential, widespread networks create a reservoir to be drawn upon at some later, unspecified time.

The new elites leading these associations have broad choices of institutional venue for achieving their symbolic capital, social influence, and recognition. If a kin organization appeals to potential members, most elites opt for kin idioms. Assuming leadership in smaller groups is a far easier task than within large, national charities and political parties. Whether seeking social status or being called upon as a result of achievement and prestige, leaders of kin associations shine in the relatively small sphere of associations. Members describe leaders as well-known, providing free services such as medical care to kin, aiding kin in job searches, providing funds, and rejuvenating the association. Running campaigns for these independent candidates is less expensive than national political party candidacies, discussed below. Not only do the elites become big fish in a small pond, more easily establishing influence on this subnational scale, but they are also able to institutionalize, channel, and potentially limit demands upon them for monetary or employment assistance.[14] Prestige has a cost, as community, friends, and family call upon the successful for jobs and loans. Some of the successful attempt to escape their obligations to kin by living a distance away; others prefer to support nonrelatives, as this furnishes prestige among non-kin whereas assisting relatives may be viewed not as charity but as a duty without social reward.[15] Through institutionalization, claims for aid can be limited or denied. Elites can restrict the amount of aid they provide.[16] The existence of the kin institution itself is a concrete demonstration that the leader cares for family, while particular claims can be deflected through the channels and priorities of the organization.

KIN ASSOCIATIONS IN ELECTIONS

The reputation, recognition, and networks created in kin associations can be used for direct electoral purposes in state political institutions by the leader of the association or prominent elites members.[17] Through the differentiation of genealogical lineages, elites outside the traditionally powerful families are able to build upon service provision to amass a potential clientele.[18] Both Jordan and Lebanon are characterized by the importance of the middleman, or *wasit;* connections in politics and services are the rule. Parliament and cabinet seats have been allocated to distribute benefits to clients and districts. In such circumstances, charitable and kin organizations can serve a double use, as both providers of aid and sources of political networks.[19] A reputation for charitable works can be used to build specific networks of friendship, loyalty, and obligation, generating a clientele increasingly dependent upon the leader. Kin associations have also been used as locations for candidates to campaign, garner support, or reach a collective decision on a member to support in elections. The latter are called primaries. Kin groups have allied with ideological trends, and politicized individuals have used kinship as a way to displace long-entrenched leaders who support the current regime.[20] Ideological stances allow the candidate to benefit from necessary votes outside the family group or succeed within the family against competing kin candidates.

The use of kin associations for electoral politics is not the rule, nor is it generally successful. Most never enter elections. When they do, electoral bids by kin association leaders have proven most successful where few votes are needed, as at the municipal level, and when candidates draw upon party or outside networks to increase votes beyond kin.[21] Size is important; generally around three thousand or four thousand votes are needed to win a parliamentary seat in Jordan, a number close to the size of the average kin association. In Lebanon the necessary votes vary widely by district. Within the association, agreeing on a candidate is not easy, and members do not necessarily vote for the candidate even when agreement is reached. Significant, too, is that individuals cite political factors as a disincentive to joining kin associations. Potential members scrutinize the political interests of founders, wary that the association would be overtly political.[22] In many cases involvement in elections splits the family, for instance, when a candidate pushes his political party onto members or when several members run for office simultaneously. Some families "help" the member vote, taking her voting card and family book and voting for her, or being present at the polling station. Numerous interviewees cited factionalism among the family as a problem that "only brings fatigue."

In Jordan, although the record of kin associations contributing overall to success in elections is mixed, there is evidence that the associations are becoming more important to electoral politics over time. In Jordan, in the 1989 elections, six parliamentarians (out of an eighty-person elected body) were identified by electoral watch organizations as leaders or members of village or family organizations.[23] In these elections few kin associations are listed among the elected parliamentarians' affiliations.[24] Instead, parliamentarians stated that memberships consisted mainly of professional memberships, labor unions, chambers of commerce, the engineers association, or Islamist groups. Two tribal sheikhs were among those elected. Nine doctors and thirty-three Islamists, the latter largely directors or leaders of Islamic charities, were among the eighty parliamentarians. Two were Islamists active in B'ir Sab'a, a Palestinian kin charity organized along village lines. Three others had kin associations,[25] and several more listed involvement in neighborhood organizations and charitable welfare activities. Four were members of national-level welfare charities.[26] For the 1993 elections, four parliamentarians and one sheikh had kin associations.[27] In the 1997 elections, kin associations of all types were listed, now clearly identified as civil society organizations. Almost one-fourth of elected representatives in those elections were listed as active members of local kinship associations.[28]

Most associations in Jordan taking a political stance stated that they would support any candidate working for their causes.[29] Large and successful associations such as Lifta (Palestinian) and al-Naber (Jordanian

Christian) have not advanced their own parliamentary candidates. One association, whose leaders are Muslim Brothers, supported opposition candidates. The association provided a forum for the liberal opposition candidate Toujan Feisal in her bid for reelection in 1997, hosting her rallies and speeches, until the Ministry of the Interior threatened to pull the association's license if they continued. (As noted in the previous chapter, Feisal was the only woman elected to the Jordanian parliament prior to the government implementing a quota for women.) In one case an elected (1989) candidate's kin group set up an informal diwan in 1994 subsequent to his withdrawal from electoral politics. A member of the kin group was elected in 1997.[30] The president of one Amman-area association was elected to parliament in 1993 but was not reelected in the next elections.[31]

Having a kin base does not assure victory, even in a country deemed as tribal as Jordan.[32] Heads of tribes who committed their members' votes for a particular candidate found that these commitments were not credible. Tribal members made their own independent voting decisions.[33] The more common occurrence was multiple kin competing for the group's vote. As one analyst stated, had the candidates been truly tribal, they would not have been so numerous. The lack of intra-tribal agreement and that multiple candidates from each tribe ran for election assured the failure to elect any kin to parliament. The Christian Azeizat tribe in Madaba, the largest tribe there, supported three candidates, a doctor (former president of the family association), a businessman, and a former minister. All three lost. In the 1997 elections five members of the Shishani tribe ran in Zarqa, three al-Jazi from the Huwaytats, and four Qoudat in Ajloun.[34] The democratic questionnaire of the Center for Strategic Studies revealed that only 8 percent of the Jordanian population felt pressured to vote for a specific electoral candidate. Of those, half voted for the candidate that was promoted and half did not.[35] Voting decisions, according to the Center's surveys, were made according to the provision of services in the voter's district, independent of opinion, and the candidate's qualifications. Kinship was listed seventh on the list of factors determining voting preference, cited by 4.6 percent of those polled.[36] Additionally, research on villagers within Jordan demonstrates that the backing of kin in internal tribal conflicts is not easily forthcoming. In elections, only about one-fourth of these villagers voted for kin. Most voted for whomever they believed promoted general societal development goals.[37]

Parliamentary bids can succeed when the kin member is able to draw support from outside sources. In some cases leaders of tribes utilize outside networks and support in order to gain prominence within the tribe and overcome internal factions.[38] In Jordan Nash'at Hamarneh, who won the Christian seat in Madaba in 1997, received additional votes because of his status as a Ba'th party member and his established neighborhood networks.[39] In Irbid a member of the al-'Omari family won in 1989 owing to support from the Muslim Brotherhood. In the 1993 elections, when another member from the family ran under the banner of the Islamic Action Front (the political wing of the Muslim Brotherhood), votes were split and no family member was elected.[40]

In Lebanon there is both a longer record of kin associations in politics and more reluctance to support kin in politics. Ten members of the 1996 parliament, or about 8 percent, were identified as affiliated with a kin association.[41] The majority of associations stated that they remained out of politics but supported members if they ran for election. Overall 20 percent of Lebanese associations in my survey supported candidates for parliament since the end of the civil war; at least one-fifth of those parliamentary bids were unsuccessful. Sixty percent of Sunni associations did not enter politics, but some of these would vote for a candidate from the family if there was one. The remainder supported Hariri's list. One Sunni association encountered resistance among potential members, because many feared that they would become subject to the will of Members of Parliament (MPs). Another Sunni association "feared submission" to a member of parliament and thus did not accept aid from him. Two-thirds of the Druze associations in my survey stay out of politics; the remaining support the Progressive Socialist Party (PSP). Two Druze associations had successful candidates from their family in parliamentary elections. Seventy percent of Christian associations reported that they did not enter politics, and one pointed out that this issue caused problems in the past by dividing the family. The remainder supported whatever candidate the family proffered in elections. A Maronite association formed in 1992 included a female candidate who won a seat in parliament in 2005. The Shi'a associations were much less politically active, yielding the field to political parties. Of the Shi'a family associations in my survey, more than half supported a candidate in elections if he or she happened to come from the family but otherwise did not expressly enter elections. The rest supported either party candidates or none at all. Families among the Shi'a community now attempt to ally themselves with parties in order to secure political success.[42] The majority of Palestinians are not able to vote, but some said that if they were eligible, they would vote for Hizbullah.

Kin associations have more success at the local municipal level than the parliamentary level in Lebanon. Twenty-three percent of responding associations supported a candidate in municipal elections, and several of those associations had three or more members in municipal government. Municipal seats in the more than 600 municipalities only require between 300 and 7,000 votes, as opposed to the 20,000–120,000 votes needed for parliament. Still, kin associations have scattered success at the municipal level. No institutional support was furnished for the greatest percentage of municipal presidents (40%), followed closely by those supported by a kin association (36%). Political leaders supported 8 percent of municipal presidents' bids. Most did not declare their participation in kin associations. This was downplayed by candidates or listed under cultural activities.[43] A study of the 1998 municipal elections revealed that almost 60 percent of elected municipal council members belonged to one of the five largest families in their area.[44] The role of major families appears to decline in larger municipalities, where half the municipal presidents come from smaller families. Coming from the largest family does not insure success, as half of all the municipal presidents from their area's largest family competed against a relative from the same family in elections.[45] Municipal seats are not usually a starter on the path to parliament; most municipal representatives limit their interest to the local realm.

Generally, in both countries, groups organizing on a kin basis were not able to be national parties. Notables or leading families have long dominated both Jordanians and Lebanese, but those families are distinct from kin mutual aid associations. In fact, political families distance themselves from kin associations, as it is believed that such affiliations pose a conflict. Kin associations limit the group to a small constituency, preventing it from being national.[46] Issues dominating kin associations are confined to internal ones.[47] One national political leader admitted that his family did not have a kin association, because "we are for all people."[48] A few years later this family initiated a kin association, a phenomenon coinciding with their downfall from national politics in favor of the Hariri family.[49] The perception is that leading families would be limited in their appeal by such associations, that it is an introversion, not an expansion into a larger political party or platform for political power, and is used by weaker families.[50] In fact, these prominent families utilize a broad genealogy of long vintage to appeal to as much of the population as possible, even tracing their heritage back thousands of years to the largest possible tribal link. For example, as noted earlier, the Khalil kin association in Lebanon's mandate era traced its descent back to the biblical Abraham.[51] In the same period Emile Lahoud chose to publicize his candidacy under the broad Daw tribe, expanding his base of support by newspaper appeals for cousins to support him.[52]

THE POLITICAL PARTY CONTEXT

The effects of kin associations on political institutions are tied to the nature of political parties and legislatures in Jordan, Lebanon, and the broader Middle East. Jordan and Lebanon share many similarities, but Lebanon has been far more democratic, with more prominent secular and sectarian politics. In the Arab world, in general, much of political party history has been leftist or socialist; for example, Arab nationalism, variants of Marxism, and socialism ruled the 1950s and 1960s.[53] Islamism is the current non-personalistic ideology capable of conquering subnational regionalism and divisions. Some recent parties are environmental, democratic, and secular. All these have an ideology that addresses an ethnic group, the state, or a group crossing national boundaries. By contrast, tribal, subnational, village, or kin group allegiances have not spawned enduring political parties. In the colonial and early independence periods notables and patronage parties were common, organizing intermittently around an individual of prominence. Such particularistic or personal patronage groups can and do occur often, and indeed characterize much of Jordanian and Lebanese politics. They differ from political parties in that they focus on the individual and patronage rather than on long-term ideological platforms.

Kin association and tribal leaders partake in campaigns as independent candidates; that is, they stand apart from a political party platform and run as individuals. Nonparty candidates in the Middle East are common; in fact, they constitute a majority of campaigners in many countries. They are often mainstream candidates, viewed by the regimes as conservative supporters of the status quo. They ally with political trends and parties but do not pledge their allegiance or subordination to them. Independents are not linked to political party discipline and hierarchies. Often, independent candidates focus on pork barrel politics or services for their particular constituency. In Jordan and Lebanon, the locales where family reigns over party support neatly correspond to the election of independent candidates.

Whereas in other regions coalitions of individuals can sustain a political party, here they do not. The goals of individual leaders detract from their taking part in a political hierarchy in which they are not the ultimate leader. Although the leadership of kin groups changes, and does not conform to the static depiction of a singular, uncontested tribal sheikh, this does not indicate that new leaders are willing to submit to the external hierarchy entailed in political parties. Even when an attempt is made to bridge kin and party allegiances, the coalition is temporary and opportunistic. In the end, one or the other is prioritized. In the case of formal kinship associations, kin usually wins out. In some cases kin associations have been allied with parties. This occurs when the leader is affiliated with a political party, and that political leaning spreads to all members whether or not they belong to the party or believe in its precepts. Tension continues between the two allegiances, and the leader must prioritize one over the other. A stark example of this is leftist parties that believe in meritocracy and eschew traditional obligations, implying that kin are not prioritized in services. Since the entire kin association is structured around receiving preferential access to jobs and services, meritocracy clearly interferes with the functioning of the kin association.

The Jordanian political system is not a democracy but a monarchy with ultimate control in the hands of the King. Long under martial law, elections returned in 1989 following large-scale demonstrations against economic reforms. Political parties were allowed a few years later. Parliament had some power, which it exercised. District size and the allocation of votes were manipulated by the monarchy to generate the results it favored, increasing the electoral weight of East Bank or Jordanian regions of the country to the detriment of Palestinian areas. Although electoral politics in Jordan are squarely under monarchical control, they have proceeded further than most in the Arab world,[54] and have afforded the population more organizational freedom than it had prior to the 1990s with the important exception of the 1950s period.

Surveys by the Center for Strategic Studies show a decrease in party membership in Jordan, although conclusions are tentative given the small number of polling years.[55] Al-Urdun al-Jadid's review of civil society declared that parties have declined in favor of nonparty relationships, tribalism, political groupings, and independent leaders.[56] Only 1 percent of the population has ever been a party member, and fewer wanted to join a party in 2000 than did in 1995. Parties are small, most having only a few dozen members. More than half the survey respondents chose the Islamic Action Front as representing their political interests in 2000. This far outpaces any other party. The next most popular political party, the government's Constitutional Party, lagged, with a scant 16 percent of polled responses.[57] Government-supporting parties are constructed as ad hoc alliances, disbanding soon after elections, later forming under a new name in time for the next elections.[58] At the local level the Islamic Action Front is the only real party of consequence. In 1999 this party won seventy-nine municipal council seats and seven mayoral positions, the largest party win by far.[59]

Although, in 1989, 83 percent of MPs had a political affiliation, less than half these members of parliament in 1993 were allied to a party.[60] In 1997 only one-quarter were members of a political party.[61] Almost half of those 1997 deputies were independents, lacking any ideological membership.[62] Particularistic tendencies of the electorate increased, causing accusations that parliamentarians acted as representatives of their subnational regions, not of the country as a whole.[63] Observers described the elections as "lacklustre, issueless, and parochial," and the new parliament as docile.[64] Parties were silenced. The new electoral law "knocked the stuffing out of all the new political parties, and the ideology out of the campaign."[65] Candidates' slogans reflected this apathy. Earlier platforms and issues, addressing national problems, were replaced by regional, local, and specific concerns. Localities and families were promoted, and larger issues were left aside. In the run-up to the 1993 elections, potential parliamentarians claimed that they would try to "do their best."[66] Slogans extolled the ethical righteousness of the candidate or praised his hometown.[67] By 2007 the vast majority (73%) of survey respondents would vote for independent candidates in parliamentary elections as opposed to 17 percent voting for political party members. Results are similar at the municipal level, with 77 percent voting for independent candidates against a meager 7 percent voting for party candidates. The majority voting for a party would vote for the Islamic Action Front at both the national and local levels.[68] Independent candidates were the big winners in the 2007 municipal elections. Among the majority of voters, tribe, family, and village of origin determined their vote, even in areas where there previously had been strong support for political parties. Issues, platforms, and campaign promises mattered little, as voters made up their minds more than a month before the political campaigns began.[69] The dearth of political parties outside Islamism has become a notable problem,[70] and Jordan's king called for a renewal of parties, including those on the left. The very parties his father had avidly fought—leftist ones—are now sought as a solution to the lack of secular opposition.

Lebanon is more democratic; indeed, it is one of the most democratic systems in the Arab world. The Lebanese political system was put in place through a census taken in 1932 and the national pact in 1943 consolidating the allocation of political offices by confession. The president would be Christian, and the prime minister Sunni Muslim. The speaker of parliament (the Chamber of Deputies) was to be Shi'a Muslim. This arrangement included all the major religious divisions and gave supreme power to Christians. The 1932 census, conducted with significant bias toward particular religious groups, concluded that Christians were the majority. Parliament was divided by a 6:5 Christian to Muslim ratio. This division of power remained through the years, though the number of parliament members increased. Prior to the 1975 civil war, Lebanon was deemed to be the only Arab democracy. On the eve of that war, political parties were numerous, strong, and active, as was civil society, many calling for an end to the confessional system. The Ta'if Accord in 1989 ending the civil war altered the allocation of parliamentary seats, now distributed evenly between Christians and Muslims. Presidential powers were downgraded, and parliamentary and cabinet powers enhanced. The Christians lost influence in this deal to the benefit of the Sunnis. However, authority ultimately resided with the Syrian-affiliated power holders in the various sects, as the Syrians occupied the country in accord with the Ta'if agreement. Their formal Syrian backing ended in 2005. A significant amount of district manipulation occurred, and the electoral law was a major point of contention.

Lebanon's reputation for democracy hides the lopsided reality of political parties. With the exception of Hizbullah and Amal, another Shi'a political party, and recently the Free Patriotic Movement (Christian) of Michel Aoun, parties are weak. Large numbers of independent candidates and elected members of parliament have not joined any party. The parties were almost exclusively Islamist after the civil war.[71] As a percentage of parliament, the number of party members has decreased slightly in the post–civil-war era, and almost all are Islamist or Hizbullah members.[72] Between 25 and 30 percent of MPs were members of political parties from 1992 to 2000.[73] The sole geographical area of party strength was in southern Lebanon, a stronghold of Hizbullah and Amal. Only there did party membership reach 30 percent.[74] By contrast to the party trend in Shi'a areas, notables increased in the Christian areas after the war. This revival of older political families[75] contrasts with their decline in power during the civil war.[76] Heavily Christian areas sport a larger number of competing candidates than other regions, the overwhelming majority of whom are independents.[77] Similarly the number of independent, nonaffiliated candidates in the Druze areas has increased, and are based on local and neighborhood groups. At the municipal level, political parties supported less than 4 percent of Maronite municipal presidents compared to almost 37 percent of Shi'a presidents. Overall, almost 70 percent of municipal presidents declared no political or ideological affinities. The ratio among Christians was higher, and lower among Shi'a and Druze.[78] This pattern continued in the 2005 elections, after the departure of the Syrians. Temporary and loose blocs were formed for elections. Candidates are identified as close or sympathetic to major political figures or trends. Political trends or umbrella groups are called "gatherings" (the Bristol Gathering, for example), taking the name of the location where a key meeting to consolidate the alliance was held.

In both countries the lack of parties accompanied an increase in the age of deputies and a decrease in their educational level. In Jordan almost two-thirds of elected deputies in 1997 had only a bachelor's degree. Twenty percent more had less-formal education than a bachelor's degree.[79] By contrast, 60 percent of the 1989 representatives had achieved higher than a bachelor's degree, and 39 percent had a doctorate, medical, or law degree.[80] In Lebanon the age of parliamentarians decreased outside the Christian mainstay, which is also the most likely to field independent candidates. Maronite candidates are about sixty years old on average, and the average Shi'a candidate is in his forties.[81] In municipal elections, elected presidents who are allied with a party have a higher level of education and are younger. Hizbullah and Druze (PSP) party allies are more educated; almost 70 percent have a university education.[82]

A TRADE-OFF BETWEEN POLITICAL PARTIES AND KIN?

The relationship between political party membership and kin associations appears in many cases to be mutually exclusive.[83] Sometimes an entire association acquires the affiliation of the leader or supports him in elections. But for many associations and members, the two types of activism do not coexist. External political party allegiances are viewed as detrimental to the solidarity of the association. Since competition between potential leaders has most often led to the demise of kin associations, political affiliations are subordinated to kin interests. The first priority is aiding the family, and thus the association reinforces that one's primary identity is based on one's locale and kin.[84] In other cases political considerations prevent kin from forming an association. A Jordanian Christian family had been unable to establish a kin association because of the presence of two powerful and electorally competing political figures in the family. The withdrawal of both from active politics permitted the family to form an association. Members generally do not actively participate in political parties, as that is deemed antithetical and detrimental to the kin association. Former political party candidates join the associations, drawn first by the pull of the membership and their quest for intermediation from an elite and, second, by easier and less-expensive campaigns for political office. Since the groups are small, there is no need to compete with party officials for a place in the electoral list. Becoming independent, provided that the electoral system furnishes seats for fewer votes, enables a candidate to skip a party organization and its battles. Campaign stances become simple. Some bill themselves as the tribal son, who would try to give the family a place in government structures.

The associations often attempt to remove political choice among members. If a leader or prominent kin member is associated with a political trend, the entire association, correctly or not, is identified with it. Some members stated that the leaders attempted to impose their views and voting preferences on members. Alternatively the leadership's political stance is assumed to be that of the association as a whole. Family leaders politically allied to the Muslim Brotherhood, with kin members predominantly in the private sector, have demonstrated organizing tendencies akin to Palestinian organizers, broadening the kin network away from Jordanian tribes and toward private-sector contacts. Owing to the mixing of religious with kin organizing, at least two Palestinian village associations are now also publicly viewed and formally listed as Islamic charities.[85] The Sons of Southern Jordan Charitable Association, formed in 1977, is built on regional ties.[86] It is popularly believed to be tribal, based in the Majali family, and is politically allied with East Bank Jordanian nationalism.[87] In other kin groups the family book, or *deftar 'a'ili*, which is necessary for individuals to register their vote, is picked up by kin representatives. They then register the individuals' votes for them or, alternatively, are present at the polling center to "help" their kin vote.

The media perceives the relationship between parties and kin associations as a trade-off. A number of Lebanese newspapers, spanning the political spectrum, ran article series on the history of Lebanese families.[88] The roots of Lebanese families were traced and the benefits of tribal culture lauded and juxtaposed to the horrors of war and the militias. One newspaper stated its reasons for beginning the series, defensively, in 1989. Because all belonging stems from familial belonging, and families had positive effects during the war, the newspaper answered its self-criticism. Familial allegiance, according to the paper, is opposed to the parties and ideological politics that characterized the war. This rewriting of history entailed denying the involvement of tribes in the war, and positioning tribalism as distinct from sectarianism. According to the paper, tribes do not kill for a sect or religion; they fight only for their leader. Tribes also replaced the government and created law and order during the war, according to this version of history.[89] Articles delineated the tribes that include numerous sects (Atallah) and those that are friendly with other tribes (Dandash).[90] The paper celebrated certain families, such as al-Khoury, that it considered secular and nonparty-oriented.[91] The media celebrated tribal practices, while emphasizing that families do not enter parties—they are neither political nor ideological.[92] But the media also described the ongoing politicization of family associations and tribes, as when they allied with different ideological trends or supported prominent politicians.[93] Though the papers clearly focused on the large, apolitical, and multireligious tribes, their writers had to note that in all cases the tribes' roles decreased with the rise of parties, unions, and even civil society organizations.[94]

Numerous interviewees reiterated this rivalry between families and parties, implicitly or explicitly. In Jordan the small number of leftists have begun organizing through kin instead of parties, as do the most politically active and those formerly opposed on principle to kin-based organizing.[95] In Lebanon one interviewee hoped that the youth of the family would be active in the association, so that they would be distanced from party participation. Another stated that with the decline in parties, young people had nowhere to go except to families. The absence of party strength worked to the advantage of kin associations, in his view.[96] One interviewee stated that he preferred a political party with a known program; if he had to be subject to an ideology, he did not want it to be a family one. Parties have social and political projects, one interviewee stated, which he felt were superior to the activities of kin associations. Members of an organization were presumed to share the politics of the association's leader—society identified the group's stance with individual members. Leaders with a political affiliation would inevitably taint members with that affiliation. The party membership of family trumps kin organizing, another interviewee claimed. One association said that it limited its services only to what the political party Amal does not provide.

An interviewee stated how deeply he felt for his family and that he desired to help others, but he also wanted all to be free to choose individually. He felt that a kin association would prevent this choice and thus would threaten to divide the family over issues within the association.

Another interviewee did not want to be drawn into politics and does not like politics, and so avoided kin associations. Others fear a prominent political actor among their kin elite would lead the association and bring it into politics. Lebanese Sunnis whom I interviewed feared political subordination to particular MPs, part of the ruling coalition, and wished to be independent of the Sunni trend. Shiʿa were concerned that the community would perceive the formation of a kin association as a politically separatist trend against the dominant parties, even though they were not seeking to escape their community's political party. Such an association would be considered in opposition to the existing parties, another stated. Sect membership became more important than family during the war, one interviewee pointed out. Parties limit kin associations, another said, not because the parties prevent kin organizing but because individuals become uninterested.

The opposition between parties and kin is related to the provision of services. A survey of voting priorities in Lebanon revealed that individuals were concerned that the candidate would not provide them services, a sentiment held particularly by middle-class youth in the university. This is especially true of those living in the north, the Baqaa, or Byblos, the least served and poorest regions of Lebanon. The fear of not finding a job and the desire for a support network brought about these feelings, according to the survey analyst. Most voted in agreement with their immediate family (87%), two-fifths voted in unison with their village or locale, and only one-third agreed with the electoral choices of their sect.[97] In Jordan more than half the survey respondents who voted for independent candidates declared that the most important qualification for office was service provision. Political inclinations were the least consideration (8%).[98] A Lebanese interviewee explained that his villagers do not need a kin association since the head of a major party comes from his village. All villagers thus receive social services from that leader. Another interviewee said that they did not need kin mutual aid, as the family gathers in the political party. Confirming this, a prominent Lebanese think tank identified an opposition between kin associations and political parties.[99] In one Lebanese village, villagers who are members of a party ask for aid or mediation from the party, not from kin.[100]

The opposition between party and kin can extend to authority and crime. When the PLO was viable in Lebanon it substituted for the authority of traditional elders and village leaders, and even vied with parents regarding internal family matters such as marriage.[101] In fact, numerous cases of parties interceding to end or prevent tribal feuds were noted in Lebanon. Most recently Hizbullah and Amal moderated armed clashes between tribes in Baalbek.[102] Sheikh Fadlallah, an ally of Hizbullah, presided over a truce between tribes that remained in effect for years, and Hizbullah regularly intervenes to pay the blood price to a murdered tribal member's family in order to avoid revenge killings. It intervened in more than two hundred such feuds since the mid-1980s.[103]

RELATIONSHIP TO STATE INSTITUTIONS

Kin associations are not state creations or subordinate to the state, but neither are they wholly independent of the state realm. The regime in Jordan and the postwar governments in Lebanon have not remained unaware of the short-term potential of kin associations to substitute for political parties. The tendency to aid independent electoral candidates and fragment the electorate into competing voting blocs has been viewed by states favorably, as aiding de-politicization. Yet the associations have not been entirely welcome. Although the state relies upon civil society organizations to provide services that it is unable to, at the same time it is suspicious of organizing outside its own purview. Perceived as potential threats, even liberal Arab states took steps to temper the independence of civil organizing. Both Jordan and Lebanon currently encourage and regulate the associations, providing institutional support preferentially while monitoring members and activities. Just as international donors attempt to award financial grants to NGOs directly, governments are inserting themselves deeper into the workings, approval, and management of these organizations.

Like other Arab state institutions, Jordan's and Lebanon's bureaucracies have been increasing their regulatory power and control over civil society and kin organizations. The associations are subject to ongoing administrative supervision and arbitrary legal decisions. Their budgets and membership books are audited by the state, and technically open to state examination at any time. A state representative attends internal elections, and members must be cleared by the government's internal security.[104] The supervising body records members' names, professions, ages, and places of residence, and can investigate their past activities once they are listed as a member. By virtue of its data gathering, monitoring, and approval functions, the supervisory organization for charities has been described as a corporatist mechanism, enhancing the state's ability to control and discipline society.[105] Even with the new regulations, the authorities do not treat all organizations equally. State institutions have broad latitude in shutting associations down or refusing to register them. In Jordan the official rationales include political activism, activities outside the scope of the association's stated goals, and low membership.[106] The proliferation of regulations and imprecise laws exacerbate the state's discretionary authority and add to the dependence of small charities on larger ones and on the supervising body.[107]

Similarly, in Lebanon, the government increased its regulatory oversight of NGOs in the mid-1980s, decreeing that political NGOs must ask permission to form.[108] Previously associations merely informed the Ministry of Interior of their existence, but now they had to receive prior approval. The move was subsequently canceled, but since 1992 the Ministry of Interior has been enacting it informally, refusing to acknowledge receipts of notification of NGOs that the Ministry believes to be political, such as human rights groups. Now even nonpolitical NGOs cannot operate without permission, contravening the existing laws. In one extreme case, in 1994, the government appointed the president and board members of the Lebanese Red Cross as leaders of an NGO. Recently oversight to the charitable associations has been stepped up. New regulations have been introduced or existing regulations rigorously enforced. Government representatives now attend internal association elections, and the Ministry of the Interior examines the association's budget.[109] Prior to the Syrian withdrawal in 2005, these moves, which seemingly aligned the traditionally liberal Lebanese surveillance system with that of fellow Arab states, were commonly attributed to the Syrian occupation. However, Prime Minister Hariri himself had a major role in the changes, and they persisted long after the departure of the Syrians.

In Jordan long-standing regime policy turns a blind eye to familial organizing, despite the fact that legally neither cooperatives nor charitable voluntary organizations can limit membership to a particular tribe, religion, or ethnic group. In practice, the original founders restrict membership, and these founders have the right legally to choose or reject new members at will. The supervisory organizations merely request that the association's name not be that of the family. Officials ask the family to change the name slightly, leave out a letter or two, or adopt an entirely new name and then return to register. Village names are acceptable, making the associations appear to be local grass-roots organizations. Charities often adopt the name of the family's ancestral village to escape this regulation. Some family cooperatives choose an unrelated, upbeat name such as Progress, the Goal, or the Green Plains (al-Taqaddum, al-Hadaf, or al-Basat al-Akhdar). Often, if the supervising organization believes that the association is exclusive to kin, officials suggest adding some non-kin members. But if the association is based on village of origin, even if all are related, as is often the case, officials do not suggest adding people from outside the village.[110] Kinship associations face less scrutiny in registration, funding requests, and membership than non-ascriptive organizations.[111]

Funding is also provided preferentially, increasing the weight of the supervising agency's decisions and preferences. In Jordan funds are provided to charities via a point system that evaluates the programs of each charity according to priorities set by the state.[112] Through this point system, the government is able to encourage private charities to take over health care, child care, regular aid to the poor, and vocational training.[113] The state allocates around $3.6 million a year to the charities through its administrative agency.[114] The state in turn obtains this money mainly through the national charitable lottery and some international funding institutions. Foreign donors' contributions must be channeled through a state intermediary, the Royal NGOs,[115] the Ministry of Social Development, or the GUVS. Overall the GUVS provides an estimated 30 percent of all charitable NGO funds, a figure that includes kin associations and non-kin charities.[116] The regulatory agency awards points for productive projects and trainings, associations located in rural and remote areas, and anything geared toward women. Points are allocated based on providing care for the disabled (which is rarely listed among the goals of kinship associations), establishing nurseries and kindergartens, the number of families aided monthly, and constructing or renting the association's headquarters.[117] Associations in my survey received funding for general budget support, operating kindergartens, productive projects such as sewing, running a health clinic, items such as furniture, and regularly supporting a number of families. Most receive a small amount of aid, generally between $600 and $900 yearly; all but one (successful) charitable family association received aid.[118] Financial records for families of Jordanian origin revealed higher funding and less scrutiny of their achievements or future plans.[119] Some associations had none of the targeted activities but nevertheless received yearly funding.[120]

In Lebanon the Ministry of Social Affairs subcontracts many services to local, mutual aid, and confessional organizations.[121] The amount of funding is much lower than in Jordan, and most associations do not receive aid, the opposite of Jordan's situation. Funding for such NGOs prior to the war was furnished through the proceeds of a lottery, as in Jordan. Funding networks revolve around the Department of Associations in the

Ministry of Social Affairs. The state in 2004 aided ninety-three religious and civil society NGOs, through the Ministry of Social Affairs.[122] Other aid comes through individuals who use state money partly to funnel aid in return for political support, as in the Ministry of the South, associated with the political party Amal. Associations that formed health clinics in particular received funding. Two associations in my survey obtained aid for clinics from the Ministry of Health.

Further, kin associations have begun to benefit from symbolic legitimacy by being recognized as civil society organizations. Jordanian think tanks have recently begun identifying these associations as potential civil society affiliations. The progressive think tank al-Urdun al-Jadid only began including family association memberships in earnest in its listing of parliamentary members with the 1997 elections.[123] The move began tentatively, with some village associations mentioned for the 1993 parliament, whereas only large, high-profile charities had been listed for the previous parliament. The Center for Strategic Studies' yearly democratic survey recently began including questions on kin associations. As of 1999 quite a few family associations from Amman and the provinces were listed on the government's Web site as NGOs,[124] and a couple were advertised internationally.[125] The importance of family and tribal associations is reiterated in Jordan by the regime, which affirms tribalism. The king is often depicted as Bedouin, nationally and internationally.[126] When tribalism was criticized, the king defended it.[127] In Lebanon, family associations are praised as charitable and peaceful. One president of an association promoted this form of organization, saying that "families are about peace, militias about war."[128] The events of kin associations are covered in the "society" pages of Lebanese magazines.[129] Meetings of the associations are reported, as are their activities for the poor, graduation parties the family holds, and their dinner parties.[130]

In both countries state encouragement of kin associations does not stop at symbolism, funding, and administrative ease, but extends as well to electoral manipulation. In Lebanon Hariri promoted Sunni and Beiruti organizations, now considered political, advancing the Union of Beiruti Families, some say as an alternative to a political party to support the former prime minister.[131] The Sunni Muslim families that were included in the union, founded in 1997, were divided among themselves. Still, Hariri called it a political party.[132] The main opposition to Hariri, apart from Hizbullah, was located in the Association of Engineers.[133] In Jordan the electoral law was altered to diminish the Islamist presence in parliament and aid kin-based organizing.[134] The new law, instituting one vote in multi-member districts, was viewed as increasing the chances of kin candidates. Amawi writes that the law "led politicians as well as kinship units such as tribes and clans to feel that they stood a better chance at winning seats under the new law by mobilizing their kin/affiliates to vote."[135] With only one vote to cast, the populace would choose a relative who could serve as a liaison with the government, and effectively support the political ambition of the individual responsible for their social provision. Previously voters had split their loyalties, voting both for a kin and an ideological candidate. Families and groups had swapped votes, resulting in cross-cutting alliances such as Christian-Muslim coalitions. In the rural areas the state more directly encouraged government-affiliated local elites to form associations along the family association pattern after the associations had become dominant in the cities.

SOCIAL AND CIVIL SOCIETY EFFECTS OF KIN ASSOCIATIONS

The implications of kin associations go beyond elections. Whether or not they are classified as civil society organizations, which is debatable because of the exclusive identity criterion of membership, the associations potentially affect individual behavior and social activism. The political and social effects of kin associations come from the use of a traditional idiom, albeit reworked, to generate an identity-based mutual aid institution, and from the concomitant need to monitor group solidarity and responsibilities informally. Though only some participate in elections, all attempt to cement solidarity, trust, and a sense of duty among members by reinforcing their separate subnational identity ideologically and through the provision of services only to kin members.[136] Many associations substitute for certain state and political party functions. Central here is the provision of services, which have been a key variable in voting decisions. Further, the organizations can be characterized as relatively "greedy" in terms of allegiance.[137] Kinship or common heritage is used to mitigate collective-action problems, but shirking and free riding are still options. Commitment and allegiance to the group must be constantly reinforced and demanded of members. As a result, kin associations continually reinforce internal group solidarity and the distinction of the kin group from the rest of society.

Members disliked the social implications of kin associations. Of the nonparticipants in Lebanon who were surveyed, half disagreed with the framework of kin organizing, citing their preference for a universalistic or civil society rubric. Instead of creating a sense of cooperation or belonging, one leader, a former leftist political dissident, believed that kin associations cause feelings of marginalization among the populace, now internally weak and divided, and separated from the nation. In his words: "The foundation for the idea of family organizations is wrong—it runs against belonging to the country or nation. It fragments, and can turn families against each other. It can be separationist. If my family in my particular city is the primary allegiance, my city should be independent." He could easily imagine that, given a threat to the city's resources, those families would unite.[138] Members' heightened importance of family reputation and their involvement in family matters could impinge on personal freedoms; fights with other groups may erupt because of the actions of one person over which the group had no control, or membership could cause a lack of choice in political candidates. Both members and nonmembers stated that any disagreement between a family member and someone else could force the group as a whole to take a stance that they really did not want to take.

These kin welfare associations were viewed as both providing services and potentially controlling members' lives, a double-edged sword, and a trade-off that Suad Joseph termed the "care/control paradigm."[139] Possible implications encompass limitations on behavior, the ability to transgress the larger group, the creation of a political identity based on ascriptive, non-universalizable affiliations, and concepts of rights limited to this subnational group. Kin organizations control behavior and limit unacceptable actions and lifestyles.[140] The use of patriarchal idioms increases the relational nature of social citizenship for women, obtained through male relatives. Interviewees, aside from the founders, were generally not enthusiastic to form or join mutual aid identity associations. They continually emphasized their lack of choice in joining because of economic conditions and spoke of the disadvantages of joining the group. Many felt that the associations were traditional, a throwback to older forms of organizing, and that they replace and undermine alternative collective politics. One member said, "Of course, I am personally against this community system—I am more for an individualistic approach—but in this economy and country, you have to do this."[141] Other members stated that kin organizing was traditional and outdated. One Jordanian association leader joined the association as president after previous years as a leftist dissident. His opinion of the associations remained unchanged: their fundamental organizing concept is wrong, he stated. His aversion to tribalism, however, coexists with his desire to provide services for his relatives.[142] Some associations complain that members do not participate adequately. One interviewee stated that because the priorities of individuals differ, kin associations are an inappropriate solution. In my survey of nonmembers, 16 percent stated that the organizing form did not resonate with family members, and they were unable to amass support for the idea. One interviewee could not convince his children to start an association despite meeting regularly as a family.

Kin associations attempt to monopolize members' allegiances, replacing a multitude of alternative organizations for members from recreation to culture. Kin associations forestall involvement in other associations by providing members with a range of activities they desire and meeting their possible needs.[143] These all-encompassing goals reveal much, but the vast majority of associations are unable to achieve such a full range of services. A sufficient number of them do meet the basic criteria of a providing a meeting place, emergency aid, and connections to represent a credible claim on members' time and allegiance, detracting from alternatives. There is evidence for their success in this endeavor. Interviews indicated that even recently reconstituted lineages contained in kin associations were felt as real, and even those who are not formal members felt a sense of identity with the group.[144]

Many associations mix nationalism with religion or culture. The Lifta Association, a Palestinian kin association in Jordan, was established in 1969 as a locale to gather the Palestinians from that village with implicit political undertones.[145] Only later did the association enter service provision, particularly in the 1990s.[146] The association leaders originally asked the PLO head (prior to Yasser Arafat) to be chairman. When he refused, they started the association as a club. The public practice of 'ashura, a Shi'a religious holiday, was an innovation utilized to tie new urbanites to one Lebanese Shi'a association in the 1950s.[147] The associations replay kin history, publish texts on the group's culture and tradition, and celebrate important events that affected kin, such as their exodus from their home village or wars with Israel. Religion is also stressed, except in inter-religious associations, and religious holidays are focal points for association activities. Aid is typically given during holidays.

Kin association publications laud the historical and religious specificity of the group with treatises on its origins. In Jordan the main distinctions are religion and national origin, mainly Palestinian or Jordanian, from the West or East Bank territory, respectively, prior to 1948. Association programs teach children their special and different identity vis-à-vis society at large. In Jordan the charter of the al-Ramla Association includes a long history lesson on the original village and its role in Islamic civilization. In the words of the charter, the association took the name of the village to keep the memory and history of that city alive.[148] The Silwan Association's charter begins with a religious convocation, as do many others.[149] Another association's publication praises the traditions and customs of "true Arabs," such as hospitality and even—guardedly—blood vengeance.[150] Associations hold cultural and nationalistic programs. Khalil al-Rahman puts on nationalistic plays. Abna' al-Harith sponsors cultural programs and lectures explaining the family's history or the importance of family unity. In Lebanon the larger families published books on their history, including the Abu Jawdeh and Imad families right before the war, Atallah in the 1960s, and Tarabey, Sinou, and Hubeiysh during the war years.[151] One Lebanese interviewee wanted to publish historical texts on the family. Palestinians in Lebanon now produce village books commemorating ancestral villages over political allegiances.

The associations also demonstrate the social power and weight of the family and its distinct nature relative to the rest of society. The associations established identity markers between themselves and others, lines of inclusion and exclusion. Beiruti families attempted to establish themselves as the authentic inhabitants of a city quickly being overwhelmed by migrants. In the process, the determination of who is Beiruti became associated exclusively with Sunnis, despite the Beirut pedigree of Orthodox, Shi'a, and other families.[152] Identity contributes to the economic and political benefit of members.[153] The philanthropic, socially responsible, and family-oriented actions of prominent kin are displayed in the associations, often publishing the names of benefactors and the amount of their donations. In political disputes or disagreements with other families, having a family association strengthens the elite's position. The associations are used to compete with others.[154] Numbers matter in this system of informal negotiation. Services such as funerals and health clinics are viewed as a demonstration of the association's strength and numbers. Health care provides legitimacy and serves as the association's "face," its public manifestation.[155] The government meets formally with the leaders of prominent kin associations in Jordan. Kin associations demonstrate leaders' influence in the government, and help them secure services or meetings with key officials. In Lebanon, new elites used their kin associations as a foundation for successful leadership claims in the 1958 civil war.[156]

The current trend of kin associations coincides with an overall increase in subnational identity politics since economic liberalization in Jordan and since the end of the civil war in Lebanon. In Jordan, where, previously, a number of authors described a decline in tribal identity and an increase in national assimilation, the espousal of ascriptive identity is now commonly noted.[157] Tribal and family histories have been newly written, celebrating those identities.[158] Returning expatriates learn that they are members of a clan for the first time. Christian Jordanians, having experienced a de-tribalization along with the rest of the society, are re-tribalizing.[159] Even previously assimilated "Jordanian nationalistic" elites, of Palestinian background, have begun identifying themselves in terms of their ancestral origin.[160] The family association trend is part of this wave of identity politics.[161] In Lebanon the war left a legacy of legitimatized identity politics. Whereas before the war protests against the confessional system threatened to destroy it, now that system of separate identities and divided politics was institutionalized, and any "taboo" on discussing it was lifted.[162] The increase in sect and kin associations is viewed by think tanks and observers as unparalleled in Lebanon's history, and kin associations are seen as "the dominant form" shaping Beirut.[163] Palestinians have eschewed their prior national unity in favor of village ties and kinship, even commemorating particularistic holidays. Street names have changed from prior political party designations to village names. Television and radio feature village stories by elders.[164] In place of prior national organizations, Palestinians have split into subnational (kin/village) and supranational (Islamist) allegiances.[165]

CONCLUSION

Kin associations have profound effects on the constitution of society and on social and political organizing. Often significantly democratic internally, the membership does learn the mechanics of voting and the power of the individual to effect an outcome, as civil society theories assert. Outside the organization, the effect of kin associations may counter the march of democracy in the national realm by hindering the solidarity power of social movements and withdrawing a key demand against the state, that of welfare. Kin associations can influence the political activities of elites and members alike. Though the kin association trend began before elections were an option in both countries, kin associations have served as electoral blocs or mass recruitment in times of war, as demonstrated by the Lebanese civil war. Kin associations were incorporated wholesale into militias.

To date, seeking election to parliament has been the preserve of a minority of kin associations. Most leaders have little or no intention of entering politics. When they do, their efforts are often unsuccessful, as they are unable to secure the votes or the unity necessary to win, or, worse, their attempts backfire by splitting the association into competing political factions supporting rival candidates. Political party allegiances are thus viewed as detrimental to kinship solidarity, as they often threaten group unity. To avoid controversies, the associations usually either stay out of politics or utilize the kin group as a platform for candidacy. In the latter case, the idiom and solidarity remain family, and the candidate campaigns as an independent, without an outside political program, helping the family and channeling state goods to them. Municipal office bids have been more successful, still outside political parties, a trend that could become increasingly relevant if these states significantly decentralize.

Kin groups and political parties are not necessarily incompatible, yet the Middle Eastern combination of the two is not stable. Kin groups remain particularistic and subnational in their priorities, and political parties in this context have generally been national, religious, or ethnic, encompassing larger numbers. Political parties built upon personalistic appeal and patronage relations have not endured as parties in this region. When a leader of a kin association belongs to a political party, the membership and ideology of the association are marginalized. If party ideology is prioritized, such a leader is viewed as detrimental to the interests of formal kin associations both because of the threat of politics tearing the association apart and subordination of kin to party goals. A leader who does not prioritize his fellow kin in jobs and services will not last long as leader, or the association itself will fall into decay.

A more wide-ranging dynamic is the affirmation of subnational identities and the displacement of formerly state-level services onto the kin group. The extent of this effect is unclear. Kin associations pull individuals into private, disconnected, and mutually exclusive organizations of redefined kinship. Without completely removing themselves from interaction with the state, these organizations attempt to re-create the plethora of goods furnished by the state, from education to employment. The state is only marginally relevant to the associations. At the same time, kin associations generate and promote subnational identities attached to their provision of goods. In their realm, the national arena is often ignored.

Conclusion: Insight into Identity and Institutions

This book has shown that mutual aid organizations based on kin solidarity in Jordan and Lebanon are spurred by economic need and vary according to that need. Kin mutual aid associations are self-help redistributive organizations grounded in social classes with resources to invest in the future but lacking long-term financial security. As a large-scale trend, the associations arose in the absence of public social provisioning. In the current period of economic liberalization, kin mutual aid associations have reached new heights. Jordanians and Lebanese did not passively acquiesce to changes in national-level welfare institutions, but neither did they protest nationally for long. National protests to reestablish social provisioning were ineffective, and activism soon turned from the politics of protest to the politics of accommodation and self-advancement.[1] The response to welfare changes came through identity as a result of the specific regulatory and employment characteristics of these economies; the lack of judicial capacity foreclosed reliance upon legal institutions to enforce mutual aid obligations, and nonprofessional service jobs, dominating the economies, prevented social insurance through employment or skill-based organizations. It was not the market or globalization that was alienating but the lack of market and state institutions.

These traditional-sounding changes in grass-roots organizing have largely escaped the social science radar, but their analysis reveals much about the dynamics of identity change and institutional creation. When noticed, kin-based identity associations are interpreted as traditional groupings that have either been constant or have arisen from a renewal of previous patterns. Yet society is not returning to some prior identity origins. Kinship was not only rediscovered but was re-created along new lines often altering previous conceptions of lineage. The reconstitution of identity along differing subnational lines alters the landscape of primary identities, generating a fluidity of identity that belies characterizations of the Middle East as driven by age-old identity antagonisms. Establishing these associations is a forward-looking action, widening the network of reciprocal obligations and employment connections in an attempt to cope with changes wrought by economic reforms that accompanied international integration. Studying the dynamics of private-sector welfare provision illuminates one specific, material mechanism through which changes concomitant with globalization seemingly promote local identities.

The brisk institutional creation and identity reshuffling in these cases are explained by the search for social insurance through an institutional form that can monitor commitment and guarantee obligations. These cases encourage social science to look beyond cultural forms and trappings, as well as assertions of identity for its own sake, and instead examine the purposes of identities. The book demonstrates the potential lines of unity that can be spun as primary identities and the extent to which identity can be stretched or created. Individuals calculated and acted instrumentally, even as they organized under the solidarity of kinship and identity. Drawing upon various cultural repertoires, the associations' founders have fashioned a substantively new associational type, at once providing welfare and economic contacts for the middle class while altering genealogical definitions and segmenting a noncompetitive labor pool. Not everyone in need was able to cobble together a group with resources, a credible identity idiom, and a method of monitoring members. Those that exceed the size of internal policing capabilities suffer a higher rate of moral hazards and shirking. Those with smaller numbers are unable to form at the outset or cannot provide services and aid once they are established.

Though generally not motivated by political concerns, the organizations have broad political effects by changing the composition of social identities, demands, and mobilization. The associations alter the structure of civic life and prefigure social and political organizing, creating social groups and altering lines of political division. They affect the nature of the interaction between the state and groups or individuals, displacing the locus of demands for redistribution and services onto reconstituted, formal identity organizations. The organizations further fracture the national social and political realm, affecting the potential of national organizing against the state. Kin groups can be active in elections, although most are not, but they do not embrace a political party or platform besides aid for the family. As such, they further the trend toward independent, nonparty politics.

In this conclusion I review the argument and then discuss the lessons learned from this book. I examine the limits of the research and the importance of the key dynamic, the search for social welfare, to various situations and regions. I look at the conclusion regarding identity changes and the establishment of institutions, along with situations when institutions are unable to be established. Finally, I outline the social and political implications of kin mutual aid associations and how they affect social movements contesting the state.

FROM ECONOMIC INSECURITY TO KIN ASSOCIATIONS

The end of state welfare policies in Jordan and the end of militia welfare in Lebanon started the current large-scale trend toward self-help through kinship. For Jordan and most of the Middle East, a social contract in the post-independence period provided economic goods in return for political quiescence. State policies served as social insurance, providing the range of goods furnished under other social welfare systems. Generous public employment along with consumer price supports and subsidies buffered families from labor market risk and economic downturns. Employment came with access to loans, health care, and pensions. In Jordan, like other Middle Eastern countries, only a portion of the populace was completely included in this benefit scheme, while others were left out. Lebanon's case differed. There social insurance came during a briefer time and through nonstate institutions. The Lebanese state initiated some subsidies on the eve of the civil war in 1975 but otherwise provided no social welfare. In the early stages of Lebanon's history, when public welfare was similarly absent, people organized through kin associations as they urbanized. During the civil war the militias that consolidated territory provided an extensive range of social welfare goods for all classes under their rule. They established mini-states, replacing and surpassing state services. These militias provided numerous services such as unemployment insurance, consumer protection, health care, jobs, loans, and education. In all, the militias directly supported approximately 30 percent of the Lebanese population. Welfare in both these cases was not limited to relief for the poor but also provided for the middle classes. It is these middle classes with resources, namely, money to save for the future and job connections, that took the initiative to form kin-based mutual aid associations when welfare ended.

The social contract trading political voice for economic goods has been viewed only in its political guise in the Middle East literature, maintaining authoritarian leaders in office owing to the disbursement of state funds. But the economic goods fulfilled another, nonpolitical purpose, that of effective social insurance for the middle and lower classes. In economic reforms, no alternative was forthcoming for the middle class. Aid to the poor, however inadequate, was provided, and benefits, pensions, and insurance for the military increased substantially. The new scheme left unaddressed middle-class concerns for the future and the maintenance of their middle-class status. Economic reforms targeted precisely the cornerstones of welfare—public employment and price subsidies[2]—sparing only military jobs. Non-oil states are the most affected. As oil prices rebounded, oil states were able to continue their generous social expenditures. But even in the richer states, welfare benefits have narrowed to focus more exclusively on the regime-supporting citizens. For the rest of the region, social policies have been progressively dismantled.

Economic reforms brought a decrease in job stability and an increase in expenses. Regional labor markets shrank just as state social insurance ended. In Jordan, starting in 1989, consumer price subsidies were cut, resulting in steep cost-of-living increases. Progressively state-owned enterprises were privatized and the bloated ranks of state employment cut. Taxes were imposed on goods, along with fees for government services and additional taxes. The result was an increase in poverty from a total absence in the mid-1980s to 30 percent soon after economic reforms, and a growing income gap. Per capita income declined to almost half its mid-1980s level by the late 1990s. Food prices rose, and debts to friends, family, and local grocers increased. In Lebanon the end of the civil war ended the militias' provision of welfare, with the exception of Hizbullah, and brought economic liberalization reforms. Employment decreased as the militias disbanded, the state began privatizing and laying off employees, and employment in local neighborhoods declined as individuals could now circulate in the country. Taxes, fees on services, and the cost of living increased, and subsidies ended. Rampant inflation during the war left an altered economy at war's end. Health costs doubled after the war, and the income structure became polarized.

In much of the developing world, including the Middle East, the removal of state policies that served as welfare for middle and lower classes alike leaves few alternatives for insurance against economic vulnerability. In these areas, work and daily life in the developing world is often more risky and precarious, and mechanisms to cope with that risk are fewer.[3] The middle classes in particular have an effective interest in social insurance; they have the resources to invest for the future but not the financial independence to insure against sudden expenses that could lead to financial ruin. When market buffers and state guarantees are removed, middle classes are exposed to increased risk of future downturns. In the context of little state regulatory capacity, measures that were deemed by international and national economic planners as wasteful and indeed were not targeted to the most needy had, in fact, been a main source of social insurance. As a result, this class has strong incentive to locate alternative sources of welfare.

Choices for social insurance turned upon the welfare opportunity structure, made up of skill base, employment profile, and potential private-sector associations based on skills. Loans, health and life insurance, and alternative labor possibilities are all lacking. The structure of alternatives for welfare is limited. Credit and insurance markets in the developed world allow individuals to access money periodically when in need, financing extra expenses through loans or insurance. In the developing world, such solutions are not common. Not only is supply of consumer credit, loan availability, and private health insurance lacking, but labor-based options also provide a solution for only a small minority of private-sector workers. Pension schemes and firm-based insurance are made difficult by the widespread nonparticipation of employers in social security, the absence of job stability, and the lack of effective regulatory and monitoring institutions.[4] The establishment of collective institutions based on straightforward economic problems, common profession, or place of employment is hindered by precarious employment and the long-standing difficulty of organizing service workers. Professional associations furnish health insurance, pensions, and other benefits to members. Unions can impose a collective, private-sector solution furnishing intermittent aid, health insurance, and pensions, but only for workers in manufacturing, which is notably absent in the greater Middle East.

Where individual solutions such as market loans and private insurance are lacking, collective solutions are sought but are not easily found. To unite, new allegiances are fashioned, drawing upon notions of primary identity as criterion for membership. Prevailing concepts of kinship itself are often reworked in the process. Employment contacts, integral to organizational success in this context, can be effectively provided by cross-class kinship institutions owing to the nature of the service-based economy. When no specialized skill is involved and employment is predominantly volatile and temporary, as is common in these service economies, labor-based collective or employer solutions are not available. This skill structure also means that cross-class, cross-sector organizing makes economic sense, bringing the possibility of wide-ranging networks, unlimited by skill or know-how, furnishing employment. The solidarity that creates mutual obligations does not have to result from similar relations to work but instead from a commonly felt vulnerability shared across a wide range of employment.

Institutions from burial societies to mutual aid associations furnished welfare, but assuring cooperation is not unproblematic. While cooperation can raise the well-being of all participants, providing benefits greater than individual reliance alone, such cooperation is often difficult absent enforced legal sanctions. Collective action and free rider problems must be overcome. Well-enforced legal systems, where existing, can prevent these problems, providing clear repercussions for the nonpayment of dues or delinquency on loans. Thus, in developed countries, mutual aid associations with open membership can serve welfare purposes with legal backup.

In most of the developing world, collective economic institutions must provide their own regulation. Mutual aid identity associations offer the most effective means to secure social insurance given the absence of contract enforceability and the service character of the labor market. Distinct from mutual aid associations in developed countries, here kinship is the basis for membership. Elites lead and benefit from the organizations, but are not the driving force behind them. Members are the variable responsible for association formation, seeking to broaden their networks by pooling resources and connections. To substitute for contracts and effective legal institutions, kin associations generate mechanisms to enhance their reputation and monitor members' compliance through direct meetings and by sharing information about members. Kin institutions utilize narratives of origin and identity to create peer pressure among members so that duties will be met. The difference between these institutions is the result of divergent regulatory environments. No external enforcement is forthcoming in the Jordanian and Lebanese cases. The institutions attempt to mitigate moral hazards through peer monitoring and the affirmation of a unique, exclusive identity. Indeed, the danger of shirking and concern for it is manifest in the effort of organizations to create a unique identity, setting the group apart from the rest of society. The group then privileges members in jobs, and social and business contacts, even when members themselves complain of the prevalence of personal connections over qualifications in determining employment and business connections. The particular identity used—class, family, region, or religion—unites private-sector employees while minimizing collective-action problems. Reputation is an important source of guarantees in informal economies and indeed in segments of industrialized countries as well. Behavior, personal character, and genealogical lineage become economic assets or liabilities.

Mutual aid kin associations in Jordan and Lebanon demonstrate the confluence of identity with economic goals. Identity is a resource; in economic terms, it is a way to build enforceable, trusted networks. But it is also distinct from other resources. Identity can be superior to civil society networks in particular economic circumstances, providing networks and accountability when other affiliations cannot. Informal and flexible workforces utilize identity, tradition, and kinship idioms, transforming coworkers into "cousins" who will volunteer their work time or locate jobs for one another.[5]

Kin associations establish the personal communication necessary to build trust and reciprocity and to sanction shirkers. Regular meetings held weekly, monthly, and annually for elections provide members opportunities to see which members are paying dues. Emergency aid is collected in special meetings, when members pass the hat to help pay other members' bills. This provides witness and pressure against nonparticipation. Aside from the overt monitoring in meetings, the group is sufficiently small as to allow gossip and word of mouth to promote active participants and decry those not meeting their obligations. Some of the membership meet informally more often than the regular meetings because of their close kinship ties. Members keep tabs and pass information on favors owed or repaid. Elections in which members elect kin group leaders are another means of enforcement. Leaders are subject to approval by vote, turning on the provision of requested services and networks.

The economic use of kin associations and their tie to the economic conditions of members is demonstrated in several ways. First, the timing of the organizations corresponds to periods of hard times when state or state-like social insurance was absent. The original rise of kin associations occurred with the initial entrance of the social group into the city when informal traditional village mutual aid mechanisms were no longer operative and new conditions of uncertainty prevailed in the city. When state or state-like welfare (through militias) was provided to all classes of the social group, the associations did not form among those benefiting, and existing kin associations fell into disuse. Second, the stated rationale for forming the organizations, at the time of establishment, was economic need. Ethnographic evidence confirms this economic role. Members stated that they pushed for the organization or joined because they felt vulnerable economically. In fact, many members remain unenthusiastic or hostile to what they perceive as the negative repercussions of formal obligations to fellow kin. Still, the economic security of aid in hard times motivated them to become members or even leaders of the organizations.[6] Third, organization services are economic. Members report that the key benefits they obtain are job networks and resources. Fourth, kin definitions changed in the process of creating these associations, altering to conform to a group with resources and internal accountability. The rationale for including or excluding relatives in the operative kin definition would be unintelligible save acknowledgment of the regulatory and resource needs of institutions functioning through informal contracts and voluntary aid.

CREATING IDENTITY AND INSTITUTIONS

Various insights emerge on the expansiveness of identity, the requisites for establishing and succeeding as institutions, the substance of membership and institutional services, the varying role of elites, and the function of legacy or culture. Identity can be generated, refashioned, and resurrected from a forgotten past, but its fluidity is limited. Created kin identity expands in an iterative fashion, starting from accepted understandings of kin. It expands or contracts along the lines of a plausible story or genealogy linking people together but also separating them from the rest of society. Different families from the same hometown can unite and consider one another related, just as some families are so close, though unrelated, that they become "aunts" and "uncles." A common religion also expands the concept of kin identity, when a minority religion sets the group apart from the majority. This corresponds to Chandra and Laitin's bounded repertoire of attributes, but the cases here proved more innovative than an inherited profile of possibilities (such as language, religion, kinship, and region).[7] Geographic proximity generated new kin, either by adding them to the associations as "friends of the association" or considering them straightforward relatives. This demonstrates the role of monitoring members' conduct in choosing the basis for kinship. In many cases neighbors have more thorough knowledge of one another's behavior than close families do, and many reciprocal lending networks are based on common locale.[8]

Economic need may spur the desire for risk-mitigating institutions like mutual aid associations, but not all are able to establish the organizations.

The cases show that only those with resources to invest and redistribute were able to form and sustain the associations. Poor and rural groups, despite much need, were often unable to organize. Interviews of individuals who did not form associations but wanted to revealed that they viewed such associations as the purview of those wealthier than themselves. In uniting, they felt they could do little more than spread the poverty, that they would not be able to help one another. Poorer associations functioned little and provided few if any services. Successful associations are almost all middle-class and urban. Once the example is well established, it can possibly have second-order effects, becoming the organizing form in vogue even in labor markets unsuited to it.

Size contributes to the success of organizations but can also spell its inability to secure member compliance. Small associations, like poor ones, often have difficulty functioning and providing the numerous services members desire. When an organization is too small, networking capability is limited as is the generation of resources. Kinship thus expanded to seek more resources to redistribute, but in some cases the expanded definition of kinship yielded a group that was unwieldy. Utilizing the kinship of hometown or village of origin, some large Palestinian associations in Jordan boasted that their membership reached nearly ten thousand but also complained of members shirking their dues and not repaying loans. Even using an identity idiom to solidify unity, moral hazards still occur. Too large an association also pushes control away from the general membership, as monitoring members and leaders becomes more difficult. Aside from these extremes of unsuccessful sizes, large and small, this research yielded only a general idea of the optimal number of members, one thousand to two thousand. This number still allowed for monitoring but also expanded the association's resources and members' job connections. Notably, founding members of the associations had a sense of the number of members they desired and altered kinship accordingly. The necessity of sufficiently large amounts of resources and networks must be counterbalanced against the requisites of enforceable commitments and maintaining control over leaders.

The role of culture and legacy is important. Potential associations with middle-class members and resources fail if they cannot cobble together a large enough kin group to redistribute. Many urban families are in this situation, as tribal lineage has long been forgotten. This accident of history, not having access to a kin definition large enough to create a mutual aid association, leaves some families without this form of social insurance. Unity can be threatened by political disagreements and internal power struggles. Disputes over relative family power prevented some associations from joining families long resident in the same village, joining families of the same religion, or joining several related clans. In some cases a number of potential identity bases were tried before finding (or not) a viable kin definition for the association. One association tried to unite with only its own family, but then tried to unite all the families in the village. Both efforts proved unsuccessful. Though fictive kinship is a part of many cultures, the relative accessibility of the kinship model may vary widely. Kin groups may not be possible in regions where repertoires of kin are absent or kinship is a non-concept, although other bases of identity may be used.

Individuals create or change collective institutions in order to improve their circumstances. Cultural organizing models and identity were innovated to create this association, and thus active, purposeful involvement is required. Usually this is associated with elites, who take on the responsibility of organizing and registering the association, incurring the expenses to do so. The desire for a new institution does generate opportunities for social-climbing entrepreneurs, but the role of elites varies in these associations. Small and very large organizations afford the elite leaders more prerogatives and rely on them more for funding. Thus the contributions and participation of elites are more important when members do not have resources or connections to share. Likewise, in very large organizations, member dues (and repayment) decrease as the main funding source. Large donations become methods of demonstrating importance and social prestige; donated amounts are listed by name in annual publications of large kin associations. Large organizations afford more potential for symbolic capital or actions promoting the good works of wealthier members. The trend through time in Jordan and Lebanon has been an increase in the horizontal nature of kin associations, demonstrating a growing preference among those now establishing for member accountability and visibility of member behavior. In a number of associations surveyed, potential members would not join unless the association was formed as a cooperative, owned by the members themselves. Founding members are not necessarily elites. In a number of cases, kin associations are founded by a small group of like-minded people seeking economic security for the future. Someone has to contribute his time and energy to establish and register the association, and to inform potential members, and, as such, the associations depend on volunteer initiative.

This book also revealed a grass-roots limiting factor in the ability of elites to champion subnational identities. At the local level elites achieve both social prestige and electoral success with less effort than national involvement would entail. This desire for social prestige is separate from, but can overlap with, electoral incentives. Most associations are unconnected to electoral ambitions. In these cases the desire among elites for subnational organizing is relatively constant, but member opinions change through time. Many elites long promote the idea of a kin association but find no takers. Unless potential members feel economically vulnerable, they are not willing to contribute aid for their kin. The varying establishment and use of the associations demonstrate the hesitancy to contribute and the fundamental nature of the association as a risk-mitigating mechanism. These examples also show the role of social and market change in creating new elites, and the requirements that members demand of their leaders. Elites without employment connections mainly contribute resources to the association but do not lead.

REMAINING QUESTIONS: WELFARE AND ECONOMIC RISK AS CAUSE

A general economic crisis, in the form of the end of state social policies, was necessary for individuals to be willing to participate in re-worked, collective kin institutions in large numbers. The feeling of economic need clearly motivated the formation of mutual aid associations. Common risks and the existence of resources to solve those risks were necessary for economic pooling. The lack of social welfare is an instance of hard times and economic vulnerability, variables that have been tied to social change, institutional creation, demands for new institutions, and the rise of trust networks.[9]

The analytical focus on welfare institutions highlights specific local constraints on collective organizing, different labor markets, state and market capacities, and the diverse effects of economic reforms. These constraints yield organizations that can differ sharply from those posited in theory derived from the Western, industrialized experience. Private-sector accommodations for social welfare also become relevant with the increasing differentiation in forms of work and ideological change in the state's role. States are encouraged to privatize even social provisioning functions, alongside the spread of diverse and irregular forms of work. The differing labor markets exhibited here—service-sector, informal, and irregular work—characterize a larger portion of labor, particularly in developing countries. The deindustrialization of the labor market in the advanced states can increase risk even apart from welfare withdrawal.[10]

International integration has been accompanied by a normative shift in state duties. Nations around the world are altering the boundaries between households and the state, explicitly calling upon the private sector, including families, to shoulder duties previously held by the state.[11] Though clearly not disappearing, some ask if the state's shrinking borders translate into the "uncaging" of society, unraveling the prior unification of society that occurred under a national welfare system and capitalist economy.[12]

The basic dynamic of seeking social insurance, in light of the existing local potential and constraints for social welfare, is a generalizable analytical window into changing societal organizing. At the local level, the character of economic networks and local provisioning are important. The forms of this search may differ because of varying cultural and organizing models. The institutional requirements of monitoring in mutual aid associations remain, but the specific form of the identity can alter. The nature of services provided by kin associations and the member profile are linked to the local context of what is not provided alternatively and who is left out of social insurance. These factors can vary, along with the idiom of solidarity, by labor market and cultural context.

Although social welfare is a popular concern with broad explanatory power, motivating bread riots and concepts of citizenship alike, the precise components of social insurance that cause organizing remain to be specified.[13] Several important research questions were beyond the scope of this book. First, what degree of economic risk or vulnerability spur popular action? What is the relative influence of subsidies on necessities, such as bread, and pensions on the saliency of economic vulnerability? Second, to what extent are feelings of insecurity tied to perception or expectation? The perception of risk may differ from objective declines in status, and both may not equally cause popular organizing. Announced cuts in welfare may have a stronger effect than economic downturns that are not perceived or publicized. A third question is the relative influence of regime type and specific types of welfare on organizing forms. As shown in this volume, the difference in regime types—one a monarchy and the other a limited democracy, did not produce different social organizing outcomes in mutual aid associations. This could be a result of the relatively similar organizing purposes of these regime types, as differentiated from socialist regimes, for example. Alternatively, economic factors could outweigh the influence of regime type.

CIVIL SOCIETY AND POLITICAL IMPLICATIONS
OF KIN WELFARE INSTITUTIONS

Whether kin associations are considered civil society or not, their effect on the realm of civil and political society is profound. At the extreme, kin associations substitute for state provisioning; they assume responsibility for that which social movements and political parties typically demand from the state. At a minimum, in states barely consolidated, the space of politics shifts. The associations alter the relationship between members and the state, including the control that associations have over members' behavior. They create or reinforce subnational identity organizing, with the potential to internalize identities in conflict with budding national unity.[14] Further, the prospects for effective demands on the state could diminish. As demonstrated by collective action analyses, democratization studies, and the social movement literature, unity and numbers are important factors in society's ability to pressure the state.[15] These findings engage debates on the advocacy of civil society as a social service provider and its link to political organizing.

Civil society has been much lauded, particularly in its role in aiding democracy. Social capital, civil society, associations, networks, and trust have been incorporated into the policy agendas of international organizations as the potential savior of developing economies, a fix-all for social ills, the source of good governance, and the prevention of ethnic conflict. The centrality of civil society and social capital to democracy and development coincided neatly with the neoliberal promotion of charity, private initiative, and the removal of the state from social provisioning.[16] Indeed, national-level organizing has been identified as a variable crucial not only for democratization but also for the generation of subnational antagonisms.[17] Essentially civil society is the idea that intermediary organizations (between state and citizen) can act as a buffer against state power and authoritarianism. By mobilizing across class and identity distinctions, moreover, civil society can lessen violence and intolerance, and create trust and expectations for government responsiveness and efficiency. Intercommunal ties, cutting across subnational groups, can forestall violence.[18] These organizations train democrats with political skills and values, bringing society into development and social planning. But recent studies have qualified the celebration of local civil society, calling attention to potential adverse effects that vary according to the form of societal organizing and the political context.[19]

No consensus exists, either in local society or academic writing, on family associations as civil society organizations.[20] Though not the tribal institutions of old, they are also not based on civic bonds with open memberships; increasingly they are becoming legitimized as civil society organizations. Many of the associations surveyed expressed disapproval of this organizing form but declared that it was the only way to provide some measure of social security. Still, the associations clearly constitute a large portion of society, and are nongovernmental, private, voluntary organizations or cooperatives. NGOs are also increasingly seen as a solution for developmental problems,[21] particularly for the international community.[22] The establishment of NGOs is encouraged financially by leading international institutions and promoted by state governments.[23] Advocates praise nongovernmental and voluntary organizations as more efficient, less expensive, and more humane than state-run services.[24] Both the political Right and Left support NGOs, the former to rid government of fiscal burdens and the latter as a solution to state-level corruption and nepotism.[25] NGOs are now charged mainly with providing services that were formerly in the realm of the state. Yet little theoretical analysis has been extended to this form of civil society. Indeed, NGOs may merely be new forms of patronage.[26] Personal contacts are not absent and may be even more crucial. Though presumed to free individuals from primordial ties,[27] in reality nongovernmental organizations often build upon hierarchies and established community divisions.

Fisher, for example, maintains that 22 civil society organizations per million persons is correlated with the presence of a high-scoring democracy.[28] Although her framework is debatable, the figure demonstrates what is considered to be a significant density of associations. The corresponding number for family associations in Jordan is 150 per million persons, and more than double that number in Lebanon (333 per million persons). In other terms, there is one kin association for every 6,800 persons in Jordan and every 3,000 in Lebanon. The relationship of the associations to the state is critical; the sheer number of NGOs is not by itself an appropriate measure of civil society's strength, and may in certain circumstances indicate the weakness of civil society in contests with the state, as high density can indicate fragmentation.[29]

Both the centrality of the state as object of civil society and the potential effect of organizations on the unity of society is questionable in developing contexts. Researchers on the Middle East and NGO analysts have argued that emerging local methods of participation may actually aid the perpetuation of the authoritarian regimes by continuing the politics of patronage and channeling social movement energies into charitable and nonconfrontational activities.[30] Mutual aid associations can affect national participation by orienting key demands away from the state, furthering the trend of independent, nonparty candidates in elections, and fractionalizing the populace by identity, hindering unified movements. As an organizing form, mutual aid associations in themselves do not create these effects; these outcomes arise, instead, from a particular form of mutual aid organizing, one that uses the idiom of identity and kinship.

Kin mutual aid associations, as noted, alter the substance and space of politics. The state may not disappear or decrease in overall importance; however, the priority of state institutions is diminished in the lives of many of its citizens, as other actors and levels of interest aggregation begin to take center stage. While they do not remove members from interaction with the state as informal squatters seek to do, their relationship to the state is peripheral. Demands for redistribution have often been at the heart of democratic politics and social movements for representation aimed at the state. The de facto locus of politics shifts to locale and identity, denuding the national arena of political relevance. The new public space in liberalization is one of identity and local municipality. Forums such as village and family associations now contain the majority of debate and discussion, trumping the national-level arena. Mutual aid associations generally surpass national politics in their democratic procedures, but the relationship of the organizations to the state is one of subservience or marginality. Thus even organizations that are relatively democratic internally may have no relation to the state or ability to pressure it.

Though these organizations may train citizens for democracy, the continued authoritarian structure of the state is maintained and even strengthened. The organizations integrate members into subnational institutions at odds with one another. By providing new services previously furnished by the state, mutual aid associations create a separate source of legitimacy. In social provisioning and ideological identity, kin associations behave like mini-states and like tribes, monopolizing the allegiances of members. Stories of particular identity make membership in these organizations seem primary, superseding all other affiliations. In this situation national politics is increasingly devoid of meaning, and contenders are reduced to small, mutually exclusive subnational blocs in competition for services. As Levi argued for civil society groups, trust created within the group does not translate into trust outside the group, but can instead generate overwhelming conflicts of interests among groups.[31] This is even more valid where organizations' interests are mutually exclusive or at least have no common interests.

For a country only beginning to solidify a national identity, nascent unity can easily fall prey to new or reworked subnational divisions, now given added economic weight. This can lead to subnational allegiances with state-like strength, particularly in weak and failing states as new welfare-providing institutions channel individual identity through kin in exchange for access to fundamental economic goods. Mutual aid kin associations, according to social movement theorists, provide the institutional "free space" that helps create counter-hegemonic and alternative identities.[32] This is particularly true when the networks promote a vision of society and politics distinct from that of the state.[33] In other contexts in the Arab world, scholars debate whether the emerging civil society will be strong enough to resist the state's encroachment. Zubaida states that the new civil society is not so much against the state as outside it and irrelevant to it.[34] Whereas Christian Base Communities in Latin America have attempted to carve out a sphere of autonomous local development, kin associations accede to national development projects without contestation.

New collective welfare institutions affect the groups that interact with national politics, marginalizing some while enhancing the prominence of others. Kin associations curtail political involvement outside the group, further marginalizing the relevance of the state. Using the idiom of kinship for solidarity, mutual aid organizations remove members and leaders from national politics since such affiliations threaten group unity. Aid to members is prioritized as the association focuses inward, renewing, creating, or solidifying subnational identity groups. Members of these organizations either withdraw from national politics or lend their support to independent candidates, typically the organization's president. The organizations thwart national collective action that is central to making effective demands and are further discredited by their ideological similarity to the state. The nature of party politics in the Arab world prevents these subnational groups, which prioritize their own members' needs over national idioms, from participating in broader party coalitions.

Political affiliations present the greatest threat to group unity, and this has far-reaching implications. Because competition among potential leaders has frequently led to the demise of kin associations, political affiliations are subordinated to kin interests. The restricted advocacy of political causes by members of kin associations and the politics of group identity in elections lead to important practical outcomes. The associations interact with a political arena dominated by weak parties and thus further the tendency to elect independent, nonparty candidates in favor of maintaining the solidarity forming the basis for informal commitments in kin associations. These effects could be expected to increase if decentralization becomes significant in these countries.

Kin associations impact the personal lives of members from their behavior to the provision of services. The presence of kin associations does not indicate that the populace has welfare coverage. Services are spotty, unreliable, and unpredictable. Despite their rosy ambitions, kin associations are often unable to provide the services they advertise. The ability of associations to undertake the services foisted on them varies greatly. Funding is meager and the organizations are overstretched.[35] Yet the associations appear to be addressing the problem, filling a vacuum. Despite the incomplete nature of the services, the lack of state provisioning heightens the social importance of kin associations to members' daily lives.

In direct opposition to cultural arguments, many members highlighted their opposition to the association for ideological and personal reasons but calculated that the financial benefits they reaped took precedence. Numerous members mentioned the drawbacks of the association, and many believed kin organizing to be a backward step. After they joined there were negative repercussions: some were dragged into issues of revenge or family feuds or had to vote for specific candidates. The organizations reinforce existing patterns of nepotism and the lack of meritocracy. Institutions of cooperation do not mean that power is absent within the association or that all members benefit equally.[36] Traditional hierarchies and norms can be solidified, discriminating against those who go against the standards of the group. Women are usually not included in the decision making of the organization, although the trend is to include them in voting. Regular monthly meetings continue to be considered a male affair. Joseph demonstrates how kin idioms affect ideas of individual rights.[37] Indeed, while family and tradition are often idealized, kin mechanisms of protection come with a price.[38] Behavioral constraints can accompany the granting of loans and financial help.[39] Kin association leaders are able to control members' actions, for they can threaten to deny benefits or even to expel members from the association. As kin associations take over more realms—operating nurseries and schools, running reception halls, and holding job-training classes—an association leader's ability to maneuver members by granting or withholding favors increases. Male family members have replaced the state administration as the welfare patron to which members are the dependent clients. Increasing the male's power and prerogative in the family is probably not considered by some segments of the populace as the development of a democratic civil society.

Regimes could embrace the finding that kin associations do not assist in political party organizing but rather in de-liberalization, and then advocate kinship for this purpose. Regimes are quietly solidified and politics rearranged as kin associations are transformed into nodes of decentralized authority. Local and family leaders are placated with power over decision making within the association and a higher social profile. Fragmented and opposing families battle over the spoils of a shrinking labor market. Indeed, they were initially encouraged by the Jordanian regime and Lebanese government, but victory calls of stability and social quiescence through de-liberalization are premature. Moving the site of economic grievances from the state to kin associations could ultimately pervert and radicalize popular demands.

Along with innovative forms of organizing come new potential scenarios of conflict. At the extreme, subnational divisions and identities are created or given added strength through these associations, which can furnish new lines of conflict or lend weight to existing ones, resulting in national destabilization. Under normal political circumstances, anti-state kin blocs may not arise; however, in political crises, these subnational institutions can rapidly mobilize.[40] As the Lebanese case shows, the development of subnational ascriptive groups with power over welfare can prefigure increased social fragmentation. Kin associations in Lebanon were incorporated wholesale into militias, furnishing thousands of foot soldiers. Kin associations effectively served as the building blocks for militias in the civil war. As militias took over the duties of kin associations, in their bid to replace the state, the associations became irrelevant, a trade-off that demonstrates the potential of the state–kin association relationship. Clans in Gaza also reveal the potential violence of identity organizing.[41]

The character of societal organizing sets the scene for political conflicts and the country's future. This book demonstrated that the institutions that come to govern market interactions may be less attributable to culture, as some have posited, than to regulatory, resource, and legal conditions.[42] Further research into the connection between welfare and social organizing could prove fruitful in illuminating differential institutional and national trajectories. The effect of changes in alternative economic options and the use of kin identity organizations only in hard times, absent alternative social insurance, tells us that these associations are neither natural, inevitable, nor preferred. This insight has long-term implications for the persistence of identity politics in the Middle East, a politics viewed as inhibiting state building, state capacity, political party development, demands for representation, and domestic nationalism. These institutional outcomes are not necessarily the most efficient ones, but they reflect the circumstances and historical accident of the institution's birth. These characteristics endure, often enshrining the suboptimal. Because the key causal ingredient is social insurance, policy options exist if subnational identity organizations are not desired. The political dynamics of the Middle East will remain unintelligible without an appreciation of the incentives for new welfare institutions that alter social identifications and participation in the state.

APPENDIX 1.

Research Method and Data

As others have encountered, doing fieldwork in the Middle East is often challenging.[1] Many topics are considered political even if the politics are not apparent to analysts. My research had to contend with authorities' opinion that kin associations were a sensitive political area combined with a dearth of formal census data. Lebanon is particularly lacking in current and comparable data. I overcame these hurdles by locating the information through alternative means. Specifically I conducted open interviews, questionnaires with open questions, interviews of government officials, academic observers, and participants and nonparticipants in kin associations (see the questionnaires in Appendix 2). I gathered data and publications from government and nongovernmental organizations, including the official gazette and unpublished records from government supervising agencies. I supplemented this with secondary data. I used primary and secondary economic data, including interviews in the industrial and free trade zones. Some evidence of the difficulties in obtaining consistent data is apparent in the differential sources used for a few elements of the case data.

Research for this book took place in two waves of fieldwork. First I concentrated on Jordan for my dissertation, with some research interviews in Syria and Lebanon for comparison. Research in Jordan took place from 1998–2000, with follow-up trips in 2004 and 2005. My research design was geared toward gathering information at the micro level. I attempted to account for differential motivations at various points in time, namely, the founding or joining of the kin association versus the time of the interview, in order not to read back from the present the motivations of the past. To do this I utilized multiple questions and overlapping data, obtaining registration statistics from state agencies and from the official gazette, for example, and checking services provided by associations with those listed in the files of the state agency. Interviews were conducted in Arabic and were open-ended. Coding of the data took place after all the interviews were conducted. Questionnaires left space for comments and statements of the interviewee, and comments outside the questions were solicited. Research was completed with the help of several researchers in Lebanon, one Palestinian for the Palestinian associations in Lebanon, and one researcher for Jordan, owing to suspicions and logistical difficulties. Researchers were referred by local social scientists. Interviewees' reactions varied from gratitude for asking their opinion, the dominant response, to suspicion regarding the motivation of the questionnaire. I omitted names of interviewees and associations not wishing to be identified. Formal interviews were supplemented by dozens of informal statements to the author during my numerous visits to Jordan and Lebanon.

I used purposive sampling with randomization within the rough quota set for number of interviews per social group and time period. In other words, within the overall number of associations and individuals to be interviewed, I set the sample size of target subject populations and time periods to assure representation from all important social groups and time periods. This was theoretically driven to examine alternative explanations. Snowball sampling would produce an overrepresentation of accessible associations in the cities as well as long-established and successful associations. I attempted to counteract this by setting goals for the numbers of the different social groups, locations, and times of association formation. For Jordan, I wanted almost equal numbers of associations formed before and after economic reforms in order to examine differences in motivation, services, membership, and leadership across time. Within those two time categories I attempted to interview rural and urban organizations in equal proportions to their overall representation in the Amman governorate. Thus I aimed for two-thirds urban associations. Rural associations were often hard to interview because of suspicions and the inability to get in touch with someone from the association. In Lebanon I set goals for the number of associations from the different sects, roughly following their proportion of total associations, and an equal number formed before and after the civil war. The associations within each category of study were then chosen given the researchers' knowledge of organizations and drawing from a list of associations.

In Jordan the data set includes detailed information on 228 associations, 105 charities, and 123 cooperatives. Associations were selected from a master list obtained from the Cooperative Corporation, in charge of cooperatives, and the General Union of Voluntary Societies (GUVS), the national supervising agency for charities. Officials and registration files provided information on the nature of the association (often not apparent by the name), names of members, services, funding and budget data, and additional detailed information. The Jordanian questionnaire data set included sixty-two associations, split about evenly between older associations and those established in the 1990s. The bulk of associations interviewed were taken from a list along with a few through references or snowball sampling, and were drawn from the greater Amman area, urban and rural.[2] Interviews took place with staff or officials in positions to possess the requisite information, usually the president of the association or the on-site director. In all, 114 interviews were conducted with members and staff of the associations. The majority of member interviews were with members from one association. Most member interviews took place from February to April 2000; most questionnaires and association interviews took place during a broader period, from the fall of 1999 to the summer of 2000. The size of the data sets differs by question, since not every association answered all questions. I was able to obtain detailed information on many, particularly the charities. In the case of cooperatives, my determination of which multipurpose cooperatives were kin was conservative: in cases of doubt, they were not counted. Cooperatives from 2000–2003 are not included because I was unable to obtain data from the Cooperative Corporation.

Research in Lebanon was more difficult. The supervising agency in charge of kin association registration, a section of the Ministry of the Interior, was not forthcoming. Nor are the data published officially in any compiled form. I encountered numerous difficulties, even after the Syrian withdrawal in 2005, in obtaining information that is publicly available but disparately located. Instead, I created a master list of associations from the Official Gazette for the years 1980 through 2005. The Lebanese member questionnaire included 88 kin associations; 26 were Christian, 19 Sunni; 15 Palestinian, 8 Shi'a, 7 Druze, and three of mixed sect. Eight non-kin associations, fishing and economic cooperatives, were also included. The associations were split; that is, about half were formed before the end of the war. Of individuals, 109 were interviewed, including 18 Christians, 15 Palestinians, 8 Shi'a, 16 Sunnis, 9 Druze, and 3 of multiple sects. Thirteen, about one-fifth of the sample, were members of associations formed before the end of the war. Forty Lebanese and Palestinians who were not members of kin associations were interviewed, including oversampling from the Shi'a community to examine their lack of kin associations.

Association formation often did not coincide with the year of registration; in fact, the notice of some was published years later. This occurred not only during the hectic war period, as expected, but in the past few years as well. I utilized dates of formation or, lacking that, dates of registration, and not the date of its publication in the official gazette. Not one of the associations in the official gazette after the war was a registered association seeking to renew its permit.[3] Old associations only entered the gazette when they altered their level of membership and name, expanding or becoming more precise concerning the village or section of the family they included. I supplemented this data with an unpublished report from the Social Development Ministry from 2002 and my own interviews with think tanks and academics. Two main studies on kin associations were published for the period prior, which I used for the pre-civil-war era. I also obtained an internal collaborative document written by officials from several Lebanese ministries detailing the associations and their activities.

The numbers used in this study most likely underestimate the kin association phenomenon in Lebanon and Jordan due to data gathering problems. My list of associations in Lebanon, compiled from the official gazette, undoubtedly omitted some. Many family and village associations do not carry the name of the family or village. Kin associations can utilize the name of the village in order to exclude family in other locations, and both types of organization often have general names that do not reveal their real membership, as in the Jordan case, such as "The Charitable Association for Development," "The Association of Righteousness and Charity," or "The Association for the Protection of Morality."[4] Where possible those with nondescript names were identified, but many probably escaped my count. Other associations do not register. During the war, one estimate was that 40 percent of associations abstained from announcing their presence officially.[5] After the war this percentage decreased. Another study maintained that 20 percent worked without official permission in the late 1990s.[6]

APPENDIX 2.

Interview Questionnaires

M y research process combined a formal questionnaire with standardized, open-ended questions, incorporated into the questionnaire and separate from it. The researchers and I wrote all comments by the interviewees and allowed them to express their opinions freely. Numerous and disparate comments were obtained as a result of this process. For Lebanon, research assistants were asked to note the sect, nationality, and status of the organization during the civil war, and also to ask for this information in discussions with the interviewees. A Palestinian researcher completed the questionnaires on Palestinian mutual aid associations.

The questionnaires begin with bullet points introducing the person conducting the study, explaining the research—its educational and fact-finding purposes—and providing several examples of kin associations. Examples were particularly helpful in Jordan, as multiple terms for the associations exist.

The questionnaires below are, respectively, those for the kin associations in Jordan and Lebanon, and for individuals, both members and nonmembers, in Jordan and Lebanon.

Unless otherwise noted, all questions were open-ended. Researchers were told to inform the interviewees that providing their names was optional, and this is also written in the introduction to the questionnaire. Items in brackets are explanatory clarifications for readers and do not appear in the questionnaire itself.

1. Name of the association
   • Address; phone
2. Type of organization: [choice of] association; cooperative; rabita; family; diwan; charity
3. In what government office is the organization registered?
4. The association is made up of: village; family

5. What is the city of origin?

6. What are the families or villages belonging to this association?

7. Who were the idea people founding the association and their professions? [names optional]

8. Number founding the organization
   • Year of founding
   • Reason for founding

9. Number of general membership
   • Number members voting in association elections for the administrative board in the most recent elections

10. Amount of dues
    • Approximate association's budget

11. Who pays dues? [choice of] adult males; adult males and females; head of household; other (specify)

12. When do the members meet?
    • Who attends meetings? (for example, men, women, heads of family, etc.)

13. Does the association receive financial aid from any governmental or nongovernmental organization?
    • Funding organization; Project funded [space to list under each]

14. What are the association's services or programs? (for example, loans, emergency aid, job help, etc.)

15. Have these services or programs changed in the past 10 years? [choice of] yes; no
    • What are these changes?

16. What assets does the association have? (for example, buildings, real estate, land, businesses, etc.)

17. How does the association spend its profit?

18. If the association participates in governmental elections, what candidates did it support for parliamentary elections in the past? [Jordan: space for candidate next to dates of recent elections—1989, 1993, 1997; for Lebanon, question includes municipal elections and space is left to fill in year and candidate]

19. Who are the members of the association's administrative board and their professions? [names optional]
    Name (not necessary)
    • Date of interview
    • Role in the association
    Comments or observations

[For Lebanon: researchers were to note the sect and nationality of the association, and its fate during the civil war.]

Individuals were asked the following:

   1. Current profession
   • How did you get your job?
   • Any previous profession or job?
   2. Educational background
   3. Do you do have a job in addition to your primary job? [choice of] yes; no
   • What is that job?
   4. Steady monthly family income:
   • [for Jordan, choice of:] less than 150 dinars; 151–300 dinars; 301–500 dinars; 501–700 dinars; over 700 dinars.
   • [for Lebanon, choice of:] less than 200 USD; 200–500 USD; 500–1000 USD; 1000–1500 USD; over 1500 USD.
   5. Any irregular sources of income to the family? (for example, aid from children or family, saving from a previous job, etc.—specify)
   6. City of origin
   [For Jordan] Are you or a member of your family among those returning from Kuwait during the [1990–91] Gulf War? [choice of] yes; no
   7. Kin associations that you belong to or have belonged to
   • Date of joining; date left; reason for joining (was membership voluntary or not?)
   8. When was the last time you attended the kin association or used its services?
   • [choice of:] this month; last 3 months; last 6 months; last year; over a year
   9. Programs or services the kin association provides that you or your family benefited from:
   10. What are the benefits you obtained through the association?
   [For Lebanon] Have you received aid from a nongovernmental organization? What was it?
   11. Professional association or union memberships now or in the past:
   • [space to list] dates of joining; date left the organization; reason for joining

12. When was the last time you attended the professional association or union?
- [choice of:] this month; last 3 months; last 6 months; last year; over a year

13. What benefits did you obtain through the professional association or union membership?

Name (optional)
- Date

Comments and observations

[For Lebanon, researchers note the sect and nationality of interviewee.]

NOTES

INTRODUCTION

1. "Kinship" refers to attachments stemming from belief in a single genealogical origin and can also consist of descent from a common village of origin. In the Arab world, as in many other regions, the latter is considered a type of kinship (*quraba*). For an in-depth discussion of the various forms of kinship, see chapters 4 and 5. I examine identity institutions, not felt identity, avoiding the numerous difficulties of analyzing identity itself. Identity, as used in this book, is collective, not individual. It is based in relationships, not the individual's concept of self, and is utilized for action. See Polletta and Jasper, "Collective Identity and Social Movements," 285; and Melucci, "The Process of Collective Identity." On social identity, see Korostelina, *Social Identity and Conflict,* chap. 1.

2. "Middle class" is used here as an income category, with sufficient resources to invest but not to be financially independent. The term can be defined by its (Marxist) relation to the means of production or (Weberian) life-chances corresponding to its position in the market, social status, and income. See Wright, *Class Counts,* 28. The two definitions coincide in the middle classes that neither own the means of production nor work in them. Instead, the middle classes often occupy a professional, educated, and skilled stratum of semi-autonomous employees, earning in the middle of the income distribution. I include self-employed professionals and small retail owners in this category, as they share that class's social networks and economic outlooks.

3. Ghabra, *Palestinians in Kuwait,* 122.

4. A classic example and similar dynamic is Weber's analysis of American Protestant sects. Membership increased credit and business worthiness by serving as a guarantee of upstanding behavior. See Weber, "The Protestant Sects and the Spirit of Capitalism."

5. Maclean, "State Social Policies and Social Support Networks."

6. International Crisis Group, "Inside Gaza"; on Lebanon, see chap. 2.

7. Magnet, "Introduction"; Willetts, *"The Conscience of the World."*

8. Edwards and Hulme, "Introduction: NGO Performance and Accountability."

9. Some NGOs promote business and are used by the middle class,

but these are few and specific to business. See chapter 4 for an overview of charities.

10. Clark, *Islam, Charity, and Activism.*

11. Goldstein, Janvry, and Sadoulet, "Is a Friend in Need a Friend Indeed?"

12. Clunan and Trinkunas, "Conceptualizing 'Ungoverned Spaces,'" forthcoming.

13. See examples in Ismail, *Political Life in Cairo's New Quarters;* and Bayat, "Un-civil Society."

14. "Institutions are the prescriptions that humans use to organize all forms of repetitive and structured interactions including those within families, neighborhoods, markets, firms, sports leagues, churches, private associations, and governments at all scales" (Ostrom, *Understanding Institutional Diversity,* 3).

15. The numbers of associations here are conservative, limited to those verified as kin associations. Figures are only those of new, not renewing, licenses. Although many do not register and some fail after registering, the trend is clear and supported by officials working with or overseeing this organizational sector. Hometown or village associations are not agricultural organizations or cooperatives, which are listed separately.

16. Center for Strategic Studies, "Istitlaa' lil-ra'i hawla al-dimuqratiyya fil-Urdun 1996 [Opinion Survey on Democracy in Jordan 1996]," 18.

17. Shteiwi, "al-Niqabat al-mihaniyya ka-juz' min al-mujtam' al-madani [Professional associations as a part of civil society]," 217.

18. Khalaf, *Lebanon's Predicament,* 171, 73–74, al-Husseini, Muhi al-Deen, and al-Haraka, "Dirasat mash minathamat al-qita' al-ahli fi Lubnan [Study of civil society organizations in Lebanon]," unpublished ms.

19. Lebanese Center for Policy Studies, "The Civil Society Report 1997."

20. Estimates are that the Shi'a represent between 34 and 41 percent of Lebanese. Since 1932 no official census has been taken because of its political sensitivity, which found Christians the majority. Birth rates among Christians are lowest in the country, and are highest among Muslims, Shi'a in particular (Prados, "Lebanon," 3). The Library of Congress uses the higher number (*Lebanon Country Study*).

21. Khuri, *From Village to Suburb: Order and Change in Greater Beirut* (Chicago: University of Chicago Press, 1975).

22. Harik, *The Public and Social Services of the Lebanese Militias.*

23. Lebanese Center for Policy Studies, "The Civil Society Report 1997."

24. Shryock, "Bedouin in Suburbia,"

25. Thelen, *How Institutions Evolve.*

26. Van Evera, "Primordialism Lives!"; Horowitz, *Ethnic Groups in Conflict.*

27. Picard, "Les habits neufs du communautarisme libanais."

28. Khalaf, *Civil and Uncivil Violence in Lebanon,* 264; Joseph, "Civic Myths, Citizenship, and Gender in Lebanon," 120.

29. Snider, "The Lebanese Forces," 5.

30. Shryock, *Nationalism and the Genealogical Imagination;* Brand, "Palestinians and Jordanians"; Abu-Odeh, *Jordanians, Palestinians, and the Hashemite Kingdom in the Middle East Peace Process.*

31. My interviews and questionnaire; Hanssen-Bauer, Pedersen, and Tiltnes, *Jordanian Society,* 302, 305; Chatelard and al-'Omari, "Primordial Ties and Beyond."

32. Swidler, "Culture in Action"; Tilly, *Popular Contention in Great Britain, 1758–1834.*

33. A number of held or possible identities can be politicized. Cleavages of family, nation, region, religion, ethnic background, or origin are some potential lines of identification.

34. Posner, *Institutions and Ethnic Politics in Africa.*

35. Chandra, *Why Ethnic Parties Succeed.*

36. Wilkinson, *Votes and Violence.*

37. Snyder, *From Voting to Violence.*

38. Cachafeiro, *Ethnicity and Nationalism in Italian Politics.*

39. Piattoni, "Clientelism in Historical and Comparative Perspective," 4.

40. Chaudhry, *The Price of Wealth;* Öniş, "The Logic of the Developmental State (Review Article)"; Berry, *Fathers Work for Their Sons.*

41. Schatz, *Modern Clan Politics.*

42. Rubin, "Russian Hegemony and the State Breakdown in the Periphery."

43. Yashar, *Contesting Citizenship in Latin America.*

44. Bates, "Modernization, Ethnic Competition, and the Rationality of Politics in Contemporary Africa."

45. Berry, *Fathers Work for Their Sons.*

46. Roy, "État et recompositions identitaires: l'exemple du Tadjikistan"; idem, "Patronage and Solidarity Groups."

47. Ferrera, *The Boundaries of Welfare.*

48. Steinmo, Thelen, and Longstreth, *Structuring Politics;* Katzenstein, *Small States in World Markets.*

49. Laitin, *Hegemony and Culture.*

50. Makdisi, *The Culture of Sectarianism.*

51. Chaudhry, *The Price of Wealth.*

52. Waterbury, *The Egypt of Nasser and Sadat;* Beinin and Stork, "On the Modernity, Historical Specificity, and International Context of Political Islam."

53. DiMaggio and Powell, "The Iron Cage Revisited."

54. Ghulum, "Ta'theer al-diwaniyyat 'ala 'amaliyya al-masharika al-siyasiyya fi al-Kuwait [Influence of diwan-s on the process of political participation in Kuwait]"; Dazi-Heni, "Hospitalité et politique."

55. Collins, "The Logic of Clan Politics."

56. Khoury and Kostiner, *Tribes and State Formation in the Middle East.*

57. Brand, "Palestinians and Jordanians"; Abu-Odeh, *Jordanians,*

Palestinians, and the Hashemite Kingdom; Sayigh, "Jordan in the 1980s: legiti-macy, entity and identity," in *Politics and the Economy in Jordan;* Boulby, *The Muslim Brotherhood and the Kings of Jordan;* Wiktorowicz, *The Management of Islamic Activism.*

58. Massad, *Colonial Effects.*

59. Shryock, *Nationalism and the Genealogical Imagination;* Layne, "'Tribalism.'"

60. Whitmeyer, "Prestige from the Provision of Collective Goods."

61. Roeder, "Liberalization and Ethnic Entrepreneurs in the Soviet Succes-sor States."

62. Laitin, "Marginality: A Microperspective," *Rationality and Society* 7, no. 1 (1995). See also the example in Erder, "Where Do You Hail From?"

63. Laitin, *Identity in Formation,* 11, 30.

64. Laitin, "Marginality"; idem, *Identity in Formation.*

65. Fearon and Laitin, "Violence and the Social Construction of Ethnic Identity."

66. Gereffi, Korzeniewicz, and Korzeniewicz, "Introduction: Global Com-modity Chains"; Denoeux, *Urban Unrest in the Middle East;* Ong, *Flexible Citizenship.*

67. Alarcon, "Mexican Hometown Associations"; Pierre-Louis, "The Limits of the State in Promoting Hometown Associations."

68. Jenkins, "Introduction: Immigration, Ethnic Associations, and Social Services."

69. Pierre-Louis, "The Limits of the State in Promoting Hometown Associations."

70. Erder, "Where Do You Hail From?"; Pratten and Baldo, "'Return to the Roots.'"

71. Biggart, "Banking on Each Other."

72. Hirsch, *Urban Revolt.*

73. Jenkins, "Introduction," 75.

74. Glenn, "Understanding Mutual Benefit Societies, 1860–1960 (Review Essay)," 638–39.

75. Ensminger, *Making a Market.*

76. Maclean, "Empire of the Young."

77. White, *Money Makes Us Relatives.*

78. Mingione, "Life Strategies and Social Economies in the Postford-ist Age"; Sabel, "Flexible Specialisation and the Re-emergence of Regional Economies."

79. Arlacchi, "The Mafioso"; Mingione, "Life Strategies and Social Economies."

80. Jabar, "Sheikhs and Ideologues," 94.

81. Migrants have organized through interest and class-based parties, as witnessed with the returned migrants to Jordan from the First Gulf War. On

interest and class organizing in other time periods here, see Anderson, *Nationalist Voices in Jordan;* idem, "The History of the Jordanian National Movement"; and Khuri, *From Village to Suburb.*

82. Social insurance, social provisioning, or social welfare is the system of programs, institutions, and policies that provide aid to vulnerable classes, benefits reducing household expenditures, and collective insurance. State welfare policies utilize national-level government institutions to modify the effect of market forces. Social welfare includes insurance that is pooled and redistributive, and aid for those who did not contribute (Nasr, "Issues of Social Protection in the Arab Region," 33–34). Systems of social protection can extend well beyond poverty prevention into public services such as health care, worker protection, and wage determinations.

83. Mares, "Social Protection around the World."

84. World Bank, *Unlocking the Employment Potential in the Middle East and North Africa;* Middle East and North Africa Region World Bank, *Reducing Vulnerability and Increasing Opportunity;* Nasr, "Issues of Social Protection in the Arab Region."

85. Doriad, "Human Development and Poverty in the Arab States."

86. Timothy, "Nonmarket Institutions for Credit and Risk Sharing in Low-Income Countries," 115.

87. Goldstein, De Janvry, and Sadoulet, "Is a Friend in Need a Friend Indeed?"; De Weerdt, "Risk-Sharing and Endogenous Network Formation"; Case, "Symposium on Consumption Smoothing in Developing Countries."

88. Rudra, "Globalization and the Decline of the Welfare State in Less-Developed Countries"; Kirby, "Theorising Globalisation's Social Impact."

89. Glenn, "Understanding Mutual Benefit Societies," 645.

90. Kuran, "Ethnic Norms and Their Transformation through Reputational Cascades."

91. On mechanisms, see Chandra, "Mechanisms vs. Outcomes."

92. Anderson, *Nationalist Voices in Jordan;* Petran, *The Struggle over Lebanon,* chap. 9.

93. Nasr, "Issues of Social Protection in the Arab Region," 40.

94. Brumberg, "Authoritarian Legacies and Reform Strategies in the Arab World," 253.

95. Toufic K. Gaspard, *A Political Economy of Lebanon,* 69; World Bank, *Unlocking the Employment Potential,* 103.

96. World Bank, *Unlocking the Employment Potential,* 62.

97. Brand, "'In the Beginning was the State . . .'"; Massad, *Colonial Effects.*

98. Nasr, "The New Social Map," 145.

99. The methodology was informed chiefly by the following perspectives: Brady and Collier, *Rethinking Social Inquiry;* Adcock and Collier, "Measurement Validity"; Collier, "The Comparative Method"; Collier, "Data, Field Work, and Extracting New Ideas at Close Range"; Bourdieu, "Social Space

and Symbolic Power"; Burawoy, "The Extended Case Method"; and Hall, "Beyond the Comparative Method," 4.

I. WELFARE, WORK, AND COLLECTIVE ACTION

1. This should not be taken as an endorsement of the application of economic institutionalism to explain history itself, but only its ability to understand institutional creation and sustenance. I agree, with Toye, that economic institutionalism is a useful micro-level theory, addressing the reality of self-interested behavior, but it is inappropriate as a theory of development or world history (Toye, "The New Institutional Economics," 64–65, 67). See also Gregory Clark's analysis in "A Review of Avner Greif's *Institutions and the Path to the Modern Economy.*"

2. Hall and Taylor, "Political Science and the Three New Institutionalisms," 55–56; Tilly, *Popular Contention in Great Britain.*

3. In fact, the criticisms in each literature about the others can enrich our analysis by highlighting typical problems and gaps, including functionalism or reading intent from the consequences or role the institution plays, omitting power and the politics of institutions, neglecting legacy and the playing field of options, assuming collective action occurs easily, correcting the tendency toward static analyses that cannot accommodate change, or assuming consequences are necessarily optimal economically. On combining different approaches, see also Ostrom, "Rational Choice Theory and Institutional Analysis"; Hall and Taylor, "Political Science and the Three New Institutionalisms."

4. Geddes, "The Great Transformation in the Study of Politics in Developing Countries," 363.

5. Thanks to Jeff Knopf for suggesting this phrase.

6. Baldwin, *The Politics of Social Solidarity.*

7. Esping-Andersen, *The Three Worlds of Welfare Capitalism;* Wimmer, *Nationalist Exclusion and Ethnic Conflict.*

8. Soskice, "Divergent Production Regimes"; Hollingsworth, Schmitter, and Streeck, *Governing Capitalist Economies;* Huber and Stephens, *Development and Crisis of the Welfare State.*

9. Esping-Andersen and Kolberg, "Welfare States and Employment Regimes"; Estevez-Abe, Iversen, and Soskice, "Social Protection and the Formation of Skills."

10. Haggard and Kaufman, *Development, Democracy, and Welfare States,* chap. 1.

11. Huber and Stephens, *Development and Crisis of the Welfare State;* Bradley et al., "Distribution and Redistribution in Postindustrial Democracies"; Pierson, "The New Politics of the Welfare State."

12. Huber, "Options for Social Policy in Latin America."

13. Karshenas and Moghadam, "Social Policy in the Middle East," 4.

14. Usui, "Welfare State Development in a World System Context."

15. Baldwin, *The Politics of Social Solidarity*, 292; Moene and Wallerstein, "Inequality, Social Insurance, and Redistribution."

16. Bledstein, "Introduction: Storytellers to the Middle Class," 5, 18.

17. Baldwin, *The Politics of Social Solidarity.*

18. Consider the example of the mischaracterization of the United States as being late in providing welfare. Because the policies took a different form than in European countries, scholars overlooked them (Skocpol, *Protecting Soldiers and Mothers*).

19. Rodrik, "What Drives Public Employment in Developing Countries?"

20. Huber, "Options for Social Policy in Latin America," 142.

21. Haggard and Kaufman, *Development, Democracy, and Welfare States.*

22. Rudra, "Welfare States in Developing Countries."

23. Moene and Wallerstein, "Inequality, Social Insurance, and Redistribution"; Iversen, *Capitalism, Democracy, and Welfare.*

24. Singerman, *Avenues of Participation;* Baaklini, Denoeux, and Springborg, *Legislative Politics in the Arab World;* Waterbury, "From Social Contracts to Extraction Contracts"; World Bank, *Unlocking the Employment Potential in the Middle East and North Africa*, 26.

25. Robalino, "Pensions in the Middle East and North Africa," 54.

26. Ibid., 54–56.

27. Abrahart, Kaur, and Tzannatos, "Government Employment and Active Labor Market Policies in MENA," 22.

28. Nasr, "Issues of Social Protection in the Arab Region."

29. Markets can also provide these goods. Some gated housing facilities approximate state-like public goods for those able to afford them, including security, utilities, and sports facilities (Glasze and Alkhayyal, "Gated Housing Estates in the Arab World").

30. Kingston, "Introduction: States-Within-States"; Bryden, "State-Within-a-Failed-State."

31. Spears, "States-Within-States," 16.

32. Zahar, "Fanatics, Mercenaries, Brigands . . . and Politicians"; Harik, *The Public and Social Services of the Lebanese Militias;* Sayigh, *Armed Struggle and the Search for State.*

33. Taylor-Gooby and Zinn, "The Current Significance of Risk"; Ryan, "Civil Society as Democratic Practice"; Glenn, "Understanding Mutual Benefit Societies."

34. Sibalis, "The Mutual Aid Societies of Paris."

35. Skocpol and Oser, "Organization Despite Adversity."

36. Townsend, "Consumption Insurance"; Massey et al., *Worlds in Motion*, 21.

37. Platteau and Abraham, "An Inquiry into Quasi-Credit Contracts," 462; Besley, "Nonmarket Institutions for Credit and Risk Sharing in Low-Income Countries," 116.

38. Eswaran and Kotwal, "Credit as Insurance in Agrarian Economies"; Dercon, "Risk, Insurance, and Poverty"; Case, "Symposium on Consumption Smoothing in Developing Countries."

39. Goldstein, Janvry, and Sadoulet, "Is a Friend in Need a Friend Indeed?"

40. Townsend, "Consumption Insurance."

41. Sekhri and Savedoff, "Private Health Insurance," 3.

42. Singerman, *Avenues of Participation*, 210–11.

43. Biggart, "Banking on Each Other"; Tripp, "Local Organizations, Participation, and the State in Urban Tanzania"; Carapico, *Civil Society in Yemen*.

44. Olson, *The Logic of Collective Action*; Hardin, *Collective Action*.

45. Little and Austin, "Women and the Rural Idyll."

46. Townsend, "Consumption Insurance."

47. Hart, "Gender and Household Dynamics."

48. Weingast, "Rational-Choice Institutionalism."

49. Greif, "Reputation and Coalitions in Medieval Trade"; North, "Markets and Other Allocation Systems in History." Heydemann shows that although these methods can help debunk culture as an explanation, culture is still often assumed to be the operative variables in the Arab world, even by those who marginalize culture as an explanation in other regions (Heydemann, "Institutions and Economic Performance").

50. Townsend, "Optimal Multiperiod Contracts"; Biggart and Castanias, "Collateralized Social Relations."

51. North, *Structure and Change in Economic History*; idem, *Institutions, Institutional Change, and Economic Performance*; Ostrom, "A Behavioral Approach to the Rational Choice Theory of Collective Action."

52. Milgrom, North, and Weingast, "The Role of Institutions in the Revival of Trade"; Greif, "Reputation and Coalitions in Medieval Trade."

53. Greif, "Reputation and Coalitions in Medieval Trade"; North, "Markets and Other Allocation Systems in History"; idem, *Structure and Change in Economic History.*

54. This is specific trust active at the micro level between individuals, not the generalized variety referred to in discussions of social capital, citizenship, and governance. For discussions of the two, see Cook, Hardin, and Levi, *Cooperation Without Trust?* chap. 1.

55. Ellickson, *Order without Law.*

56. Hyden, "Governance and the Study of Politics," 9; Mingione, *Fragmented Societies*, 25.

57. Sik and Wellman, "Network Capital in Capitalist, Communist, and Postcommunist Countries," 231.

58. Ben-Porath, "The F-Connection."

59. Besley, "Nonmarket Institutions for Credit and Risk Sharing," 118.

60. Tilly, *Trust and Rule*, 57.

61. Weingast, "Rational-Choice Institutionalism," 671.

62. Wall et al., "Families and Informal Support Networks in Portugal"; De Weerdt, "Risk-Sharing and Endogenous Network Formation," 197.

63. De Weerdt, "Risk-Sharing and Endogenous Network Formation."

64. Espinoza, "Social Networks among the Urban Poor"; Singerman, *Avenues of Participation.*

65. Cook, Hardin, and Levi, *Cooperation Without Trust?* 85.

66. Landa, *Trust, Ethnicity, and Identity,* 28.

67. Ibid., 17.

68. Kuran, "Ethnic Norms and Their Transformation through Reputational Cascades."

69. Sabel, "Flexible Specialisation and the Re-emergence of Regional Economies."

70. Among neighbors, see Ellickson, *Order without Law,* 233, 235. For a discussion of how mutual benefit societies in the United States use ritual and ceremonies to solidify obligations, see Glenn, "Understanding Mutual Benefit Societies," 638–39.

71. Pratten and Baldo, "'Return to the Roots,'" 146.

72. Portes and Sensenbrenner, "Embeddedness and Immigration," 1325, 1336.

73. Collins, "The Logic of Clan Politics."

74. Poros, "The Role of Migrant Networks in Linking Local Labour Markets."

75. Roberts, "Informal Economy and Family Strategies."

76. Portes and Sensenbrenner, "Embeddedness and Immigration."

77. Muldrew, *The Economy of Obligation.*

78. Ostrom, "A Behavioral Approach to the Rational Choice Theory of Collective Action."

79. Oliver and Marwell, "The Paradox of Group Size in Collective Action; Olson, *The Logic of Collective Action.*

80. Ellickson, *Order without Law,* 177–78.

81. Biggart, "Banking on Each Other," 146.

82. De Weerdt, "Risk-Sharing and Endogenous Network Formation," 197.

83. I conceptualize the decision making as an individual choice, usually representing the household. I do not problematize immediate and close extended family's mutual aid. I am aware that this does violence to the contentious reality of relations within the household, as gender and household studies have analyzed. See Redclift and Mingione, "Introduction: Economic Restructuring and Family Practices." Breaking apart the household at this stage would unnecessarily complicate the analysis. My interviews were based on household decisions and did not delve within that unit. The analysis does demonstrate negative consequences of kin organizing for women and ideological minorities or behavioral nonconformists, as the association dictates social norms in return for aid. See the concluding chapter.

84. Sullivan, Warren, and Westbrook, *The Fragile Middle Class.*

85. Saleh and Harvie, "An Analysis of Public Sector Deficits and Debt in Lebanon."

86. Oxford Business Group, "Emerging Lebanon," 125.

87. Figuié, *Le Point sur le Liban,* 289; Gaspard, *A Political Economy of Lebanon,* 71.

88. Sekhri and Savedoff, "Private Health Insurance."

89. Barr, *The Economics of the Welfare State,* III, 17–18. The risk must also be individual, not collective, and therefore, in light of widespread under- and unemployment, it is not clear that even with functioning legal institutions the market could make up for social welfare during recessions.

90. World Bank, *Economic Developments and Prospects,* 83.

91. World Bank, *Doing Business 2009: Country Profile for Jordan,* 41; idem, *Doing Business 2009: Country Profile for Lebanon,* 41.

92. De Weerdt, "Risk-Sharing and Endogenous Network Formation," 197.

93. Iversen, *Capitalism, Democracy, and Welfare.*

94. Hani Hourani et al., *Directory of Civil Society Organizations in Jordan,* 317; Lebanese Center for Policy Studies, "The Civil Society Report 1997"; Figuié, *Le Point sur le Liban,* 275–79.

95. el-Mikawy and Posusney, "Labor Representation in the Age of Globalization, 53.

96. Figures are for 1992. Hamarneh, *al-Urdun [Jordan],* 174.

97. World Bank, *Unlocking the Employment Potential,* 62.

98. Iversen, *Capitalism, Democracy, and Welfare.*

99. Ibid.; Thelen, *How Institutions Evolve.* For more on the relationship between skills and social insurance, see Estevez-Abe, Iversen, and Soskice, "Social Protection and the Formation of Skills." Note that the situation here differs from that described by Iversen and Soskice, since in their case the specialized skills are firm-specific, and those with generalized skills face a much more favorable employment market than in the Middle East (Iversen and Soskice, "An Asset Theory of Social Policy Preferences").

100. Middle East and North Africa Region World Bank, *Reducing Vulnerability and Increasing Opportunity,* Table A2.10, p. 126.

101. Charmes, "Trends in Informal Sector Employment in the Middle East," 170–71.

102. World Bank, *Unlocking the Employment Potential,* 131.

103. Rollins, *The Index of Global Philanthropy,* 32.

104. Gaspard, *A Political Economy of Lebanon,* 96.

105. McCann, "Patrilocal Co-residential Units (PCUs) in Al-Barha."

106. Figuié, *Le Point sur le Liban,* 297–98.

107. Interviews, Beirut, May 2004, and interviews and questionnaires, various dates, Lebanon, 2005.

108. Iversen, *Capitalism, Democracy, and Welfare,* 10.

109. Johnson, *Class and Client in Beirut.* See also Delacroix, "The Distributive State in the World System."

110. John Mangan, *Workers Without Traditional Employment.*

111. Roberts, "Household Coping Strategies and Urban Poverty in a Comparative Perspective."

112. Johnson, *Class and Client in Beirut.*

113. Roberts and Morris, "Fortune, Risk, and Remittances"; Roberts, "Informal Economy and Family Strategies," 9.

114. Sabel, "Moebius-Strip Organizations and Open Labor Markets"; Smith, "Towards an Ethnography of Idiosyncratic Forms of Livelihood"; Espinoza, "Social Networks among the Urban Poor," 173.

115. Mangan, *Workers Without Traditional Employment;* Mingione, "Life Strategies and Social Economies."

116. Granovetter, *Getting a Job.*

117. Bian, "Getting a Job through a Web of *Guanxi* in China."

118. Beito, *From Mutual Aid to the Welfare State,* 222–31; Glenn, "Understanding Mutual Benefit Societies," 648.

119. Beito, *From Mutual Aid to the Welfare State,* 231.

120. Wellman, "Preface."

121. World Bank, *Reducing Vulnerability and Increasing Opportunity,* 51; Tzannatos, "Social Protection in the Middle East and North Africa," 130.

122. Tzannatos, "Social Protection in the Middle East and North Africa," 129.

123. Platteau and Abraham, "An Inquiry into Quasi-Credit Contracts," 470.

124. Besley, "Nonmarket Institutions for Credit and Risk Sharing," 120–21.

125. Roberts and Morris, "Fortune, Risk, and Remittances," 1268.

126. "Family" is a loose, expansive term that can mean nuclear family or extended relatives. The family embodied in kinship associations institutionalizes the kin relatives that are important to daily life, that can be turned to in need.

127. Ostrom, "A Behavioral Approach to the Rational Choice Theory of Collective Action," 7.

128. Roy, "État et recompositions identitaires"; Kuran, "Ethnic Norms and Their Transformation through Reputational Cascades"; Landa, *Trust, Ethnicity, and Identity.*

129. Polletta and Jasper, "Collective Identity and Social Movements," 285; Melucci, "The Process of Collective Identity."

130. Piore and Sabel, *The Second Industrial Divide.*

131. Sabel, "Flexible Specialisation and the Re-emergence of Regional Economies."

2. STATE AND MILITIA WELFARE AND THEIR DEMISE

1. Random statements to the author, East Beirut, 1998–2000.

2. The term "militia" refers to an armed, nonstate group fighting either for

or against the state. See Zahar, "Fanatics, Mercenaries, Brigands . . . and Politicians," 44.

3. A significant literature documents the provision of social services by some militias in other regions of the world, aiming to replace the state. See, for example, Kingston and Spears, *States Within States*.

4. The predominantly East Bank military saved the Hashemite monarchy on several occasions, namely, the ousting of the socialist government under Suleiman Nabulsi in 1957 and the Black September episode, 1970–71, that pitted the state and army against the Palestine Liberation Organization (PLO). The PLO was then forced to move to Lebanon. The army's allegiance to the Hashemite regime was crucial in these episodes. Statements on the Jordanian tribes forming the regime's social base are numerous. For a concise discussion, see Adnan Abu-Odeh, *Jordanians, Palestinians, and the Hashemite Kingdom in the Middle East Peace Process*.

5. Esping-Andersen, *The Three Worlds of Welfare Capitalism*.

6. Huber and Stephens, *Development and Crisis of the Welfare State*.

7. In the Middle East and other regions, weddings and funerals are expensive, and serve to demonstrate the family's status in society. See Bourdieu, *The Logic of Practice,* chap. 7. Poor and middle-class families often incur debt for these events.

8. Skocpol, *Protecting Soldiers and Mothers*.

9. Huber, "Options for Social Policy in Latin America," 147.

10. See, for example, World Bank, *Unlocking the Employment Potential in the Middle East and North Africa,* chap. 2; Singerman, *Avenues of Participation;* Baaklini, Denoeux, and Springborg, *Legislative Politics in the Arab World;* Waterbury, "From Social Contracts to Extraction Contracts."

11. Anderson, "Politics in the Middle East." On the development of social security up to the 1970s, see Dixon, "Social Security in the Middle East."

12. Waterbury, "From Social Contracts to Extraction Contracts"; Chaudhry, "Consuming Interests"; World Bank, *Unlocking the Employment Potential,* 131.

13. Nasr, "Issues of Social Protection in the Arab Region," 36; Robalino, "Pensions in the Middle East and North Africa," 54–56.

14. Southern Europe has been suggested as a "fourth" model of welfare, in addition to Esping-Andersen's three. See the citations below.

15. Martin, "Social Welfare and the Family in Southern Europe," 25.

16. Ferrera, "The 'Southern Model' of Welfare in Social Europe"; Martin, "Social Welfare and the Family," 33.

17. Ferrera, "The 'Southern Model' of Welfare in Social Europe."

18. Rhodes, "Southern European Welfare States," 5–6.

19. On the development of social security up to the boom decade, see Dixon, "Social Security in the Middle East."

20. Anderson, "Prospects for Liberalism in North Africa," 131.

21. The distinction is one of national origin or lineage, not current

citizenship. These categories should be taken as general descriptions only; distinctions between Jordanian and Palestinian are not hard-and-fast. Senses of identity, political factors, and societal mixing complicate rigid categorizations. The relative percentage of the groups is unknown; census statistics on the subject are considered a national secret. Palestinians are popularly believed to form the majority of the population, but without concomitant political power.

22. See the vast literature on Jordanians in public employment, including Brand, "Palestinians and Jordanians"; Sayigh, "Jordan in the 1980s."

23. Interviews with Jordanian Christian civil service official 'Azzam al-Naber, Public Relations Director, Cooperative Organization, 6 December 1999; and 'Abd al-Rahman al-Jam'aani, Director of Administration, Jordan Cooperative Corporation, various dates, spring 1998 and fall 1999.

24. Hamarneh, "Social and Economic Transformation of Trans-Jordan, 1921–1946"; Aruri, *Jordan: A Study in Political Development;* Bocco and Tell, "*Pax Britannica* in the Steppe"; Tell, "Guns, Gold, and Grain."

25. Massad, "Identifying the Nation," 111. This was a common colonial tactic paralleling French policies in the mandates of Syria and Lebanon.

26. Brynen, "Economic Crisis and Post-Rentier Democratization in the Arab World," 82; Mazur, *Economic Growth and Development in Jordan.*

27. Bocco and Tell, "*Pax Britannica* in the Steppe"; Wilson, "The Role of Commercial Banking in the Jordanian Economy."

28. The British land policy established a relatively egalitarian distribution, allowing for small peasants to remain on their plots. This arguably contributed to the antirevolution, pro-government stance of the tribal constituencies. See Fischbach, "British Land Policy in Transjordan"; and idem, *State, Society and Land in Jordan.*

29. Vatikiotis, *Politics and the Military in Jordan;* Massad, *Colonial Effects.*

30. Antoun, *Arab Village,* 27.

31. Gilbar, "The Economy of Nablus and the Hashemites"; Rivier, *Croissance Industrielle dans une Economie Assistée,* 68.

32. Abu-Odeh, *Jordanians, Palestinians, and the Hashemite Kingdom,* 190, 228; Radi, "La gestion d'appartenances multiples"; Sayigh, "Jordan in the 1980s."

33. al-Fa'ouri, *al-Wasata fil-qita' al-hukumi al-Urduni;* Cunningham and Sarayrah, *Wasta;* Fathi, *Jordan—An Invented Nation?*

34. Brand, "Palestinians and Jordanians."

35. Jreisat, "Bureaucracy and Development in Jordan," 99; Jureidini and McLaurin, *Jordan.*

36. Mazur, *Economic Growth and Development in Jordan,* 111.

37. Daves, "Biting the Hand That Feeds You"; Brynen, "Economic Crisis and Post-Rentier Democratization," 82.

38. Jaber, "The Impact of Structural Adjustment on Women's Employment

and Urban Households," 156; Hanssen-Bauer, Pedersen, and Tiltnes, *Jordanian Society,* 197; Dejong and Tell, "Economic Crisis and the Labour Market," 214.

39. Full scholarships were available after ten years of service. These places at state universities, the most prestigious educational institutions, were much coveted (Bader, *al-Ta'leem al-'ali fil-Urdun [Higher education in Jordan]*). This policy, together with military-only consumer stores, increased the military's economic role (Massad, *Colonial Effects,* 219).

40. If the employed is a woman, her dependents only have access to social security and health insurance if she is certified as head of the household, not an easy or common accomplishment (Amawi, "Gender and Citizenship in Jordan," 179).

41. *Jordan Times,* 19–20 May 2000. Private universities and community colleges are attempting to answer the excess demand. The country spent 11.2 percent of its GNP in 1992 on education (Bader, *Higher Education in Jordan*).

42. To mobilize savings of expatriate workers, dual nationals were acknowledged in 1987 and allowed to participate in the Social Security Corporation. See Massad, "Identifying the Nation," 60; Roberts, "The Political Economy of Identity." Most of those covered were men and amounted to about one-fourth of the workforce in the late 1990s (Hashemite Kingdom of Jordan, Social Security Corporation, "Overview and Tables"). About three hundred thousand workers are insured in the program (Hashemite Kingdom of Jordan, "Statistical Yearbook 1998," 222).

43. Sha'sha, "The Role of the Private Sector in Jordan's Economy," 84.

44. Hourani, *Azma al-iqtisad al-Urduni [The crisis of Jordan's economy],* 67.

45. Mazur, *Economic Growth and Development in Jordan.* The army's salary was raised after the unrest. The government had begun subsidizing wheat in the 1960s.

46. Interview with Wizarat al-Tamween, Economic Director of the Secretary General Office, Ministry of Supply, 22 April 1998.

47. Owen, "Government and Economy in Jordan"; Anani and Khalaf, "Privatization in Jordan." The Consumer Corporation began permitting purchases via credit to aid consumers, but business leaders complained about this competition. Since the government was able to import without customs duties or fees, private businesses in Karak suffered (*al-'Arab al-yawm,* 5 January 2000).

48. Wizarat al-Tamween [Ministry of Supply], "Qa'ima bil-mawaad al-ghitha'iyya al-tamweeniyya wa al-mawaad wa al-sil' al-ukhra al-mas'ra min qibl wizara al-tamween"; Andoni and Schwedler, "Bread Riots in Jordan," 40.

49. Kana'an, "The Social Dimension in Jordan's Approach to Development."

50. Satloff, "Jordan's Great Gamble; Wasif al-Wazani, *al-Jihaz al-masrifi wa al-siyasa al-naqdiyya fil-Urdun, 1989–1995.*

51. Andoni, "The Five Days That Shook Jordan," 3–4.

52. "Jordan: New Government," *Oxford Analytica Daily Brief,* 2 May 1989.

53. "Jordan: Fragile Kingdom," *Oxford Analytica Daily Brief,* 15 October 1991.

54. Country Operations Division World Bank, Country Department III, Europe, Middle East, and North Africa Region, "Jordan Public Expenditure Review," 6.

55. Kamal, "Bread Subsidy to Go," 11; Albrecht, "The Pains of Restructuring (Jordan Economy)," 20–21; Kamal, "The Price of Bread," 13.

56. Dougherty, "The Pain of Adjustment."

57. Andoni and Schwedler, "Bread Riots in Jordan," 41.

58. Andoni, "Jordan: Behind the Recent Disturbances," 17–18.

59. Many have been forced to substitute bread for other, now more expensive food items, leading to the paradoxical situation of an increase in bread consumption along with an increase in the price of bread.

60. Some estimates of poverty levels are higher. Al-Wazani, "Jordan: Strategic Options for Growth and Development Facing Poverty and Unemployment"; Suyyagh, "Poverty Management in Jordan."

61. Central Bank of Jordan, "Thirty Fifth Annual Report 1998," 38.

62. Michel Marto (Minister of Finance) and Ziad Fariz (Central Bank Governor), "Letter of Intent of the Government of Jordan to Michel Camdessus, International Monetary Fund, 28 August 1999."

63. Middle East and North Africa Region World Bank, *Reducing Vulnerability and Increasing Opportunity*, 81, Table 2.8.

64. *Jordan Times*, 25 November 1999, 28–29 April 2000. Customs for goods such as soft drinks were around 60 percent.

65. *al-Aswaq*, 28 June 2000.

66. Industry in Jordan depends heavily on imported raw materials. The government's reasoning for not eliminating them was the cost in lost revenues (interview with Abdallah A. Attieh, Assistant Director, Research Directorate, Amman Chamber of Commerce, 2 May 2000).

67. *al-Rai'*, 6 February 2000.

68. Interview with Ministry of Finance official, 23 March 2000. The value-added tax, though better for businesses, would have the same regressive effect on popular income as the sales tax.

69. *al-'Arab al-yawm*, 22 November 1999.

70. *Jordan Times*, 12 April 2000. The tax ranges from 10 to 150 Jordanian dinar (JD).

71. World Bank, *Unlocking the Employment Potential*, 98–99.

72. "Jordan: Economic Outlook," *Oxford Analytica Daily Brief*, 4 November 1988.

73. "Jordan: Government under Pressure as Violence Mounts," *Oxford Analytica Daily Brief*, 27 April 2001.

74. Interview with Wizarat al-Tamween.

75. *al-'Arab al-yawm*, 5 January 2000, 9.

76. CERMOC (Centre d'Études et de Recherches sur le Moyen-Orient Contemporain), "Chronologie decembre 1995–avril 1996." Salaries were

increased by 10 JD (Jordanian Dinars), and soon after half the members of parliament demanded an increase of 15 JD.

77. *Jordan Times,* 6 January 2000.

78. Baylouny, "Militarizing Welfare: Neo-liberalism and the Jordanian Regime."

79. Robinson, "Defensive Democratization in Jordan,"

80. Hashemite Kingdom of Jordan, "Statistical Yearbook 1998," 246.

81. Central Bank of Jordan, "Thirtieth Annual Report 1993," 66, 68; Central Bank of Jordan, "Thirty-Fifth Annual Report 1998," 82–3.

82. Interviews with Jordanian military officers, 17 April and 10 May 2004, Amman.

83. Abrahart, Kaur, and Tzannatos, "Government Employment and Active Labor Market Policies in MENA in a Comparative International Context."

84. Center for Strategic Studies, "Istitlaa' lil-ra'i hawla al-dimuqratiyya fil-Urdun 2002 [Opinion Survey on Democracy in Jordan 2002]," Table 2/1/3.

85. Amara, "Military Industrialization and Economic Development," 5.

86. Interviews with Jordanian military officers, 17 April and 10 May 2004, Amman.

87. World Bank, *Reducing Vulnerability and Increasing Opportunity,* 132.

88. Robalino, "Pensions in the Middle East and North Africa," 202.

89. World Bank, *Unlocking the Employment Potential,* 148.

90. Oxford Business Group, *Emerging Jordan* (2003), 178.

91. World Bank, *Unlocking the Employment Potential,* 135.

92. Amara, "Military Industrialization and Economic Development," 4.

93. Ibid., 18.

94. Hanssen-Bauer, Pedersen, and Tiltnes, *Jordanian Society,* 189. Military insurance is the most common form of health insurance, held by 25 percent of the population. Government insurance represents another 23 percent. Insurance coverage is high in rural areas, with a heavy proportion of military insurance. By contrast, only 20 percent of camp residents have government insurance, and 6 percent have military insurance (Tiltnes, "Poverty and Welfare in the Palestinian Refugee Camps of Jordan").

95. Dejong, "The Urban Context of Health During Economic Crisis," 277. Only about 5 percent of the population is covered by UNRWA health care, 63 percent of camp refugees. See Hanssen-Bauer, Pedersen, and Tiltnes, *Jordanian Society,* 190; and Tiltnes, "Poverty and Welfare in the Palestinian Refugee Camps." Doctors warned against privatizing the public health care system, which would further skew the distribution of care (*al-'Arab al-yawm,* 10 June 2000).

96. Hashemite Kingdom of Jordan, "Dirasa nafaqat wa dakhl al-usra 1997 [Household Expenditure and Income Survey 1997]," Table 3.14; Tiltnes, "Poverty and Welfare in the Palestinian Refugee Camps."

97. Mansur, "Social Aspects of the Adjustment Program," 63.

98. Curmi, "Les Associations de Bienfaisance à Amman"; Jaber, "The

Impact of Structural Adjustment." Interview with Jordanian social scientist, various dates, 1999–2000. Reportedly King Abdullah had to visit al-Bashir Hospital, Amman's main public hospital, three times in 1999 in order to have the elevators repaired.

99. Curmi, "Les Associations de Bienfaisance à Amman," 370.

100. Markus Loewe et al., "Improving the Social Protection of the Urban Poor and Near-Poor in Jordan," iv.

101. World Bank, *Reducing Vulnerability and Increasing Opportunity.*

102. Interview with Wizarat al-Tamween. All antipoverty and social measures are based on the family and on family-income levels, not on the individual.

103. Andoni and Schwedler, "Bread Riots in Jordan," 41.

104. Central Bank of Jordan, "Thirty-Fifth Annual Report 1998," 41; Suyyagh, "Poverty Management in Jordan."

105. Hashemite Kingdom of Jordan, *Plan for Economic and Social Development 1993–1997,* 66; Mansur, "Social Aspects of the Adjustment Program," 63.

106. Shteiwi, "Poverty Assessment of Jordan," 21; Hamarneh, *al-Urdun [Jordan].* To such charity, the population responded by asking for jobs (*Jordan Times,* 12 December 1999).

107. Shteiwi and Hejoj, "Poverty Alleviation Programs Effectiveness in Jordan."

108. Loewe et al., "Improving the Social Protection of the Urban Poor," vi.

109. *Jordan Times,* 9 February 2000.

110. Government of Jordan, "Memorandum on Economic and Financial Policies to IMF."

111. Central Bank of Jordan, "Thirtieth Annual Report 1993," 33; Central Bank of Jordan, "Thirty Fifth Annual Report 1998."

112. My assertion that militias provided their populations with social insurance should in no way be construed as denying the destruction and repression of their rule. Just as state-building in Europe was generally brutal, it nevertheless established the institutions of the modern state and social policies.

113. Salibi, *A House of Many Mansions.*

114. Gaspard, *A Political Economy of Lebanon,* 258.

115. Figuié, *Le Point sur le Liban,* 287.

116. Dagher, *L'état et l'économie au Liban,* 12:88, 106–107, 35, 37.

117. Petran, *The Struggle over Lebanon,* 56.

118. Ne'meh, "Slipping through the Cracks."

119. Dib, *Warlords and Merchants.*

120. Picard, "The Political Economy of Civil War in Lebanon," 295.

121. American Task Force for Lebanon, *Working Paper—Conference on Lebanon,* 35.

122. Makdisi, *Lessons of Lebanon,* 85.

123. Dib, *Warlords and Merchants,* 187–89.

124. Library of Congress, "A Country Study: Lebanon."

125. Makdisi, *Lessons of Lebanon,* 85.

126. Kubursi, "Reconstructing the Economy of Lebanon."

127. Dib, *Warlords and Merchants*, 191, 197.

128. Harik, *The Public and Social Services of the Lebanese Militias*, 32–33.

129. Study by Theodor Hanf, quoted in Zahar, "Fanatics, Mercenaries, Brigands," 170, 174.

130. Makdisi and Sadaka, "The Lebanese Civil War, 1975–1990," 2:66.

131. Nasr, "Anatomie d'un système de guerre interne," 91; Picard, "The Political Economy of Civil War in Lebanon," 306; Dib, *Warlords and Merchants*, 157.

132. Khalidi, "The Palestinians in Lebanon," 255, 257.

133. Hudson, "Palestinians and Lebanon," 254.

134. Rubenberg, *The Palestine Liberation Organization*, 19.

135. Yezid Sayigh, *Armed Struggle and the Search for State*, 458–60.

136. Sayigh, "Palestinians in Lebanon: Uncertain Future," 101.

137. Hudson, "Palestinians and Lebanon," 254.

138. Khalidi, "The Palestinians in Lebanon," 257–58.

139. Harik, *The Public and Social Services of the Lebanese Militias*, 15–17, 33.

140. Kingston and Zahar, "Rebuilding *A House of Many Mansions*," 90.

141. Snider, "The Lebanese Forces," 141.

142. McLaurin, "From Professional to Political," 556–58.

143. Picard, "The Political Economy of Civil War in Lebanon," 306.

144. "Liban: L'argent des milices," *Les Cahiers de l'Orient*, no. 10 (1988): 279.

145. Zahar, "Fanatics, Mercenaries, Brigands," 120, 132.

146. Harik, "Change and Continuity among the Lebanese Druze Community."

147. Picard, "The Political Economy of Civil War in Lebanon," 314.

148. Harik, *The Public and Social Services of the Lebanese Militias*, 17.

149. Richani, "The Druze of Mount Lebanon; Harik, "Change and Continuity among the Lebanese Druze Community."

150. Saad-Ghorayeb, *Hizbu'llah*.

151. "L'argent des milices," 285. A martyr is defined as anyone killed by hostile forces, whether a combatant or not. This includes those killed by Israeli action or the opposition Lebanese Christian forces during the war.

152. Hamzeh, *In the Path of Hizbullah*, 50–55.

153. Harik, *The Public and Social Services of the Lebanese Militias*.

154. Harik, *Hezbollah*.

155. Quilty, "Hariri," p. 27.

156. Makdisi, *Lessons of Lebanon*, 85.

157. Picard, "Autorité et souveraineté de l'État à l'épreuve du Liban sud," 34.

158. The state now owned part of Intra Investment Company, the Central Bank held almost 28 percent and the government itself another 10 percent. Through this source, the government had an interest in militia finances, since Intra's holdings included the Casino du Liban in Juniyeh, which was in the hands of the Lebanese Forces. Forty percent of the Casino's monthly receipts

of $2 million went to the government (Library of Congress, "A Country Study: Lebanon").

159. Dr. Toufic Gaspard, personal communication, 9 May 2005.

160. Sena Eken et al., "Economic Dislocation and Recovery in Lebanon."

161. Leenders, "Public Means to Private Ends."

162. Saleh and Harvie, "An Analysis of Public Sector Deficits and Debt in Lebanon"; Oxford Business Group, "Emerging Lebanon," 43.

163. Baroudi, "Continuity in Economic Policy in Postwar Lebanon"; Denoeux and Springborg, "Hariri's Lebanon," 164.

164. Makdisi, *Lessons of Lebanon,* 125; Saleh and Harvie, "An Analysis of Public Sector Deficits."

165. Oxford Business Group, "Emerging Lebanon," 42.

166. "Playing the Army against the Labor."

167. Oxford Business Group, "Emerging Lebanon"; Makdisi, *Lessons of Lebanon,* 127.

168. Picard, "The Political Economy of Civil War in Lebanon," 318. Interview with General Director of Subsidies Section, Lebanese Ministry of Economy, Beirut, 27 June 2005.

169. Oxford Business Group, "Emerging Lebanon," 43.

170. World Bank, *Reducing Vulnerability and Increasing Opportunity,* 64, 81.

171. Embassy of the United States of America, *Country Commercial Guide: Lebanon 2004,* 7.

172. Makdisi, *Lessons of Lebanon,* 129.

173. Congressional Research Service, "CRS Issue Brief for Congress: Lebanon."

174. Kechichian, "The Lebanese Army," 35; Barak, "Lebanon: Failure, Collapse, and Resuscitation," 326; Economist Intelligence Unit, "Lebanon: Country Profile," 16. Of this number, thirteen thousand were in the Internal Security Forces.

175. Karam, "Systèmes de protection sociale au Liban," 219.

176. United Nations Development Programme (UNDP), "A Profile of Sustainable Human Development in Lebanon," 1997.

177. Oxford Business Group, "Emerging Lebanon," 14.

178. Robalino, "Pensions in the Middle East and North Africa," 55; UNDP, "A Profile of Sustainable Human Development in Lebanon" 1997

179. World Bank, *Unlocking the Employment Potential,* 135; UNDP, "Globalization," 24.

180. Marseglia, "Welfare in the Mediterranean Countries: Lebanon"; UNDP, "Mapping of Living Conditions in Lebanon."

181. Karam, "Systèmes de protection sociale au Liban," 219; Ne'meh, "Slipping Through the Cracks."

182. Jawad, "A Profile of Social Welfare in Lebanon," 323; UNDP, "A Profile of Sustainable Human Development in Lebanon," 10.

3. HARD TIMES AND PRIVATE-SECTOR WELFARE OPTIONS

1. World Bank, *Unlocking the Employment Potential,* 44; idem, *Economic Developments and Prospects.*

2. Tzannatos, "Social Protection in the Middle East and North Africa," 124.

3. World Bank, *Unlocking the Employment Potential,* 104.

4. Iversen, *Capitalism, Democracy, and Welfare.*

5. Ibid., 4.

6. Eswaran and Kotwal, "Credit as Insurance in Agrarian Economies."

7. Interview with micro-finance NGO employee, Beirut, spring 2000.

8. On Egypt, see, for example, Wickham, "Islamic Mobilization and Political Change." On Jordan, see Azm, "The Islamic Action Front party."

9. Middle East and North Africa Region World Bank, *Reducing Vulnerability and Increasing Opportunity,* 4.

10. "Jordan: Economic Predicament," *Oxford Analytica Daily Brief,* 7 September 1999; al-Wazani, "Jordan"; Mansur, "Social Aspects of the Adjustment Program," 58. ESCWA also puts the figure at 30 percent for 1994 (Aken, "Development as a Gift"). Radi puts the figure at 40 percent (Radi, "Les Palestiniens du Koweit en Jordanie"). For the differing measures of poverty, see Suyyagh, "Poverty Management in Jordan."

11. al-Wazani, "Jordan"; Musa Shteiwi, "Poverty Assessment of Jordan."

12. Interview with Jordanian statistician and social scientist, various dates, spring 2000. Calculations from Hashemite Kingdom of Jordan, "Dirasa nafaqat wa dakhl al-usra 1997," Table 3.14; Hashemite Kingdom of Jordan, *Plan for Economic and Social Development 1993–1997,* 43. On increasing income inequality in Jordan, see also Tzannatos, "What Accounts for Earnings Inequality in Jordan and How Can Labor Policies Help Reduce Poverty?" 173.

13. *Jordan Times,* 18 September 1999; Amawi, "Scrutinizing the Nature of Economic Growth," 105; Hashemite Kingdom of Jordan, "Dirasa nafaqat wa dakhl al-usra 1997," Table 3.16. An account of one northern Jordanian village determined that almost 70 percent of households, with eight or more average members, operate on less than $280 monthly (Shunnaq, "Political and Economic Conflict within Extended Kin Groups."

14. *Jordan Times,* 12 December 1999; Jaber, "The Impact of Structural Adjustment on Women's Employment and Urban Households," 160–61.

15. Jordanians cite their main problems as the rising cost of living (almost half the survey respondents), unemployment (a quarter of respondents), and poverty (12% of respondents). These issues also top the list of problems for prior polls in 2005 and 2006 (Jordan Center for Social Research, "Democratic Transformation and Political Reform in Jordan," Table 2).

16. Dejong, "The Urban Context of Health during Economic Crisis"; Razzaz, "Law, Urban Land Tenure, and Property Disputes in Contested Settlements."

17. Mansur, "Social Aspects of the Adjustment Program," 60.

18. Interview with Jordanian statistician and social scientist. Calculations from Hashemite Kingdom of Jordan, "Household Expenditure and Income Survey 1992"; idem, "Dirasa nafaqat wa dakhl al-usra 1997"; Central Bank of Jordan, "Thirtieth Annual Report 1993," 148; idem, "Thirty-fifth Annual Report 1998," 134.

19. *Jordan Times,* 28 November 1999; Tiltnes, "Poverty and Welfare in the Palestinian Refugee Camps of Jordan,"

20. Interview with Jordanian statistician and social scientist. Calculations from Hashemite Kingdom of Jordan, "Dirasa nafaqat wa dakhl al-usra 1997," Tables 4.9, 4.12.

21. In this report the poverty line was set at less than one JD per day, 184 JD per month, for the average family of 6.2 persons; 28 percent of the population fell below this line.

22. *Jordan Times,* 1 January 1998, 24 February 2000; *al-'Arab al-yawm,* 6 January 2000; Khouri, "So much to buy, so little to buy it with," *Globe and Mail,* 27 April 2000. For the Ramadan holiday in 2000, few could even afford the traditional slaughtering of a sheep. Whereas in extended families at least one member would commonly be able to manage the expense, this year many middle-class families had no one who could do so.

23. Kubursi, "Reconstructing the Economy of Lebanon," 77; Makdisi, *Lessons of Lebanon,* 84.

24. Denoeux and Springborg, "Hariri's Lebanon," 160.

25. Kubursi, "Reconstructing the Economy of Lebanon"; Makdisi, *Lessons of Lebanon,* 84; Haddad, "The Poor in Lebanon," 83.

26. Nasr, "The New Social Map," 156.

27. Harris, "The View from Zahle," 282.

28. Nasr, "The New Social Map," 155.

29. Makdisi, *Lessons of Lebanon,* 149.

30. Ibid.

31. Nasr, "The New Social Map."

32. Coordination Forum of NGOs Working in the Palestinian Community, "Second Supplementary Report on the Rights of the Palestinian Child in Lebanon."

33. Roberts, "The Impact of Assistance on the Coping Mechanisms of Long-term Refugees."

34. Iversen, *Capitalism, Democracy, and Welfare,* 10.

35. Mingione, *Fragmented Societies,* 78.

36. Wages are also lower in a service economy than in a manufacturing economy (Sassen, *Globalization and Its Discontents*). Productivity is lower in service sectors, and has been termed Baumol's disease. See also the trilemma argument on Western Europe in Iverson and Wren, "Equality, Employment, and Budgetary Restraint"; and Pierson, "Three Worlds of Welfare State Research."

37. World Bank, *Economic Developments and Prospects,* 57.

38. World Bank, *Reducing Vulnerability and Increasing Opportunity,* Table A2.10, p. 126.

39. Figuié, *Le Point sur le Liban,* 296.

40. Services create a higher proportion of low-wage labor than does manufacturing (Sassen, *Globalization and Its Discontents*).

41. Shteiwi, "Class Structure and Inequality in the City of Amman," 418; Nasr, "Issues of Social Protection in the Arab Region," 33.

42. Arab Monetary Fund, "Joint Arab Economic Report," chap. 10, Tables 1, 2.

43. This figure includes members of kin associations as well as nonmembers.

44. As many as seventy-four income sources applied to the forty-four households in this village. See McCann, "Patrilocal Co-residential Units (PCUs) in Al-Barha."

45. Gaspard, *A Political Economy of Lebanon,* 96.

46. Although Jordanian and Palestinian categories generally imply different forms of livelihood and welfare, these divisions should be taken with caution, as a number of exceptions exist. Some Palestinians did work for the state, and there were Jordanians involved in the private sector. Despite the imprecise nature of the division, individuals are commonly termed and recognized as either Jordanian or Palestinian. Small minority groups are also present such as the Circassians, Chechens, and some Armenians. In labor market and welfare analyses, the Circassians are subsumed within the Jordanian population. Similarly the Jordanian Christians have consistently allied with the regime and are incorporated into public employ, albeit with less carte blanche than the Jordanian Muslims.

47. The Center for Strategic Studies reported the share of capital owned by individuals of Palestinian ancestry to have been 83 percent in 1996. Eleven percent was Transjordanian, and the remainder came from minority groups (Abu-Odeh, *Jordanians, Palestinians, and the Hashemite Kingdom,* 196).

48. Hashemite Kingdom of Jordan, "Jordan in Figures 2007," http://www.dos.gov.jo/jorfig/2007/jor_f_e.htm (accessed 24 August 2009).

49. Calculations from Hashemite Kingdom of Jordan, "Statistical Yearbook 1998," 9.

50. Ibid., 14.

51. Gilen et al., "Finding Ways"; Sawalha, "Identity, Self, and the Other among Palestinian Refugees in East Amman."

52. Destremau, "L'espace du camp et la reproduction du provisoire," 84, 91.

53. The Wihdat camp is inhabited primarily by 1948 refugees, Balqa by a large portion of 1967 "displaced people"—the term used in official UN documents for the 1967 refugees (Gilen et al., "Finding Ways").

54. Dejong, "The Urban Context of Health during Economic Crisis," 272.

55. Tiltnes, "Poverty and Welfare in the Palestinian Refugee Camps."

56. Suyyagh, "Poverty Management in Jordan," 10.

57. Piro, *Political Economy of Market Reform in Jordan,* 40. Estimates of the total domestic workforce employed by the government at this time generally range from 45–50 percent. The World Bank put the figure at 45 percent, or 257,000 individuals, in 1991. Of these, 90,000 were in government administration, 30,000 in autonomous institutions under the government's umbrella, and the remainder were employed by the army (Country Operations Division World Bank, "Jordan Public Expenditure Review," vii.

58. Jaber, "The Competitiveness of Jordan's Manufacturing Industry."

59. Brynen, "Economic Crisis and Post-Rentier Democratization in the Arab World"; Hashemite Kingdom of Jordan, "Dirasat al-istikhdam, fil-mu'assasat alati y'amal bi-kul min-ha 5 ashkhas aw akthar [Employment Survey for Establishments Engaging (5) Persons or More]," Tables 8, 9. Public employment was 95 percent in Mafraq, 90 percent in Ma'an, and 63 percent overall as the national average. This does not include micro firms or agricultural employment, so the figures are slightly inflated. Given the low proportion of domestic workers in agriculture, and the low incidence of small-scale firms in the regions outside the capital, it is reasonable to conclude that figures for public employment in the rural regions are more accurate than those for the capital.

60. Doan, "Class Differentiation and the Informal Sector in Amman, Jordan," 32.

61. Kanovsky, *The Economy of Jordan,* 6; Antoun, *Arab Village,* 27; Rivier, *Croissance Industrielle dans une Economie Assistée.*

62. Seccombe, "Labour Emigration Policies and Economic Development in Jordan," 123.

63. World Bank, *Unlocking the Employment Potential,* 62.

64. Tell, "Paysans, nomades et état en Jordanie orientale," 97.

65. Aken, "Development as a Gift." Farming began to be considered a spare-time activity to be done by women, old men, children, and those with no better options, including Egyptians (Shryock, "Bedouin in Suburbia"). Foreign workers, mainly Egyptians, are currently estimated as comprising 90 percent of guest workers. About one-third of the registered 150,000 guest workers are employed in agriculture, and one-quarter in construction and sanitation (*Jordan Times,* 26 April 2000).

66. This figure does not include the West Bank territories administered at the time by Jordan (Mazur, *Economic Growth and Development in Jordan,* 119).

67. Samha, "The Impact of Migratory Flows on Population Changes in Jordan," 216; Rivier, "Rente petroliere et politiques industrielles des états non petroliers, 117; Seccombe, "Labour Emigration Policies and Economic Development."

68. Reported worker remittances reached a low in 1991 of 389 million JD. They were 1032 million JD in 1997 (Hashemite Kingdom of Jordan, *Plan for Economic and Social Development 1993–1997,* 120; idem, "Statistical Yearbook 1998").

69. Arab Monetary Fund, "Joint Arab Economic Report," chap. 10, Tables 1 and 2.

70. Dejong and Tell, "Economic Crisis and the Labour Market."

71. "Family" in these statistics refers to immediate family. The data are from 1980. See Shami, "Domesticity Reconfigured," 88; Ahmed and Williams-Ahmed, "The Impact of the Gulf Crisis on Jordan's Economic Infra-Structure"; Anderson, "The History of the Jordanian National Movement." Families who received remittances from a relative working abroad did not receive income from the state, and vice versa, demonstrating the split between public and private labor markets. See Hanssen-Bauer, Pedersen, and Tiltnes, *Jordanian Society,* 290.

72. Keely and Saket, "Jordanian Migrant Workers in the Arab Region"; Saket, "Economic Uses of Remittances"; Nushiwat, "The Effect of Remittances on Investment"; Samha, "The Impact of Migratory Flows on Population Changes"; Share, "The Use of Jordanian Workers' Remittances."

73. Economic Studies Unit, "Unemployment in Jordan." In one survey, 40 percent of the younger generation from one village is in debt (McCann, "Patrilocal Co-residential Units").

74. There are indications that Jordanians have begun to accept previously rejected types of work (*Jordan Times,* 24 February 2000).

75. *Jordan Times,* 29 March 1998; Longuenesse, "Ingénieurs et marché de l'emploi en Jordanie."

76. World Bank, *Unlocking the Employment Potential,* 103; Daves, "Biting the Hand That Feeds You."

77. *al-'Arab al-yawm,* 17 May 2000.

78. The figure is for 1998. Bader, *al-Ta'leem al-'ali fil-Urdun: bayna al-mas'ouliyya al-hukumiyya wa al-qita' al-khas* [*Higher education in Jordan: Between public and private sectors*]; Hashemite Kingdom of Jordan, "Key National Indicators," http://www.dos.gov.jo/sdb_jd/jd_txt3e.htm.

79. *al-'Arab al-yawm,* 31 May 2000; Hashemite Kingdom of Jordan, "Statistical Yearbook 1998," 232.

80. Hashemite Kingdom of Jordan, *Plan for Economic and Social Development 1993–1997,* 120; idem, "Statistical Yearbook 1998," 275; Le Troquer and al-Oudat, "From Kuwait to Jordan," 43. New projects registered at the Chamber of Industry increased by two hundred or three hundred during 1991–93.

81. Since the Gulf War, most of Ma'an's ten thousand drivers are idle, and their income has fallen to one-fifth of its previous level (Feuilherade, "Iraqi Oil Keeps Flowing," 9; *Jordan Times,* 19–20 May 2000).

82. This is the result of policies promoting the nationalization of labor in the Gulf countries (Winckler, "Gulf Monarchies as Rentier States").

83. Van Aken, "Development as a Gift," 49; Department of Statistics Hashemite Kingdom of Jordan, "Dirasa al-Urduniyeen al-'a'ideen min al-kharij khilal al-fatra 8/10/1991–12/31/1992 [Survey of Jordanians returning from abroad

during the period 8/10/1991–12/31/1992]"; Le Troquer and al-Oudat, "From Kuwait to Jordan"; Radi, "Les Palestiniens du Koweit en Jordanie"; Van Hear, "L'impact des rapatriements forcés vers la Jordanie et le Yémen pendant la crise du golfe." Though the aggregate amount increased, the proportion of remittances remained lower than the prior, oil-boom level.

84. Tiltnes, "Poverty and Welfare in the Palestinian Refugee Camps"; Longuenesse, "Ingénieurs et marché de l'emploi en Jordanie."

85. Amman Ministry of Industry and Trade, "Agreement between the Hashemite Kingdom of Jordan and Israel on Irbid Qualifying Industrial Zone." Karak, Zarqa, Aqaba, and Irbid have zones; only the one in Irbid had active production as of 2000. Interview with Ministry of Industry and Trade official, 18 April 2000.

86. al-'Arab al-yawm, 31 May 2000; Jordan Times, 28 December 1999. Jordanians with whom I spoke were unaware that a minimum wage existed.

87. Interview with Labor Union official, Labor Union Central Office, Amman, 26 June 2000; Tarawneh, "Formalizing the Informal." Children typically work in the informal sector and on the streets, but they are also employed in NGOs since these are exempt from labor regulations (Shteiwi, "Poverty Assessment of Jordan," 20).

88. Moore, "The Newest Jordan."

89. For more information, see Baylouny, "Jordan's New 'Political Development' Strategy."

90. Interviews with owners, managers, and officials in the Amman, Kerak, and Irbid industrial zones, April–May 2004.

91. Dejong and Tell, "Economic Crisis and the Labour Market," 209, 11–12; Kawar, "Implications of the Young Age Structure of the Female Labour Force in Amman"; Jaber, "The Impact of Structural Adjustment," 159.

92. Mark, "CRS Issue Brief for Congress: Lebanon," 8; Figuié, Le Point sur le Liban, 46. Almost four hundred thousand are registered with the UNRWA, but analysts estimate that the actual number of Palestinians in Lebanon is closer to two hundred thousand (Ugland, Difficult Past, Uncertain Future, 17).

93. Estimates range from Muslim, Shi'a, and others comprising 60 percent of the population to Shi'a comprising 38 percent (CIA—The World Factbook, "Lebanon," http://www.cia.gov/cia/publications/factbook/print/le.html; Congressional Research Service, "CRS Issue Brief for Congress: Lebanon").

94. Mark, "CRS Issue Brief," 8.

95. Figuié, Le Point sur le Liban, 46, 58; Davie, "The Emerging Urban Landscape of Lebanon," 171.

96. American Task Force for Lebanon, Working Paper—Conference on Lebanon.

97. Interviews with Prof. Fawwaz Trabulsi, Department of Political Science, American University of Beirut, 26 January 1998; and Prof. Ahmad S. Moussalli, Department of Political Science, American University of Beirut, 15 January 1998.

98. Labaki and Abou Rjeily, *Bilan des guerres du Liban,* 177; Kubursi, "Reconstructing the Economy of Lebanon," 70; Gaspard, *A Political Economy of Lebanon,* 69.

99. Labaki and Abou Rjeily, *Bilan des guerres du Liban,* 188; Gaspard, *A Political Economy of Lebanon,* 168.

100. Nasr, "Les travailleurs de l'industrie manufacturiere au machrek," 150.

101. American Task Force for Lebanon, *Conference on Lebanon,* 61.

102. Economist Intelligence Unit, "Lebanon: Country Profile," 34; Fattouh and Leenders, "Lebanon," 19.

103. Gaspard, *A Political Economy of Lebanon,* 93.

104. Labaki, "L'exode de 1945 à 1980"; idem, "L'économie politique de l'émigration libanaise."

105. Gaspard, *A Political Economy of Lebanon,* 97; Nasr, "The New Social Map," 144–47.

106. Picard, "Trafficking, Rents, and Diaspora in the Lebanese War," 42.

107. Dib, *Warlords and Merchants,* 307.

108. Arab Monetary Fund, "Joint Arab Economic Report," chap. 10, Tables 1 and 2.

109. Longuenesse, "Guerre et decentralisation urbaine au Liban"; Beyhum, "Population Displacement in the Metropolitan District of Beirut."

110. From the start of the war, approximately 550,000 people were forced out of mixed areas (Dib, *Warlords and Merchants,* 245).

111. American Task Force for Lebanon, *Conference on Lebanon,* 100.

112. Khalaf, "On Roots and Routes," 134.

113. Nasr, "Anatomie d'un système de guerre interne," 91; American Task Force for Lebanon, *Conference on Lebanon,* 21.

114. Khalaf, "On Roots and Routes:," 127. Only 22 percent moved between the different parts of the city.

115. Makdisi, *Lessons of Lebanon,* 83; Dib, *Warlords and Merchants,* 134.

116. Gaspard, *A Political Economy of Lebanon,* 205.

117. Figuié, *Le Point sur le Liban,* 298.

118. Nasr, "The New Social Map," 156; Makdisi, *Lessons of Lebanon,* 144; Figuié, *Le Point sur le Liban,* 299; Oxford Business Group, "Emerging Lebanon," 47.

119. World Bank, *Unlocking the Employment Potential,* 62.

120. Interview with the General Director of Subsidies Section, Lebanese Ministry of Economy, Beirut, 27 June 2005.

121. Haddad, "The Poor in Lebanon."

122. World Bank, *Unlocking the Employment Potential,* 62; Oxford Business Group, "Emerging Lebanon," 159; Gaspard, *A Political Economy of Lebanon,* 92.

123. Haddad, "The Poor in Lebanon"; Amery and Anderson, "International Migration and Remittances to a Lebanese Village."

124. Oxford Business Group, "Emerging Lebanon," 28; Picard, "Trafficking, Rents, and Diaspora in the Lebanese War," 27.

125. Gaspard, *A Political Economy of Lebanon,* 155; Lebanese Center for Policy Studies, "The Civil Society Report 1997."

126. Figuié, *Le Point sur le Liban,* 297; Gaspard, *A Political Economy of Lebanon,* 87.

127. Figuié, *Le Point sur le Liban,* 261.

128. Calculations based on labor force estimates and percentages involved in liberal and independent work. In 1998 the labor force was comprised either of 1 million or 1.25 million (ibid., 59, 61).

129. Ibid., 58, 233.

130. *L'Orient le Jour,* 23 April 2004, 8.

131. Oxford Business Group, "Emerging Lebanon," 133.

132. Coordination Forum of NGOs Working in the Palestinian Community, "Second Supplementary Report."

133. Abbas et al., "The Socio-economic Conditions of Palestinians in Lebanon," 285.

134. Hudson, "Palestinians and Lebanon," 258.

135. "Citrus Workers in Tyre's Refugee Camps," vol. 9, March 2005, http://www.prc.org.uk/index.php?module=return_review&id=a940f741a1e846ed0453a1e4c88f416&offset=&month=3 (accessed 24 August 2009).

136. Hourani et al., *Directory of Civil Society Organizations in Jordan,* 317; Lebanese Center for Policy Studies, "The Civil Society Report 1997"; Figuié, *Le Point sur le Liban,* 275–79.

137. Nahas, "L'économie libanaise et ses déséquilibres," 64–65.

138. Longuenesse, "Professional Syndicates in Jordan."

139. *Al-Dustoor,* 8 May 2004.

140. Hourani et al., *Directory of Civil Society Organizations in Jordan,* 77.

141. Ibid., 317.

142. al-Husseini, al-Deen, and al-Haraka, "Dirasat mash minathamat al-qita' al-ahli fi Lubnan [Study of civil society organizations in Lebanon] (unpublished manuscript)."

143. Lebanese Center for Policy Studies, "The Civil Society Report 1997."

144. Khuri, *From Village to Suburb,* 205.

145. Lebanese Center for Policy Studies, "The Civil Society Report 1997"; Figuié, *Le Point sur le Liban,* 275–79.

146. Analyzing the incentives for rotating savings societies in Egypt, Baydas et al. conclude that the type of credit demanded by participants in these societies is not forthcoming through banks. According to their survey, the members of many such societies work in banks and thus have access to formal credit. However, the credit available is neither short-term nor are the terms easy. See Baydas, Bahloul, and Adams, "Informal Finance in Egypt."

147. Barr, *The Economics of the Welfare State,* 111, 17–18.

148. Saleh and Harvie, "An Analysis of Public Sector Deficits and Debt in Lebanon."

149. Oxford Business Group, "Emerging Lebanon," 125.

150. Moez Doriad, "Human Development and Poverty in the Arab States," 211.

151. Makdisi, *Lessons of Lebanon*, 150.

152. Oxford Business Group, "Emerging Lebanon," 71.

153. UNDP, "Globalization."

154. Loewe et al., "Improving the Social Protection of the Urban Poor and Near-Poor in Jordan."

155. Tayyar, "Lebanon's Insurance Sector," STAT-USA Market Research Reports, http://strategis.ic.gc.ca/epic/internet/inimr-ri/nsf/en/gr117403e.html; Saradar Investment House, "Lebanon's Insurance Industry," AME Info, http://www.ameinfo.com/news/Detailed/36698.html (accessed September 2005).

156. Vittas, "Insurance Regulation in Jordan."

157. Oxford Business Group, *Emerging Jordan* (2003), 101–4.

158. Loewe et al., "Improving the Social Protection of the Urban Poor," iv.

159. Gaspard, *A Political Economy of Lebanon*, 71.

160. UNDP, "A Profile of Sustainable Human Development in Lebanon," 6.

161. Figuié, *Le Point sur le Liban*, 289.

162. World Bank, "Proposed Projects on Jordan," http://www.worldbank.org/pics/pid/jo39749.txt (accessed March 2000).

163. Marseglia, "Welfare in the Mediterranean Countries: Lebanon"; Sekhri and Savedoff, "Private Health Insurance: Implications for Developing Countries, 3; World Bank, *Reducing Vulnerability and Increasing Opportunity,* 117.

164. Glasze and Alkhayyal, "Gated Housing Estates in the Arab World."

165. Loewe et al., "Improving the Social Protection of the Urban Poor," v.

166. Skocpol and Oser, "Organization Despite Adversity"; Beito, "'This Enormous Army.'"

4. KIN MUTUAL AID

1. Besley, "Nonmarket Institutions for Credit and Risk Sharing in Low-Income Countries."

2. Data in this chapter are derived mainly from my survey and interviews, verified and supplemented by published data from state agencies in Lebanon and Jordan. Additional data for Jordan came from the national supervising agency for charities, the General Union of Voluntary Societies (GUVS), and the Cooperative Corporation in charge of cooperatives. Obtaining data on Lebanon was more difficult. The supervising agency—a section of the Ministry of the Interior—was not forthcoming. Nor is the data published officially in any compiled form. I created a master list of associations from the *Official Gazette* for the years 1980 through 2005. Two main studies on kin associations were published for the previous period, which I use for the pre–civil war era. I also obtained an internal collaborative document written by officials from several

Lebanese ministries detailing the associations and their activities. The figures here regard formal registered kin associations owing to the difficulties in obtaining data on unregistered associations. Though some are informal, the trend can be seen from the number of formal associations. For more on the research method and the questionnaires, see the appendixes to this volume.

3. In Jordan mutual aid associations can register as either cooperatives, part of the business sector, or charities. They are functionally similar, perform the same services, are subject to virtually the same state regulations, and use identical idioms of organizing and tropes of family. However, kin-organized charities are not the legal property of members; when disbanded, the assets of charities devolve to the state whereas cooperatives retain their assets. Cooperatives also have more leeway and autonomy in their activities, and predominate in Jordan's richer areas. Charities, on the other hand, dominate the poorer rural south and north.

4. These initial cooperatives registered as mutual benefit cooperatives, a category reserved for kin organizing. The current trend is to register as a multi-purpose association (interview with an official of the Jordan Cooperative Corporation, 14 April 1998, and various dates in fall 1999).

5. Al-Naber is the family name. The association was registered in 1965 as a mutual-aid cooperative, *manfaʻ mutabadila*, at a time when the association was allowed to retain the family name (interview with member and Cooperative Corporation official, Aal al-Naber Cooperative, 2 February 2000).

6. Interview with al-Naber.

7. In spite of a treatise on the family's historical roots, the tribe's publication states that their original location is unimportant. What is relevant is that a section of the tribe now lives, united, under the Hashemite monarchy (Jamiʻaan and Jamiʻaan, *Maʻdaba wa ʻashira al-Karadisheh* [*Madaba and the Karadisheh tribe*], 1).

8. Ghabra, *Palestinians in Kuwait*, 17–18.

9. Sawalha, "Identity, Self and the Other among Palestinian Refugees in East Amman"; Gilen et al., "Finding Ways."

10. Interview with Mohammad Abu Saʻad, President of the Lifta Charitable Association, Amman, 11 February 2000.

11. Registered, dues-paying members in Amman number only 1,750 (interview with Abu Saʻad).

12. Silwan Social Development Association, *al-Nitham al-asasi* [*Charter*].

13. al-Ramla Charitable Association, *al-Nitham al-asasi* [*Charter*].

14. al-Husbani, "al-ʻAshaʼiriyya wa al-dawla: dirasa li-thahira al-madafat fi madinat Irbid [Tribalism and the state: The phenomenon of Madafas in the city of Irbid]." The middle class had become distanced from kinship institutions, developing professional and other overtly economic or interest-based associational ties over the previous few decades. This is apparent in statements made prior to 1990 that Jordan was detribalizing, less-fragmented, and beginning to create a unified national identity. Education and mobility were deemed

responsible for the tribe's waning influence. See Jureidini and McLaurin, *Jordan;* Abu-Odeh, *Jordanians, Palestinians, and the Hashemite Kingdom in the Middle East Peace Process,* 275; Fathi, *Jordan—An Invented Nation?;* Abu Jaber and Fathi, "The 1989 Jordanian Parliamentary Elections"; Library of Congress, "Country Studies: Jordan," http://lcweb2.loc.gov/frd/csquery.html (accessed August 2000); and Sayigh, "Jordan in the 1980s."

15. Labor possibilities in the Gulf states have shrunk considerably, making success in the domestic market crucial.

16. A large portion (41%) of previous migrants to the Gulf countries established their own businesses upon return (Keely and Saket, "Jordanian Migrant Workers in the Arab Region," 692). Returnees from the Gulf War in the 1990s found employment in banking, financial services, commercial enterprises, and the health sector, in addition to running their own businesses. These activities created an entire commercial district in the capital. See Le Troquer and al-Oudat, "From Kuwait to Jordan."

17. Gilen et al., "Finding Ways"; Rasheed, "Social Structure, Kinship, and Settlement."

18. Multiple names for the tribe exist, depending on how descent is traced, the author states. The writer's name takes up a full four lines, tracing his ancestry back to the time of the Prophet. The definition he uses of his tribe, however, is more limited than that lineage would imply (al-Kaswani, *Qabila Aal Zaydan al-Zayadna Family,* 30, 96).

19. Hanssen-Bauer, Pedersen, and Tiltnes, *Jordanian Society,* 280.

20. Interview with Mohammad al-Ardha, Researcher, Directorate of Studies and Research, General Union of Voluntary Societies, 12 October 1999.

21. Interview, Adnan Taha, member of Abna' al-Harith cooperative, 30 April 2004, Amman.

22. Hashemite Kingdom of Jordan, "Statistical Yearbook 1998," 228; idem, "Societies and Syndicates," http://www.dos.gov.jo/jorfig/1999/fiq_e_n.htm. The 1985 figure includes the West Bank, as well as business, housing, and agricultural cooperatives.

23. General Union of Voluntary Societies, "Taqreer al-majlis al-tanfeethi. al-idari wa al-mali wa al-mawazina al-taqdeeriyya [Executive report. Administration and finances and projected budget]," 58, Hashemite Kingdom of Jordan, "Statistical Yearbook 1998," 230.

24. Hanssen-Bauer, Pedersen, and Tiltnes, *Jordanian Society,* 280, 304; Center for Strategic Studies, "Istitlaa' lil-ra'i hawla al-dimuqratiyya fil-Urdun 2000 [Opinion Survey on Democracy in Jordan 2000]," 31.

25. Center for Strategic Studies, "Istitlaa' lil-ra'i hawla al-dimuqratiyya fil-Urdun 2000," 31.

26. Interview with Munther al-Qara'een, Vice President of the al-Azhaar Cooperative, 12 March 2000.

27. Khalaf, *Lebanon's Predicament,* 172.

28. Lebanese Center for Policy Studies, "The Civil Society Report 1997."

29. Personal communication with Prof. Asʿad AbuKhalil, California State University, Stanislaus, 16 May 2005.

30. Baalbaki, "Dinamiya al-taʾteer al-ijtimaʿi fi qura wa baladat qada Aaley [Dynamics of social framing in the villages and towns of Aley district]," 227.

31. Ibid., 216.

32. Nasr, "Anatomie d'un système de guerre interne: Le cas du Liban," 95.

33. Interview with Prof. Chawqi Doueihi, Department of Anthropology, Lebanese University, 23 June 2005; interview, Prof. Salim Nasr, Senior Advisor for Civil Society and Public Participation, UNDP, 21 June 2005. An attempt at civilian rule in West Beirut failed, unable to unite the various interests. Judith P. Harik, "Change and Continuity among the Lebanese Druze Community," 379–80.

34. Registration documents and Khaled Ziadé, "Trablous: al-ʿaʾila wa al-siyasa [Tripoli: Family and politics]."

35. Baalbaki, "Dynamics of Social Framing," 224.

36. Joseph, "Civic Myths, Citizenship, and Gender in Lebanon," 120–22; Hannoyer, "Introduction: Économies de la violence, dimensions de la civilité."

37. Khalaf, Civil and Uncivil Violence in Lebanon, 264.

38. Khalaf, "On Roots and Routes, 131.

39. Lebanese Center for Policy Studies, "The Civil Society Report 1997."

40. Khalili, "Grass-roots Commemorations"; Peteet, "Lebanon"; Le Monde Diplomatique, http://www.monde-diplomatique.fr/cahier/proche-orient/region-lebanon-refugee; Suleiman, "Palestinians in Lebanon and the Role of Non-governmental Organizations," 398; Roberts, "Bourj al-Barajneh: The Significance of Village Origin in a Palestinian Refugee Camp"; Jaber Suleiman, personal communication, 7 April 2005.

41. Figures do not include those associations renewing an existing license. Though figures vary and data are unreliable (see Appendix 1), the trend is clear. All interviewees and research institutions affirmed this.

42. These are distinct from agricultural organizations or cooperatives.

43. This is a conservative estimate, limited to those verified as kin associations.

44. Khalaf, Lebanon's Predicament, 171, 73–74. Not all these prior associations remain active; some fail. There is much movement into and out of the mutual aid association sphere.

45. al-Husseini, Muhi al-Deen, and al-Haraka, "Dirasat mash minathamat al-qitaʿ al-ahli fi Lubnan [Study of civil society organizations in Lebanon]" (unpublished manuscript).

46. Lebanese Center for Policy Studies, "The Civil Society Report 1997."

47. al-Husseini, Muhi al-Deen, and al-Haraka, "Dirasat mash minathamat al-qitaʿ al-ahli fi Lubnan."

48. United Nations Development Programme, Programme on Governance

in the Arab Region (UNDP-POGAR), "Country Index: State—Civil Society Relations. Lebanon," http://www.pogar.org/countries/civil.asp?cid=9 (accessed September 2005), Chawqi Doueihy, "al-Sira'a 'ala al-madina: madkhal ila dirasa rawabit al-ahiya' fi Beirut [The struggle for the city: Introduction to the study of neighborhood associations in Beirut]."

49. Baalbaki, "Dynamics of Social Framing"; Lebanese Center for Policy Studies, "The Civil Society Report 1997."

50. *L'Express*, 7 March 2005.

51. Ibid.

52. al-Husseini, Muhi al-Deen, and al-Haraka, "Study of Civil Society Organizations in Lebanon."

53. Interview with Ghassan Jamous, US AID, Beirut, 4 May 2004.

54. *al-Diyar*, 3 October 1998.

55. Neighborhood associations also fulfilled local law and order roles, particularly during the civil war (Doueihy, "The Struggle for the City").

56. Interview with Abu Sa'ad.

57. Interview with al-Qara'een.

58. Interview with Aal al-Naber, Member and Cooperative Corporation Official.

59. Silwan Social Development Association, *al-Nitham al-asasi* [*Charter*].

60. This association interviewee complained that the family had lost its work ethic as a result of receiving so much welfare from the family association.

61. Silwan Social Development Association, *al-Nitham al-asasi*.

62. al-Ramla Charitable Association, *al-Nitham al-asasi*.

63. General Union of Voluntary Societies, "Taqreer al-majlis al-tanfeethi. al-idari wa al-mali wa al-mawazina al-taqdeeriyya [Executive report. Administration and finances and projected budget]" (1987–88, p. 43; 1994–95, p. 39); idem, "Tarikh . . . baramij . . . meshari'a [Profile, programs, projects]," 7.

64. General Union of Voluntary Societies, "Tarikh . . . baramij . . . meshari'a," 7.

65. Lebanese Center for Policy Studies, "The Civil Society Report 1997."

66. Interview with Shuwayka Charitable Association official.

67. The leader referred to Bangladesh's Grameen Bank. Interview with al-Qara'een.

68. The association also has a school and clinics, provides transportation to its school and aid to the poor, and holds trainings (Khalil al-Rahman Charitable Association, *al-Taqreer al-sinnawi li-'am* [*Yearly report for the year*] *1983, 1984, 1985, 1986;* idem, *al-Taqreer al-sinnawi li-'am . . . 1987, 1988, 1989.* The Lifta association also rents out its hall, albeit at a more reasonable rate.

69. Interviews, Aleppo and Damascus, Syria, summer 1998 and January 2000. The phenomenon of receptions held in the home was previously more frequent in Jordan but is now associated with lower-class status. Interviews in Amman.

70. There is a disconnect between training and labor-market needs. Participants acknowledge that the skills most needed do not coincide with the training that they take. Further, those outside the labor market, not seeking employment, attend the same type of training as those seeking employment. See al-Jomard, "al-Mutaghayyerat al-mu'athira 'ala al-musharika fi dawraat al-tadreeb li-tanmiyya al-mahaarat fil-Urdun [Variables affecting participation in skills training courses in Jordan]," 81; and Economic Studies Unit, "Unemployment in Jordan—1996," 72. For a critical assessment of women's training programs, see Shteiwi and Hejoj, "Poverty Alleviation Programs Effectiveness in Jordan"; and Suyyagh, "Poverty Management in Jordan." One association stated as a priority the need to raise the educational level of "girls" in the family, a term which in the Arab world refers to unmarried females of any age. Increasing female education could reflect the desire to marry well, since educated women are now in high demand as marriage partners, and women represent a very small percentage of the urban workforce in Jordan.

71. al-Fa'ouri, "al-Jama'iyyat al-khayriyya fi muhafatha Irbid [Charitable associations in Irbid]."

72. Interview with Aal al-Naber, member and Cooperative Corporation official.

73. Interview with al-Qara'een; interview with Bassam F. Ma'ayeh, Former President of the al-Basat al-Akhdar Cooperative, 24 June 2000.

74. Interview with Youssef Antoine Daccache, Association President, Byblos, Lebanon, 5 May 2004.

75. Interview with a member of the Abna' al-Harith Cooperative, 7 May 2000.

76. Hashemite Kingdom of Jordan, "Statistical Yearbook 1998," 118. In my survey of central Jordan, about 10 percent of associations added a kindergarten at the end of the 1990s.

77. Irbid's nurseries increased from three in 1993 to fifteen in 1999. Mafraq went from having seven to ten nurseries, and Irbid from nine to fifteen (Hamarneh, al-Urdun [Jordan], 194); General Union of Voluntary Societies, "Ri'aya al-tufoula [Childhood care]."

78. Hashemite Kingdom of Jordan, "Dirasa nafaqat wa dakhl al-usra 1997," 34; de Bel-Air, "La gestion politique, economique et sociale des phenomenes demographiques en Jordanie."

79. In Jordan 57 percent of working women are married, and 42 percent of all working women have a child under the age of six (Flynn and Oldham, "Women's Economic Activities in Jordan").

80. Establishment of an association does not indicate its success or failure. Many organizations disband or become inactive, or lack capacity to deliver the promised services. This fleeting nature does not detract from the motivation spurring their formation. Efficacy is unrelated to the impetus for forming an association. The establishment of associations in itself tells us much about the

deficiencies in the market and the ability to provide for themselves; in this context the solution necessitates linkages with others which in turn limits political and social independence.

81. Clark, *Islam, Charity, and Activism*.

82. The only similar membership organizations are the profession-based associations discussed in chapter 3. However, in kin associations, membership is delineated by non-market identity criterion that cuts transaction costs but also excludes and draws a line between insiders and outsiders.

83. Brand, *Women, the State, and Political Liberalization*.

84. Hamarneh, *Jordan;* Hammad, "Islamists and Charitable Work in Jordan." See also Clark, *Islam, Charity, and Activism*.

85. Hammad, "Islamists and Charitable Work in Jordan," 181–82.

86. Dabbas, "Islamic Centers, Associations, Societies, Organizations, and Committees in Jordan"; Hammad, "Islamists and Charitable Work in Jordan," 176.

87. Hammad, "Islamists and Charitable Work in Jordan," 172. See also el-Said, *Between Pragmatism and Ideology*.

88. Hammad, "Islamists and Charitable Work in Jordan," 176–77.

89. Ibid.

90. Wiktorowicz, "Islamists, the State, and Cooperation in Jordan," 10.

91. Directorate of Research and Social Studies General Union of Voluntary Societies, "Dalil al-jama'iyyat al-khayriyya fil-Urdun [Directory of voluntary societies in Jordan]"; Hammad, "Islamists and Charitable Work in Jordan."

92. Hammad, "Islamists and Charitable Work in Jordan," 173. The yearly beneficiaries increase incrementally up to 1990 and then jump dramatically.

93. Curmi, "Les Associations de Bienfaisance à Amman," 364–64.

94. *Jordan Times,* 9 February 2000, 3.

95. *al-Rai,* 3 May 2004.

96. Interview with Ministry of Social Development official in charge of women's affairs, 26 April 2004.

97. Jawad, "A Profile of Social Welfare in Lebanon," 324.

98. al-Husseini, Muhi al-Deen, and al-Haraka, "Study of Civil Society Organizations in Lebanon."

99. Ibid.

100. Jawad, "A Profile of Social Welfare in Lebanon," 324.

101. UNDP, "A Profile of Sustainable Human Development in Lebanon."

102. Deeb, "An Enchanted Modern."

103. Lebanese Center for Policy Studies, "The Civil Society Report 1997."

104. Jawad, "A Profile of Social Welfare in Lebanon," 335.

105. Sayigh, "Palestinians in Lebanon," 101.

106. Roberts, "The Impact of Assistance on the Coping Mechanisms of Long-term Refugees," 217.

107. Personal communication, independent researcher and former educator in PLO institutions, Beirut, 17 June 2005.

108. Roberts, "The Impact of Assistance on the Coping Mechanisms," 219–20. Most Palestinian groups operating in the camps in Lebanon are not in the PLO coalition but are groups that reject the Oslo Accords.

109. Coordination Forum of NGOs Working in the Palestinian Community, "Second Supplementary Report on the Rights of the Palestinian Child in Lebanon," May 2001, http://www.palcoordinationforum.org.

110. Coordination Forum of NGOs Working in the Palestinian Community, "Achievements" and "Members," http://www.palcoordinationforum.org/maine .htm.

111. Suleiman, "Palestinians in Lebanon and the Role of Non-governmental Organizations," 403.

112. Follis, "Micro-credit Can Fill Holes Left by Banks."

113. Norton, *Hezbollah*, 109–10.

5. CREATING KIN AND NEW INSTITUTIONS

1. Analyzing the post-independence period in Lebanon, Khuri states that manipulating kin ties for influence is not new, but the form used, the kin as-sociation, is qualitatively new (*From Village to Suburb*, 227).

2. A few very old associations used a form of *waqf*, an endowment or trust, for the family. Although associated with Islam, Christian associations in Leba-non used it also.

3. Shryock, "Bedouin in Suburbia"; al-Husbani, "al-'Asha'iriyya wa al-dawla [Tribalism and the state]."

4. In Syria and Jordan it is called *madafa*, in Kuwait and Jordan *diwan*, *rabita* in Palestine, *manzul* or *majlis* in Lebanon, and *mafraj* in Kuwait and Yemen. In general, East Bank Jordanians refer to these as *diwan* or *madafa*, and Palestinians as *rabita*.

5. Shryock, "Bedouin in Suburbia"; al-Husbani, "Tribalism and the State."

6. Hannoyer, "L'hospitalité, économie de la violence"; Hanssen-Bauer, Ped-ersen, and Tiltnes, *Jordanian Society*, 280, 303–4; Antoun, "Civil Society, Tribal Process, and Change in Jordan."

7. Baalbaki, "Dinamiya al-ta'teer al-ijtima'i fi qura wa baladat qada Aaley [Dynamics of social framing in the villages and towns of Aley district]," 227.

8. Aleppo and Damascus, interviews, summer 1998.

9. Ghabra, *Palestinians in Kuwait*, 108.

10. Jordan and Syria, interviews, fall 1999–spring 2000. The practice is still common and is called *sunduq nisa'i* (women's treasury). One-third of women in a northern Jordanian village participated in such savings clubs (McCann, "Patrilocal Co-residential Units (PCUs) in Al-Barha." In Cairo they are called

jama'iyyat. See Singerman, *Avenues of Participation,* chap. 3; see also Aili Mari Tripp, "Local Organizations, Participation, and the State in Urban Tanzania," 232–33.

11. Khuri, *From Village to Suburb,* 228.

12. The general term "kin" or "family association" was not always immediately recognized by Jordanians, in contrast to Lebanese. When presented with prominent examples of associations, Jordanians immediately identified their own association and the trend as a whole. A wide variety of exemplars were used with the same result. Survey institutions in Jordan have encountered the same problems and have solved the dilemma by listing several alternative names for kin associations.

13. Relatives can refuse to join; however, once a majority of the potential kin group has agreed, individual families find it hard to opt-out or not participate. Some attempt to avoid paying dues, but those same individuals recognize the need to eventually become dues-paying members, which is necessary if they request services from the organization. For the most part, informal methods of social control, gossip, and peer pressure assure continued payment of dues and participation. In Kuwait Ghabra found that only two out of fifteen Palestinian families from one association did not pay their dues (*Palestinians in Kuwait,* 140). In northern Jordan al-Husbani found that 84 percent of respondents contributed to the financial upkeep of the association ("Tribalism and the State," 134).

14. Ghabra, *Palestinians in Kuwait,* 18. Similarly Fandy states that family is expansive, extending to non-kin (*Saudi Arabia and the Politics of Dissent,* 31).

15. The term "tribe" is over-used and ill-defined. See Tapper, "Anthropologists, Historians, and Tribespeople on Tribe and State Formation in the Middle East." The definition often includes a cultural component, that is, the group believes it shares a culture distinct from that of other groups. Historically, in the Middle East, tribes moved, lived, and produced together, based on a nomadic or agricultural life-style or both. Khoury and Kostiner loosely define tribes as "large kin groups organized and regulated according to ties of blood or family lineage" ("Introduction: Tribes and the Complexities of State Formation in the Middle East," 4).

16. In the Arab world, as in many other world regions, this is considered kinship (*quraba*). Village as a form of kinship has generally not been explicitly spelled out in the literature, but it is often implied, conflated with tribe or clan, or referred to as locational or regional identity. See Rubin, "Russian Hegemony and the State Breakdown in the Periphery"; Roy, "État et recompositions identitaires"; Berry, *Fathers Work for Their Sons;* Baram, "Neo-Tribalism in Iraq"; Batatu, *The Old Social Classes and the Revolutionary Movements of Iraq,* chap. 58; Jabar, "Shaykhs and Ideologues"; Khalaf, "Changing Forms of Political Patronage in Lebanon," 190; and Denoeux, *Urban Unrest in the Middle East,* 215.

17. Berry, *Fathers Work for Their Sons;* Pratten and Baldo, "'Return to the

Roots'"; Pierre-Louis, "The Limits of the State in Promoting Hometown Associations"; Biggart, "Banking on Each Other."

18. Some Jordanian associations include non-relatives under the category "friends of the association." They do not have voting rights in the association.

19. Khuri, *From Village to Suburb*, 178.

20. Interview with the founding member of Mdan Cooperative.

21. Calculated from the Lebanese official gazette, 1984–2005.

22. Lebanese official gazette and interviews.

23. Khalaf, *Lebanon's Predicament*, 167.

24. Khuri, *From Village to Suburb*, 176.

25. Doueihy, "al-Sira'a 'ala al-madina [The struggle for the city]."

26. *al-Diyar*, 15 December 1997.

27. Riedel, *Who's Who in the Jordanian Parliament 1989–1993*, 36.

28. Interview with Rana Taha, Amman, Jordan, 3 May 1998, and other members of Abna' al-Harith, various dates, fall 1999–spring 2000.

29. Jungen, "Tribalism in Kerak."

30. Khuri, *From Village to Suburb*, 175, 78.

31. By contrast, other types of associations formed for the purposes of uniting fishermen, providing services to farmers, doing charity work, and improving agriculture.

32. General Union of Voluntary Societies, "al-Sira al-thatiyya lil-jama'iyyat al-muta'ddida al-aghrad [Profile of multipurpose associations] (Internal document)"; al-Fa'ouri, "al-Jama'iyyat al-khayriyya fi muhafatha Irbid [Charitable associations in Irbid]"; Hamarneh, *al-Urdun [Jordan]*, 185.

33. Lebanese Center for Policy Studies, "The Civil Society Report 1997."

34. Beito, *From Mutual Aid to the Welfare State.*

35. The trend is toward registering all members, male and female.

36. Interview with Awad Hamdan, the director of the Silwan Association, 3 May 2004.

37. Fathi, *Jordan—An Invented Nation?*

38. al-Husbani, "Tribalism and the State," 115, 21–22, 34.

39. Fathi, *Jordan—An Invented Nation?*

40. Interview with al-Qara'een.

41. Interview with Abu Sa'ad; interview with Daccache.

42. Khuri, *From Village to Suburb*, 78.

43. Significantly the traditional tribal *jaha*, often assumed as a purpose for family associations, was barely mentioned as a benefit.

44. Interview with official at the Shuwayka Charitable Association, 8 February 2000.

45. Interview with Ma'ayeh.

46. The director of one cooperative stated that a minority of members are employees, which generally refers to government employees (interview with al-Naber).

47. al-Husbani, "Tribalism and the State," chap. 5.

48. Interview with the founding member of the Mdan Cooperative.

49. The percentage of attendees was based on frequent attendees, not the aggregate membership. The remaining 10 percent of employment consisted of farmers, labor supervisors (one trained in a service profession), students, and retirees.

50. Interview with a member of the Abna' al-Harith Cooperative.

51. This was a village-based Palestinian charity. Interview with founding member, the Sour Bahir Charity, 9 February 2000.

52. Al-Ramla employs thirty individuals, twenty-four as teachers (Al-Ramla Charitable Association, *al-Nitham al-asasi* [*Charter*].

53. Interview with Daccache.

54. Ibid.

55. According to one Jordanian leader, less than one-third of this category was interested in kinship organizations in the past. Their attendance has tripled and now includes almost all these professions. This observation was confirmed by interviews with members of other societies who are themselves part of the intellectual community.

56. Lebanese Center for Policy Studies, "The Civil Society Report 1997."

57. al-Husbani, "Tribalism and the State."

58. The leaders in Jordan are overwhelmingly male, with the exception of one Christian association in my survey with a woman on its board. In Lebanon a much higher percentage of associations have women leaders, particularly among the Druze associations in my survey.

59. I separated data on leaders and founders of kin associations into two main categories: the primary founders, the individual singly responsible for the organization's founding, and the secondary founders, those in the initial group forming the core of the organization's official registration. I further subdivided these categories into national origin and period of time the organization formed. The questionnaire was open-ended, and coding took place subsequently. Occupational categories were chosen for two reasons. First, they are large enough to encompass a number of smaller categories, all of which share the same characteristics that theory indicates could be relevant motivations for uniting the family. For example, lawyers, doctors, and engineers are classified as professionals. They share a potential incentive for enlarging their networks of influence in order to generate business contacts, to rise in social influence, and to be used as a possible springboard for a political career. Many representatives of parliament derive from the professions. For current government officials and high-level employees, the benefits are limited to social and political influence. Second, breaking down the categories more finely was not helpful because of the limited data available. No pattern was evident as to whether doctors or lawyers, for example, are more prone to initiating family associations. Similarly lower-level, private-sector employees were among the secondary founders, but

there was no pattern evident among them. They have neither contacts nor goods and services to offer, and derive their income from a salary, not commission or sales; they are therefore placed in a single category.

60. Despite the temporal coincidence, the return of thousands of Palestinian workers from Kuwait during the Gulf War was not directly tied to the formation of family associations. The returnees themselves were not among the founders or leaders of the new organizations.

61. Khuri, *From Village to Suburb*, 188.

62. The information is from the survey of 126 associations. For key founders, 64 associations were in the data pool.

63. Jami'aan and Jami'aan, *Ma'daba wa 'ashira al-Karadisheh*.

64. The president of the municipality wields more power than the *mukhtar* or mayor. The tribal *mukhtar* can represent the descent group, but the president of the municipality is more connected to the central government and able to reap the benefits of that relationship. In many places there are multiple *makhateer*. See Shunnaq, "Political and Economic Conflict within Extended Kin Groups and Its Effects on the Household in a North Jordanian Village."

6. ELITES, ELECTIONS, AND CIVIL SOCIETY

1. Petran, *The Struggle over Lebanon*, 35.

2. One association president stated that kin association leaders were outside the upper classes, driven by a desire to expand their social contacts and relationships through the provision of services, or possibly religious or personal motivations. Unable to increase their social network by themselves, they create a kin association for that purpose (interview with Abu Sa'ad).

3. Compare the similar reputational and good-works criteria for new and rising elites to become local authorities and social players of influence in Ismail, *Political Life in Cairo's New Quarters*.

4. al-Radi, "La famille comme mode de gestion et de contrôle du social chez les élites traditionnelles Palestiniennes"; Shryock and Howell, "'Ever a Guest in Our House,'" 247; Khalaf, "Changing Forms of Political Patronage in Lebanon."

5. Doueihy, "al-Sira'a al-madina [The struggle for the city]."

6. Azm, "The Islamic Action Front Party," 101, 28–31.

7. See Bourdieu, *The Logic of Practice*, 112–21.

8. Definitional problems for the concept of social capital abound. The World Bank defines it as "the institutions, relationships, and norms that shape the quality and quantity of a society's social interactions." In a word, social cohesion (World Bank, "Social Capital," http://www.worldbank.org/poverty/scapital/whatsc.htm [accessed February 2001]). For definitions of social capital, see Putnam, "Bowling Alone"; and World Bank, "Social Capital." For a critical review, see Fine, *Social Capital versus Social Theory*.

9. On the United States, see Seibel and Anheier, "Sociological and Political Science Approaches to the Third Sector." For other regions, see Roy, "The Transformation of Islamic NGOs in Palestine"; Sullivan, "Extra-State Actors and Privatization in Egypt"; Ghabra, "Voluntary Associations in Kuwait"; Anheier, "Private Voluntary Organizations and the Third World"; Ilchman, Katz, and Queen II, "Introduction"; Denoeux, *Urban Unrest in the Middle East;* Wickham, "Islamic Mobilization and Political Change"; and Destremau, "The Systemic Relations of the State and Poverty," http://www.crop.org/rosa3bkp.htm.

10. Ilchman, Katz, and Queen II, "Introduction," xiii. In the Islamic Empire, elites used philanthropic donations, which also served as charity for the poor, to improve or maintain their status in relation to other elites. See Arjomand, "Philanthropy, the Law, and Public Policy in the Islamic World before the Modern Era."

11. Ostrower, *Why the Wealthy Give.* Church groups dating to the sixteen century are the oldest international aid organizations in the West (Smith, *More Than Altruism,* 27). In present-day Saudi Arabia, financial aid to institutions and governments appears to be one of the main elements of Saudi foreign public relations (Kozlowski, "Religious Authority, Reform, and Philanthropy in the Contemporary Muslim World"). In Nigeria, private voluntary organizations represented political parties in the 1950s and more recently have been tied to religion. International aid organizations mirror these trends (Anheier, "Private Voluntary Organizations and the Third World"; Smith, *More Than Altruism*).

12. Smith uses the example of Herbert Hoover's large-scale charitable activities in Western Europe (*More Than Altruism,* 32). A contemporary example would be Colin Powell's leadership of a charitable NGO prior to assuming a government post.

13. Bourdieu, *The Logic of Practice,* 112, 18–19. See also the example of descent-based groups in Africa, in Berry, *Fathers Work for Their Sons,* 79–81; and idem, "Social Institutions and Access to Resources," 44–46.

14. Schatz, *Modern Clan Politics,* 156. Greater economic rewards and social prestige are sometimes obtained by achieving importance among a smaller, rather than a larger, group. Even if elites do attempt to move into the majority group and give up their marginal status, in many cases members of their minority nonetheless call upon them for help with in-group affairs and promotion. See Laitin, "Marginality: A Microperspective"; Fearon and Laitin, "Explaining Interethnic Cooperation"; Hardin, "Contested Community"; and Jenkins, "Conclusion: The States and the Associations," 275–76.

15. Khuri, *From Village to Suburb,* 50, 108.

16. Schatz, *Modern Clan Politics,* 156.

17. These usually, but not always, coincide: prominent elites are generally among the association's leadership, on the board of directors, for example, or are presidents of kin associations.

18. Though they resemble patron-client relations, political clientelism is not an explanation for multiclass networks. As Gilsenan notes, Lebanon's elaborate patronage networks do not add up to a social order, or even a sufficient framework for analysis. Patronage may be prevalent, but it cannot explain outcomes, particularly since the term is used to cover networks ranging from Chicago to the Arab world. To view it as causal would mistake "symptom for cause" (Gilsenan, "Against Patron-Client Relations," 179). Further, the motivations and benefits for individuals participating in the client end of the network have been given short shrift (Singerman, *Avenues of Participation*).

19. Singerman, *Avenues of Participation*, 249.

20. Amawi, "The 1993 Elections in Jordan," 22; Chatelard and al-'Omari, "Primordial Ties and Beyond."

21. Precise numbers of kin associations attempting to elect a member to government are not available; no data currently exist on nonelected candidates' affiliations across time. What follows therefore represents available data and examples. As the current system becomes increasingly institutionalized, and welfare remains in the hands of kin associations, kin electoral blocs may well prove more effective than currently.

22. Interview with founding member of the Sour Bahir Charity in Jordan.

23. Changes in the reporting of these affiliations could be a factor, since in the 1990s kin associations began to gain legitimacy as civil society organizations.

24. Elected candidates were clearly political or ideologically motivated, in contrast to later elections. All but fourteen are members of parties or electoral blocs. Two of those had previously been exiled for plotting against the government, leaving twelve out of eighty nonpolitical members of parliament. See Riedel, *Who's Who in the Jordanian Parliament 1989–1993*.

25. This includes Kawar, a Christian association dating from 1965, and a Bedouin charity (ibid.).

26. I do not include Circassian charities in this data.

27. Hourani, Dabbas, and Power-Stevens, *Who's Who in the Jordanian Parliament 1993–1997*.

28. The figure came to fifteen out of eighty representatives. This count does not include religious or ethnic-based associations, professional associations, or local cultural and sports clubs. Calculations from Hourani and Yassin, *Who's Who in the Jordanian Parliament 1997–2001*.

29. The majority of Jordanian associations did not comment on their role in politics, as political involvement is one reason for the state to dissolve associations.

30. This was the al-'Omari kin group in Irbid. See Riedel, *Who's Who in the Jordanian Parliament 1989–1993*, 64; Hourani and Yassin, *Who's Who in the Jordanian Parliament 1997–2001*, 147; and Chatelard and al-'Omari, "Primordial Ties and Beyond."

31. Hourani, Dabbas, and Power-Stevens, *Who's Who in the Jordanian Parliament 1993–1997*, 133.

32. Carapico, *Civil Society in Yemen*, 122.

33. In one Jordanian case, tribal ('Abbadi) candidates were defeated by a Christian doctor from outside the tribe. The women voted for him because he had delivered their children (Layne, *Home and Homeland*, 116–17).

34. Duclos, "Political Science's Perspective on the Electoral Process." Bocco comments that "tribal unity" is more a myth than reality ("L'état producteur d'identités locales").

35. Center for Strategic Studies, "Istitlaaʻ lil-raʼi hawla al-dimuqratiyya fil-Urdun 1998 [Opinion Survey on Democracy in Jordan 1998]," 43. Eighty-nine percent of the respondents experienced no pressure to vote for a kin or tribal candidate.

36. Moaddel, *Jordanian Exceptionalism*, 124.

37. Shunnaq, "Political and Economic Conflict within Extended Kin Groups and Its Effects on the Household in a North Jordanian Village."

38. Jungen, "Tribalism in Kerak," 202.

39. Hamarneh is allied to the Karadsheh kin group, although he is not part of that lineage. Interview with member of al-Sahl al-Akhdar; interview with al-Qaraʻeen; Chatelard and al-ʻOmari, "Primordial Ties and Beyond." Another Christian tribe, the Azeizat, had previously elected Samih al-Farah in 1993. There are three Christian tribes in Madaba: Maʻayah, Azeizat, and Karadisheh. A loose coalition of other Christian families in the Madaba area is referred to as the "fourth brother" families.

40. Chatelard and al-ʼOmari, "Primordial Ties and Beyond."

41. Lebanese Center for Policy Studies, "Biographical Briefs of the 1996 Deputies by Region."

42. *al-Mustaqbal*, 18 September 1999.

43. Favier, "Annexe 1—Tableau des municipalitès du Liban (en 1999)"; idem, "Annexe 3—Questionnaires SOFRES-CERMOC, 1999."

44. Mrad, "Annexe 4—Composition sociale des conseils municipaux élus au Liban Sud en 1998," 422.

45. Krayyem, "Les présidents de municipalité élus en 1998 au Liban," 48–49.

46. Saab, "Municipal Elections in Southern Mount Lebanon" (in Arabic).

47. Ziadé, "Trablous: al-ʻaʼila wa al-siyasa [Tripoli: Family and politics]."

48. Saʼib Sallam to Prof. Chawqi Doueihi, Department of Anthropology, Lebanese University. Recounted to me during an interview with Doueihi, 23 June 2005.

49. *al-Safir*, 24 May 2005.

50. Interview with Doueihi.

51. Khuri, *From Village to Suburb*, 176.

52. *al-Diyar*, 1 October 1998.

53. On Jordan, see Anderson, *Nationalist Voices in Jordan*; and Abidi, *Jordan*,

A Political Study 1948–1957. On Lebanon, see Trabloulsi, *A History of Modern Lebanon*.

54. Baaklini, Denoeux, and Springborg, *Legislative Politics in the Arab World*, chap. 2.

55. Center for Strategic Studies, "Istitlaa' lil-ra'i hawla al-dimuqratiyya fil-Urdun 2000 [Opinion Survey on Democracy in Jordan 2000]," 19–20.

56. Hourani et al., *Directory of Civil Society Organizations in Jordan*, 245.

57. Center for Strategic Studies, "Opinion Survey," 23.

58. Hourani, "Prospects for the Development of Political Parties and Strategies for Enhancing Political Party Processes in Jordan."

59. All but eight of the remaining seats, out of around twenty-five hundred, went to independent and "tribal" candidates ("Jordan: Fundamental Difficulties," *Oxford Analytica Daily Brief*, 27 July 1999).

60. Brynen, "The Politics of Monarchical Liberalism: Jordan."

61. Hourani and Yassin, *Who's Who in the Jordanian Parliament 1997–2001*, 29.

62. This was thirty-six of the eighty members (ibid., 118).

63. Hourani, "Intikhabat 1993 al-Urduniyya [The 1993 Jordanian elections]."

64. Hawatmeh, "Lacklustre Campaign," 10–11.

65. "Tribal Heat: Jordan (Electoral Law Changes)," *Economist* 329, no. 7836 (6 November 1993), 50–51.

66. Amawi, "The 1993 Elections in Jordan," 19.

67. Omaar, "Elections a Tribal Affair," 4–5; Jaber, "Elections and Civil Society."

68. Jordan Center for Social Research, "Democratic Transformation and Political Reform in Jordan," Tables 12, 13, 23, 24.

69. Jordan Center for Social Research, "The 2007 Municipal Elections in Jordan."

70. *Al-Dustur*, 27 and 30 April 2004.

71. el Khazen, "Lebanon's First Postwar Parliamentary Election, 1992," 65.

72. el Khazen, "Political Parties in Postwar Lebanon," 620–21.

73. Ishtay, "Political Parties in the 2000 Elections," 91; Lebanese Center for Policy Studies, "Biographical Briefs of the 1996 Deputies." Six are identified as "former" party members.

74. Khalaf, "On Roots and Routes," 125.

75. el-Husseini, "Lebanon: Building Political Dynasties"; Ziadé, "Tripoli."

76. American Task Force for Lebanon, *Working Paper—Conference on Lebanon*, 41.

77. Harik, "Citizen Disempowerment and the 1996 Parliamentary Elections in the Governate of Mount Lebanon," 179.

78. Krayyem, "Les présidents de municipalité élus en 1998 au Liban," 50–51.

79. Hourani and Yassin, *Who's Who in the Jordanian Parliament 1997–2001*, 218.

80. Four percent had a secondary-school education or lower. Computations from Riedel, *Who's Who in the Jordanian Parliament 1989–1993.*

81. Bahout, "Les élites parlementaires Libanaises de 1996," 22.

82. Krayyem, "Les présidents de municipalité élus en 1998 au Liban," 51.

83. For condemnations of the kin association as detracting from national identity or alternative political activism and increasing fragmentation, see al-Husbani, "al-'Asha'iriyya wa al-dawla [Tribalism and the state]"; Shryock, "Bedouin in Suburbia"; Khalaf, *Lebanon's Predicament;* Fathi, *Jordan—An Invented Nation?* chap. 6.

84. Ziadé, "Tripoli."

85. Dabbas, "Islamic Centers, Associations, Societies, Organizations, and Committees in Jordan," 259.

86. The association's primary goal is to enable students to obtain higher education by providing housing for them. With fifty registered members, they wield a budget of well over 300,000 JD (Jordanian Dinar) (Sons of Southern Jordan Charitable Association, *Unpublished Report.*

87. Interviews; Layne, *Home and Homeland;* Brynen, "The Politics of Monarchical Liberalism." The association has spurred resentment by its perceived monopolization of state employment to the detriment of other southern Jordanians.

88. These were *al-Diyar* in the late 1990s, and *al-Afkar* and *al-Safir* after 2000. The goal of *al-Nahar's* series was to demonstrate the Arab origins of the Lebanese (*al-Nahar,* 7 December 1996).

89. *al-Diyar,* 12 December 1989.

90. Ibid., 17 July 1999; *al-Diyar,* 16 December 1997.

91. *al-Diyar,* 15 May 1999.

92. *al-Safir,* 24 May 2005.

93. *al-Diyar,* 2 October 1998.

94. *al-Safir,* 24 May 2005.

95. Hanssen-Bauer, Pedersen, and Tiltnes, *Jordanian Society,* 302, 305; Chatelard and al-'Omari, "Primordial Ties and Beyond."

96. Interview with Daccache.

97. Sha'oul, "Elections 2000."

98. Jordan Center for Social Research, "National Public Opinion Poll #4," Table 23.

99. Lebanese Center for Policy Studies, "The Civil Society Report 1997."

100. Makhoul and Harrison, "Intercessory *Wasta* and Village Development in Lebanon," 31.

101. Peteet, "Socio-Political Integration and Conflict Resolution in the Palestinian Camps in Lebanon."

102. *al-Nahar,* 4 June 2005.

103. *al-Safir,* 7 April 1997; Hamzeh, *In the Path of Hizbullah,* 107–108.

104. Legally this is to determine that the individual is morally upright, not a criminal, and is not facing a lawsuit.

105. Wiktorowicz, *The Management of Islamic Activism*.

106. Wiktorowicz reports that the most common rationale for closing an organization is the failure to provide the state with requested information ("Civil Society as Social Control," 53).

107. The number of laws governing these organizations is surpassed only by the number of agencies in charge of supervising them, fifty-two at last count (Maamsir, "al-Tajriba al-Urduniyya fi muhariba al-faqr wa al-battala [The Jordanian experience in battling poverty and unemployment]," 208). A new law is in the works for charitable associations, and the oversight body, the General Union of Voluntary Societies (GUVS), which was established in 1959 and answers to the Ministry of Social Development, plays a central role in these discussions (*al-'Arab al-yawm*, 8 May 2000; *al-'Arab al-yawm*, 25 June 2000). The law for charitable associations is Law #33 of 1966, and it spells out regulations on fund-raising activities and permits, including making donations and holding bazaars, parties, and concerts. The laws governing mutual aid associations are the following: Emirate of TransJordan, "Qanun al-jama'iyyat al-muwaqqat li-sinna 1936 [Provisional Association Law of 1936]"; Hashemite Kingdom of Jordan, "Qanun raqm 17 li-sinna 1956 qanun jama'iyyat al-ta'wun [Law #17 of 1956: Cooperative Associations Law]"; idem, "Qanun raqm (33) li-sinna 1966: qanun al-jama'iyyat wa al-hay'at al-ijtima'iyya [Law #33 of 1966: Law of Associations and Social Organizations]"; idem, "Nitham al-awal: Nitham jam' al-tabarru'at lil-wujuh al-khayriyya [Regulation #1: Regulation on Collecting Donations for Charitable Purposes]"; idem, "Nitham raqm 13 li-sinna 1998 nitham al-jama'iyyat al-taa'wuniyya [Regulation #13 of 1998: Regulation for Cooperative Associations]"; idem, "al-Nitham al-asasi al-mu'adal lil-ittihad al-'am lil-jama'iyyat al-khayriyya li-'am 1995 [The Basic Amended Charter for the General Union of Voluntary Societies of 1995]"; Jordan Cooperative Organization, "al-Taqreer al-sanawi li-'am 1991 [Annual Report for 1991]," 15; and idem, "Qanun raqm 18 li-sinna 1997 qanun al-taa'wun [Law #18 of 1997: Cooperative Law]."

108. The Special Law of 1909 under the Ottomans regulates associations, together with Article 13 of the 1926 Lebanese Constitution providing for freedom of association (Government of Lebanon, "Qanun al-jama'iyat [Associations Law]."

109. Lebanese Center for Policy Studies, "The Civil Society Report 1997." Interview with Ghassan Jamous, USAID, Beirut, 4 May 2004.

110. Interview with Khalil Na'mat, Director of Research and Studies, General Union of Voluntary Societies. Amman, 28 April 2004.

111. Cultural organizations, for example, were targeted by the state, particularly after 1997, and women's organizations even earlier. See Wiktorowicz, "The

Limits of Democracy in the Middle East"; and Brand, *Women, the State, and Political Liberalization*, 164.

112. Internally this is called a curriculum vitae and is done through the GUVS.

113. Hashemite Kingdom of Jordan, *Plan for Economic and Social Development 1993–1997*, 157–61.

114. The organizational structure is decentralized. The GUVS provides funding to the regional unions, which in turn unite all the charitable associations in that governorate, and these regional unions fund the local associations. The bulk of funding goes to charities in the central region, containing the majority of the population (General Union of Voluntary Societies, "Tarikh . . . baramij . . . meshari'a [Profile, programs, projects]"; idem, "Taqreer al-majlis al-tanfeethi" [Executive report]."

115. These NGOs, Nour al-Hussein Foundation, for example, are distinct administratively and financially from the state, yet are run by members of the royal family and need not abide by the usual laws. They are large, have the inside track on obtaining external, international funding, and are able to push smaller NGOs out of the competition.

116. Wiktorowicz, *The Management of Islamic Activism*, 36.

117. General Union of Voluntary Societies, "Taqreer al-majlis al-tanfeethi [Executive report]," 64. Five thousand dinars are given for the first construction project, twenty-five hundred dinars for expansions and improvements, and GUVS contributes one-forth of the estimated cost for maintenance of the association's buildings.

118. This was the Lifta Charity, which had received eight hundred dinars per year when it was starting out. It currently receives no budget support but has received funds from UNICEF in the past. Fourteen out of twenty-five declined to specify the amounts of aid they receive. Three of the remaining associations receive between three hundred and six hundred dinars yearly, four receive around one thousand dinars, and another four receive two thousand or more dinars. The higher amounts of aid were usually for particular projects, such as purchasing a bus with money obtained from another NGO or a large loan to acquire a new building for the association. Five thousand dinars yearly was allocated to the southern regional association, heavily financed and supported by present and former ministers, whose main goal is higher education for young men from the southern region.

119. By contrast, the accomplishments of non-kin associations were questioned, and their requests to add additional goals (and thus obtain more funding) denied, one on the basis that its goals remained unfulfilled. While seemingly reasonable, kin associations typically have numerous programs that are only partly, if at all, realized in a given year. Yet the associations are regularly permitted to increase their services and obtain more funding.

120. General Union of Voluntary Societies, "al-Sira al-thatiyya lil-jama'iyyat al-muta'ddida al-aghrad [Profile of multipurpose associations]."

120. General Union of Voluntary Societies, "al-Sira al-thatiyya lil-jama'iyyat al-muta'ddida al-aghrad [Profile of multipurpose associations]."

121. Jawad, "A Profile of Social Welfare in Lebanon."

122. Mimeo of state-funded associations, Ministry of Social Affairs. Obtained through the USAID office, the American Embassy in Beirut, May 2004.

123. Riedel, *Who's Who in the Jordanian Parliament 1989–1993;* Hourani, Dabbas, and Power-Stevens, *Who's Who in the Jordanian Parliament 1993–1997;* Hourani and Yassin, *Who's Who in the Jordanian Parliament 1997–2001.*

124. Royal Hashemite Court International Press Office, "Non-Governmental Organizations (NGO's)." National Information Centre, Government of Jordan, http://www.nic.gov.jo/society/ngo.html. Aside from the unions, one per governorate, Amman has the highest number of non-kin associations listed as NGOs on the government's Web site, with eleven out of fifty-seven. In Irbid four out of the five listed are family; in Balqa, five out of ten; in Karak, also five out of ten; in Ma'an, nine out of ten; in Zarqa, 19 out of 34; in Mafraq, twenty-five out of thirty-two; in Tafileh, all five; in Madaba, fourteen out of nineteen; in Jerash, sixteen out of seventeen; in Ajloun, sixteen out of twenty; and in Aqaba, two out of five. The ones in Amman are of older vintage, generally from the 1970s and 1980s, whereas the associations in the governorates are mostly from the 1990s.

125. Ibid.; Sustainable Development Network Programme, "NGO's in Jordan." Internationally, see EuroCom, "Social Development Organizations—Jordan."

126. Layne, *Home and Homeland;* Shryock, *Nationalism and the Genealogical Imagination;* Shryock and Howell, "'Ever a Guest in Our House.'"

127. Layne, "'Tribalism,'" 189; Amawi, "Gender and Citizenship in Jordan," 158.

128. Interview with Dr. Hassan Hallak, Professor of History, Lebanese University, Beirut, 22 June 2005.

129. *al-Diyar,* 2 October 1998.

130. *al-Shiraa,* various issues, 2003–2004.

131. Lebanese Center for Policy Studies, "The Civil Society Report 1997," 36.

132. *al-Safir,* 24 May 2005; interview with Hallak.

133. Lebanese Center for Policy Studies, "The Civil Society Report 1997."

134. Hourani, "The 1993 Jordanian Elections"; Brand, "'In the Beginning was the State . . .'"; Robinson, "Can Islamists Be Democrats? The Case of Jordan."

135. Amawi, "The 1993 Elections in Jordan," 16.

136. I focus on identity institutions, not the amorphous issue of identity itself, since identity is multiple and changing, and also difficult to measure. More important, institutionalists and social movement analysts have shown how identification is created through involvement in concrete institutions. See Thelen and Steinmo, "Historical Institutionalism in Comparative Politics"; Polletta and Jasper, "Collective Identity and Social Movements."

137. Porta, "Introduction," 18.

138. Interview with al-Qara'een.

139. Joseph, "Civic Myths, Citizenship, and Gender in Lebanon," 110.

140. Khalaf, *Lebanon's Predicament*, chap. 8.

141. Interview with a member of the al-Sahl al-Akhdar Cooperative, 3 May 1998.

142. Interview with al-Qara'een.

143. Doueihy, "The Struggle for the City."

144. In the case of a kin association joining Palestinians and Jordanians, an educated Palestinian member, only five years after discovering his new kinship, strongly expressed his identity as that of the Jordanian tribe (interview with a member of Abna' al-Harith; interviews with family members of Palestinian kin associations who do not pay dues or attend meetings, spring 2000).

145. Interviews; Shafeeq N. Ghabra, *Palestinians in Kuwait*, 153. The PLO did not participate or explicitly encourage these types of associations at this time.

146. Interview with Abu Sa'ad. "When we started, there was no place to hold large meetings, and we wanted to gather the family in one place," another leader stated (interview with al-Twal).

147. Khuri, *From Village to Suburb*, 185.

148. al-Ramla Charitable Association, *al-Nitham al-asasi [Charter]*, 23.

149. Silwan Social Development Association, *al-Nitham al-asasi*.

150. Jami'aan and Jami'aan, *Ma'daba wa 'ashira al-Karadisheh*, chap. 8.

151. Khalaf, *Lebanon's Predicament*, 177.

152. Doueihy, "The Struggle for the City"; Douayhi, "Beyrouth et ses étrangers."

153. Berry, "Social Institutions and Access to Resources."

154. Lebanese Center for Policy Studies, "The Civil Society Report 1997."

155. Doueihy, "The Struggle for the City."

156. Lebanese Center for Policy Studies, "The Civil Society Report 1997."

157. See the survey by the Center for Strategic Studies in 1994 which found that 65 percent of (Trans)Jordanians and 72 percent of Palestinians stated that they had effectively become one people. The figures are lower for elites of both origins: 65 percent of Palestinian elites, and only 49 percent of Jordanian elites, believe that the two communities have become one (Abu-Odeh, *Jordanians, Palestinians, and the Hashemite Kingdom in the Middle East Peace Process*, 275.

158. Noted by Shryock, "Bedouin in Suburbia"; and Brand, "Palestinians and Jordanians." For example, al-Kurdi, *Tarikh al-Salt wa al-Balqa wa dour-huma fi bina' al-Urdun al-hadeeth [History of Salt and Balqa and their role in building modern Jordan]*; al-Manzilaawi, *al-Turath al-sha'bi fil-'Aqaba [People's history of Aqaba]*; al-Kaswani, *Qabila Aal Zaydan al-Zayadna [The Tribe of Zaydan al-Zayadna]*; Jami'aan and Jami'aan, *Madaba and the Karadisheh Tribe*.

159. Haddad, "'Detribalizing' and 'Retribalizing,'" 87.

160. In 1991 a Jordanian MP, who was part of the Transjordanian nationalist

movement, suggested to the king that he fire his "Palestinian" adviser. This incident inspired the political adviser Abu-Odeh to contemplate what had changed during the two preceding decades to cause a rise in Jordanian separatism (Abu-Odeh, *Jordanians, Palestinians, and the Hashemite Kingdom,* 4–5). This same adviser now identifies himself as a "Jordanian of Palestinian origin," as opposed to his prior self-declared identity simply as a Jordanian. See Kassim, "The Palestinians," 203 and n. 13.

161. Although a few kin associations in Jordan have expanded to include members of other previously antagonistic social groups, this does not foretell social reconciliation. Despite having previously been on the opposing side of the nationalistic divide, those groups continued to pick an allegiance, either Palestinian or Jordanian, and did not bridge both identities.

162. Picard, "Les habits neufs du communautarisme libanais," 52; Khalaf, "On Roots and Routes."

163. Lebanese Center for Policy Studies, "The Civil Society Report 1997."

164. Khalili, "Grass-roots Commemorations."

165. Ibid., 10.

CONCLUSION

1. Bayat, "Un-civil Society."

2. World Bank, *Unlocking the Employment Potential in the Middle East and North Africa,* 28.

3. Besley, "Nonmarket Institutions for Credit and Risk Sharing in Low-Income Countries," 115.

4. The potential for private welfare markets to develop is currently limited. Private social insurance requires perfect information and no moral hazard problem; it cannot accommodate large-scale collective shocks. This is because the probability of one person's insurance need would have to be independent of others' needs for welfare (Barr, *The Economics of the Welfare State,* 117–18).

5. Smith, "Towards an Ethnography of Idiosyncratic Forms of Livelihood."

6. Individuals with alternative, non-kin sources of social insurance, such as professional associations, do not spearhead the drive to establish the organization and avoid it when possible. Since the organizations use a kin identity idiom, relatives are pressured to join, and these individuals often use the organization as a method of achieving social status as new elites. On peer pressure among identity groups formally analyzed as reputational cascades, see Kuran, "Ethnic Norms and Their Transformation through Reputational Cascades."

7. Chandra and Laitin, "A Framework for Thinking about Identity Change.

8. See, for example, Singerman, *Avenues of Participation;* Stack, *All Our Kin;* Weerdt, "Risk-Sharing and Endogenous Network Formation"; Ellickson,

Order without Law; Espinoza, "Social Networks among the Urban Poor"; and Ismail, *Political Life in Cairo's New Quarters.*

9. Gourevitch, *Politics in Hard Times;* Iversen and Soskice, "An Asset Theory of Social Policy Preferences," 875; Tilly, *Trust and Rule,* 56; Polanyi, *The Great Transformation.*

10. Iversen and Cusack, "The Causes of Welfare State Expansion," 313–14.

11. Teeple, *Globalization and the Decline of Social Reform.*

12. Weiss, *The Myth of the Powerless State,* 11. See also Amin, "Post-Fordism," 33; Brodie, "New State Forms, New Political Spaces."

13. Wimmer, *Nationalist Exclusion and Ethnic Conflict;* Thompson, "The Moral Economy of the English Crowd."

14. The question of internalization of that identity remains, but my research indicates that, for many, their new memberships have become a real, operative force in daily life.

15. For example, see Collier, *Paths Toward Democracy;* Younis, *Liberation and Democratization;* Tilly, *Social Movements.*

16. Seibel and Anheier, "Sociological and Political Science Approaches to the Third Sector."

17. Snyder, *From Voting to Violence.*

18. Varshney, *Ethnic Conflict and Civic Life.*

19. Foley and Edwards, "The Paradox of Civil Society"; Encarnación, "On Bowling Leagues and NGOs"; Jamal, *Barriers to Democracy.*

20. Questions on participation in different types of civil society organizations, listing choices such as charitable and professional associations, existed prior to 1997. Only one-third of 1 percent of those surveyed said that they belonged to civil society organizations in 1996. When the question of participation in kin associations was framed separately from civil society, the response increased to 40 percent or more, and the participation rate in civil society organizations similarly increased to 15 percent (Center for Strategic Studies, "Istitlaa' lil-ra'i hawla al-dimuqratiyya fil-Urdun [Opinion Survey on Democracy in Jordan]." For 1996, 1998, and 2000, respectively, see pages 18, 36, and 31.

21. Arab Thought Forum and Bruno Kreisky Forum, *The Role of NGOs in the Development of Civil Society;* Carapico, "NGOs, INGOs, GO-INGOs and DO-NGOs."

22. Khilnani, "The Development of Civil Society."

23. Teeple, *Globalization and the Decline of Social Reform,* 113; Anheier and Seibel, "The Third Sector in Comparative Perspective."

24. The dominant stereotype of charities as small, grass-roots groups of caring and dedicated individuals is juxtaposed to the image of a large and inhuman public bureaucracy (Willetts, *"The Conscience of the World"*).

25. Tvedt, *Angels of Mercy or Development Diplomats?* 4.

26. Bayat, "Activism and Social Development in the Middle East."

27. Seligman, *The Idea of Civil Society.*

28. Fisher, *Non-Governments,* 161.

29. Langohr, "Too Much Civil Society, Too Little Politics."

30. Zubaida, "Islam and the Politics of Community and Citizenship," 23; Johnson, "Political Bosses and Their Gangs"; Hammami, "Palestinian NGOs since Oslo"; Wiktorowicz, "Civil Society as Social Control"; Joseph, "Civic Myths, Citizenship, and Gender in Lebanon."

31. Levi, "Social and Unsocial Capital," 47.

32. Polletta and Jasper, "Collective Identity and Social Movements," 288.

33. Denoeux, *Urban Unrest in the Middle East,* 22, 24. See, for example, Dazi-Heni, "Hospitalité et politique."

34. Zubaida, "Religion, the State, and Democracy," 61; Zubaida, "Islam and the Politics of Community and Citizenship," 23.

35. Clark, "The Economic and Political Impact of Economic Restructuring on NGO-State Relations in Egypt."

36. Moe, "Power and Political Institutions."

37. Joseph, "The Public/Private—The Imagined Boundary in the Imagined Nation/State/Community."

38. Castel, "The Model of the 'Employment Society' as a Principle of Comparison between Systems of Social Protection in Northern and Southern Europe," 29.

39. Portes and Sensenbrenner, "Embeddedness and Immigration."

40. Existing organized groups are easier to mobilize for all types of social movements than unorganized ones. See Oberschall, *Social Conflict and Social Movements.* Oberschall, however, did not imagine families performing the role of bloc recruitment.

41. International Crisis Group, "Inside Gaza."

42. Although Avner Greif posits that cultural orientations influenced the individualist or collectivist solutions to principal-agent problems, in some circumstances there may be little alternative ("Cultural Beliefs and the Organization of Society").

APPENDIX 1

1. Clark, "Field Research Methods in the Middle East."

2. Biernacki and Waldorf, "Snowball Sampling."

3. This explanation for the rise in associations was stated by an academic, namely, that they were forced to renew their registrations and thus showed as an increase in association numbers, and I investigated it.

4. Lebanese Center for Policy Studies, "The Civil Society Report 1997."

5. Baalbaki, "Dinamiya al-ta'teer al-ijtima'i fi qura wa baladat qada Aaley [Dynamics of social framing in the villages and towns of Aley district]."

6. Lebanese Center for Policy Studies, "The Civil Society Report 1997."

BIBLIOGRAPHY

NEWS PERIODICALS
International

The Economist
Middle East International
Oxford Analytica Daily Brief

Amman

al-ʿArab al-yawm
al-Aswaq
al-Raiʾ
Jordan Times

Beirut

al-Afkar
al-Anwar
al-Diyar
al-Mustaqbal
al-Nahar
al-Safir
al-Shiraa

SELECTED INTERVIEWS AND PERSONAL COMMUNICATIONS
(NAMED INDIVIDUALS)
Jordan

Abu-Hammour, Dr. Mohammad S. Ministry of Finance, 23 March 2000.
Abu Saʿad, Mohammad. President, Lifta Charitable Association, 11 February 2000.
al-Ardha, Mohammad. Researcher, Directorate of Studies and Research, General Union of Voluntary Societies, 12 October 1999.
al-Jamʿaani, ʿAbd al-Rahman. Director of Administration, Jordan Cooperative Corporation, various dates, spring 1998–fall 1999.

al-Naber, ʿAzzam. Public Relations Director, Cooperative Organization, 6 December 1999.

al-Naber, Jamal. Director, Aal al-Naber Cooperative, 9 January 2000.

al-Twal, Suhail, M.D. Former president of al-Sahl al-Akhdar Cooperative, 2 June 2000.

Attieh, Abdallah A. Assistant Director, Research Directorate, Amman Chamber of Commerce, 2 May 2000.

Hamdan, Awad. Director, Jamaʿiyya Silwan, 3 May 2004.

Hamdan, Dr. Muhammad Mumtaz. Public Relations, Ministry of Finance, 8 March 1998.

Khalial, Atef (Ph.D). Director of Studies and Research, Ministry of Planning, 7 March 2000.

Maʿayeh, Bassam F. Former president of al-Basat al-Akhdar Cooperative, 24 June 2000.

Qaraʿeen, Munther. Vice President of al-Azhaar Cooperative, 12 March 2000.

Shteiwi, Musa. Professor of Sociology, University of Jordan, 4 October 1999 and 7 May 2000.

Wizarat al-Tamween, Economic Director of the Secretary General Office, Ministry of Supply, 22 April 1998.

Lebanon

AbuKhalil, Asʿad. Professor, California State University Stanislaus, 16 May 2005.

Bou-Merhi, Farud H. Mayor Elect and Association President, Dammour, 5 May 2004.

Daccache, Youssef Antoine. President, Syndicat des Commercants des legume et Fruits en Gros, Byblos, 5 May 2004.

Doueihi, Chawqi. Professor, Department of Anthropology, Lebanese University, 23 June 2005.

Gaspard, Toufic Gaspard, Ph.D. Personal communication, 19 October 2005.

Hafez, Fadi. Political Section, American Embassy in Beirut, 4 May 2004.

Hallak, Hassan. Professor of History, Lebanese University, 22 June 2005.

Jannouse, Ghassan. USAID, 4 May 2004.

Murr, Lina. Director, Ministry of Interior, Associations Section, 16 June 2005.

Nasr, Salim Nasr. Professor and Senior Adviser for Civil Society and Public Participation, UNDP, 21 June 2005.

PRIMARY SOURCES
Jordan

al-Jomard, Atheel A. "al-Mutaghayyerat al-muʾathira ʿala al-musharika fi dawraat al-tadreeb li-tanmiyya al-mahaarat fil-Urdun [Variables affecting participation in skills training courses in Jordan]." Amman: Center for Strategic Studies, University of Jordan, 1998.

———. "al-Mutaghayyerat al-mu'athira 'ala istithmar al-qita' al-khas al-mahali fil-Urdun [Variables affecting local private sector investment in Jordan]." Amman: Center for Strategic Studies, University of Jordan, 1997.

Amman Chamber of Industry. "Liqa' al-'amal ma' m'ali wazeer al-maliyya/al-jamarik al-duktoor Mishil Marto [Working meeting with the Minister of Finance and Customs Doctor Mishil Marto]." Amman: Amman Chamber of Industry, 2000.

Center for Strategic Studies. "Istitlaa' lil-ra'i hawla al-dimuqratiyya fil-Urdun [Opinion Survey on Democracy in Jordan]." Amman: Markaz al-dirasat al-stratijiyya, University of Jordan, various years.

Central Bank of Jordan. "Annual Report." Amman: Department of Research and Studies, various years.

General Union of Voluntary Societies. "al-Sira al-thatiyya lil-jama'iyyat al-muta'ddida al-aghrad [Profile of multipurpose associations] (Internal document)." Amman: Ittihad al-'am lil-jama'iyyat al-khayriyya, 1999.

———. "al-Tarbiyya wa al-ta'leem [Upbringing and education] (Promotional pamphlet)." Amman: Ittihad al-'am lil-jama'iyyat al-khayriyya, 1999.

———. "Dalil al-jama'iyyat al-khayriyya fil-Urdun [Directory of voluntary societies in Jordan]." Amman: Ittihad al-'am lil-jama'iyyat al-khayriyya, 1999.

———. Internal Buget Records and Financial Files of Associations. Amman: Ittihad al-'am lil-jama'iyyat al-khayriyya, 2000.

———. "Ri'aya al-tufoula [Childhood care] (Promotional pamphlet)." Amman: Ittihad al-'am lil-jama'iyyat al-khayriyya, 1999.

———. "Taqreer al-majlis al-tanfeethi. al-idari wa al-mali wa al-mawazina al-taqdeeriyya [Executive report. Administration and finances and projected budget]." Amman: Ittihad al-'am lil-jama'iyyat al-khayriyya, various years.

———. "Taqreer al-majlis al-tanfithi [Report of the executive committee]." Amman: Ittihad al-'am lil-jama'iyyat al-khayriyya, 2002–2003.

———. "Tarikh . . . baramij . . . meshari'a [Profile, Programs, Projects]." Amman: Ittihad al-'am lil-jama'iyyat al-khayriyya, 2000.

General Union of Voluntary Societies, Directorate of Research and Social Studies. "Dalil al-jam'aiyyat al-khayriyya wa al-tanmawiyya al-ijtima'iyya fil-mamlaka al-Urduniyya al-Hashimiyya [Directory of voluntary societies and social development in the Hashemite Kingdom of Jordan (updated)]." Amman: Ittihad al-'am lil-jama'iyyat al-khayriyya, 1999.

Hashemite Kingdom of Jordan. "al-Hisabat al-qawmiyya [National accounts 1952–1992]." Amman: Department of Statistics, 1994.

———. "al-Nitham al-asasi al-mu'adal lil-ittihad al-'am lil-jama'iyyat al-khayriyya li-'am 1995 [The basic amended charter for the General Union of Voluntary Societies of 1995]." *Mawsu'a al-tashree' al-urduni* [*Encyclopaedia of Jordanian Law 1998*] 1995, 70–89.

———. "Dirasa al-Urduniyeen al-ʿaʾideen min al-kharij khilal al-fatra 8/10/1991–12/31/1992 [Survey of Jordanians returning from abroad during the period, 8/10/1991–12/31/1992]." Amman: Department of Statistics, 1993.

———. "Dirasa nafaqat wa dakhl al-usra 1992 [Household Expenditure and Income Survey 1993]." Amman: Department of Statistics, 1993.

———. "Dirasa nafaqat wa dakhl al-usra 1997 [Household Expenditure and Income Survey 1997]." Amman: Department of Statistics, 1999.

———. "Dirasat al-istikhdam, fil-muʾassasat alati yʿamal bi-kul min-ha 5 ashkhas aw akthar [Employment Survey, for Establishments Engaging (5) Persons or More]." Amman: Department of Statistics, 1992.

———. "Statistical Yearbook." Amman: Department of Statistics, various years.

———. *Plan for Economic and Social Development 1993–1997*. Amman: Jordan Press Foundation, 1993?

Jordan Cooperative Corporation. "List of cooperatives by type and governate (Internal documents)." Amman: al-Muʾassasa al-tʿawuniyya al-Urduniyya, al-Maʿhad al-tʿawuni, 2000.

———. "al-Taqreer al-sanawi li-ʿam 1991 [Annual Report for 1991]." Amman: al-Munathama al-tʿawuniyya al-Urduniyya, al-Maʿhad al-tʿawuni, 1991.

Ministry of Industry and Trade, Amman. "Agreement between the Hashemite Kingdom of Jordan and Israel on Irbid Qualifying Industrial Zone." Mimeograph, n.d.

Ministry of the Interior. Internal Documents: List of Registered Associations. Amman: Ministry of the Interior, Mimeograph, 2000.

Royal Hashemite Court International Press Office, "Non-Governmental Organizations (NGO's)." National Information Centre, Government of Jordan, http://www.nic.gov.jo/society/ngo.html (accessed September 1999).

Sawt al-Taʿawun [The Voice of Cooperation]. "al-Jamaʿiyyaat al-tʿawuniyya fil-Urdun: tatawwuru-ha wa intisharuha wa al-muʿawwaqat allati tuwajihu-ha [Cooperative associations in Jordan: Their development, expansion, and difficulties they face]" 24 (December 1991): 12–29.

Wizarat al-Tamween [Ministry of Supply]. "Qaʾima bil-mawaad al-ghithaʾiyya al-tamweeniyya wa al-mawaad wa al-silʿ al-ukhra al-masʿra min qibl wizara al-tamween [List of provided food and other commodities and goods priced by the Ministry of Supply]." Mimeograph, 1998.

Lebanon

al-Husseini, Hashem, Abdullah Muhi al-Deen, and Munthir al-Haraka. "Dirasat mash minathamat al-qitaʿ al-ahli fi Lubnan [Study of civil society organizations in Lebanon] (unpublished manuscript)." Beirut: Ministry of Social Affairs, 2002.

Embassy of the United States of America. *Country Commercial Guide: Lebanon*

2004. Beirut: Embassy of the United States of America, Beirut, Lebanon, 2003.
Government of Lebanon. "Qanun al-jama'iyat (jam'aiyat wa ijtima'iyat wa andiya wa riyadiya) [Associations Law (associations, societies, clubs, sports)] of 1909 and amendments." *al-Majalla al-qadaiya (Beirut).*
Lebanon, *Official Gazette*, 1980–2005.
Ministry of Social Affairs, Mimeograph of state-funded associations. Obtained through the USAID office at the American Embassy in Beirut, May 2004.
Ministry of Social Affairs. Social Welfare Institutions. Lebanese Republic, http://www.socialaffairs.gov.lb (accessed September 2005).

KIN ASSOCIATION PUBLICATIONS

al-Azhaar Cooperative Association. *Charter.* Mimeograph, n.d.
al-Falouja Charitable Association. *al-Nitham al-asasi [Charter].* Amman, 1987.
al-Kaswani, 'Abdullah Isma'el. *Qabila Aal Zaydan al-Zayadna Family [The Tribe of Zaydan al-Zayadna].* Amman: al-Maktaba al-wataniyya, 1994.
al-Kurdi, Muhammad 'Ali al-Suwayriki. *Tarikh al-Salt wa al-Balqa wa dourhuma fi bina' al-Urdun al-hadeeth [History of Salt and Balqa and their role in building modern Jordan].* Amman: Wizarat al-thaqafa; jam'iyya 'ummal al-mataabi' al-t'aawuniyya, 1998.
al-Manzilaawi, 'Abd allah Karam. *al-Turath al-sha'bi fil-'Aqaba [People's history of Aqaba].* Jam'iyya 'ummal al-mataabi' al-t'aawuniyya: Published under the supervision of the Sons of Aqaba Charitable Association, 1993.
al-Ramla Charitable Association. *al-Nitham al-asasi [Charter].* Amman: al-Safadi, 1997.
Daccache Family Association. *Al Daccache Charitable Dispensary and Association*, Okaibe, Bakaa-ed-Dine, and Kesrawan, 2005.
Hallaq Family Asssociation. *al-Nitham al-asasi [Charter].* Beirut, 1998.
Jami'aan, Mika'il Khalil, and Amjad 'Adnan Jami'aan. *Ma'daba wa 'ashira al-Karadisheh: tarikhaan wa haadhiraan wa hadaaratan [Madaba and the Karadisheh tribe: Historically, presently, and culturally].* Amman: al-Matab'a al-'askiriyya, 1997.
Khalil al-Rahman Charitable Association. *al-Taqreer al-sinnawi li-'am [Yearly report for the year] 1983, 84, 85, 86.* Amman: al-Ta'awuni, 1987.
———. *al-Taqreer al-sinnawi li-'am [Yearly report for the year] 1987, 88, 89.* Amman: al-Ta'awuni, 1990?
Silwan Social Development Association. "al-Taqreer al-sinnawi al-thani wa al-'ashroun 'an al-sinna al-maliyya 1998 [Twenty-second Annual Report for the Fiscal Year 1998]." Amman: al-Dustoor, 1998.
———. *al-Nitham al-asasi [Charter].* Amman: al-Ta'awuni, 1993.
Sons of Southern Jordan Charitable Association. Association pamphlet. Amman, 1998?

Tabarbour Charitable Association. *al-Nitham al-asasi* [*Charter*] (established 1992). Amman, n.d.

Union of Beiruti Family Associations [Ittihad jama'iyyat al-'a'iliyyat al-Bayruti-yya]. *Union of Beiruti Family Associations* [*Ittihad jama'iyyat al-'a'iliyyat al-Bayrutiyya*]. Beirut, 2001.

———. *Union of Beiruti Family Associations* [*Ittihad jama'iyyat al-'a'iliyyat al-Bayrutiyya*]. Beirut. 2004–2005.

OTHER REFERENCES

Abbas, Mahmoud, Hussein Shaaban, Bassem Sirhan, and Ali Hassan. "The Socio-economic Conditions of Palestinians in Lebanon (Review Articles)." *Journal of Refugee Studies* 10, no. 3 (1997): 378–96.

Abdel Jaber, Tayseer. "The Competitiveness of Jordan's Manufacturing Industry." In *The Industrialization of Jordan: Achievements and Obstacles,* ed. Matthes Buhbe and Sami Zreigat, 11–20. Amman, Jordan: Friedrich Ebert Stiftung Research Institute, 1989.

Abi Saab, Fares. "Municipal Elections in Southern Mount Lebanon (in Arabic)." In *Municipal Elections in Lebanon 1998* (in Arabic), ed. Fares Abi Saab et al., 25–106. Beirut: Lebanese Center for Policy Studies, 1999.

Abidi, Aquil Hyder Hasan. *Jordan, A Political Study 1948–1957.* New York: Asia Publishing House, 1965.

Abrahart, Alan, Iqbal Kaur, and Zafiris Tzannatos. "Government Employment and Active Labor Market Policies in MENA in a Comparative International Context." In *Employment Creation and Social Protection in the Middle East and North Africa,* ed. Heba Handoussa and Zafiris Tzannatos, 21–48. New York: American University in Cairo Press, 2002.

Abu Jaber, Kamel S., and Shirin H. Fathi. "The 1989 Jordanian Parliamentary Elections." *Orient (Orient Institute)* 31, no. 1 (March 1990): 67–86.

Abu-Odeh, Adnan. *Jordanians, Palestinians, and the Hashemite Kingdom in the Middle East Peace Process.* Washington, D.C.: United States Institute of Peace Press, 1999.

Adcock, Robert, and David Collier. "Measurement Validity: A Shared Standard for Qualitative and Quantitative Research." *American Political Science Review* 95, no. 3 (September 2001): 529–46.

Ahmed, Hisham H., and Mary A. Williams-Ahmed. "The Impact of the Gulf Crisis on Jordan's Economic Infra-structure: A Study of the Responses of 207 Displaced Palestinian and Jordanian Workers." *Arab Studies Quarterly* 15, no. 4 (1993): 33–62.

al-Fa'ouri, Rif'at. "al-Jama'iyyat al-khayriyya fi muhafatha Irbid: waq'a wa tumou-hat [Charitable associations in Irbid—between theory and practice]." *Majalla abhath al-Yarmûk musalsilla al-'uloum al-insaniyya wa al-ijtima'iyya* [*Yarmouk studies journal, series on human and social sciences*] 13, no. 3 (1995): 31–48.

————. *al-Wasata fil-qita' al-hukumi al-Urduni: dirasa maydaniyya lil-idara al-wusta* [*Intermediation in Jordan's government sector: A study of the middle administration*]. Edited by Yarmouk University Jordanian Studies Center, Abhath markaz al-dirasat al-Urduniyya [Researches of Jordanian Studies Center]. Irbid: Yarmouk University Publications, 1997.

al-Husbani, Abd el-Hakim K. "al-'Asha'iriyya wa al-dawla: dirasa li-thahira al-madafat fi madinat Irbid [Tribalism and the state: The phenomenon of Madafas in the city of Irbid]." M.A. thesis, Yarmouk University, 1991.

al-Husseini, Hashem, Abdullah Muhi al-Deen, and Munthir al-Haraka. "Dirasat mash minathamat al-qita' al-ahli fi Lubnan [Study of civil society organizations in Lebanon] (unpublished manuscript)." Beirut: Ministry of Social Affairs, 2002.

al-Jomard, Atheel A. "al-Mutaghayyerat al-mu'athira 'ala al-musharika fi dawraat al-tadreeb li-tanmiyya al-mahaarat fil-Urdun [Variables affecting participation in skills-training courses in Jordan]." Amman: Center for Strategic Studies, University of Jordan, 1998.

al-Radi, Lamia. "La famille comme mode de gestion et de contrôle du social chez les élites traditionnelles Palestiniennes." In *Palestine, Palestiniens: territoire national, espaces communautaires*, ed. Riccardo Bocco, Blandine Destremau and Jean Hannoyer, 351–66. Amman: CERMOC (Centre d'Études et de Recherches sur le Moyen-Orient Contemporain), 1997.

al-Wazani, Khaled. "Jordan: Strategic Options for Growth and Development Facing Poverty and Unemployment." Paper presented at the Workshop on the Economy conducted under CSS former director Mustapha Hamarneh, Amman, June 1999.

al-Wazani, Khaled Wasif. *al-Jihaz al-masrifi wa al-siyasa al-naqdiyya fil-Urdun, 1989–1995* [*The banking system and financial policy in Jordan, 1989–1995*]. Amman: Center for Strategic Studies (Economic Studies Unit), University of Jordan, 1996.

Alarcon, Rafael. "Mexican Hometown Associations: A Model of Economic Cooperation Between Diasporas and Homelands." Paper presented at the Diaspora and Homeland Development Conference, Berkeley Center for Globalization and Information Technology, University of California, Berkeley, April 13, 2004, http://bcgit.berkeley.edu/diaspora.html.

Amara, Jomana. "Military Industrialization and Economic Development: Jordan's Defense Industry." In *Working Paper Series*, ed. Defense Resources Management Institute. Monterey, Calif.: Naval Postgraduate School, 2006.

Amawi, Abla. "Gender and Citizenship in Jordan." In *Gender and Citizenship in the Middle East*, ed. Suad Joseph, 158–84. Syracuse: Syracuse University Press, 2000.

————. "Scrutinizing the Nature of Economic Growth: UNDP's Human Development Report for 1996." *Jordanies*, no. 2 (December 1996): 100–106.

Amawi, Abla M. "The 1993 Elections in Jordan." *Arab Studies Quarterly* 16, no. 3 (1994): 15–27.

American Task Force for Lebanon. *Working Paper—Conference on Lebanon.* Washington, D.C.: American Task Force for Lebanon, 1991.

Amery, Hussein A., and William P. Anderson. "International Migration and Remittances to a Lebanese Village." *Canadian Geographer* 39, no. 1 (1995): 46–59.

Amin, Ash. "Post-Fordism: Models, Fantasies, and Phantoms of Transition." In *Post-Fordism: A Reader,* ed. Ash Amin, 1–39. Cambridge: Blackwell, 1994.

Anani, Jawad, and Rima Khalaf. "Privatization in Jordan." In *Privatization and Structural Adjustment in the Arab Countries,* ed. Said El-Naggar, 210–23. Washington, D.C.: International Monetary Fund, 1989.

Anderson, B. S. "The History of the Jordanian National Movement: Its Leaders, Ideologies, Successes, and Failures." Ph.D. diss., University of California, Los Angeles, 1997.

Anderson, Betty S. *Nationalist Voices in Jordan: The Street and the State.* Austin: University of Texas Press, 2005.

Anderson, Lisa. "Politics in the Middle East: Opportunities and Limits in the Quest for Theory." In *Area Studies and Social Science: Strategies for Understanding Middle East Politics,* ed. Mark Tessler, 1–10. Bloomington: Indiana University Press, 1999.

———. "Prospects for Liberalism in North Africa: Identities and Interests in Preindustrial Welfare States." In *Islam, Democracy, and the State in North Africa,* ed. John P. Entelis, 127–40. Bloomington: Indiana University Press, 1997.

Andoni, Lamis, and Jillian Schwedler. "Bread Riots in Jordan." *Middle East Report,* no. 201 (1996): 40–42.

Anheier, Helmut K. "Private Voluntary Organizations and the Third World: The Case of Africa." In *The Third Sector: Comparative Studies of Nonprofit Organizations,* ed. Helmut K. Anheier and Wolfgang Seibel, 361–76. New York: Walter de Gruyter, 1990.

Anheier, Helmut K., and Wolfgang Seibel. "The Third Sector in Comparative Perspective: Four Propositions." In *The Third Sector: Comparative Studies of Nonprofit Organizations,* ed. Helmut K. Anheier and Wolfgang Seibel, 379–87. New York: Walter de Gruyter, 1990.

Antoun, Richard T. *Arab Village: A Social Structural Study of a Trans-Jordanian Peasant Community.* Bloomington: Indiana University Press, 1972.

———. "Civil Society, Tribal Process, and Change in Jordan: An Anthropological View." *International Journal of Middle East Studies* 32 (2000): 441–63.

Arab Monetary Fund. "Joint Arab Economic Report." Abu Dhabi, 2006.

Arab Thought Forum and Bruno Kreisky Forum, eds. *The Role of NGOs in the Development of Civil Society: Europe and the Arab Countries (Proceedings of a Seminar Held in Amman, Jordan on December 6–7, 1997).* Amman: al Kutba, 1999.

Arjomand, Said Amir. "Philanthropy, the Law, and Public Policy in the Islamic

World before the Modern Era." In *Philanthropy in the World's Traditions*, ed. Warren F. Ilchman, Stanley N. Katz, and Edward L. Queen II, 109–32. Bloomington: Indiana University Press, 1998.

Arlacchi, Pino. "The Mafioso: From Man of Honour to Entrepreneur." *New Left Review*, no. 118 (1979): 53–72.

Aruri, Naseer H. *Jordan: A Study in Political Development (1921–1965)*. The Hague: Martinus Nijhoff, 1972.

Azm, Ahmad Jamil. "The Islamic Action Front Party." In *Islamic Movements in Jordan*, ed. Hani Hourani, 95–141. Amman: al-Urdun al-Jadid Research Center and Friedrich Ebert Stiftung, 1997.

Baaklini, Abdo, Guilain Denoeux, and Robert Springborg. *Legislative Politics in the Arab World: The Resurgence of Democratic Institutions*. Boulder, Colo.: Lynne Rienner, 1999.

Baalbaki, Ahmad. "Dinamiya al-ta'teer al-ijtima'i fi qura wa baladat qada Aaley [Dynamics of social framing in the villages and towns of Aley district]." In *La vie publique au Liban: expressions et recompositions du politique*, ed. Joseph Bahout and Chawqi Douayhi, 211–40. Beirut: CERMOC, 1997.

Bader, Majed. *al-Ta'leem al-'ali fil-Urdun: bayna al-mas'ouliyya al-hukumiyya wa al-qita' al-khas [Higher education in Jordan: Between public and private sectors]*. Amman: CERMOC, 1994.

Bahout, Joseph. "Les élites parlementaires Libanaises de 1996: étude de composition." In *La vie publique au Liban: expressions et recompositions du politique*, ed. Joseph Bahout and Chawqi Douayhi. Beirut: CERMOC, 1997.

Baldwin, Peter. *The Politics of Social Solidarity: Class Bases in the European Welfare State, 1875–1975*. New York: Cambridge University Press, 1990.

Barak, Oren. "Lebanon: Failure, Collapse, and Resuscitation." In *State Failure and State Weakness in a Time of Terror*, ed. Robert I. Rotberg, 305–39. Washington, D.C.: World Peace Foundation, 2003.

Baram, Amatzia. "Neo-Tribalism in Iraq: Saddam Hussein's Tribal Policies, 1991–96." *International Journal of Middle East Studies* 29 (1997): 1–31.

Baroudi, Sami E. "Continuity in Economic Policy in Postwar Lebanon: The Record of the Hariri and Hoss Governments Examined, 1992–2000." *Arab Studies Quarterly* 24, no. 1 (winter 2002).

Barr, Nicholas. *The Economics of the Welfare State*. 2nd ed. Stanford, Calif.: Stanford University Press, 1993.

Batatu, Hanna. *The Old Social Classes and the Revolutionary Movements of Iraq*. Princeton, N.J.: Princeton University Press, 1978.

Bates, Robert H. "Modernization, Ethnic Competition, and the Rationality of Politics in Contemporary Africa." In *State Versus Ethnic Claims: African Policy Dilemmas*, ed. Donald Rothchild and Victor A. Olorunsola, 152–71. Boulder, Colo.: Westview, 1983.

Bayat, Asef. "Activism and Social Development in the Middle East." *International Journal of Middle East Studies* 34 (2002): 1–28.

———. "Un-civil Society: The Politics of the Informal People." *Third World Quarterly* 18, no. 1 (1997): 53–72.

Baydas, Mayada M., Zakaria Bahloul, and Dale W. Adams. "Informal Finance in Egypt: 'Banks' within Banks." *World Development* 23, no. 4 (1995): 651–61.

Baylouny, Anne Marie. "Jordan's New 'Political Development' Strategy." *Middle East Report*, no. 236 (2005).

———. "Militarizing Welfare: Neo-liberalism and the Jordanian Regime." *Middle East Journal* 62, no. 2 (2008): 277–303.

Beinin, Joel, and Joe Stork. "On the Modernity, Historical Specificity, and International Context of Political Islam." In *Political Islam: Essays from Middle East Report*, ed. Joel Beinin and Joe Stork, 3–25. Berkeley: University of California Press, 1997.

Beito, David T. *From Mutual Aid to the Welfare State: Fraternal Societies and Social Services, 1890–1967.* Chapel Hill: University of North Carolina Press, 2000.

———. "'This Enormous Army': The Mutual Aid Tradition of American Fraternal Societies before the Twentieth Century." *Social Philosophy and Policy* 14, no. 2 (1997): 20–38.

Ben-Porath, Yoram. "The F-Connection: Families, Friends, and Firms and the Organization of Exchange." *Population and Development Review* 6, no. 1 (1980): 1–30.

Berry, Sara. *Fathers Work for Their Sons: Accumulation, Mobility, and Class Formation in an Extended Yoruba Community.* Berkeley: University of California Press, 1985.

———. "Social Institutions and Access to Resources." *Africa* 59, no. 1 (1989): 41–55.

Besley, Timothy. "Nonmarket Institutions for Credit and Risk Sharing in Low-Income Countries." *Journal of Economic Perspectives* 9, no. 3 (1995): 115–27.

Beyhum, Nabil. "Population Displacement in the Metropolitan District of Beirut: Are the Displacements Over?" In *Population Displacement and Resettlement: Development and Conflict in the Middle East*, ed. Seteney Shami, 13–23. New York: Center for Migration Studies, 1994.

Bian, Yanjie. "Getting a Job through a Web of *Guanxi* in China." In *Networks in the Global Village*, ed. Barry Wellman, 255–77. Boulder, Colo.: Westview, 1999.

Biernacki, Patrick, and Dan Waldorf. "Snowball Sampling." *Sociological Methods and Research* 10, no. 2 (1981): 141–64.

Biggart, Nicole Woolsey. "Banking on Each Other: The Situational Logic of Rotating Savings and Credit Associations." *Advances in Qualitative Organization Research* 3 (2001): 129–53.

Biggart, Nicole Woolsey, and Richard P. Castanias. "Collateralized Social Relations: The Social in Economic Calculation." *American Journal of Economics and Sociology* 60, no. 2 (2001): 471–500.

Bledstein, Burton J. "Introduction: Storytellers to the Middle Class." In *The*

Middling Sorts: Explorations in the History of the American Middle Class, ed. Burton J. Bledstein and Robert D. Johnston, 1–25. New York: Routledge, 2001.

Bocco, Ricardo. "L'état producteur d'identités locales: lois electorales et tribus bedouines en Jordanie." *URBAMA* 20 (1989): 271–87.

Bocco, Riccardo, and Tariq M. M. Tell. "*Pax Britannica* in the Steppe: British Policy and the Transjordan Bedouin." In *Village, Steppe and State: The Social Origins of Modern Jordan,* ed. Eugene L. Rogan and Tariq Tell, 108–27. New York: British Academic Press, 1994.

Boulby, Marion. *The Muslim Brotherhood and the Kings of Jordan, 1945–1993.* Atlanta, Ga.: Scholars Press, 1999.

Bourdieu, Pierre. "Social Space and Symbolic Power." *Sociological Theory* 7, no. 1 (1989): 14–25.

———. *The Logic of Practice.* Translated by Richard Nice. Stanford, Calif.: Stanford University Press, 1990.

Bradley, David, Evelyne Huber, Stephanie Moller, François Nielsen, and John D. Stephens. "Distribution and Redistribution in Postindustrial Democracies." *World Politics* 55 (2003): 193–228.

Brady, Henry E., and David Collier, eds. *Rethinking Social Inquiry: Diverse Tools, Shared Standards.* New York: Rowman and Littlefield, 2004.

Brand, Laurie. "'In the Beginning Was the State . . .': The Quest for Civil Society in Jordan." In *Civil Society in the Middle East, Volume 1,* ed. Augustus Richard Norton, 148–85. New York: E. J. Brill, 1995.

———. *Women, the State, and Political Liberalization: Middle Eastern and North African Experiences.* New York: Columbia University Press, 1998.

Brand, Laurie A. "Palestinians and Jordanians: A Crisis of Identity." *Journal of Palestine Studies* 24, no. 4 (summer 1995): 46–61.

Brodie, Janine. "New State Forms, New Political Spaces." In *States against Markets: The Limits of Globalization,* ed. Robert Boyer and Daniel Drache, 383–98. New York: Routledge, 1996.

Brumberg, Daniel. "Authoritarian Legacies and Reform Strategies in the Arab World." In *Political Liberalization and Democratization in the Arab World,* Vol. 1, *Theoretical Perspectives,* ed. Rex Brynen, Bahgat Korany and Paul Noble, 229–59. Boulder, Colo.: Lynne Rienner, 1995.

Bryden, Matt. "State-Within-a-Failed-State: Somaliland and the Challenge of International Recognition." In *States-Within-States: Incipient Political Entities in the Post–Cold War Era,* ed. Paul Kingston and Ian S. Spears, 167–88. New York: Palgrave Macmillan, 2004.

Brynen, Rex. "Economic Crisis and Post-Rentier Democratization in the Arab World: The Case of Jordan." *Canadian Journal of Political Science* 25, no. 1 (March 1992): 69–97.

———. "The Politics of Monarchical Liberalism: Jordan." In *Political Lib-*

eralization and Democratization in the Arab World, vol. 2, *Comparative Experiences,* ed. Bahgat Korany, Rex Brynen, and Paul Noble, 71–100. Boulder, Colo.: Lynne Rienner, 1998.

Burawoy, Michael. "The Extended Case Method." In *Ethnography Unbound: Power and Resistance in the Modern Metropolis,* ed. Michael Burawoy et al., 271–87. Berkeley: University of California Press, 1991.

Cachafeiro, Margarita Gomes-Reino. *Ethnicity and Nationalism in Italian Politics: Inventing the Padania: Lega Nord and the Northern Question.* Burlington, Vt.: Ashgate, 2002.

Carapico, Sheila. *Civil Society in Yemen: The Political Economy of Activism in Modern Arabia.* New York: Cambridge University Press, 1998.

———. "NGOs, INGOs, GO-INGOs and DO-NGOs: Making Sense of Non-Governmental Organizations." *Middle East Report,* no. 214 (2000): 12–15.

Case, Anne. "Symposium on Consumption Smoothing in Developing Countries." *Journal of Economic Perspectives* 9, no. 3 (1995): 81–82.

Castel, Robert. "The Model of the 'Employment Society' as a Principle of Comparison between Systems of Social Protection in Northern and Southern Europe." In *Comparing Social Welfare Systems in Southern Europe,* ed. Bruno Palier, 27–46. Paris: MIRE, 1997.

Center for Strategic Studies. "Istitlaaʿ lil-raʾi hawla al-dimuqratiyya fil-Urdun 1996 [Opinion Survey on Democracy in Jordan 1996]." Amman: Markaz al-dirasat al-stratijiyya, University of Jordan, 1996.

———. "Istitlaaʿ lil-raʾi hawla al-dimuqratiyya fil-Urdun 1998 [Opinion Survey on Democracy in Jordan 1998]." Amman: Markaz al-dirasat al-stratijiyya, University of Jordan, 1998.

———. "Istitlaaʿ lil-raʾi hawla al-dimuqratiyya fil-Urdun 2000 [Opinion Survey on Democracy in Jordan 2000]." Amman: Markaz al-dirasat al-stratijiyya, University of Jordan, 2000.

———. "Istitlaaʿ lil-raʾi hawla al-dimuqratiyya fil-Urdun 2002 [Opinion Survey on Democracy in Jordan 2002]." Amman: Markaz al-dirasat al-stratijiyya, University of Jordan, 2002.

———. "Istitlaaʿ lil-raʾi hawla al-dimuqratiyya fil-Urdun [Opinion Survey on Democracy in Jordan]." Amman: Markaz al-dirasat al-stratijiyya, University of Jordan, various years.

Central Bank of Jordan. "Thirtieth Annual Report 1993." Amman: Department of Research and Studies, 1994?

———. "Thirty-fifth Annual Report 1998." Amman: Department of Research and Studies, 1999.

CERMOC (Centre d'Études et de Recherches sur le Moyen-Orient Contemporain). "Chronologie decembre 1995–avril 1996." *Jordanies,* no. 1 (June 1996): 115–48.

Chandra, Kanchan. "Mechanisms vs. Outcomes." *Qualitative Methods Newsletter* (*American Political Science Association*) (spring 2006): 6–13.

————. *Why Ethnic Parties Succeed: Patronage and Head Counts in India*. New York: Cambridge University Press, 2004.

Chandra, Kanchan, and David Laitin. "A Framework for Thinking about Identity Change, Paper Prepared for Presentation at LICEP 5." Paper presented at the Laboratory in Comparative Ethnic Processes, Stanford University, 11 May 2002, http://www.yale.edu/macmillan/ocvprogram/licep/5/chandra-laitin/chandra -laitin.pdf.

Charmes, Jacques. "Trends in Informal Sector Employment in the Middle East." In *Trade Policy and Economic Integration in the Middle East and North Africa: Economic Boundaries in Flux*, ed. Hassan Hakimian and Jeffrey B. Nugent, 165–83. New York: RoutledgeCurzon, 2004.

Chatelard, Géraldine, and Asem al-'Omari. "Primordial Ties and Beyond. Two Case Studies: The Muslim Seats in Irbid and the Christian Seat in Madaba." *Jordanies. Special issue: The 1997 Parliamentary Elections*, no. 5–6 (June–December 1998): 273–96.

Chaudhry, Kiren Aziz. "Consuming Interests: Market Failure and the Social Foundations of Iraqi Etatisme." In *Iraq's Economic Predicament*, ed. Kamil Mahdi, 233–65: University of Exeter Press, 2002.

————. *The Price of Wealth: Oil and Labor Exporters in the International Economy*. Ithaca, N.Y.: Cornell University Press, 1997.

CIA—The World Factbook. "Lebanon." http://www.cia.gov/cia/publications/ factbook/print/le.html.

"Citrus Workers in Tyre's Refugee Camps." Vol. 9, March 2005, http://www .prc.org.uk/index.php?module=return_review&id=a94f741a1e4c88f516&offs et=&month=3 (accessed 24 August 2009).

Clark, Gregory. "A Review of Avner Greif's *Institutions and the Path to the Modern Economy:* Lessons from Medieval Trade." *Journal of Economic Literature* 45, no. (September 2007): 725–41.

Clark, Janine A. "Field Research Methods in the Middle East." *PS: Political Science & Politics* (2006): 417–23.

————. *Islam, Charity, and Activism: Middle-Class Networks and Social Welfare in Egypt, Jordan, and Yemen*. Bloomington: Indiana University Press, 2004.

————. "The Economic and Political Impact of Economic Restructuring on NGO-State Relations in Egypt." In *Economic Liberalization, Democratization, and Civil Society in the Developing World*, ed. Remonda Bensabat Kleinberg and Janine A. Clark, 157–79. New York: Palgrave, 2000.

Clunan, Anne L., and Harold Trinkunas. "Conceptualizing 'Ungoverned Spaces': Territorial Statehood, Contested Authority and Softened Sovereignty." In *Ungoverned Spaces? Alternatives to State Authority in an Era of Softened Sovereignty*, ed. Anne L. Clunan and Harold Trinkunas (forthcoming, Stanford University Press).

Collier, David. "Data, Field Work, and Extracting New Ideas at Close Range

(Letter from the President)." *ASPSA Comparative Politics Section Newsletter* (winter 1999).

———. "The Comparative Method." In *Political Science: The State of the Discipline II*, ed. Ada W. Finifter, 105–19. Washington, D.C.: American Political Science Association, 1993.

Collier, Ruth Berins. *Paths Toward Democracy: The Working Class and Elites in Western Europe and South America.* New York: Cambridge University Press, 1999.

Collins, Kathleen. "The Logic of Clan Politics: Evidence from the Central Asian Trajectories." *World Politics* 56 (2004): 224–61.

Congressional Research Service. "CRS Issue Brief for Congress: Lebanon." Washington, D.C.: Library of Congress, 2005.

Cook, Karen S., Russell Hardin, and Margaret Levi. *Cooperation without Trust?* Russell Sage Foundation Series on Trust. New York: Russell Sage Foundation, 2005.

Coordination Forum of NGOs Working in the Palestinian Community. "Second Supplementary Report on the Rights of the Palestinian Child in Lebanon." http://www.crin.org/resources/infoDetail.asp?ID=2462 (accessed August 2009).

Cunningham, Robert B., and Yasin K. Sarayrah. *Wasta: The Hidden Force in Middle Eastern Society.* Westport, Conn.: Praeger, 1993.

Curmi, Brigitte. "Les Associations de Bienfaisance à Amman: le Jabal Achrafiyyeh." In *Amman, Ville et Societe—The City and Its Society*, ed. Jean Hannoyer and Seteney Shami, 359–71. Beirut, Lebanon: CERMOC, 1996.

Dabbas, Hamed. "Islamic Centers, Associations, Societies, Organizations, and Committees in Jordan." In *Islamic Movements in Jordan*, ed. Hani Hourani, 195–259. Amman: al-Urdun al-Jadid Research Center and Friedrich Ebert Stiftung, 1997.

Dagher, Albert. *L'état et l'économie au Liban: Action gouvernementale et finances publique de l'independence a 1975.* Vol. 12, *Les Cahiers du CERMOC.* Beirut: CERMOC, 1995.

Daves, Bryan. "Biting the Hand That Feeds You: The Dilemma of Economic Reform and Regime stability. Jordan in Comparative Perspective." Paper presented at the Politique et état en Jordanie, 1946–1996, Conference, Paris, 24–25 June 1997.

Davie, Michael F. "The Emerging Urban Landscape of Lebanon." In *Lebanon's Second Republic: Prospects for the Twenty-first Century*, ed. Kail C. Ellis, 159–74. Gainesville: University Press of Florida, 2002.

Dazi-Heni, Fatiha. "Hospitalité et politique: La dîwâniyya au Koweit." *Maghreb-Machrek*, no. Spécial 1er trimestre (1994): 109–23.

de Bel-Air, Françoise. "La gestion politique, economique et sociale des phenomenes demographiques en Jordanie." Paper presented at the Politique et état en Jordanie, 1946–1996. Conference, Paris, 24–25 June 1997.

De Weerdt, Joachim. "Risk-Sharing and Endogenous Network Formation." In *Insurance against Poverty*, ed. Stefan Dercon, 197–216. New York: Oxford University Press, 2005.

Deeb, Lara. "An Enchanted Modern: Gender and Public Piety among Islamist Shi'i Muslims in Beirut." Ph.D. diss., Emory University, 2003.

Dejong, Jocelyn. "The Urban Context of Health during Economic Crisis." In *Amman, Ville et Societe—The City and Its Society*, ed. Jean Hannoyer and Seteney Shami, 265–94. Beirut, Lebanon: CERMOC, 1996.

Dejong, Jocelyn, and Tariq Tell. "Economic Crisis and the Labour Market: A Case-study of Palestinian Workers in Low-income East Amman." In *Palestine, Palestiniens: Territoire national, espaces communautaires*, ed. Riccardo Bocco, Blandine Destremau, and Jean Hannoyer, 195–217. Amman: CERMOC, 1997.

Delacroix, Jacques. "The Distributive State in the World System." *Studies in Comparative International Development* (fall 1980): 3–21.

Della Porta, Donatella. "Introduction: On Individual Motivations in Underground Political Organizations." In *Social Movements and Violence: Participation in Underground Organizations*, ed. Donatella Della Porta, 3–28. Greenwich, Conn.: JAI Press, 1992.

Denoeux, Guilain. *Urban Unrest in the Middle East: A Comparative Study of Informal Networks in Egypt, Iran, and Lebanon*. Albany: State University of New York Press, 1993.

Denoeux, Guilain, and Robert Springborg. "Hariri's Lebanon: Singapore of the Middle East or Sanaa of the Levant?" *Middle East Policy* 6, no. 2 (1998): 158–73.

Dercon, Stefan. "Risk, Insurance, and Poverty: A Review." In *Insurance against Poverty*, ed. Stefan Dercon, 9–37. New York: Oxford University Press, 2005.

Destremau, Blandine. "L'espace du camp et la reproduction du provisoire: les camps de refugiés Palestiniens de Wihdat et de Jabal Hussein à Amman." In *Moyen-Orient: migrations, démocratisation, mediations*, ed. Riccardo Bocco and Mohammad-Reza Djalili, 83–99. Paris: Presses Universitaires de France, 1994.

Destremau, Blandine. "The Systemic Relations of the State and Poverty. Background Paper, The Role of the State in Poverty Alleviation III Conference." Comparative Research Programme on Poverty of the International Social Science Council (Bergen, Norway), http://www.crop.org/rosa3bkp.htm.

Dib, Kamal. *Warlords and Merchants: The Lebanese Business and Political Establishment*. Reading, U.K.: Ithaca Press, 2004.

DiMaggio, Paul J., and Walter W. Powell. "The Iron Cage Revisited: Institutional Isomorphism and Collective Rationality in Organizational Fields." *American Sociological Review* 48, no. 2 (1983): 147–60.

Dixon, John. "Social Security in the Middle East." In *Social Welfare in the Middle East*, ed. John Dixon, 163–200. Wolfeboro, N.H.: Croom Helm, 1987.

Doan, Rebecca Miles. "Class Differentiation and the Informal Sector in Amman, Jordan." *International Journal of Middle East Studies* 24, no. 1 (February 1992): 27–38.

Doriad, Moez. "Human Development and Poverty in the Arab States." In *Employment Creation and Social Protection in the Middle East and North Africa*, ed. Heba Handoussa and Zafiris Tzannatos, 195–236. New York: American University in Cairo Press, 2002.

Douayhi, Chawqi. "Beyrouth et ses étrangers." In *Guerres civiles: Économies de la violence, dimensions de la civilité*, ed. Jean Hannoyer, 203–19. Paris: Karthala, 1999.

Doueihy, Chawqi. "al-Sira'a 'ala al-madina: madkhal ila dirasa rawabit al-ahiya' fi Beirut [The struggle for the city: Introduction to the study of neighborhood associations in Beirut]." In *La vie publique au Liban: expressions et recompositions du politique*, ed. Joseph Bahout and Chawqi Doueihy, 275–312. Beirut: CERMOC, 1997.

Dougherty, Pamela. "The Pain of Adjustment—Kerak's Bread Riots as a Response to Jordan's Continuing Economic Restructuring Programme: A General Overview." *Jordanies*, no. 2 (December 1996): 95–99.

Duclos, Louis-Jean. "Political Science's Perspective on the Electoral Process: The November 1997 Parliamentary Elections." *Jordanies. Special Issue: The 1997 Parliamentary Elections*, no. 5–6 (June–December 1998): 210–35.

Economic Studies Unit. "Unemployment in Jordan—1996: Preliminary Results and Basic Data." Amman: Center for Strategic Studies, University of Jordan, 1997.

Economist Intelligence Unit. "Lebanon: Country Profile." New York: The Economist Intelligence Unit Limited, 2004.

Edwards, Michael, and David Hulme. "Introduction: NGO Performance and Accountability." In *Beyond the Magic Bullet: NGO Performance and Accountability in the Post–Cold War World*, ed. Michael Edwards and David Hulme, 1–20. West Hartford, Conn.: Kumerian, 1996.

Eken, Sena, Paul Cashin, S. Nuri Erbas, Jose Martelino, and Adnan Mazarei. "Economic Dislocation and Recovery in Lebanon." Washington, D.C.: International Monetary Fund, 1995.

el Khazen, Farid. "Lebanon's First Postwar Parliamentary Election, 1992: An Imposed Choice." Oxford: Centre for Lebanese Studies, 1998.

———. "Political Parties in Postwar Lebanon: Parties in Search of Partisans." *Middle East Journal* 57, no. 4 (2003): 605–24.

el-Husseini, Rola. "Lebanon: Building Political Dynasties." In *Arab Elites: Negotiating the Politics of Change*, ed. Volker Perthes, 239–66. Boulder, Colo.: Lynne Rienner, 2004.

el-Mikawy, Noha, and Marsha Pripstein Posusney. "Labor Representation in the Age of Globalization: Trends and Issues in Non-Oil-Based Arab Economies." In *Employment Creation and Social Protection in the Middle East and North Africa*, ed. Heba Handoussa and Zafiris Tzannatos, 49–94. New York: American University in Cairo Press, 2002.

el-Said, Sabah. *Between Pragmatism and Ideology: The Muslim Brotherhood in Jordan, 1989–1994*. Policy Papers Number 39 ed. Washington, D.C.: Washington Institute for Near East Policy, 1995.

Ellickson, Robert C. *Order without Law: How Neighbors Settle Disputes*. Cambridge, Mass.: Harvard University Press, 1991.

Embassy of the United States of America. *Country Commercial Guide: Lebanon 2004*. Beirut: Embassy of the United States of America, Beirut, Lebanon, 2003.

Emirate of TransJordan. "Qanun al-jama'iyyat al-muwaqqat li-sinna 1936 [Provisional association law of 1936]." *al-Jarideh al-rasmiyya [Official Gazette]*, 16 July 1936, 288–91.

Encarnación, Omar G. "On Bowling Leagues and NGOs: A Critique of Civil Society's Revival (Book Review)." *Studies in Comparative International Development* 36, no. 4 (2002): 116–31.

Ensminger, Jean. *Making a Market: The Institutional Transformation of an African Society*. New York: Cambridge University Press, 1992.

Erder, Sema. "Where Do You Hail From? Localism and Networks in Istanbul." In *Istanbul: Between the Global and the Local*, ed. Çaglar Keydar, 161–71. New York: Rowman and Littlefield, 1999.

Esping-Andersen, Gøsta. *The Three Worlds of Welfare Capitalism*. Princeton, N.J.: Princeton University Press, 1990.

Esping-Andersen, Gøsta, and Jon Eivind Kolberg. "Welfare States and Employment Regimes." In *The Study of Welfare State Regimes*, ed. Jon Eivind Kolberg, 3–36. Armonk, N.Y.: M. E. Sharpe, 1992.

Espinoza, Vicente. "Social Networks among the Urban Poor: Inequality and Integration in a Latin American City." In *Networks in the Global Village*, ed. Barry Wellman, 147–84. Boulder, Colo.: Westview, 1999.

Estevez-Abe, Margarita, Torben Iversen, and David Soskice. "Social Protection and the Formation of Skills: A Reinterpretation of the Welfare State." In *Varieties of Capitalism: The Institutional Foundations of Comparative Advantage*, ed. Peter A. Hall and David Soskice, 145–83. New York: Oxford University Press, 2001.

Eswaran, Mukesh, and Ashok Kotwal. "Credit as Insurance in Agrarian Economies." *Journal of Development Economics* 31, no. 1 (1989): 37–53.

EuroCom. "Social Development Organizations—Jordan." http://www.eurocomberlin.de/eurocom/jordan/NGO/Social_Development.htm.

Fandy, Mamoun. *Saudi Arabia and the Politics of Dissent*. New York: St. Martin's, 1999.

Fathi, Schirin. *Jordan—An Invented Nation? Tribe-State Dynamics and the Formation of National Identity*. Hamburg: Deutches Orient-Institut, 1994.

Fattouh, Bassam, and Reinoud Leenders. "Lebanon: The Emerging Regional Financial Center?" *Amsterdam Middle East Papers*, no. 6 (1996).

Favier, Agnès. "Annexe 1—Tableau des municipalitès du Liban (en 1999)." In

Municipalités et Pouvoirs Locaux au Liban, ed. Agnès Favier, 357–81. Beirut: CERMOC, 2001.

———. "Annexe 3—Questionnaires SOFRES-CERMOC, 1999." In *Municipalités et Pouvoirs Locaux au Liban,* ed. Agnès Favier, 383–415. Beirut: CERMOC, 2001.

Fearon, James D., and David Laitin. "Violence and the Social Construction of Ethnic Identity." *International Organization* 54, no. 4 (2000): 845–77.

———. "Explaining Interethnic Cooperation." *American Political Science Review* 90, no. 4 (December 1996): 715–35.

Ferrera, Maurizio. "The 'Southern Model' of Welfare in Social Europe." *Journal of European Social Policy* 6, no. 1 (1996): 17–37.

———. *The Boundaries of Welfare: European Integration and the New Spatial Politics of Social Protection.* New York: Oxford University Press, 2005.

Figuié, Gérard. *Le Point sur le Liban.* Beirut, 2005.

Fine, Ben. *Social Capital versus Social Theory: Political Economy and Social Science at the Turn of the Millennium.* New York: Routledge, 2001.

Fischbach, Michael R. "British Land Policy in Transjordan." In *Village, Steppe and State: The Social Origins of Modern Jordan,* ed. Eugene L. Rogan and Tariq Tell, 80–107. New York: British Academic Press, 1994.

———. *State, Society, and Land in Jordan.* Boston: Brill, 2000.

Fisher, Julie. *Non-Governments: NGOs and the Political Development of the Third World.* West Hartford, Conn.: Kumerian, 1998.

Flynn, Donna K., and Linda Oldham. "Women's Economic Activities in Jordan: Research Findings on Women's Participation in Microenterprise, Agriculture, and the Formal Sector." Washington, D.C.: Office of Women in Development, U.S. Agency for International Development, with Development Alternatives, Inc., 1999.

Foley, Michael W., and Bob Edwards. "The Paradox of Civil Society." *Journal of Democracy* 7, no. 3 (1996): 38–52.

Follis, Louisa. "Micro-credit Can Fill Holes Left by Banks: NGOs Are Distributing Small Loans That Are Helping the Poor to Help Themselves." *Daily Star,* 30 November 2000.

Gaspard, Toufic K. *A Political Economy of Lebanon, 1948–2002: The Limits of Laissez-faire.* Boston: Brill, 2004.

Geddes, Barbara. "The Great Transformation in the Study of Politics in Developing Countries." In *Political Science: The State of the Discipline,* ed. Ira Katznelson and Helen V. Milner, 342–70. New York: W. W. Norton, 2002.

General Union of Voluntary Societies. "al-Sira al-thatiyya lil-jama'iyyat al-muta'ddida al-aghrad [Profile of multipurpose associations] (Internal document)." Amman: Ittihad al-'am lil-jama'iyyat al-khayriyya, 1999.

———. "Ri'aya al-tufoula [Childhood care] (Promotional pamphlet)." Amman: Ittihad al-'am lil-jama'iyyat al-khayriyya, 1999.

———. "Taqreer al-majlis al-tanfeethi. al-idari wa al-mali wa al-mawazina al-taqdeeriyya [Executive report. Administration and finances and projected budget]." Amman: Ittihad al-'am lil-jama'iyyat al-khayriyya, 1994–95.

———. "Taqreer al-majlis al-tanfeethi. al-idari wa al-mali wa al-mawazina al-taqdeeriyya [Executive report. Administration and finances and projected budget]." Amman: Ittihad al-'am lil-jama'iyyat al-khayriyya, 1987–88.

———. "Taqreer al-majlis al-tanfeethi. al-idari wa al-mali wa al-mawazina al-taqdeeriyya [Executive report. Administration and finances and projected budget]." Amman: Ittihad al-'am lil-jama'iyyat al-khayriyya, 1995–96.

———. "Taqreer al-majlis al-tanfeethi. al-idari wa al-mali wa al-mawazina al-taqdeeriyya [Executive report. Administration and finances and projected budget]." Amman: Ittihad al-'am lil-jama'iyyat al-khayriyya, 1996–97.

———. "Taqreer al-majlis al-tanfeethi. al-idari wa al-mali wa al-mawazina al-taqdeeriyya [Executive report. Administration and finances and projected budget]." Amman: Ittihad al-'am lil-jama'iyyat al-khayriyya, 1997–98.

———. "Tarikh . . . baramij . . . meshari'a [Profile, programs, projects]." Amman: Ittihad al-'am lil-jama'iyyat al-khayriyya, 2000.

General Union of Voluntary Societies, Directorate of Research and Social Studies. "Dalil al-jama'iyyat al-khayriyya fil-Urdun [Directory of voluntary societies in Jordan]." Amman: Ittihad al-'am lil-jama'iyyat al-khayriyya, 1999.

Gereffi, Gary, Miguel Korzeniewicz, and Roberto P. Korzeniewicz. "Introduction: Global Commodity Chains." In *Commodity Chains and Global Capitalism*, ed. Gary Gereffi and Miguel Korzeniewicz, 1–14. Westport, Conn.: Greenwood, 1994.

Ghabra, Shafeeq. "Voluntary Associations in Kuwait: The Foundation of a New System?" *Middle East Journal* 45, no. 2 (spring 1991): 199–215.

Ghabra, Shafeeq N. *Palestinians in Kuwait: The Family and the Politics of Survival*. Boulder, Colo.: Westview, 1987.

Ghulum, Yusef. "Ta'theer al-diwaniyyat 'ala 'amaliyya al-masharika al-siyasiyya fi al-kuwait [Influence of diwan-s on the process of political participation in Kuwait]." *Majella al-'ulum al-ijtima'iyyeh [Magazine of social sciences]* 24, no. 3 (1996): 9–30.

Gilbar, Gad G. "The Economy of Nablus and the Hashemites: The Early Years, 1949–56." *Middle Eastern Studies* 25, no. 1 (January 1989): 51–63.

Gilen, Signe, Are Hovdenak, Rania Maktabi, Jon Pederson, and Dag Tuastad. "Finding Ways: Palestinian Coping Strategies in Changing Environments." Oslo, Norway: FAFO, 1994.

Gilsenan, Michael. "Against patron-client relations." In *Patrons and Clients in Mediterranean Societies*, ed. Ernest Gellner and John Waterbury, 167–83. London: Duckworth, 1977.

Glasze, Georg, and Abdallah Alkhayyal. "Gated Housing Estates in the Arab World: Case Studies in Lebanon and Riyadh, Saudi Arabia." *Environment and Planning B: Planning and Design* 29, no. 3 (2002): 321–36.

Glenn, Brian J. "Understanding Mutual Benefit Societies, 1860–1960 (Review Essay)." *Journal of Health Politics, Policy, and Law* 26, no. 3 (2001): 638–51.

Goldstein, Markus, Alain De Janvry, and Elisabeth Sadoulet. "Is a Friend in Need a Friend Indeed? Inclusion and Exclusion in Mutual Insurance Networks in Southern Ghana." In *Insurance against Poverty*, ed. Stefan Dercon, 217–46. New York: Oxford University Press, 2005.

Gourevitch, Peter. *Politics in Hard Times: Comparative Responses to International Economic Crises*. Ithaca, N.Y.: Cornell University Press, 1986.

Government of Jordan. "Memorandum on Economic and Financial Policies to IMF, 4 July." http://www.imf.org/external/np/loi/2000/jor/01/index.htm.

———. "Qanun al-jama'iyat (jam'aiyat wa ijtima'iyat wa andiya wa riyadiya) [Associations Law (associations, societies, clubs, sports)] of 1909 and amendments." *al-Majalla al-qadaiya* (Beirut).

Granovetter, Mark S. *Getting a Job: A Study of Contacts and Careers*. Cambridge, Mass.: Harvard University Press, 1974.

Greif, Avner. "Cultural Beliefs and the Organization of Society: A Historical and Theoretical Reflection on Collectivist and Individualist Societies." *Journal of Political Economy* 102, no. 5 (1994): 912–50.

———. "Reputation and Coalitions in Medieval Trade: Evidence on the Maghribi Traders." *Journal of Economic History* 49, no. 4 (1989): 857–82.

Haddad, Antoine. "The Poor in Lebanon." *Lebanon Report*, no. 3 (1996).

Haddad, M. "'Detribalizing' and 'Retribalizing': The Double Role of Churches among Christian Arabs in Jordan: A Study in the Anthropology of Religion." *The Muslim World* 82, no. 1–2 (January–April 1992): 67–89.

Haggard, Stephan, and Robert R. Kaufman. *Development, Democracy, and Welfare States: Latin America, East Asia, and Eastern Europe*. Princeton, N.J.: Princeton University Press, 2008.

Hall, Peter A. "Beyond the Comparative Method (Letter from the President)." *APSA-CP Newsletter* 15, no. 2 (2004): 1–4.

Hall, Peter A., and Rosemary C. R. Taylor. "Political Science and the Three New Institutionalisms." *Political Studies* 44 (1996): 936–57.

Hamarneh, Mustafa. *al-Urdun [Jordan]*. Edited by Sa'ad al-Deen Ibrahim, Dirasat mashru' al-mujtam' al-madani wa al-tahawwul al-dimuqrati fi al-watan al-'arabi [Studies in the civil society project and the democratic transformation of the Arab world]. Cairo: Markaz Ibn Khaldoun and Dar al-Ameen, 1995.

Hamarneh, Mustafa B. "Social and Economic Transformation of Trans-Jordan 1921–1946." Ph.D. diss., Georgetown University, 1985.

Hammad, Waleed. "Islamists and Charitable Work in Jordan: The Muslim Brotherhood as a Model." In *Islamic Movements in Jordan*, ed. Hani Hourani, 169–92. Amman: Al-Urdun al-Jadid Research Center and Friedrich Ebert Stiftung, 1997.

Hammami, Rema. "Palestinian NGOs Since Oslo: From NGO Politics to Social Movements?" *Middle East Report* 30, no. 214 (2000): 16–19, 27, 48.

Hamzeh, Ahmad Nizar. *In the Path of Hizbullah*. Syracuse, N.Y.: Syracuse University Press, 2004.

Hannoyer, Jean. "Introduction: Économies de la violence, dimensions de la civilité." In *Guerres civiles: Économies de la violence, dimensions de la civilité*, ed. Jean Hannoyer, 9–30. Paris: Karthala, 1999.

———. "L'hospitalité, économie de la violence." *Maghreb-Machrek*, no. 123 (janv–mars 1989): 226–40.

Hanssen-Bauer, Jon, Jon Pedersen, and Age A. Tiltnes, eds. *Jordanian Society: Living Conditions in the Hashemite Kingdom of Jordan*, Fafo-report 253. Oslo: Fafo Institute for Applied Social Science, 1998.

Hardin, Russell. *Collective Action*. Baltimore, Md.: John Hopkins University Press, 1982.

———. "Contested Community." *Society* 32, no. 5 (July/August 1995): 23–29.

Harik, Judith. "Citizen Disempowerment and the 1996 Parliamentary Elections in the Governate of Mount Lebanon." *Democratization* 15, no. 1 (1998): 158–82.

———. *The Public and Social Services of the Lebanese Militias*. Edited by Centre for Lebanese Studies, Papers on Lebanon 14. Oxford: Oxonian Rewley Press, 1994.

Harik, Judith P. "Change and Continuity among the Lebanese Druze Community: The Civil Administration of the Mountains, 1983–90." *Middle Eastern Studies* 29, no. 3 (1993): 377–98.

Harik, Judith Palmer. *Hezbollah: The Changing Face of Terrorism*. New York: I. B. Tauris, 2004.

Harris, William. "The View from Zahle: Security and Economic Conditions in the Central Bekaa 1980–1985." *Middle East Journal* 39, no. 3 (1985): 270–86.

Hart, Gillian. "Gender and Household Dynamics: Recent Theories and Their Implications." In *Critical Issues in Asian Development: Theories, Experiences, and Policies*, ed. M. G. Guibria, 39–74. New York: Oxford University Press, 1995.

Hashemite Kingdom of Jordan. "al-Nitham al-asasi al-mu'adal lil-ittihad al-'am lil-jama'iyyat al-khayriyya li-'am 1995 [The Basic Amended Charter for the General Union of Voluntary Societies of 1995]." *Mawsu'a al-tashree' al-Urduni [Encyclopaedia of Jordanian Law 1998]* 1995, 70–89.

———. "Dirasa al-Urduniyeen al-'a'ideen min al-kharij khilal al-fatra 8/10/1991–12/31/1992 [Survey of Jordanians returning from abroad during the period 8/10/1991–12/31/1992]." Amman: Department of Statistics, 1993.

———. "Dirasa nafaqat wa dakhl al-usra 1997 [Household Expenditure and Income Survey 1997]." Amman: Department of Statistics, 1999.

———. "Dirasat al-istikhdam, fil-mu'assasat alati y'amal bi-kul min-ha 5 ashkhas aw akthar [Employment Survey, for Establishments Engaging (5) Persons or More]." Amman: Department of Statistics, 1992.

———. Household Expenditure and Income Survey 1992 [Dirasa nafaqat wa dakhl al-usra 1992]." Amman: Department of Statistics, 1993.

————. "Jordan in Figures 1999: Population Density and Area." http://www
.dos.gov.jo/jorfig/1999/fig_e_n.htm.

————. "Key National Indicators." http://www.dos.gov.jo/sdb_jd/jd_txt3e.htm.

————. "Nitham al-awal: Nitham jam' al-tabarru'at lil-wujuh al-khayriyya
[Regulation #1: Regulation on collecting donations for charitable purposes]."
Amman, 1957.

————. "Nitham raqm 13 li-sinna 1998 nitham al-jama'iyyat al-taa'wuniyya
[Regulation #13 of 1998: regulation for cooperative associations]." *al-Jarida
al-rasmiyya* [*Official Gazette*], 3 May [Ayar] 1998, 1382–96.

————. *Plan for Economic and Social Development 1993–1997.* Amman: Jordan
Press Foundation, 1993?

————. "Qanun raqm 17 li-sinna 1956 qanun jama'iyyat al-ta'wun [Law #17 of
1956: Cooperative associations law]." *al-Jarida al-rasmiyya* [*Official Gazette*],
29 February 1956, 1419–35.

————. "Qanun raqm 18 li-sinna 1997 qanun al-taa'wun [Law #18 of 1997:
Cooperative law]." *al-Jarida al-rasmiyya* [*Official Gazette*], 22 March 1997,
1683–91.

————. "Qanun raqm (33) li-sinna 1966: qanun al-jama'iyyat wa al-hay'at al-
ijtima'iyya [Law #33 of 1966: Law of associations and social organizations]."
Mawsu'a al-tashree' al-Urduni [*Encyclopaedia of Jordanian Law 1998*] 1966,
32–43.

————. Social Security Corporation, "Overview and Tables." http://www.ssc.
gov.jo.

————. "Societies and Syndicates." http://www.dos.gov.jo/jorfig/1999/fiq_e_n
.htm.

————. "Statistical Yearbook 1998." Amman: Department of Statistics, 1999.

Heydemann, Steven. "Institutions and Economic Performance: The Use and
Abuse of Culture in New Institutional Economics." *Studies in Comparative
International Development* 43 (2008): 27–52.

Hirsch, Eric L. *Urban Revolt: Ethnic Politics in the Nineteenth-Century Chicago
Labor Movement.* Berkeley: University of California Press, 1990.

Hollingsworth, J. Rogers, Philippe Schmitter, and Wolfgang Streeck, eds. *Governing Capitalist Economies.* New York: Oxford University Press, 1994.

Horowitz, Donald. *Ethnic Groups in Conflict.* Berkeley: University of California
Press, 1985.

Hourani, Hani. *Azma al-iqtisad al-Urduni* [*The crisis of Jordan's economy*]. Nico-
sia, Cyprus: al-Urdun al-Jadid, 1989.

————. "Intikhabat 1993 al-Urduniyya: qira'a fi khalfiyyatiha; thuroufiha; wa
nata'ijiha [The 1993 Jordanian elections: A reading on their background; conditions; and results]." *Qira'at siyassiyya* [*Political readings*] 4, no. 2, rabi' (1994).

————. "Prospects for the Development of Political Parties and Strategies for
Enhancing Political Party Processes in Jordan." *Middle East Report,* no. 209
(1998): 30.

Hourani, Hani, Hamed Dabbas, and Mark Power-Stevens. *Who's Who in the Jordanian Parliament 1993–1997.* Translated by George Musleh. Amman: Al-Urdun al-Jadid Research Center, 1995.

Hourani, Hani, and Ayman Yassin. *Who's Who in the Jordanian Parliament 1997–2001.* Translated by Lola Keilani and Lana Habash. Amman: Al-Urdun al-Jadid Research Center, 1998.

Hourani, Hani, et al. *Directory of Civil Society Organizations in Jordan.* Translated by Sadik Ibrahim Odeh. Amman: Sindbad Publishing House and al-Urdun al-Jadid Research Center, 2001.

Huber, Evelyne. "Options for Social Policy in Latin America: Neoliberal versus Social Democratic Models." In *Welfare States in Transition: National Adaptations in Global Economies,* ed. Gøsta Esping-Andersen, 141–91. Thousand Oaks, Calif.: Sage, 1996.

Huber, Evelyne, and John D. Stephens. *Development and Crisis of the Welfare State: Parties and Policies in Global Markets.* Chicago: University of Chicago Press, 2001.

Hudson, Michael C. "Palestinians and Lebanon: The Common Story." *Journal of Refugee Studies* 10, no. 3 (1997): 243–60.

Hyden, Goran. "Governance and the Study of Politics." In *Governance and Politics in Africa,* ed. Goran Hyden and Michael Bratton, 1–267. Boulder, Colo.: Lynne Rienner, 1992.

Ilchman, Warren F., Stanley N. Katz, and Edward L. Queen II. "Introduction." In *Philanthropy in the World's Traditions,* ed. Warren F. Ilchman, Stanley N. Katz, and Edward L. Queen II, ix–xv. Bloomington: Indiana University Press, 1998.

International Crisis Group. "Inside Gaza: The Challenge of Clans and Families." In *Middle East Report N 71,* 2007.

International Press Office, The Royal Hashemite Court. "Non-Governmental Organizations (NGO's)." National Information Centre, Government of Jordan, http://www.nic.gov.jo/society/ngo.html.

Ishtay, Chawkat. "Political Parties in the 2000 Elections: The Presence of the Name and the Absence of Institutions." In *Legislative Elections 2000: Between Reproduction and Change* (in Arabic), ed. Melhem Chaoul et al., 83–142. Beirut: Lebanese Center for Policy Studies, 2002.

Ismail, Salwa. *Political Life in Cairo's New Quarters: Encountering the Everyday State.* Minneapolis: University of Minnesota Press, 2006.

Iversen, Torben. *Capitalism, Democracy, and Welfare.* New York: Cambridge University Press, 2005.

Iversen, Torben, and Thomas R. Cusack. "The Causes of Welfare State Expansion: Deindustrialization or Globalization?" *World Politics* 52 (2000): 313–49.

Iversen, Torben, and David Soskice. "An Asset Theory of Social Policy Preferences." *American Politcal Science Review* 95, no. 4 (2001): 875–93.

Iverson, Torben, and Anne Wren. "Equality, Employment, and Budgetary Restraint: The Trilemma of the Service Economy." *World Politics* 50, no. 4 (1998): 507–46.

Jabar, Faleh A. "Shaykhs and Ideologues: Detribalization and Retribalization in Iraq, 1968–1988." *Middle East Report,* no. 215 (summer 2000): 28–31, 48.

———. "Sheikhs and Ideologues: Deconstruction and Reconstruction of Tribes under Patrimonial Totalitarianism in Iraq, 1968–1998." In *Tribes and Power: Nationalism and Ethnicity in the Middle East,* ed. Faleh Abdul-Jabar and Hosham Hawod, 69–109. London: Saqi, 2003.

Jaber, Hana'. "Elections and Civil Society: Typology of the slogans in Amman's second and fourth electoral constituencies." *Jordanies. Special issue: The 1997 Parliamentary Elections,* no. 5–6 (June–December 1998): 253–60.

———. "The Impact of Structural Adjustment on Women's Employment and Urban Households." *Jordanies,* no. 4 (décembre 1997): 148–66.

Jamal, Amaney A. *Barriers to Democracy: The Other Side of Social Capital in Palestine and the Arab World.* Princeton, N.J.: Princeton University Press, 2007.

Jawad, Rana. "A Profile of Social Welfare in Lebanon: Assessing the Implications for Social Development Policy." *Global Social Policy* 2, no. 3 (2002): 319–42.

Jenkins, Shirley. "Conclusion: The States and the Associations." In *Ethnic Associations and the Welfare State: Services to Immigrants in Five Countries,* ed. Shirley Jenkins, 275–81. New York: Columbia University Press, 1988.

———. "Introduction: Immigration, Ethnic Associations, and Social Services." In *Ethnic Associations and the Welfare State: Services to Immigrants in Five Countries,* ed. Shirley Jenkins, 1–19. New York: Columbia University Press, 1988.

Johnson, Michael. *Class and Client in Beirut: The Sunni Muslim Community and the Lebanese State 1840–1985.* Atlantic Highlands, N.J.: Ithaca Press, 1986.

———. "Political Bosses and Their Gangs: Zu'ama and qabadayat in the Sunni Muslim quarters of Beirut." In *Patrons and Clients in Mediterranean Societies,* ed. Ernest Gellner and John Waterbury, 207–24. London: Duckworth, 1977.

Jordan Center for Social Research. "Democratic Transformation and Political Reform in Jordan: National Public Opinion Poll #4." Amman, 2007.

———. "The 2007 Municipal Elections in Jordan: An Exit Poll Conducted in Six Electoral Districts Located in Six Municipalities." Amman, 2007.

Jordan Cooperative Organization. "al-Taqreer al-sanawi li-'am 1991 [Annual Report for 1991]." Amman: al-Munathama al-t'awuniyya al-Urduniyya, al-Ma'had al-t'awuni, 1991.

Joseph, Suad. "Civic Myths, Citizenship, and Gender in Lebanon." In *Gender and Citizenship in the Middle East,* ed. Suad Joseph, 107–36. Syracuse, N.Y.: Syracuse University Press, 2000.

———. "The Public/Private—The Imagined Boundary in the Imagined Nation/State/Community: The Lebanese Case." *Feminist Review* 57, no. (fall 1997): 73–92.

Jreisat, Jamil E. "Bureaucracy and Development in Jordan." *Journal of Asian and African Studies* 24, no. 1–2 (1989): 94–105.

Jungen, Christine. "Tribalism in Kerak: Past Memories, Present Realities." In *Jordan in Transition*, ed. George Joffé, 191–207. New York: Palgrave, 2002.

Jureidini, Paul A., and R. D. McLaurin. *Jordan: The Impact of Social Change on the Role of the Tribes*. New York: Praeger, 1984.

Kana'an, Taher H. "The Social Dimension in Jordan's Approach to Development." In *Income Distribution in Jordan*, ed. Kamel Abu Jaber, Matthes Buhbe, and Mohammad Smadi, 9–16. San Francisco: Westview (in cooperation with the Friedrich Ebert Stiftung), 1990.

Kanovsky, E. *The Economy of Jordan: The Implications of Peace in the Middle East*. Tel Aviv: University Publishing Projects, 1976.

Karam, Nadim. "Systèmes de protection sociale au Liban." In *Médecins et protection sociale dans le monde Arabe*, ed. Brigitte Curmi and Sylvia Chiffoleau, 203–209. Beirut: CERMOC, 1993.

Karshenas, Massoud, and Valentine M. Moghadam. "Social Policy in the Middle East: Introduction and Overview." In *Social Policy in the Middle East: Economic, Political, and Gender Dynamics*, ed. Massoud Karshenas and Valentine M. Moghadam, 1–30. New York: Palgrave Macmillan and the United Nations Research Institute for Social Development (UNRISD), 2006.

Kassim, Anis F. "The Palestinians: From Hyphenated to Integrated Citizenship." In *Citizenship and the State in the Middle East: Approaches and Applications*, ed. Nils A. Butenschon, Uri Davis, and Manuel Hassassian, 201–24. Syracuse, N.Y.: Syracuse University Press, 2000.

Katzenstein, Peter J. *Small States in World Markets: Industrial Policy in Europe*. Ithaca, N.Y.: Cornell University Press, 1985.

Kawar, Mary. "Implications of the Young Age Structure of the Female Labour Force in Amman." In *Amman, Ville et Societe—The City and Its Society*, ed. Jean Hannoyer and Seteney Shami, 233–63. Beirut: CERMOC, 1996.

Kechichian, Joseph A. "The Lebanese Army: Capabilities and Challenges in the 1980s." *Conflict Quarterly* 5 (1985): 15–39.

Keely, Charles B., and Bassam Saket. "Jordanian Migrant Workers in the Arab Region: A Case Study of Consequences for Labor Supplying Countries." *Middle East Journal* 38, no. 4 (fall 1984): 685–98.

Khalaf, Samir. "Changing Forms of Political Patronage in Lebanon." In *Patrons and Clients in Mediterranean Societies*, ed. Ernest Gellner and John Waterbury, 185–205. London: Duckworth, 1977.

———. *Civil and Uncivil Violence in Lebanon: A History of the Internationalization of Communal Conflict*. New York: Columbia University Press, 2002.

———. *Lebanon's Predicament*. New York: Columbia University Press, 1987.

———. "On Roots and Routes: The Reassertion of Primordial Loyalties." In *Lebanon in Limbo: Postwar Society and State in an Uncertain Regional*

Environment, ed. Theodor Hanf and Nawaf Salam, 107–41. Baden-Baden: Nomos Verlagsgesellschaft, 2003.

Khalidi, Rashid. "The Palestinians in Lebanon: Social Repercussions of Israel's Invasion." *Middle East Journal* 38, no. 2 (1984): 255–66.

Khalili, Laleh. "Grass-roots Commemorations: Remembering the Land in the Camps of Lebanon." *Journal of Palestine Studies* 34, no. 1 (2004): 6–22.

Khilnani, Sunil. "The Development of Civil Society." In *Civil Society: History and Possibilities,* ed. Sudipta Kaviraj and Sunil Khilnani, 11–32. New York: Cambridge University Press, 2001.

Khoury, Philip S., and Joseph Kostiner. "Introduction: Tribes and the Complexities of State Formation in the Middle East." In *Tribes and State Formation in the Middle East,* ed. Philip S. Khoury and Joseph Kostiner, 1–22. Berkeley: University of California Press, 1990.

———, eds. *Tribes and State Formation in the Middle East.* Berkeley: University of California Press, 1990.

Khuri, Fuad I. *From Village to Suburb: Order and Change in Greater Beirut.* Chicago: University of Chicago Press, 1975.

Kingston, Paul. "Introduction: States-Within-States: Historical and Theoretical Perspectives." In *States-Within-States: Incipient Political Entities in the Post–Cold War Era,* ed. Paul Kingston and Ian S. Spears, 1–13. New York: Palgrave Macmillan, 2004.

Kingston, Paul, and Ian S. Spears, eds. *States-Within-States: Incipient Political Entities in the Post–Cold War Era.* New York: Palgrave Macmillan, 2004.

Kingston, Paul, and Marie-Joëlle Zahar. "Rebuilding *A House of Many Mansions:* The Rise and Fall of Militia Cantons in Lebanon." In *States-Within-States: Incipient Political Entities in the Post–Cold War Era,* ed. Paul Kingston and Ian S. Spears, 81–97. New York: Palgrave Macmillan, 2004.

Kirby, Peadar. "Theorising Globalisation's Social Impact: Proposing the Conept of Vulnerability." *Review of International Political Economy* 13, no. 4 (2006): 632–55.

Korostelina, Karina V. *Social Identity and Conflict: Structures, Dynamics, and Implications.* New York: Palgrave Macmillan, 2007.

Kozlowski, Gregory C. "Religious Authority, Reform, and Philanthropy in the Contemporary Muslim World." In *Philanthropy in the World's Traditions,* ed. Warren F. Ilchman, Stanley N. Katz, and Edward L. Queen II, 279–308. Bloomington: Indiana University Press, 1998.

Krayyem, Hassan. "Les présidents de municipalité élus en 1998 au Liban: des 'élites' locales non dirigeantes." In *Municipalités et Pouvoirs Locaux au Liban,* ed. Agnès Favier, 33–57. Beirut: CERMOC, 2001.

Kubursi, Atif A. "Reconstructing the Economy of Lebanon." *Arab Studies Quarterly* 21, no. 1 (1999): 69–93.

Kuran, Timur. "Ethnic Norms and Their Transformation through Reputational Cascades." *Journal of Legal Studies* 27, no. 2 (1998): 623–59.

Labaki, Boutros. "L'économie politique de l'émigration libanaise." *Le Commerce du Levant*, no. 2 (February 1981): 9–15.

———. "L'exode de 1945 à 1980." *Le Commerce du Levant*, no. 9 (February 1981): 10–25.

Labaki, Boutros, and Khalil Abou Rjeily. *Bilan des guerres du Liban, 1975–1990*. Paris: Éditions L'Harmattan, 1993.

Laitin, David D. *Hegemony and Culture*. Chicago: University of Chicago Press, 1986.

———. *Identity in Formation: The Russian-Speaking Populations in the Near Abroad*. Ithaca, N.Y.: Cornell University Press, 1998.

———. "Marginality: A Microperspective." *Rationality and Society* 7, no. 1 (1995): 31–57.

Landa, Janet Tai. *Trust, Ethnicity, and Identity: Beyond the New Institutional Economics of Ethnic Trading, Networks, Contract Law, and Gift Exchange*. Ann Arbor: University of Michigan Press, 1994.

Langohr, Vickie. "Too Much Civil Society, Too Little Politics: Egypt and Liberalizing Arab Regimes." *Comparative Politics* (2004): 181–204.

Layne, Linda L. *Home and Homeland: The Dialogics of Tribal and National Identities in Jordan*. Princeton, N.J.: Princeton University Press, 1994.

———. "'Tribalism': National Representations of Tribal Life in Jordan." *Urban Anthropology* 16, no. 2 (1987): 183–203.

Le Troquer, Yann, and Rozenn Hommery al-Oudat. "From Kuwait to Jordan: The Palestinians' Third Exodus." *Journal of Palestine Studies* 28, no. 3 (spring 1999): 37–51.

Lebanese Center for Policy Studies. "Biographical Briefs of the 1996 Deputies by Region." *Lebanon Report*, no. 3 (1996).

———. "The Civil Society Report 1997." Beirut: Lebanese Center for Policy Studies, 1997.

Leenders, Reinoud. "Public Means to Private Ends: State Building and Power in Post-war Lebanon." In *Politics from Above, Politics from Below: The Middle East in the Age of Economic Reform*, ed. Eberhard Kienle, 304–35. London: Saqi, 2003.

Levi, Margaret. "Social and Unsocial Capital: A Review Essay of Robert Putnam's *Making Democracy Work*." *Politics & Society* 24, no. 1 (1996): 45–55.

"Liban: L'argent des milices." *Les Cahiers de l'Orient*, no. 10 (1988): 271–87.

Library of Congress. "A Country Study: Lebanon." Country Studies, Federal Research Division, http://lcweb2.loc.gov/frd/cs/lbtoc.html.

———. "Country Studies: Jordan." http://lcweb2.loc.gov/frd/csquery.html.

Little, Jo, and Patricia Austin. "Women and the Rural Idyll." *Journal of Rural Studies* 12, no. 2 (1996): 101–11.

Loewe, Markus, et al. "Improving the Social Protection of the Urban Poor and Near-Poor in Jordan: The Potential of Micro-Insurance." Bonn: German Development Institute, 2001.

Longuenesse, Elisabeth. "Guerre et decentralisation urbaine au Liban: le cas de Zghorta." In *Petites villes et villes moyennes dans le monde Arabe*, ed. Centre d'Études et de Recherches URBAMA, 345–60. Tours: Université de Tours, 1986.

———. "Ingénieurs et marché de l'emploi en Jordanie." In *Bâtisseurs et Bureaucrates: Ingénieurs et Société au Maghreb et au Moyen-Orient*, ed. Elisabeth Longuenesse, 127–45. Lyon: Maison de l'Orient, 1990.

———. "Professional Syndicates in Jordan (Talk given to CERMOC)." Amman, 1998.

Maamsir, Muhammad Kayr. "al-Tajriba al-Urduniyya fi muhariba al-faqr wa al-battala [The Jordanian experience in battling poverty and unemployment]." In *al-Battala wa al-faqr: waqi' wa tahaddiyyat. al-Urdun, al-Maghreb, Masr, Tunis, Lubnan* [*Unemployment and poverty: The reality and challenges. Jordan, Morocco, Egypt, Tunisia, Lebanon*], ed. Khalid al-Wazani, 199–208. Amman: 'Abd al-Hameed Shooman, 2000.

Maclean, Lauren Morris. "Empire of the Young: The Legacies of State Agricultural Policy on Local Capitalism and Social Support Networks in Ghana and Côte d'Ivoire." *Comparative Studies in Society and History* 46, no. 3 (2004): 469–96.

———. "State Social Policies and Social Support Networks: The Unintended Consequences of State Policymaking on Informal Networks in Ghana and Côte d'Ivoire." *International Journal of Public Administration* 26, no. 6 (2003): 665–91.

Magnet, Myron. "Introduction." In *What Makes Charity Work? A Century of Public and Private Philanthropy*, ed. Myron Magnet, vii–xiii. Chicago: Ivan R. Dee, 2000.

Makdisi, Samir. *Lessons of Lebanon: The Economics of War and Development*. New York: I. B. Tauris, 2004.

Makdisi, Samir, and Richard Sadaka. "The Lebanese Civil War, 1975–1990." In *Understanding Civil War: Evidence and Analysis*. Vol. 2, *Europe, Central Asia, and Other Regions*, ed. Paul Collier and Nicholas Sambanis, 59–85. Washington, D.C.: World Bank, 2005.

Makdisi, Ussama. *The Culture of Sectarianism: Community, History, and Violence in Nineteenth-Century Ottoman Lebanon*. Berkeley: University of California Press, 2000.

Makhoul, Jihad, and Lindsey Harrison. "Intercessory *Wasta* and Village Development in Lebanon." *Arab Studies Quarterly* 26, no. 3 (2004): 25–41.

Mangan, John. *Workers without Traditional Employment: An International Study of Non-standard Work*. Northampton, Mass.: Edward Elgar, 2000.

Mansur, Ahsan. "Social Aspects of the Adjustment Program: Strengthening of the Social Safety Net." In *Jordan: Strategy for Adjustment and Growth (Occasional Paper #136)*, ed. Edouard Maciejewski and Ahsan Mansur, 58–65. Washington, D.C.: International Monetary Fund, 1996.

Mares, Isabela. "Social Protection around the World: External Insecurity, State Capacity, and Domestic Political Cleavages." *Comparative Political Studies* 38, no. 6 (2005): 623–51.

Mark, Clyde R. "CRS Issue Brief for Congress: Lebanon." Washington, D.C.: Congressional Research Service, Library of Congress, 2004.

Marseglia, Manuela. "Welfare in the Mediterranean Countries: Lebanon." Arco Felice, Italy: Centre for Administrative Innovation in the Euro-Mediterranean Region (CAIMED.).

Martin, Claude. "Social Welfare and the Family in Southern Europe." In *Southern European Welfare States: Between Crisis and Reform*, ed. Martin Rhodes, 23–41. Portland, Ore.: Frank Cass, 1997.

Marto, Michel (Minister of Finance), and Ziad Fariz (Central Bank Governor). "Letter of Intent of the Government of Jordan to Michel Camdessus, International Monetary Fund, 28 August 1999." International Monetary Fund, http://www.imf.org/external/np/loi/1999/082899.htm.

Massad, Joseph A. *Colonial Effects: The Making of National Identity in Jordan.* New York: Columbia University Press, 2001.

Massad, Joseph Andoni. "Identifying the Nation: The Juridical and Military Bases of Jordanian National Identity." Ph.D. diss., Columbia University, 1998.

Massey, Douglas S., Joaquin Arango, Graeme Hugo, Ali Kouaouci, Adela Pellegrino, and J. Edward Taylor. *Worlds in Motion: Understanding International Migration at the End of the Millennium.* New York: Clarendon, 1998.

Mazur, Michael P. *Economic Growth and Development in Jordan.* London: Croom Helm, 1979.

McCann, Lisa M. "Patrilocal Co-residential Units (PCUs) in Al-Barha: Dual Household Structure in a Provincial Town in Jordan." *Journal of Comparative Family Studies (Special Issue: The Arab Family)* 28, no. 2 (summer 1997): 113–35.

McLaurin, Ronald D. "From Professional to Political: The Redecline of the Lebanese Army." *Armed Forces & Society* 17, no. 4 (1991): 545–68.

Melucci, Alberto. "The Process of Collective Identity." In *Social Movements and Culture*, ed. Hank Johnston and Bert Klandermans, 41–63. Minneapolis: University of Minnesota Press, 1995.

Milgrom, Paul, Douglass C. North, and Barry R. Weingast. "The Role of Institutions in the Revival of Trade: The Medieval Law Merchant, Private Judges, and the Champagne Fairs." *Economics and Politics* 1 (1990): 1–23.

Mingione, Enzo. *Fragmented Societies.* Oxford: Blackwell, 1991.

———. "Life Strategies and Social Economies in the Postfordist Age." *International Journal of Urban and Regional Relations* 18, no. 1 (1994): 24–45.

Ministry of Industry and Trade, Amman. "Agreement between the Hashemite Kingdom of Jordan and Israel on Irbid Qualifying Industrial Zone." Mimeograph, n.d.

Moaddel, Mansoor. *Jordanian Exceptionalism: A Comparative Analysis of State-Religion Relationships in Egypt, Iran, Jordan, and Syria.* New York: Palgrave, 2002.

Moe, Terry M. "Power and Political Institutions." *Perspectives on Politics* 3, no. 2 (2005): 215–33.

Moene, Karl Ove, and Michael Wallerstein. "Inequality, Social Insurance, and Redistribution." *American Politcal Science Review* 95, no. 4 (2001): 859–74.

Mrad, Mohammad. "Annexe 4—Composition sociale des conseils municipaux élus au Liban Sud en 1998." In *Municipalitès et Pouvoirs Locaux au Liban,* ed. Agnès Favier, 417–26. Beirut: CERMOC, 2001.

Muldrew, Craig. *The Economy of Obligation: The Culture of Credit and Social Relations in Early Modern England.* New York: St. Martin's, 1998.

Nahas, Charbel. "L'économie libanaise et ses déséquilibres." *Maghreb-Machrek,* no. 169 (2000): 55–69.

Nasr, Salim. "Anatomie d'un système de guerre interne: Le cas du Liban." *Cultures et conflits,* no. 1 (1990–91): 85–99.

———. "Issues of Social Protection in the Arab Region: A Four-Country Overview." *Cooperation South,* no. 2 (2001): 31–48.

———. "Les travailleurs de l'industrie manufacturiere au machrek: Irak, Jordanie-Palestine, Liban, Syrie." In *Industrialisation et changements sociaux dans l'orient Arabe,* ed. André Bourgey, 145–70. Beirut: CERMOC, 1982.

———. "The New Social Map." In *Lebanon in Limbo: Postwar Society and State in an Uncertain Regional Environment,* ed. Theodor Hanf and Nawaf Salam, 143–58. Baden-Baden: Nomos Verlagsgesellschaft, 2003.

Ne'meh, Adib. "Slipping Through the Cracks: Social Safety Nets in Lebanon." *Lebanon Report,* no. 3 (1996).

North, Douglass. "Markets and Other Allocation Systems in History: The Challenge of Karl Polanyi." *Journal of European Economic History* 6 (1977): 703–16.

North, Douglass C. *Institutions, Institutional Change, and Economic Performance.* New York: Cambridge University Press, 1990.

———. *Structure and Change in Economic History.* New York: W. W. Norton, 1981.

Norton, Augustus Richard. *Hezbollah: A Short History.* Princeton, N.J.: Princeton University Press, 2007.

Nushiwat, Munther Issa. "The Effect of Remittances on Investment: The Case of Jordan." Ph.D. diss., New School for Social Research, 1994.

Oberschall, Anthony. *Social Conflict and Social Movements.* Englewood Cliffs, N.J.: Prentice Hall, 1973.

Oliver, Pamela E., and Gerald Marwell. "The Paradox of Group Size in Collective Action: A Theory of the Critical Mass. II." *American Sociological Review* 53, no. 1 (1988): 1–8.

Olson, Mancur. *The Logic of Collective Action: Public Goods and the Theory of Groups.* Cambridge, Mass.: Harvard University Press, 1971.

Ong, Aihwa. *Flexible Citizenship: The Cultural Logic of Transnationality.* Durham, N.C.: Duke University Press, 1999.

Öniş, Ziya. "The Logic of the Developmental State (Review Article)." *Comparative Politics* 24 no. 1 (October 1991): 109–26.

Ostrom, Elinor. "A Behavioral Approach to the Rational Choice Theory of Collective Action (Presidential Address, American Political Science Association, 1997)." *American Political Science Review* 92, no. 1 (1998): 1–22.

———. "Rational Choice Theory and Institutional Analysis: Toward Complementarity." *American Political Science Review* 85, no. 1 (1991): 237–43.

———. *Understanding Institutional Diversity.* Princeton, N.J.: Princeton University Press, 2005.

Ostrower, Francie. *Why the Wealthy Give: The Culture of Elite Philanthropy.* Princeton, N.J.: Princeton University Press, 1995.

Owen, Roger. "Government and Economy in Jordan: Progress, Problems and Prospects." In *The Shaping of an Arab Statesman: Sharif Abd al-Hamid Sharaf and the Modern Arab World,* ed. Patrick Seale, 85–104. New York: Quartet Books, 1983.

Oxford Business Group. *Emerging Jordan,* 2003.

———. *Emerging Lebanon.* 2002.

Peteet, Julie. "Socio-Political Integration and Conflict Resolution in the Palestinian Camps in Lebanon." *Journal of Palestine Studies* 16, no. 2 (1987): 29–44.

Peteet, Julie M. "Lebanon: Palestinian Refugees in the Post-war Period (HCR Report December 1997)." *Le Monde Diplomatique,* http://www.monde-diplomatique.fr/cahier/proche-orient/region-lebanon-refugee.

Petran, Tabitha. *The Struggle over Lebanon.* New York: Monthly Review Press, 1987.

Piattoni, Simona. "Clientelism in Historical and Comparative Perspective." In *Clientelism, Interests, and Democratic Representation: The European Experience in Historical and Comparative Perspective,* ed. Simona Piattoni, 1–30. New York: Cambridge University Press, 2001.

Picard, Elizabeth. "Autorité et souveraineté de l'État à l'épreuve du Liban sud." *Maghreb-Machrek,* no. 169 (2000): 32–42.

———. "Les habits neufs du communautarisme libanais." *Cultures et conflits* 15/16 (1994): 49–70.

———. "The Political Economy of Civil War in Lebanon." In *War, Institutions, and Social Change in the Middle East,* ed. Steven Heydemann, 292–322. Berkeley: University of California Press, 2000.

———. "Trafficking, Rents, and Diaspora in the Lebanese War." In *Rethinking the Economics of War: The Intersection of Need, Creed, and Greed,* ed. Cynthia J. Arnson and I. William Zartman, 23–51. Baltimore, Md.: Johns Hopkins University Press, 2005.

Pierre-Louis, François. "The Limits of the State in Promoting Hometown

Associations: The Case of Haiti." Paper presented at the Diaspora and Homeland Development Conference, Berkeley Center for Globalization and Information Technology, University of California, Berkeley, April 13, 2004, http://bcgit.berkeley.edu/diaspora.html.

Pierson, Paul. "The New Politics of the Welfare State." *World Politics* 48, no. 2 (1996): 143–80.

———. "Three Worlds of Welfare State Research." *Comparative Political Studies* 33, no. 6/7 (2000): 791–821.

Piore, Michael, and Charles Sabel. *The Second Industrial Divide: Possibilities for Prosperity.* New York: Basic Books, 1984.

Piro, Timothy. *Political Economy of Market Reform in Jordan,* 1998.

Platteau, Jean-Philippe, and Anita Abraham. "An Inquiry into Quasi-Credit Contracts: The Role of Reciprocal Credit and Interlinked Deals in Small-scale Fishing Communities." *Journal of Development Studies* 23 (1987): 461–90.

"Playing the Army against the Labor." *Lebanon Report,* no. 1 (1996).

Polanyi, Karl. *The Great Transformation: The Political and Economic Origins of Our Time.* Boston: Beacon Hill, 1957.

Polletta, Francesca, and James M. Jasper. "Collective Identity and Social Movements." *Annual Review of Sociology* 27 (2001): 283–305.

Poros, Maritsa V. "The Role of Migrant Networks in Linking Local Labour Markets: The Case of Asian Indian Migration to New York and London." *Global Networks* 1, no. 3 (2001): 243–59.

Portes, Alejandro, and Julia Sensenbrenner. "Embeddedness and Immigration: Notes on the Social Determinants of Economic Actions." *American Journal of Sociology* 98, no. 6 (1993): 1320–50.

Posner, Daniel N. *Institutions and Ethnic Politics in Africa.* New York: Cambridge University Press, 2006.

Prados, Alfred B. "Lebanon." In *CRS Issue Brief for Congress.* Washington, D.C.: Congressional Research Service, The Library of Congress, 2007.

Pratten, David T., and Suliman Ali Baldo. "'Return to the Roots': Processes of Legitimacy in Sudanese Migrant Associations." In *Beyond the Magic Bullet: NGO Performance and Accountability in the Post–Cold War World,* ed. Michael Edwards and David Hulme, 142–55. West Hartford, Conn.: Kumerian, 1996.

Putnam, Robert D. "Bowling Alone: America's Declining Social Capital." *Journal of Democracy* 6, no. 1 (January 1995): 65–78.

Radi, Lamia. "La gestion d'appartenances multiples." *Les Cahiers de l'Orient,* no. 35 (1994): 97–111.

———. "Les Palestiniens du Koweit en Jordanie." *Maghreb-Machrek,* no. 144 (April–June 1994): 55–65.

Rasheed, Khalid M. "Social Structure, Kinship and Settlement: A Case Study from Southern Jordan." M.A. thesis, Yarmouk University, 1991.

Razzaz, Omar Munif. "Law, Urban Land Tenure, and Property Disputes in

Contested Settlements: The Case of Jordan." Ph.D. diss., Harvard University, 1991.

Redclift, N., and E. Mingione. "Introduction: Economic Restructuring and Family Practices." In *Beyond Employment: Household, Gender, and Subsistence*, ed. N. Redclift and E. Mingione, 1–11. Oxford: Blackwell, 1985.

Rhodes, Martin. "Southern European Welfare States: Identity, Problems and Prospects for Reform." In *Southern European Welfare States: Between Crisis and Reform*, ed. Martin Rhodes, 1–22. Portland, Ore.: Frank Cass, 1997.

Richani, Nazi. "The Druze of Mount Lebanon: Class Formation in a Civil War." *Middle East Report*, no. 162 (1990): 26–30.

Riedel, Tim. *Who's Who in the Jordanian Parliament 1989–1993*. Amman: Friedrich Ebert Stiftung Amman, 1993.

Rivier, François. *Croissance Industrielle dans une Economie Assistée: Le Cas Jordanien*. Beirut: CERMOC, 1980.

———. "Rente petroliere et politiques industrielles des états non petroliers: Egypte, Jordanie, Liban, Syrie." In *Industrialisation et changements sociaux dans l'orient Arabe*, ed. André Bourgey, 69–143. Beirut: CERMOC, 1982.

Robalino, David A. "Pensions in the Middle East and North Africa: Time for Change." Washington, D.C.: World Bank, 2005.

Roberts, B. R. "Household Coping Strategies and Urban Poverty in a Comparative Perspective." In *Urban Life in Transition*, ed. M. Gottdiener and C. G. Pickvance. Newbury Park, Calif.: Sage, 1991.

Roberts, Bryan. "Informal Economy and Family Strategies." *International Journal of Urban and Regional Relations* 18, no. 1 (1994): 71–87.

Roberts, John M. "The Political Economy of Identity: State and Society in Jordan." Ph.D. diss., University of Chicago, 1994.

Roberts, Kenneth D., and Michael D. S. Morris. "Fortune, Risk, and Remittances: An Application of Option Theory to Participation in Village-Based Migration Networks." *International Migration Review* 37, no. 4 (2003): 1252–81.

Roberts, Rebecca. "Bourj al-Barajneh: The Significance of Village Origin in a Palestinian Refugee Camp." M.A. thesis, University of Durham, 1999.

———. "The Impact of Assistance on the Coping Mechanisms of Long-term Refugees: The Case of Palestinian Refugees in Lebanon." Ph.D. diss., University of York, 2004.

Robinson, Glenn E. "Can Islamists Be Democrats? The Case of Jordan." *Middle East Journal* 51, no. 3 (summer 1997): 373–87.

———. "Defensive Democratization in Jordan." *International Journal of Middle East Studies* 30 (1998): 387–410.

Rodrik, Dani. "What Drives Public Employment in Developing Countries?" *Review of Development Economics* 4, no. 3 (2000): 229–43.

Roeder, Philip G. "Liberalization and Ethnic Entrepreneurs in the Soviet Successor States." In *The Myth of "Ethnic Conflict": Politics, Economics, and "Cultural" Violence*, ed. Beverly Crawford and Ronnie D. Lipschutz, 78–107.

Berkeley: University of California Press/University of California International and Area Studies Collection, 1998.

Rollins, Karina, ed. *The Index of Global Philanthropy.* Washington, D.C.: Hudson Institute, 2006.

Roy, Olivier. "État et recompositions identitaires: l'exemple du Tadjikistan." In *Guerres civiles: Économies de la violence, dimensions de la civilité,* ed. Jean Hannoyer, 221–34. Paris: Karthala, 1999.

———. "Patronage and Solidarity Groups: Survival or Reformation?" In *Democracy without Democrats? The Renewal of Politics in the Muslim World,* ed. Ghassan Salamé, 270–81. New York: I. B. Tauris, 1994.

Roy, Sara. "The Transformation of Islamic NGOs in Palestine." *Middle East Report* 30, no. 214 (2000): 24–26.

Rubenberg, Cheryl. *The Palestine Liberation Organization: Its Institutional Infrastructure,* IAS Monograph Series: Palestine Studies, No. 1. Belmont, Mass.: Institute of Arab Studies, 1983.

Rubin, Barnett R. "Russian Hegemony and the State Breakdown in the Periphery: Causes and Consequences of the Civil War in Tajikistan." In *Post-Soviet Political Order: Conflict and State Building,* ed. Barnett R. Rubin and Jack Snyder, 128–61. New York: Routledge, 1998.

Rudra, Nita. "Globalization and the Decline of the Welfare State in Less-Developed Countries." *International Organization* 56, no. 2 (2002): 411–45.

———. "Welfare States in Developing Countries: Unique or Universal?" *Journal of Politics* 69, no. 2 (2007): 378–96.

Ryan, Mary P. "Civil Society as Democratic Practice: North American Cities during the Nineteenth Century." *Journal of Interdisciplinary History* 29, no. 4 (1999): 559–84.

Saad-Ghorayeb, Amal. *Hizbu'llah: Politics and Religion.* Sterling, Va.: Pluto, 2002.

Sabel, Charles. "Moebius-Strip Organizations and Open Labor Markets: Some Consequences of the Reintegration of Conception and Execution in a Volatile Economy." In *Social Theory for a Changing Society,* ed. Pierre Bourdieu and James S. Coleman. San Francisco: Westview, 1991.

Sabel, Charles F. "Flexible Specialisation and the Re-emergence of Regional Economies." In *Post-Fordism: A Reader,* ed. Ash Amin, 101–56. Cambridge: Blackwell, 1994.

Saket, Bassam K. "Economic Uses of Remittances—The Case of Jordan." In *Jordan's Place within the Arab Oil Economies,* ed. Monther Share', 55–73. Irbid, Jordan: Yarmouk University Press, 1986.

Saleh, Ali Salman, and Charles Harvie. "An Analysis of Public Sector Deficits and Debt in Lebanon: 1970–2000." *Middle East Review of International Affairs* 9, no. 4 (2005).

Salibi, Kamal. *A House of Many Mansions: The History of Lebanon Reconsidered.* Berkeley: University of California Press, 1988.

Samha, M. "The Impact of Migratory Flows on Population Changes in Jordan: A Middle Eastern Case Study." *International Migration* 28, no. 2 (June 1990): 215–28.

Saradar Investment House. "Lebanon's insurance industry." AME Info, http://www.ameinfo.com/news/Detailed/36698.html.

Sassen, Saskia. *Globalization and Its Discontents.* New York: New Press, 1998.

Satloff, Robert. "Jordan's Great Gamble: Economic Crisis and Political Reform." In *The Politics of Economic Reform in the Middle East,* ed. Henri Barkey, 130–52. New York: St. Martin's, 1992.

Sawalha, Aseel. "Identity, Self and the Other among Palestinian Refugees in East Amman." In *Amman, Ville et Société—The City and Its Society,* ed. Jean Hannoyer and Seteney Shami, 345–57. Beirut: CERMOC, 1996.

Sayigh, Rosemary. "Palestinians in Lebanon: Uncertain Future." In *Peace for Lebanon? From War to Reconstruction,* ed. Deirdre Collings, 97–108. Boulder, Colo.: Lynne Rienner, 1994.

Sayigh, Yezid. *Armed Struggle and the Search for State: The Palestinian National Movement 1949–1993.* New York: Oxford University Press, 1999.

———. "Jordan in the 1980s: Legitimacy, Entity and Identity." In *Politics and the Economy in Jordan,* ed. Rodney Wilson, 167–83. New York: Routledge, 1991.

Schatz, Edward. *Modern Clan Politics: The Power of "Blood" in Kazakhstan and Beyond.* Seattle: University of Washington Press, 2004.

Seccombe, Ian J. "Labour Emigration Policies and Economic Development in Jordan: From Unemployment to Labour Shortage." In *The Economic Development of Jordan,* ed. Bichara Khader and Adnan Badran, 118–32. London: Croon Helm, 1987.

Seibel, Wolfgang, and Helmut K. Anheier. "Sociological and Political Science Approaches to the Third Sector." In *The Third Sector: Comparative Studies of Nonprofit Organizations,* ed. Helmut K. Anheier and Wolfgang Seibel, 7–20. New York: Walter de Gruyter, 1990.

Sekhri, Neelam, and William Savedoff. "Private Health Insurance: Implications for Developing Countries. Discussion Paper Number 3." Geneva: World Health Organization, 2004.

Seligman, Adam B. *The Idea of Civil Society.* New York: Free Press, 1992.

Sha'oul, Melhem. "Elections 2000: Analysis of Opinion Poll Results" (in Arabic). In *Lebanese Parliamentary Elections in 2000,* ed. Melhem Chaoul et al., 27–56. Beirut: Lebanese Center for Policy Studies, 2002.

Sha'sha, Zayd J. "The Role of the Private Sector in Jordan's Economy." In *Politics and the Economy in Jordan,* ed. Rodney Wilson, 79–89. New York: Routledge, 1991.

Shami, Seteney. "Domesticity Reconfigured: Women in Squatter Areas of Amman." In *Organizing Women: Formal and Informal Women's Groups in the Middle East,* ed. Dawn Chatty and Annika Rabo, 81–99. New York: Berg, 1997.

Share, M. A. J. "The Use of Jordanian Workers' Remittances." In *The Economic Development of Jordan*, ed. Bichara Khader and Adnan Badran, 32–44. London: Croon Helm, 1987.

Shryock, Andrew. "Bedouin in Suburbia: Redrawing the Boundaries of Urbanity and Tribalism in Amman, Jordan." *Arab Studies Journal* (1997): 40–56.

———. *Nationalism and the Genealogical Imagination: Oral History and Textual Authority in Tribal Jordan*. Berkeley: University of California Press, 1997.

Shryock, Andrew, and Sandy Howell. "'Ever a Guest in Our House': The Emir Abdullah, Shaykh Majid al-'Adwan, and the Practice of Jordanian House Politics, as Remembered by Umm Sultan, the Widow of Majid." *International Journal of Middle East Studies* 33 (2001): 247–69.

Shteiwi, Musa. "al-Niqabat al-mihaniyya ka-juz' min al-mujtam' al-madani [Professional associations as a part of civil society]." In *al-Niqabat al-mihaniyya wa tahaddiyat al-tahawwul al-dimuqratiyya fil-Urdun [Professional associations and the challenge of democratic transformation in Jordan]*, ed. Hani Hourani et al. Amman: al-Urdun al-Jadid Research Center and Sindbad Publishing, 2000.

———. "Class Structure and Inequality in the City of Amman." In *Amman, Ville et Societe—The City and Its Society*, ed. Jean Hannoyer and Seteney Shami, 405–24. Beirut: CERMOC, 1996.

———. "Poverty Assessment of Jordan." Paper presented at the Workshop on the Economy conducted under former director Mustapha Hamarneh, Amman, June 1999.

Shteiwi, Musa, and Ibrahim Hejoj. "Poverty Alleviation Programs Effectiveness in Jordan." Paper presented at the Workshop on the Economy conducted under former director Mustapha Hamarneh, Amman, June 1999.

Shunnaq, Mohammed. "Political and Economic Conflict within Extended Kin Groups and Its Effects on the Household in a North Jordanian Village." *Journal of Comparative Family Studies (Special Issue: The Arab Family)* 28, no. 2 (summer 1997): 136–50.

Sibalis, Michael David. "The Mutual Aid Societies of Paris, 1789–1848." *French History* 3, no. 1 (1989): 1–30.

Sik, Endre, and Barry Wellman. "Network Capital in Capitalist, Communist, and Postcommunist Countries." In *Networks in the Global Village*, ed. Barry Wellman, 225–53. Boulder, Colo.: Westview, 1999.

Singerman, Diane. *Avenues of Participation: Family, Politics, and Networks in Urban Quarters of Cairo*. Princeton, N.J.: Princeton University Press, 1995.

Skocpol, Theda. *Protecting Soldiers and Mothers: The Political Origins of Social Policy in the United States*. Cambridge, Mass.: Harvard University Press, 1992.

Skocpol, Theda, and Jennifer Lynn Oser. "Organization Despite Adversity: The Origins and Development of African American Fraternal Associations." *Social Science History* 28, no. 3 (2004): 367–437.

Smith, Brian H. *More Than Altruism: The Politics of Private Foreign Aid.* Princeton, N.J.: Princeton University Press, 1990.

Smith, Gavin. "Towards an Ethnography of Idiosyncratic Forms of Livelihood." *International Journal of Urban and Regional Relations* 18, no. 1 (1994): 71–87.

Snider, Lewis W. "The Lebanese Forces: Their Origins and Role in Lebanon's Politics." *Middle East Journal* 38, no. 1 (1984): 1–33.

———. "The Lebanese Forces: Wartime Origins and Political Significance." In *The Emergence of a New Lebanon: Fantasy or Reality?* ed. Edward E. Azar, 117–61. New York: Praeger, 1984.

Snyder, Jack. *From Voting to Violence: Democratization and Nationalist Conflict.* New York: W. W. Norton, 2000.

Soskice, David. "Divergent Production Regimes: Coordinated and Uncoordinated Market Economies in the 1980s and 1990s." In *Continuity and Change in Contemporary Capitalism,* ed. Herbert Kitschelt, Peter Lange, Gary Marks, and John D. Stephens, 101–34. New York: Cambridge University Press, 1999.

Spears, Ian S. "States-Within-States: An Introduction to Their Empirical Attributes." In *States-Within- States: Incipient Political Entities in the Post–Cold War Era,* ed. Paul Kingston and Ian S. Spears, 15–34. New York: Palgrave Macmillan, 2004.

Stack, Carol B. *All Our Kin: Strategies for Survival in a Black Community.* New York: Harper and Row, 1975.

Steinmo, Sven, Kathleen Thelen, and Frank Longstreth, eds. *Structuring Politics: Historical Institutionalism in Comparative Analysis.* New York: Cambridge University Press, 1992.

Suleiman, Jaber. "Palestinians in Lebanon and the Role of Non-governmental Organizations." *Journal of Refugee Studies* 10, no. 3 (1997): 397–410.

Sullivan, Denis J. "Extra-State Actors and Privatization in Egypt." In *Privatization and Liberalization in the Middle East,* ed. Iliya Harik and Denis J. Sullivan, 24–45. Bloomington: Indiana University Press, 1992.

Sullivan, Teresa A., Elizabeth Warren, and Jay Lawrence Westbrook. *The Fragile Middle Class: Americans in Debt.* New Haven, Conn.: Yale University Press, 2000.

Sustainable Development Network Programme. "NGO's in Jordan." http://www.sdnp.jo/ngo.html (accessed October 1999).

Suyyagh, Fayiz. "Poverty Management in Jordan: A Critical Assessment of Institutional Structures and Processes." Paper presented at the Workshop on the Economy conducted under former director Mustapha Hamarneh, Amman, June 1999.

Swidler, Ann. "Culture in Action: Symbols and Strategies." *American Sociological Review* 51, no. 2 (1986): 273–86.

Tapper, Richard. "Anthropologists, Historians, and Tribespeople on Tribe and State Formation in the Middle East." In *Tribes and State Formation in the*

Middle East, ed. Philip S. Khoury and Joseph Kostiner, 48–73. Berkeley: University of California Press, 1990.

Tarawneh, Mohammad. "Formalizing the Informal: A New Approach to Poverty Alleviation in Jordan." Paper presented at the Conference on Assessing Foreign Aid to Jordan (1989–1999), University of Jordan, Amman, 23 April 2000.

Taylor-Gooby, Peter, and Jens O. Zinn. "The Current Significance of Risk." In *Risk in Social Science,* ed. Peter Taylor-Gooby and Jens O. Zinn, 1–19. New York: Oxford University Press, 2006.

Tayyar, Naaman. "Lebanon's Insurance Sector." STAT-USA Market Research Reports, http://www.strategis.ic.gc.ca/epic/internet/inimr-ri/nsf/en/gr117403e.html (accessed September 2005).

Teeple, Gary. *Globalization and the Decline of Social Reform: Into the Twenty-first Century.* New York: Humanity Books, 2000.

Tell, Tareq. "Paysans, nomades et état en Jordanie orientale: les politiques de développement rural (1920–1989)." In *Steppes d'Arabies. États, pasteurs, agriculteurs et commerçants: le devenir des zones sèches,* ed. Riccardo Bocco, Ronald Jaubert, and Françoise Métral, 87–102. Paris: Presses Universitaires de France, 1993.

Tell, Tariq. "Guns, Gold, and Grain: War and Food Supply in the Making of Transjordan." In *War, Institutions, and Social Change in the Middle East,* ed. Steven Heydemann, 33–58. Berkeley: University of California Press, 2000.

Thelen, Kathleen. *How Institutions Evolve: The Political Economy of Skills in Germany, Britain, the United States, and Japan.* New York: Cambridge University Press, 2004.

Thelen, Kathleen, and Sven Steinmo. "Historical Institutionalism in Comparative Politics." In *Structuring Politics: Historical Institutionalism in Comparative Analysis,* ed. Sven Steinmo, Kathleen Thelen, and Frank Longstreth. New York: Cambridge University Press, 1992.

Thompson, E. P. "The Moral Economy of the English Crowd." In *Customs in Common,* ed. E. P. Thompson, 185–351. New York: New Press, 1993.

Tilly, Charles. *Popular Contention in Great Britain, 1758–1834.* Cambridge, Mass.: Harvard University Press, 1995.

———. *Social Movements, 1768–2004:* Paradigm, 2004.

———. *Trust and Rule.* New York: Cambridge University Press, 2005.

Tiltnes, Aage. "Poverty and Welfare in the Palestinian Refugee Camps of Jordan: Portrait of Living Conditions Based on a Household Survey." Paper presented at the conference "Palestinian Refugees and UNRWA [United Nations Relief and Works Agency] in Jordan, the West Bank, and Gaza, 1949–1999," Dead Sea, Jordan, 1 September 1999.

Townsend, Robert M. "Consumption Insurance: An Evaluation of Risk-Bearing Systems in Low-Income Economies." *Journal of Economic Perspectives* 9, no. 3 (1995): 83–102.

——. "Optimal Multiperiod Contracts and the Gain from Enduring Relationships under Private Information." *Journal of Political Economy* 90, no. 6 (1982): 1166–86.

Toye, John. "The New Institutional Economics and Its Implications for Development Theory." In *The New Institutional Economics and Third World Development*, ed. John Hariss, Janet Hunter, and Colin M. Lewis, 49–68. New York: Routledge, 1995.

Trabloulsi, Fawwaz. *A History of Modern Lebanon.* Ann Arbor: Pluto, 2007.

Tripp, Aili Mari. "Local Organizations, Participation, and the State in Urban Tanzania." In *Governance and Politics in Africa*, ed. Goran Hyden and Michael Bratton, 221–42. Boulder, Colo.: Lynne Rienner, 1992.

Tvedt, Terje. *Angels of Mercy or Development Diplomats? NGOs and Foreign Aid.* Trenton, N.J.: Africa World Press, 1998.

Tzannatos, Zafiris. "Social Protection in the Middle East and North Africa: A Review." In *Employment Creation and Social Protection in the Middle East and North Africa*, ed. Heba Handoussa and Zafiris Tzannatos, 121–71. New York: American University in Cairo Press, 2002.

——. "What Accounts for Earnings Inequality in Jordan and How Can Labor Policies Help Reduce Poverty?" In *Earnings Inequality, Unemployment, and Poverty in the Middle East and North Africa*, ed. Wassim Shahin and Ghassan Dibeh, 171–83. Westport, Conn.: Greenwood, 2000.

Ugland, Ole Fr., ed. *Difficult Past, Uncertain Future: Living Conditions among Palestinian Refugees in Camps and Gatherings in Lebanon.* Norway: FAFO, 2003.

United Nations Development Programme (UNDP). "A Profile of Sustainable Human Development in Lebanon," 1997.

——. "Globalization: Towards a Lebanese Agenda," 2002.

——. "Mapping of Living Conditions in Lebanon," 1998.

United Nations Development Programme, Programme on Governance in the Arab Region (UNDP-POGAR). "Country Index: State–Civil Society Relations. Lebanon." http://www.pogar.org/countries/civil.asp?cid=9.

Usui, Chikako. "Welfare State Development in a World System Context: Event History Analysis of First Social Insurance Legislation among 60 Countries, 1880–1960." In *The Comparative Political Economy of the Welfare State*, ed. Thomas Janoski and Alexander M. Hicks, 254–77. New York: Cambridge University Press, 1994.

Van Aken, Mauro. "Development as a Gift: Patterns of Assistance and Refugees' Strategies in the Jordan Valley." Paper presented at the conference "Palestinian Refugees and UNRWA in Jordan, the West Bank, and Gaza, 1949–1999," Dead Sea, Jordan, 1 September 1999.

Van Evera, Stephen. "Primordialism Lives! (Symposium—Cumulative Findings in the Study of Ethnic Politics)." *APSA-CP Newsletter* (winter 2001): 20–22.

Van Hear, Nicholas. "L'impact des rapatriements forcés vers la Jordanie et le

Yémen pendant la crise du golfe." In *Moyen-Orient: migrations, démocratisa-tion, mediations*, ed. Riccardo Bocco and Mohammad-Reza Djalili, 101–16. Paris: Presses Universitaires de France, 1994.

Varshney, Ashutosh. *Ethnic Conflict and Civic Life: Hindus and Muslims in In-dia*. New Haven, Conn.: Yale University Press, 2002.

Vatikiotis, P. J. *Politics and the Military in Jordan: A Study of the Arab Legion 1921–1957*. London: Frank Cass, 1967.

Vittas, Dimitri. "Insurance Regulation in Jordan: New Rules—Old System. Policy Research Working Paper #3298." Washington, D.C.: World Bank, 2004.

Wall, Karin, Sofia Aboim, Vanessa Cunha, and Pedro Vasconcelos. "Families and Informal Support Networks in Portugal: The Reproduction of Inequal-ity." *Journal of European Social Policy* 11, no. 3 (2001): 213–33.

Waterbury, John. "From Social Contracts to Extraction Contracts: The Political Economy of Authoritarianism and Democracy." In *Islam, Democracy, and the State in North Africa*, ed. John P. Entelis, 141–76. Bloomington: Indiana University Press, 1997.

Waterbury, John. *The Egypt of Nasser and Sadat: The Political Economy of Two Regimes*. Princeton, N.J.: Princeton University Press, 1983.

Weber, Max. "The Protestant Sects and the Spirit of Capitalism." In *From Max Weber: Essays in Sociology*, ed. H. H. Gerth and C. Wright Mills, 302–22. New York: Oxford University Press, 1975.

Weingast, Barry R. "Rational-Choice Institutionalism." In *Political Science: The State of the Discipline*, ed. Ira Katznelson and Helen V. Milner, 660–92. New York: W. W. Norton, 2002.

Weiss, Linda. *The Myth of the Powerless State*. Ithaca, N.Y.: Cornell University Press, 1998.

Wellman, Barry. "Preface." In *Networks in the Global Village*, ed. Barry Wellman, xi–xxii. Boulder, Colo.: Westview, 1999.

White, Jenny B. *Money Makes Us Relatives: Women's Labor in Urban Turkey*. Austin: University of Texas Press, 1994.

Whitmeyer, Joseph M. "Prestige from the Provision of Collective Goods." *Social Forces* 85, no. 4 (2007): 1765–86.

Wickham, Carrie Rosefsky. "Islamic Mobilization and Political Change: The Islamist Trend in Egypt's Professional Associations." In *Political Islam: Essays from Middle East Report*, ed. Joel Beinin and Joe Stork, 120–35. Berkeley: University of California Press, 1997.

Wiktorowicz, Quintan. "Civil Society as Social Control: State Power in Jordan." *Comparative Politics* 34, no. 1 (October 2000): 43–61.

———. "Islamists, the State, and Cooperation in Jordan." *Arab Studies Quar-terly* 21, no. 4 (fall 1999): 1–17.

———. "The Limits of Democracy in the Middle East: The Case of Jordan." *Middle East Journal* 53, no. 4 (fall 1999): 606–20.

———. *The Management of Islamic Activism: Salafis, the Muslim Brotherhood, and State Power in Jordan.* Albany: State University of New York Press, 2001.

Wilkinson, Steven I. *Votes and Violence: Electoral Competition and Ethnic Riots in India.* New York: Cambridge University Press, 2004.

Willetts, Peter, ed. *"The Conscience of the World": The Influence of Non-Governmental Organisations in the UN System.* Washington, D.C.: Brookings Institution, 1996.

Wilson, Rodney. "The Role of Commercial Banking in the Jordanian Economy." In *The Economic Development of Jordan,* ed. Bichara Khader and Adnan Badran, 45–61. London: Croon Helm, 1987.

Wimmer, Andreas. *Nationalist Exclusion and Ethnic Conflict: Shadows of Modernity.* New York: Cambridge University Press, 2002.

Winckler, Onn. "Gulf Monarchies as Rentier States: The Nationalization Policies of the Labor Force." In *Middle East Monarchies: The Challenge of Modernity,* ed. Joseph Kostiner, 27–256. Boulder, Colo.: Lynne Rienner, 2000.

Wizarat al-Tamween [Ministry of Supply]. "Qa'ima bil-mawaad al-ghitha'iyya al-tamweeniyya wa al-mawaad wa al-sil' al-ukhra al-mas'ra min qibl wizara al-tamween [List of provided food and other commodities and goods priced by the Ministry of Supply]." Mimeograph, 1998.

World Bank. *Doing Business 2009: Country Profile for Jordan,* Comparing Regulation in 181 Economies. Washington, D.C.: World Bank, 2008.

———. *Doing Business 2009: Country Profile for Lebanon,* Comparing Regulation in 181 Economies. Washington, D.C.: World Bank, 2008.

———. *Economic Developments and Prospects: Job Creation in an Era of High Growth,* Middle East and North Africa Region. Washington, D.C.: World Bank, 2007.

———. "Proposed Projects on Jordan." http://www.worldbank.org/pics/pid/j039749.txt.

———. "Social Capital." http://www.worldbank.org/poverty/scapital/whatsc.htm.

———. *Unlocking the Employment Potential in the Middle East and North Africa: Toward a New Social Contract (MENA Development Report).* Washington, D.C.: World Bank, 2004.

World Bank, Country Operations Division, Country Department III, Europe, Middle East and North Africa Region. "Jordan Public Expenditure Review." Washington, D.C.: World Bank, 1991.

World Bank, Middle East and North Africa Region. *Reducing Vulnerability and Increasing Opportunity: Social Protection in the Middle East and North Africa.* Washington, D.C.: World Bank, 2002.

Wright, Erik Olin. *Class Counts.* New York: Cambridge University Press, 1997.

Yashar, Deborah J. *Contesting Citizenship in Latin America: The Rise of Indigenous Movements and the Postliberal Challenge.* New York: Cambridge University Press, 2005.

Younis, Mona N. *Liberation and Democratization: The South African and Palestinian National Movements*. Edited by Bert Klandermans. Vol. II, *Social Movements, Protest, and Contention*. Minneapolis: University of Minnesota Press, 2000.

Zahar, Marie-Joëlle. "Fanatics, Mercenaries, Brigands . . . and Politicians: Militia Decision-Making and Civil Conflict Resolution." Ph.D. diss., McGill University, 1999.

Ziadé, Khaled. "Trablous: al-ʿaʾila wa al-siyasa [Tripoli: family and politics]." In *La vie publique au Liban: expressions et recompositions du politique*, ed. Joseph Bahout and Chawqi Douayhi, 241–74. Beirut: CERMOC, 1997.

Zubaida, Sami. "Islam and the Politics of Community and Citizenship." *Middle East Report*, no. 221 (winter 2001): 20–27.

———. "Religion, the State, and Democracy: Contrasting Conceptions of Society in Egypt." In *Political Islam: Essays from Middle East Report*, ed. Joel Beinin and Joe Stork, 51–63. Berkeley: University of California Press, 1997.

INDEX

'Abd al-Hameed Shooman Foundation, 113
Abna' al-Harith association, 125, 126, 163, 240n144
agriculture: employment in, 40, 81, 82, 85–87, 219n59; Green Plan (Lebanon), 61; impact of economic recession on, 55; impact of oil boom on, 81; loans to women farmers, 115; subsidies for, 53, 64, 66, 67
Ajloun, Jordan, 99f4.5, 145, 239n124
Aley (Druze area), 102, 122
Al-Faori, Rifat, 129
al-Hawamdeh, Dr. 'Ali, 125, 126
al-Husbani, Abd el-Hakim K., 228n13
al-Majmoua, 115
al-Naber Association, 94, 95f4.1, 109, 136–137, 144–145, 221nn5,7, 225n72
al-Quds, 110
al-Ramla Association, 96, 108, 110, 162–163
al-Urdun al-Jadid (think tank), 149, 159
Amal, 124, 151, 154, 156, 159
Amawi, Abla M., 160
Ameen (NGO), 115
Amman, Jordan: Aal al-Naber Association migration to, 94; charities in, 100, 112, 113; kin associations in, 99f4.5; Lifta (village outside Jerusalem) association, 95–96, 96f4.2;

mutual aid societies in, 112; non-kin associations as NGOs, 239n124; Palestinian public-sector employment in, 81
Aoun, Michel, 151
Aqaba, 99f4.5, 239n124
Arab Free Trade Area, 69
ascriptive identity, espousal of, 164, 240n157
'ashura (Shi'a regious holiday), 162
Atallah family (Lebanon), 154, 163
'Ayn Karam, 110
Azeizat tribe (Christian), 145, 234n39

Baalbek, Lebanon, 102, 156
Ba'th party, 146
Baghdad Pact, 125
Bagot Glubb, John, 52
Baldwin, Peter, 28
Balqa, Jordan, 76, 80, 81, 96, 99f4.5, 113, 239n124
Baumol's disease, 213n36
Bedouins, 52, 159
Beirut, Lebanon: authentic identity in, 163; kin associations in, 86, 101, 102, 104, 122–123, 135, 163; large business access to credit, 89; militias in, 63, 102; population flight during civil war, 86; Union of Beiruti Families, 159
Beito, David, 43
B'ir Sab'a (Palestinian kin charity), 144

287

birth rate, 49, 74, 84, 110
Bourdieu, Pierre, 141–142
bread riots, 55–56, 177, 207n59
Byblos, Lebanon, 123

candidates for political office, 143–144, 148–153, 165, 180–182
Caritas (Catholic organization), 115
Center for Strategic Studies, 100, 145, 149, 159
Chandra, Kanchan, 11, 173
charities: family fund (*sunduq al-'a'ili*), 119; foreign funding of, 112, 114; government involvement in, 158, 237n107, 238n118; horizontal participation networks of, 45; Islamist charities in Jordan, 112–113; kin associations and, 100, 112, 129, 221n3; Lifta Charitable Association, 95–96, 96f4.2, 106, 109, 144–145, 162, 238n118; motives for giving, 141–142, 143, 232n11; neoliberal promotion of, 178; religious charities, 111–112, 232n11; stereotypes of, 179, 242n24
children: agricultural work, 81, 215n65; child care, 83–84, 93, 110, 158, 225nn76,79; child labor, 83, 217n87; kin association programs for, 162; LF social services for, 65; mutual aid association services for, 106, 107f4.7; PLO-supported social services for, 64; training programs for girls in Jordan, 108. *See also* education
Christian Base Communities (Latin America), 181
Christian Jordanians: access to state social provisioning, 51t2.1; al-Naber Association, 94, 95f4.1, 109, 221nn5,7, 225n72; mutual aid associations of, 52, 94, 122–123; state employment, 50, 51, 214n46; tribal identities of, 164

Christian kin associations (Lebanon), 101, 102, 107, 122, 127, 146, 187, 227n2
Christian Lebanese Forces, 7, 63, 65
Christians in Lebanon: demographics of, 84, 194n20; employment of, 93, 94, 101, 102; forced migration to East Beirut, 86; impact of civil war on, 9; kin associations, 9, 13, 101, 102, 107, 122, 127, 146, 187, 227n2; LF (Lebanese Forces), 7, 63, 64, 65, 66; militia welfare, 51, 63, 63t2.2, 102; privilege of, 60, 151; social insurance organizations of, 93; in state-building, 48, 50; urbanization of, 101
Circassians, 214n46
Civil Administration of the Mountain (CAOM), 66
civil society organizations, 4, 159, 160, 178, 179, 242n20
civil war (Lebanon): democracy prior to, 151; economic status of Lebanon after, 66–68, 77, 85, 210n158; government aid during, 61–62; identity politics of, 164; kin associations and, 9–10, 13, 101–102, 103; military welfare as source of social services, 50; militia welfare during, 47, 48, 50, 63–67, 63t2.2, 102, 168; population dislocations during, 85, 86; reconstruction after, 48, 68; state social aid during, 47, 60–62; Ta'if agreement, 61, 69, 151; tribalism during, 154
clientelism, 43, 50, 142–143, 183, 233n18
Community Infrastructure Development Program, 59–60
confessional system, 9, 103, 164
Constitutional Party (Jordan), 149
construction industry, 82, 84, 87
consumer goods and services:

consumer credit, 170; cooperatives, 54, 58, 61, 65, 70, 100, 187, 221nn3,4; food supply, 54, 55–56, 177, 207n59; mutual aid associations in Jordan, 109, 128; in postwar Jordan, 76–77, 212n22; poverty and access to, 76–77, 213nn21,22; price supports/controls, 48, 49, 54–56, 58, 61, 64, 168–169; PSP (Progressive Socialist Party), 66; public employment in Jordan, 52; subsidies in Jordan, 50, 93; taxation of, 56, 169; work remittances as payment for, 82, 216n71

consumer spending, decreases in, 76–77, 213n22

consumer tax (Jordan), 56

Cooperative Corporation, 186, 187

Cooperative of Public-Sector Employees (Lebanon), 61

cooperatives, 54, 58, 61, 70, 100, 187, 221nn3,4

Coordination forum of NGOs Working in the Palestinian Community, 114

credit, 35, 37, 37t1.1, 38f1.1, 39, 74–75, 79, 88, 89, 219n146

culture, 25, 32, 45, 46, 125–126, 129, 174, 200n49

currency devaluation (Jordan), 55, 77

Dahiyya, 63

Dandash (tribe), 154

Daw tribe, 148

debt, 67–69, 76, 77, 78–79, 169

Department of Consumer Protection (LF), 65

diwan, 98, 100, 117, 119, 120, 125, 145, 227n4

diwaniyya, 12

Druze communities (Lebanon), 60; Aley (Druze area), 102, 122; Christian kin associations in, 102; militia

welfare, 51, 63, 63t2.2, 102; political involvement, 135, 146, 151, 152; population of, 84; service-sector employment, 94; Shouf, 102

Druze Foundation of Social Welfare, 114

Druze kin associations (Lebanon), 146, 187, 230n58

Druze Progressive Socialist Party (PSP), 7, 63, 66, 146, 152

dues payments, 171, 172, 228n13

East Amman refugee camp, 80

East Bankers, 58; army service, 57, 80, 204n4, 214n46; defined, 51; electoral power of, 149; kin associations, 52; labor market for, 80, 214n46; national assimilation, 240n157; Palestinians and, 122, 250n157; preferential treatment of, 50, 51, 52, 53, 57, 204n4; public employment, 81; Sons of Southern Jordan Charitable Association, 153, 236nn86,87; Um Batma, 99

economic liberalization: income distribution after, 75–76; international aid, 41; labor market after, 41, 48, 56, 57, 169; protests, 55–56, 166, 207n59; reconstruction policies, 48; and the rise of kin associations, 52, 98, 166; subnational identity politics in Jordan, 163–164; taxation, 56; welfare services, 16–17, 47

education: financial aid for, 55, 56, 58, 107, 111, 113, 114, 129, 132f5.1; funding from work remittances, 82, 216n71; Jordanian state spending for, 54; kin association support for, 110, 114, 224n68, 225n76; kindergartens, 110, 114, 129, 158, 225n76; military service, 54, 206n39; militias as providers of, 65, 66, 67, 168; nursery schools, 110, 225n77;

Palestinian welfare services, 114; PLO support of, 64, 65; skill sets for employment, 26, 36–37, 40, 41, 42–43, 75, 78, 170–171, 225n70; UNRWA (United Nations Relief and Works Agency), 80; women and, 108, 225n70

Egypt, 11–12, 34, 40, 41, 219n146, 227n10

elections: internal association elections, 130; in Jordan, 13, 144, 145–146, 149, 150; kin associations and, 13, 125, 143–147, 159–160, 165, 180, 233n21; manipulation of, 159–160; municipal elections, 147, 151–152; Palestinians, 149; parliamentary elections, 126, 127, 140, 145–146, 150, 165; patronage, 49, 50, 143; politics of group identity in, 181; use of outside support, 145–146

elites: as association leaders, 134–135; as championing subnational identities, 175–176; electoral politics, 13, 176; identity construction of, 14; and kin associations, 14, 122, 124, 135–136, 140, 163, 175, 176; new elites, 140, 141; social prestige, 176; social responsibility, 141. *See also* leadership of kin associations

Ellickson, Robert C., 201n70

employment: access to social welfare, 39–40, 49, 50, 51t2.1; Gulf returnees, 222n16; kin association assistance for, 2–3, 107f4.7, 117; of Lebanese Christians, 93, 94, 101, 102; multiple jobs, 42, 78, 79, 86–87; Palestinians' access to, 51, 64, 72, 78, 81, 87, 94–95; preferential treatment, 39, 53; in public-sector institutions, 28–29; of refugee camp residents, 81; skill sets for, 26, 36–37, 38f1.1, 40, 41, 42–43, 75, 78, 170–171, 225n70. *See also* labor

force; labor market; training programs; unemployment; wages

employment networks: incentives for, 230n59; job opportunities, 132; and kin association membership, 117, 118, 125–126, 132f5.1; middle-class employees, 131; parties for (*tawaasul*), 133, 134; *wasta* (connections), 39, 53, 138; young adults in, 131, 133, 134

EU (European Union), 56, 69

Euro-Med (Euro-Mediterranean Partnership), 69

expatriate labor, 54, 79, 81–82, 83, 85, 98, 206n42

Fadlallah, Sheikh, 156

Fafo Institute for Applied Social Science, 100

families: birth rate, 49, 74, 84, 110; *diwan*, 98, 100, 117, 119, 120, 125, 145, 227n4; genealogies of, 95f4.1, 96f4.2, 97f4.3, 97f4.4, 98, 123, 125, 147–148, 159, 172, 222n18; language of, in group identity, 34; League of United Families, 122–123; marriage, 110, 121, 122; measures of poverty among, 76; names of family associations, 157–158; patriarchalism in, 113, 182–183; political involvement of, 144, 146–147, 154–155; and social mobility, 105, 124, 141; social services for, 31, 59, 115–116, 158, 177, 201n83, 224n60; use of term, 98, 203n126; voting strategies of, 144, 150, 155, 160; wife's kin, 95. *See also* children; *headings for specific families* (e.g., Lifta Charitable Association); *kin association headings;* women

family fund (*sunduq al-'a'ili*), 119

Fandy, Mamoun, 228n14

Fatah militiamen, 65

Feisal, Toujan, 127, 145
fieldwork in Jordan, 185–188
Fisher, Julie, 179
food supply, 52, 54, 55–56, 76–77,
169, 177, 207n59
foreign workers, 81, 83–84, 87–88
free riders, 25, 31, 120, 121, 171
fuel supply, 55, 62, 65
Fund for the Sick and the Poor, 113
funerals: association assistance at, 8,
106, 126, 132f5.1, 163; as economic
risk, 26, 49, 204n7; *maqar* (reception hall) for, 105, 109; NGOs in
Lebanon aid for, 114; Pharmacist
Association (Jordan), 88; Silwan
Social Development Association
(Palestinian) aid for, 129; state
employee loans for, 53–54; tribal
guesthouses as venues for, 119

Gaza Strip, 52, 183
Geddes, Barbara, 25
genealogies, 95f4.1, 96f4.2, 97f4.3,
97f4.4, 98, 123, 125, 147–148, 159,
172, 222n18
General Union of Voluntary Services
(GUVS), 158, 186–187, 237n107,
238n114
Ghabra, Shafeeq, 95, 228n13
Gilsenan, Michael, 233n18
gossip, 140, 172, 228n13
Granovetter, Mark, 43
Green Crescent (Red Cross), 112
Green Plan (Lebanon), 61
Grief, Avner, 243n42
guesthouses, 100, 117, 119, 125, 130,
227n4. *See also diwan; madafa*
(guesthouse); *rabita* (guesthouse)
Gulf states: expatriate Lebanese
workers in, 85; nationalization of
work force, 74, 83, 216n82; Palestinian labor migration to, 51, 52, 54,
206n42, 216n71; remittances from

expatriate workers, 54, 79, 81–83,
206n42, 215n68, 216n71; return
migration, 98, 222n16, 231n60
Gulf War, 83, 98, 216n81

hadana (nursery schools), 110, 225n77
Haggard, Stephan, 27, 28
Hamadeh (Sh'ia mutual aid associations [Lebanon]), 101
Hamarneh, Nash'at, 129, 146, 234n39
handicraft industries, 109, 126, 129, 158
Hariri, Prime Minister Rafiq, 68, 114,
146, 147, 157, 159
Hashemite regime, 94, 204n4
health care: charities in support of,
112–113, 114, 158, 224n68; costs in
postwar Jordan, 77; employment
opportunities in, 126; expenditures
in post-civil-war Lebanon, 68; gender bias in access to, 54, 206n40;
health education for women, 129;
hospitals, 39, 59, 90, 114; Islamic
Health Organization (Hizbullah),
66, 67; kin association funding
of, 106, 107, 108, 111, 128; military
service, 54, 58, 90; militias and, 54,
64, 65, 66, 168; NGOs and, 70, 80,
108, 114, 126, 132f5.1, 163; Palestinian support for, 64, 82, 111, 129;
social class and access to, 58–59,
208n94; state employment and, 52,
53, 54, 90, 168
Health Care Society, 114
health insurance, 28–29, 39, 58, 90,
169, 208n94
Heydemann, Steven, 200n49
High Relief Committee, 70
Hizbullah, 151; authority of, 156; in
Beirut, 63, 86; construction projects of, 67; intervention in feuds,
156; Palestinian support of, 146;
political candidates in, 152; in
post-civil-war era in Lebanon, 169;

Shi'a community and, 6, 7, 66, 124; social services of, 66–67, 112, 114, 115
Horizon 2000 (post-civil-war reconstruction), 68
horizontal networks, 44, 45, 93, 118, 139, 175
hospitals, 39, 59, 70, 114
housing, 29, 39, 54, 57, 80–81, 88, 90
Hussein, King, 55–56
Huwaytats, 145

IMF (International Monetary Fund), 55, 69, 72
independent candidates, 148–149, 150, 153, 180, 181, 182
industrial zones, 83–84, 110, 225n79
informal labor, 31, 41, 42–43, 49, 78, 79, 81, 87
information and information networks: for collective social insurance, 40; individual behavior influenced by, 35; information asymmetry, 39, 40, 241n4; kin idioms in, 44; in private-sector insurance, 39, 241n4
insurance: health insurance, 28–29, 39, 58, 90, 169, 208n94; job-based insurance, 37t1.1; life insurance, 30, 39, 90; military insurance, 208n94; nonstate collective accommodations for, 30; for service-sector workers, 78
internet services, 88, 106, 107f4.7, 109
International Monetary Fund. See IMF
Iraq, 55, 58, 82–83
Irbid, Jordan, 76, 99f4.5, 109, 129, 146
Islamic Action Front, 146, 149, 150
Islamic Health Organization (Hizbullah), 66, 67
Islamism, 112–113, 114–115, 141, 144, 148, 150, 159–160

Islamist Center Charity Society, 112–113
Israel, 52, 64, 86, 162

jaha, 132f5.1, 229n43
jama'iyya, 9, 120, 228n10
Jerash, Jordan, 99f4.5, 239n124
Jordan: business accountability, 39; currency devaluation, 55, 77; declining income levels, 76–77; defense industry, 58; economic recession in, 54–55; elections in, 13, 144, 145–146, 149, 150; fieldwork in, 185; Hashemite regime, 94, 204n4; individual options for aid and insurance in, 38–39; industrial zones, 83–84, 110, 225n79; Lebanon compared with, 19–20; the military, 53, 54, 58, 70; multiple jobs per worker in, 79; Palestinian population in, 47; parliament in, 144, 149, 150, 159–160; post-independence social contract, 168; removal of collective welfare, 2; women-run savings associations (*sunduq nisa'i*), 227n10
Jordanian Muslims, 13, 51t2.1, 93, 98, 214n46
Joseph, Suad, 161, 182

Karak, Jordan, 55, 76, 81, 94, 99f4.5, 125–126, 239n124
Kaufman, Robert R., 27, 28
Khalil al-Rahman (Hebron association), 109, 110, 163, 224n68
Khalil family, 123, 147–148
Khoury, Philip S., 228n15
Khuri, Fuad, 127
kin associations: allegiances of, 163–164, 240nn157,160, 241n161; as civil society organizations, 4, 159, 160, 178, 179, 242n20; configuration of services provided by, 7–8, 106–108,

107f4.7, 111, 162, 163, 225n80; dues, 98, 119–120, 129–130, 171, 172, 174, 228n13, 288n13; enforcement of behavioral norms, 32, 33, 34, 36, 139–140, 201n70; financial resources of, 121, 129–130; formation of, 1–2, 104, 121, 124–129, 152–153, 172–174, 188, 225n80, 243n3; guesthouses, 100, 117, 119, 227n4; identification with, 162–163, 172, 240n144; impact of civil war on, 7, 9; incorporation of family networks, 122–123, 127–128, 132; as *jama'iyya*, 9, 120, 228n10; *maqar* (reception hall) for, 105–106, 108, 109; meetings of, 98, 99, 105–106, 126, 132–133, 171, 172, 230n49; militias and, 101, 102–103, 183; nonkin affiliations with, 106, 121, 122, 229n18; political participation of, 112, 124–126, 147, 149, 152–156, 167, 233n21; reciprocity, 32–33, 43–44, 117, 129, 142; registration of, 104, 188, 243n3; rituals, 34, 36, 91, 201n70; rural communities, 98–99; state monitoring of, 104, 156, 157, 179–181, 188, 237n107, 243n3; subnational identities in, 163–164, 165, 166–167, 175–176, 180, 181, 183, 242n14; use of term in Jordan, 228n12; voting decisions of, 144–145; weddings, 8, 26, 49, 54, 105, 109, 119, 126, 132f5.1, 204n7. *See also* charities; elections; funerals; leadership of kin associations; membership; NGOs; size of kin associations

kin associations (Jordan): formation of, 93, 94, 99–100, 99t4.5, 128–129, 221n3; government employment and, 132–133; government relations with, 93, 157–158, 163, 238nn118,119; health care coverage by, 108; impact of U.S. foreign aid

on, 98–99, 221n14; leadership profiles, 135–136; leftist organization through, 154; meeting attendance, 98, 99, 105–106, 132–133, 171, 172, 230n49; names of, 157, 188; nonkin affiliations with, 158, 229n18; political participation of, 125, 143–147, 154–155; real estate holdings, 109–110; savings funds, 107; state oversight of, 157–158; use of term, 228n12; young adults in, 131, 133

kin associations (Lebanon), 104f4.6, 228n12; education financial assistance, 107; educational backgrounds, 131; educational programs of, 110; government allocations to, 158–159; health care coverage by, 107, 108; job networks of, 133; leadership profiles, 135; military service during civil war, 164; multireligious associations, 122; Official Gazette listings of, 187; political involvement of, 144, 146, 147; postwar services, 108; publications of, 163; real estate holdings of, 110; services of, 106, 107f4.7; support for members in elections, 146, 147; training programs of, 109; urbanization of, 101; women in leadership roles, 230n58; young adults in, 134

kindergartens, 110, 114, 129, 158, 225n76

King Abdullah II Design and Development Bureau (KADDB), 58

kinship: culture and legacy in determination of, 174; definitions of, 92–93, 94, 98, 120–123, 125, 157, 166–167, 181, 193n1, 228nn15,16; genealogies, 95f4.1, 96f4.2, 97f4.3, 97f4.4, 98, 123, 125, 147–148, 159, 172, 222n18; villages as defining, 95–96, 96f4.2, 97, 101, 120, 122–123, 174, 228n16

Kisrawan, Lebanon, 123
Kostiner, Joseph, 228n15
Kuwait, 82, 83, 95, 228n13

labor force: access to pension systems, 50; expatriate labor, 51–54, 79, 81–82, 83, 85, 98, 206n42; military employees, 53, 58; motivation for organizing, 41; multiple sources of income, 42, 78, 79, 86–87; networks in, 42–43; Palestinians in, 64–65, 78; postwar employment statistics, 86–87; remittances from expatriate workers, 54, 79, 81–83, 87, 206n42, 215n68, 216n71; social insurance coverage for, 40; state employment, 51–55, 57, 60, 81, 90, 101, 168, 215n57; unions, 40, 41, 74, 88–89, 169
labor market: child care services, 83–84, 93, 110, 158, 225n79; comparison between Jordan and Lebanon, 78–79; in determining membership, 125; ethnic group participation in, 80, 214n46; flexible specialization in, 42–43; informal labor, 31, 41, 42–43, 49, 78, 81, 87; job security in, 40, 41–42, 78; national identity and access to, 51; postwar reconstruction in Lebanon, 86; skill sets for, 26, 36–37, 40, 41, 42–43, 75, 78, 170–171, 225n70. See also training programs
Lahoud, Emile, 148
Laitin, David, 11, 25, 173
Lamaʿiyyah (Christian organization), 123
land ownership, 53, 77, 109–110, 141
Landa, Janet Tai, 34
Latin America, 11, 49, 50, 74, 120, 181
leadership of kin associations: association founders compared with, 230n59; changing definitions of

kinship, 121; control of members' actions, 182–183; elections of, 129, 130, 172; group membership recruitment, 123; motivations for, 141, 231n2; obligations of, 142–143; in Palestinian associations in Jordan, 136–137; political involvement of, 122, 144, 148, 149, 155, 163, 165; research methods on, 230n59; rural associations in Jordan, 123; social hierarchy, 103, 122, 134–136, 136–137, 142, 231n2; women as, 230n58
League of United Families, 122–123
Lebanese National Movement, 66
Lebanese Red Cross, 157
Lebanon: bank ownership, 67, 210n58; business accountability, 39; challenges of research in, 186, 187; democracy in, 148; economic liberalization after civil war, 66–67, 210n58; fieldwork in, 185; Jordan compared with, 19–20; the military, 50, 69–70, 164; national identity of, 60; parliament, 146, 151; state ownership of businesses, 67, 68, 210n58; trade initiatives of, 69. *See also* civil war (Lebanon); Hizbullah; *kin association headings;* post-civil-war Lebanon
Levi, Margaret, 180
LF (Lebanese Forces), 63, 64, 65, 66
Lifta Charitable Association, 95–96, 96f4.2, 106, 109, 144–145, 162, 238n118
loans, 37, 37t1.1, 38f1.1; availability, 170; behavioral constraints as, 182; collateral for, 39, 89; educational loans, 132f5.1; government-sponsored, in Lebanon, 61; Hizbullah, 67, 115; housing loans, 39; interest rates, 39; large business access to, 89; for life-cycle events (e.g., weddings, funerals), 8, 26, 49, 54,

204n7; for micro-enterprises, 89; nonkin sources of, 43; Palestinian kin associations in Lebanon as providers of, 111; professional associations, 88; public employment in Jordan, 53, 168; repayment of, 39, 40, 106, 111, 129, 171, 202n89; to women farmers, 115. *See also* NGOs

Ma'an, Jordan, 55, 59, 76, 81, 99f4.5, 215n59, 216n81
Madaba, Jordan, 80, 99f4.5, 145, 146, 234n39, 239n124
madafa (guesthouse), 100, 117, 119, 227n4
Mafraq, Jordan, 76, 215n59, 239n124
Majali family, 153, 236nn86,87
manufacturing sector, 40, 78, 79, 82–85, 169
maqar (reception hall), 105–106, 108, 109
Maqassed Society, 114
Maronite Christian kin associations, 131–132, 135, 146, 150
martyrs, 64, 65, 210n151
membership: accountability, 25, 31, 34–35, 124, 129–130, 175; on association affiliation, 10, 160–161, 171–173, 182; benefits of, 10, 132–133; eligibility requirements for, 35, 121–123, 125; enforcement of behavioral norms, 32–36, 33, 34, 37, 139–140, 201n70; family ties and, 92–93, 117, 119, 121, 122–123, 127–128, 182–183, 228n15; free riders, 25, 31, 120, 121; internal association elections, 130; interviews with, 187; on kin associations as civil society organizations, 197, 242n20; and nonparticipation by relatives, 228n13; political participation of, 127, 132f5.1, 144, 152–153, 165, 167, 181, 229n18; social services requests (*talabat*), 126; withdrawal

from kin mutual aid groups, 129; of young adults, 131, 133, 134. *See also* leadership of kin associations; size of kin associations
middle class: access to credit, 39, 76, 91; charity and, 4, 30, 111–112; defined, 193n2; economic risks of, 26; employment networks and, 131; formation of kin associations, 2–3, 102, 124, 130, 141, 168, 221n14; impact of economic liberalization on, 48, 75–76; Islamist activism, 141; postwar income structure in Lebanon, 77; risk management, 169–170; social mobility, 4, 90, 105; social services and, 27–28, 47, 115, 168, 169–170; structural adjustment policies and, 57
migration: brain drain, 87; to Gulf states, 51, 52, 54, 81–82, 206n42, 216n71; kinship formation, 15–16, 120, 172–173; of Lebanese Christians, 84; out-migration for employment, 81, 82, 83; remittances from expatriate workers, 54, 79, 81–83, 85, 206n42, 215n68; rural migration during civil war in Lebanon, 82, 86
military, the (Jordan), 53, 54, 57, 58, 70
military, the (Lebanon), 50, 69–70, 164
militias: Amal, 124, 151, 154, 156, 159; defined, 203n2; Fatah, 65; Hamas, 114; and kin organizations, 101, 102–103, 183; popular support for, 62–63; in post-civil-war era in Lebanon, 169; PSP (Druze Progressive Socialist Party), 63, 66, 146, 152; as social welfare providers, 10, 26, 30, 47, 63–64, 63t2.2, 65, 101, 102–103, 114. *See also* Hizbullah
Ministry of Social Affairs (Lebanon), 158–159

Ministry of Social Development (Jordan), 113, 158
Ministry of Supply, 54, 206n47
Ministry of the Displaced, 70
Ministry of the Interior (Lebanon), 157, 187
moral hazard problem, 25, 31, 39, 40, 118, 171, 241n4
Mount Lebanon, 63, 105
Multi-Fiber Agreement, 83
municipal elections, 147, 151–152
Muslim Brotherhood, 112, 126, 145, 146, 149, 150, 153
Muslims: Jordanian Muslims, 13, 51t2.1, 93, 98, 214n46; Muslim Brotherhood, 112, 126, 145, 146, 149, 150, 153. *See also* Shi'a Muslims (Lebanon); Sunni Muslims (Lebanon)

National Aid Fund (Jordan), 59
new elites, 140, 141, 142–143, 163
NGOs: aid for nonmember families, 124; child labor for, 217n87; compared with mutual aid associations, 129; for emergency medical aid, 64, 112, 114; family associations as, 239n124; government funding of, 48; health care for the poor, 59; kin associations as, 100, 179; kinship associations compared with, 4; Lebanon state oversight of, 157; loans, 112, 115; Palestinian, 64, 107–108, 114, 129, 144, 163; social welfare, 48; support for, 179; UNICEF, 238n118; UNRWA (United Nations Relief and Works Agency), 80, 101, 114; USAID, 105, 113; World Bank, 56, 76; WTO (World Trade Organization), 56, 69. *See also* charities; *kin association headings*
nonkin associations, 104f4.6, 187, 241n6

NSSF (National Social Security Fund), 61, 70

oil economy, 50, 54–55, 81, 82, 169
Oslo Accords, 103, 114

Palestine Red Crescent Society, 64, 114
Palestinian elites, as founders of kin associations, 135–136
Palestinian kin associations, 95f4.1, 96f4.2, 97f4.3, 97f4.4, 130; affiliation with East Bank Jordanian groups, 122; balance of power, 130; challenges of providing services, 111; *diwan*, 98, 100, 117, 119, 120, 125, 145, 227n4; founding of, 94–95, 98; interviews with, 187; leadership of, 136–137; leadership profiles, 135, 136; Lifta Charitable Association, 95–96, 96f4.2, 106, 109, 144–145, 162, 238n118; schools run by, 110, 225n76; Silwan Social Development Association, 107–108, 129, 163; village of origin as defining kinship in, 103, 123, 125, 153, 163, 174
Palestinian Martyrs Works Society (SAMED), 64
Palestinians, 47; access to health care, 58, 208n95; access to state social provisioning in Jordan, 51t2.1; affiliation with Jordanian kin networks, 125–126; as constituents of Jordanian kin networks, 125–126; defined, 51–52; demographics in Jordan, 204n21; electoral politics and, 149; employment of, 51, 64, 72, 78, 81, 87, 94–95; formation of kin groups, 231n60; Gulf states labor migration, 51, 52, 54, 82, 206n42, 216n71; Hizbullah supported by, 146; Jordanization project, 53; labor market for, 53,

prior to economic reforms, 81, 215nn57,59; reduction in, 56; urban Jordanians, 82

Qoudat, 145

rabita (guesthouse), 100, 117, 119, 120
reciprocity, 32–33, 43–44, 117, 129, 142
Reconstruction Campaign (Hizbullah), 66–67
refugee camps, 63, 63t2.2, 80–83, 95, 114, 208n94, 216n71
religious alliances, 13, 103, 111–112, 122, 123, 124, 129, 173, 232n11
rentierism, 12, 14–15, 29, 50, 52
research methodology, 19–21, 154–155, 185–188, 220n2, 230n59
risk, 24; business accountability, 39; collective risks of industrialization, 26; formation of kin associations, 177; indebtedness to kin relatives, 43; job security, 26–27, 43–44; loan repayments, 39, 202n89; management of, 169–170; mitigation of, as central to welfare, 49; moral hazard problem, 25, 31, 39, 40, 118, 171, 241n4; organization for social insurance, 41
rituals, 34, 36, 91, 201n70
Rodrik, Dani, 28
ROSCAs (rotating savings associations), 15, 31, 120
royal NGOs, 112, 113, 158
Rudra, Nita, 28
rural areas: economic status of, 75–76, 82, 86, 87; Hizbullah, 67; kin associations in, 98–99, 99f4.5, 101, 123, 130, 135, 137, 186, 188; military employees, 53, 58; social welfare for, 51t2.1, 61, 110, 114, 208n94; urban migration from, 82, 86. *See also* villages

Saudi Arabia, 125, 232n11
Sayda, 102
SCC (Social Security Corporation), 58
secular associations, 104f4.6, 114
self-employment, 41, 42, 78, 85
service-sector employment, 29, 41; employment longevity, 78; impact of Lebanon's civil war on, 86; in Jordan after economic reforms, 82; kin association networks, 133; minority populations in Lebanon in, 94; models of organization of, 42, 44; multiple jobs, 42, 78, 79; skill sets in, 42–43, 78; taxi driving, 56, 79, 84, 85
sheikhs, 119, 141, 144
Shi'a associations (Lebanon), 103; *'ashura* (Shi'a religious holiday), 162; balance of power, 130; employment, 101, 134; founding of, 101–102; interviews with, 187; political involvement of, 146; in postwar Lebanon, 104, 105
Shi'a Muslims (Lebanon): Beiruti identity of, 86, 163; demographics of, 194n20; educational achievement, 85; Hizbullah relations with, 6, 7, 66; militia welfare, 51, 63, 63t2.2, 102, 105; political parties of, 151, 152, 155; population growth of, 84; social services for, 124; urbanization of, 85, 101; village of origin as defining kinship, 101, 123
Shishani tribe, 145
Silwan Social Development Association (Lebanon), 107–108, 129, 163
Sinou family, 101, 163
size of kin associations: accountability, 120, 129, 130; and definitions of family relations, 98, 121, 228n15; and group effectiveness, 105, 118–121, 123, 174; leadership influence, 142–143,

waqf (endowment), 227n2
wasta (connections), 39, 53, 138
Weber, Max, 193nn2,4
weddings, 8, 26, 49, 54, 105, 109, 119, 126, 132f5.1, 204n7
Weingast, Barry R., 33
welfare opportunity structure (WOS), 25–26, 37, 37n1.1, 38f1.1
West Bank, 88; Aal al-Naber Association migration to, 94; family associations in Jordan, 95; health care, 108; Jordan state relations with, 55; Lifta (village outside Jerusalem) association, 95–96, 96f4.2; mortgages in exchange for state allegiance, 53; Palestinians, 52
wheat subsidies, 54, 55, 62
Wihdat refugee camp, 80
Wilkinson, Steven I., 11
women: agricultural work, 81, 115, 215n65; association roles of, 8, 135, 182; child care services, 83–84, 93, 110, 158, 225n79; education financial assistance, 107; handicraft industries, 109, 126, 129, 158; health education for, 129;
industrial zone labor, 83–84, 110, 225n79; loan services for, 115; matrilineal relatives in definitions of kinship, 120; microfinancing for women's enterprises, 59; NGOs in Lebanon aid for, 114; in nonkin associations, 125–126; in parliament, 127, 145, 146; patriarchalism, 161, 206n40; PLO-supported education for, 64; savings associations (*sunduq nisa'i*) for, 119, 227n10; small businesses, 113; voting decisions of, 144, 182, 234n33; wife's kin, 95; women-run financial services in Egypt, 34, 227n10
World Bank, 56, 76
WTO (World Trade Organization), 56, 69

Yazour, Palestine, 125

Zahleh, Lebanon, 127
Zakat Fund (Jordan), 59, 113
Zarqa, Jordan, 80–81, 95–96, 96f4.2, 99f4.5, 100, 113, 145, 239n124
Zubaida, Sami, 181

ANNE MARIE BAYLOUNY is Assistant Professor of National Security Affairs at the Naval Postgraduate School, Monterey, California.

Printed and bound by CPI Group (UK) Ltd, Croydon, CR0 4YY

13/04/2025

14656548-0005